Educational Differences

ARTHUR R. JENSEN

Educational Differences

Methuen & Co Ltd
11 New Fetter Lane
London EC4P 4EE

First published 1973
© 1973 *Arthur R. Jensen*
Printed in Great Britain
by T. & A. Constable Ltd
Hopetoun Street, Edinburgh

ISBN 0 416 75980 7

Contents

73591

To Roberta

Acknowledgements

The author gratefully acknowledges the kindness of the following publishers for permission to reprint the articles in this volume: Associated Book Publishers, Ltd. for 'Hierarchical Theories of Mental Ability'; the National Foundation for Educational Research in England and Wales for 'The Culturally Disadvantaged: Psychological and Educational Aspects' and 'Do Schools cheat Minority Children?'; the ERIC Clearinghouse on Early Childhood Education for 'Understanding Readiness'; the Journal Press for 'The Role of Verbal Mediation in Mental Development'; the Educational Testing Service for 'Another Look at Culture-Fair Testing'; the *Toledo Law Review* (1970, 403-57) for 'Selection of Minority Students in Higher Education'; Charles E. Merrill Publishing Co. for 'Varieties of Individual Differences in Learning'; the University of Chicago Press (*Perspectives in Biology and Medicine*, Autumn, 1971) for 'The Phylogeny and Ontogeny of Intelligence'; *Engineering and Science Magazine* (California Institute of Technology) for 'The Heritability of Intelligence'; and D.C. Heath & Co. (*Emerging Issues in Education*, ed. by J. E. Bruno, 1972) for 'Heritability and Teachability'.

Preface

Educational Differences is a varied and representative selection from my more recent articles that deal with the interface between differential psychology and education. Today, as in the past, it appears that, of all the branches of psychology, differential psychology – the study of individual and group behavioral differences – is the most germane to discussion of the problems of education. Developmental psychology and the psychology of human learning follow closely in importance.

The predominant relevance of differential psychology to education is viewed by some educators as a condemnation of the educational system, which they see as one vast mechanism for differentiation and selection among individuals in the population, rather than as an influence that fundamentally changes individuals, inculcates abilities, and bestows equal benefits to everyone. This charge is quite accurate. The educational process traditionally has, in fact, mainly followed the paradigm of the talent hunt – of exposing more or less everyone to similar influences and opportunities for learning, and then grading, sifting, and selecting at intervals along the way. Those who do not pan out in this process are more or less abandoned by the system or at least are relegated to second class status in terms of the eventual interest, facilities, appropriate expenditures and further opportunities that the system provides, as contrasted with those who win out in the academic talent race. Much of the injustice in this system is attributable to the overly narrow criteria for grading and selecting on which depend rising or falling in the system.

The failures of the system could not become fully apparent prior to enforced universal education, which keeps, or tries to keep, all children in school up to the age of 16 or 18. Until school attendance was mandatory it was customary for increasing numbers of children to drop out at successive stages of schooling. But as education in the United States became more universal, with compulsory school attendance taking in virtually the entire child and adolescent population, the stage was set for the educational failures and malignancies that were finally to become obvious to everyone.

The precipitating incident perhaps was the Soviet Union's technological triumph, the orbiting of Sputnik, which momentarily seemed to arouse in Americans a feeling of scientific and intellectual inferiority and thus spurred the great emphasis on academic excellence in the late 1950s. It was urged then that the schools be drastically up-graded in the academic subjects. Intellectual achievement in history, language, mathematics, and science was the badge of excellence and became the national focus for the educational enterprise.

What this general emphasis on academic achievement and the attendant assessments ultimately revealed, more fully than anything else had done, were the great disparities in scholastic performance among various segments of the population – among geographical regions, socio-economic classes, racial groups, neighborhoods, and schools.

What caused these inequalities in scholastic achievement? The prevailing theory, at the time, was that inequalities of educational opportunities were to blame – differences in school facilities, teachers' qualifications, pupil-teacher ratio, average expenditure per pupil, and the like. Thus, bringing all these factors up to a high standard common for all of the population should wipe out the observed disparities in educational outputs.

It was the fact that such disparities could not be viewed as trivial that they became of national concern. For example, the U.S. Office of Education made a study of the extent of functional illiteracy, that is, inability to read and write sufficiently for the minimum demands of today's economic and social life. An estimated 24 million persons 18 years and over are functionally illiterate, unable to read, write or cipher at a fifth-grade level. Yet, as Roger Freeman (1971, p. 79) pointed out, there were 'only 6·4 million Americans, 14 years and over, who had attended school for fewer than five years. In a study on Chicago's Southside, for example, 93% of the respondents were found to have completed at least the fifth grade; but fewer than half could read at fifth grade level.' (In American schools the fifth grade comprises children mostly between 10 and 11 years of age.)

Then, in 1964, the U.S. Congress, under the Civil Rights Act, appropriated $1·25 million for a comprehensive survey of the nation's schools, to determine the extent of educational inequality and discrimination against children from low-income backgrounds. Specifically, it was intended 'to document the lack of availability of equal educational opportunities' for minority groups in American schools. The survey was carried out by a research team of sociologists and statisticians under sociologist James Coleman at the Johns Hopkins University. The results of the survey, based on the testing of more than 645,000 pupils in 4,000 of the nation's schools, were published in 1966 in two large volumes, *Equality of Educational Opportunity*, which came to be called simply 'The Coleman Report'. The findings were a shocking and disconcerting surprise to nearly everyone. When the costly study was proposed there had been some complaints that, like so much educational research, it would only document statistically what had long been common knowledge: that socio-economic and racial inequalities in scholastic performance were mainly the result of inequities in school facilities and expenditures. But the conclusions of the Coleman report were in fact quite the contrary; it was a monumental example of empirical research shattering a popular myth.

The main conclusions of the Coleman report are by now so well known as not to require detailed summary. Briefly, in Coleman's words, 'The evidence revealed that within broad geographic regions, for each racial and ethnic group, the physical and economic resources going into a school had very little relationship to the achievements coming out of it . . . if it were otherwise we could give simple prescriptions: increase teachers' salaries, lower class size, enlarge libraries, and so on. But the evidence does not allow such simple answers.' As just one example, Coleman found that teacher-pupil ratio 'showed a consistent lack of relation to achievements among all groups under all conditions'. Eight re-analyses of the massive Coleman data by other researchers have not essentially altered the conclusions in any way. (The most searching re-evaluations are to be found in recent books by Moynihan and Mosteller [1972], and Jencks [1972]).

Just a year after the Coleman report there followed the nation-wide survey and evaluation of the large federally funded compensatory education programs, by the U.S. Commission on Civil Rights. The Commission's conclusions were entirely negative: 'The fact remains . . . that none of the programs appear to have raised significantly the achievement of participating pupils, as a group, within the period evaluated by the Commission.' The conclusions were backed up by the testimony of those very school superintendents who had put forth the greatest effort to make compensatory education work. Dr Neil Sullivan, then superintendent of schools in Berkeley, California, with one of the nation's most progressive school systems, testified before a U.S. Senate committee (May 21, 1970):

'Berkeley, as most communities in 1965, with the passage of the Elementary and Secondary Education Act, put its first money into compensatory education. We went the whole route, lowered class size, provided remedial reading teachers, bought the [teaching] machines, did those things we thought were right. The results after two and a half or three years clearly indicated that not only did the child in the inner city not improve, he had retrogressed.'

Mayor Lindsay of New York City said in 1969, in response to the decline of achievements in the New York City schools to substantially below the national average:

'Our schools are the most lushly funded school system in the nation [spending more than twice the national average per pupil] . . . it has the best teacher-pupil ratio of any city . . . but the management of the thing is such that we just don't get the production' (*New York Times*, June 6, 1969). Later, New York City's school superintendent voiced his quandary:

'We have been spending a great deal of money on solutions which have little relation to the causes. Nobody knows why certain children are not profiting from the educational program. . . .Money is being spent on new gimmicks but nobody knows the cause and effect relationship. . . . We have offered all kinds of solutions but they are not producing results and nobody knows why' (*New York Times*, December 4, 1969).

Then, the Headstart program, on which were pinned the highest hopes of any of the many compensatory education programs, after five years in existence, was evaluated in a large-scale study by the Westinghouse Corporation, a private research organization. Again, negative findings. The status of findings from all compensatory programs at that time was cautiously summarized by President Nixon in his Education Message of March 1970:

> We must stop letting wishes color our judgments about the educational effectiveness of many special compensatory programs, when – despite some dramatic and encouraging exceptions – there is growing evidence that most of them are not yet measurably improving the success of poor children in school . . . *the best available evidence indicates that most of the compensatory education programs have not measurably helped poor children catch up.*
>
> Recent findings on the two largest such programs are particularly disturbing. We now spend more than $1 billion a year for educational programs run under Title I of the Elementary and Secondary Education Act. Most of these have stressed the teaching of reading, but before-and-after tests suggest that only 19% of the children in such programs improve their reading significantly; 13% appear to fall behind more than expected; and more than two-thirds of the children remain unaffected – that is, they continue to fall behind. In our Headstart program, where so much hope is invested, we find that youngsters enrolled only for the summer achieve almost no gains, and the gains of those in the program for a full year are soon matched by their non-Headstart classmates from similarly poor backgrounds.

Next came 'performance contracting', in which experts from private educational organizations came into a school system to introduce and supervise the application of better instructional techniques, usually based upon the latest theories of learning, with control of reinforcements, motivation, sequencing, programmed instruction, and the like.

The U.S. Office of Economic Opportunity, which sponsored a large-scale evaluation of performance contracting, described its working as follows (quoted by Page, 1972, p. 40):

A contractor signs an agreement to improve students' perform-ance in certain basic skills by set amounts.

The contractor is paid according to his success in bringing students' performance up to those prespecified levels. If he succeeds, he makes a profit. If he fails, he doesn't get paid.

Within guidelines established by the school board, the con-tractor is free to use whatever instructional techniques, incentive systems, and audio-visual aids he feels can be most effective. He thus is allowed more flexibility than is usually offered a building principal or a classroom teacher.

The OEO's evaluation of the effects of performance contracting involving over 25,000 pupils and a cost of over $6 million, has been called the most important experiment in the history of American education (Page, 1972). It was, in fact, a true experi-ment, and not just a statistical survey. That is to say, it involved an experimental group which received special treatment, and a matched control group which merely had the school's ordinary program. The whole experimental design is well described by Page (1972). It is remarkably clean for such a large-scale experi-ment. The OEO's report summarized the results, in terms of achievement gains of the experimental groups as compared with the control group, as follows:

[T]he difference in gains was remarkably small in all 10 of the grade/subject combinations for which this analysis is appropriate. In half of the 10 cases, there was no difference at all between the gains of the experimental and control groups. In four of the cases there was a difference of as much as two-tenths of a grade level. These overall differences are so slight that we can conclude that performance contracting was no more effective in either reading or math than the traditional classroom methods of instruction. . . . [T]he performance of students in the experi-mental group does not appear disappointing just because students in the control group did unexpectedly well. In fact, neither group did well. In only two of the 20 possible cases was the mean gain of either the control or experimental students as much as one grade level. . . . In all cases, the average achieve-ment level of children in the experimental group was well below the norm for their grade and in all cases, in terms of grade equivalents, the average slipped even further behind during the year. . . . [There] is no evidence that performance contracting had differential results for the lowest or highest achieving students in the sample. . . . Not only did both groups do equally poorly in terms of overall averages, but also these averages were very nearly the same in each grade, in each subject, for the best and worst students in the sample, and, with few exceptions, in each site. Indeed, the most interesting aspect of these conclusions is their very consistency. This evidence does not indicate that performance contracting will bring about any great improvement in the educational status of disadvantaged children. (Quoted in Page, 1972, p. 41.)

Professor Page's concluding statement is worth quoting in full:

No matter how these data are revolved (and more elaborate analyses are forthcoming), the essential conclusion will remain, and it seems a severe blow to certain of our professional illusions. Many of us have believed, implicitly, something like this:

Applied psychology has certain powerful behavioural skills. We understand task analysis; input repertory; stimulus shaping; response elicitation; the provision of reinforcement; the arrangement of repetition, sequencing, looping; concept formation; the practicing of transfer. These are important ingredients in learning, and as psychologists we understand these things much better than traditionally trained teachers. If we as a profession are given the support, the students, the autonomy, we can make incalculable improvements in education.

This belief has been one cornerstone of our faith in ourselves.

Now the OEO has provided what may be the first really solid test of its truth: – whether the present, state-of-the-art, garden-variety, applied psychology can in fact contribute to the most important learnings in the schools. We will not make those statements so casually in the future. Our skills in training do *not* seem the immediate solution to our problems in education.

There are arguments to be raised, of course, some with validity: These PC contractors had materials and programs that were far from ideal. This is only a limited test of one year's duration. This study compared a well-bred horse (teaching) with the *first* automobile (PC). The tests are perhaps biased toward the conventional methods of teaching. We have not seen the affective changes. Perhaps the higher-order interactions. . . .

Yet this experience with performance contracting, painful as it is, should be squarely confronted. It may cause us to re-examine many of our practices and assumptions about school learning and its evaluation. We have much to reappraise. It will be exciting to see how, in the next few years, we cope with this threat to our professional confidence.

In the light of the mounting negative findings on the effects of various types of educational intervention intended to reduce the achievement gap between minority and majority pupils, it was claimed by some social scientists that the missing ingredient for success was racial integration of the schools. It had been noted, for example, that Negro pupils attending predominantly white neighborhood schools showed somewhat higher achievement levels than Negro pupils in predominantly Negro neighborhoods. The suggested solution was to break down the racial segregation in schools resulting from residential patterns by enforcing racial quotas such that in all classrooms Negro pupils should be out-numbered by their white classmates. The only feasible means of doing this in many communities was by the busing of Negro and white children into each other's neighborhoods. Except for wishful thinking, there was no good reason to expect that busing in order to obtain the desired racial balance, should have any beneficial effect on scholastic achievement *per se*, whatever other effects it might have. And so far as we are able to tell at the present time, this has turned out to be the case. Armor (1972) has made a thorough review of the evidence on the effects of busing in those schools that had the necessary data for objective evaluation. He found no significant differences on achievement tests resulting from integration by busing, but he did note a lowering of assigned school grades of Negro pupils in integrated classes. He states: 'Since black students of the same age are, on average, behind white students in all parts of the country with respect to academic achievement, we should expect their grades to fall when they are taken from the competition in an all-black school to the competition in a predominantly white school. In addition, the bused students may not be adequately prepared for this competition, at least in terms of the higher standards that may be applied in the suburban schools' (p. 101). Armor adds a necessary caution at this stage of the evidence on busing:

'In view of the fact that most of the short-term measures do not conclusively demonstrate positive effects of busing in the area of achievement, aspirations, self-concept, and race relations, it becomes even more important to consider possible long-term changes that may relate to eventual socio-economic parity between blacks and whites. Since no busing program has been in operation more than seven years or so, this area, obviously, has not been studied extensively' (p. 105).

One long-range effect which has been studied is that the bused students are more likely to start college than the control group; but Armor notes that although many more of the bused students actually start some form of higher education, the bused students also have a substantially higher drop-out rate so that not more of them remain in college than the control group who were not bused. But then, the bused students who remained in college were enrolled in what are generally considered higher quality institutions as compared with the control group. Armor concludes: 'Given the lack of positive effects in other areas, these findings may have great significance for future busing programs, and further research is urgently needed.'

But the repeated and conspicuous failures of the many efforts to equalize achievements led many observers of the educational scene to a flinty disillusionment, such as that voiced by economist and presidential adviser Roger Freeman (1971, pp. 83-4):

Experience has shown that the schools can teach almost every normal child to read, write, or count to the same extent to which it can teach him to sing, paint, sculpture, swim, run, play a musical instrument, or play basketball – that is, according to his individual capacity to perform and succeed in each of these fields. It can no more teach *all* children to read or count at the national average, than it can teach *all* children to sing or swim or sculpture or play basketball at the national average. But some people seem to feel that in a country as rich and powerful as ours *everybody* ought to be above the average, or at the least, at the average.

This reminds me of the alchemists who for nearly two thousand years, with a tremendous effort and at a huge expense, tried to do what we now know cannot be done. But they and their sponsors had a deep emotional need to believe that it could be done, so they kept trying and went undeterred from defeat to defeat, always expecting to find success around the next corner. For how much longer will we let our latter-day alchemists set goals for our public schools?

Some of the specific educational approaches and techniques which were viewed in the beginning as the most promising means of raising the achievements of the disadvantaged have subsequently led to diminished hopes for their efficacy in reducing the achievement gap. Although the overall level of achievement may be somewhat raised by a particular technique, individual and group differences are not reduced when the technique is applied to everyone, and often differences are increased. Teaching machines and programmed instruction are one example. When they were introduced in the late 1950s, they generated considerable enthusiasm. They were hailed by some psychologists as the solution to our educational problems. From what I have seen of these techniques when applied in schools, there is no doubt that they do indeed work. They are an effective and efficient means of teaching many scholastic skills, usually much more effective than ordinary classroom instruction in engaging children's attention and effort. These techniques are not used enough and their merits warrant wider use. But as far as I can determine, their applications have given no indication that they are capable of solving the problems connected with *differences* in educational performance. Where teaching machines and programmed instruction are competently and systematically used in schools they slightly raise the overall level of achievement but magnify individual and group differences. As usually happens, any improved instructional technique that proves good for the educational 'have nots' proves even better for the 'haves'. One of the main virtues of teaching machines and programmed lessons, however, may be that they permit children to learn at their own pace, with little or no knowledge of just how their classmates are doing, so that the children's learning is not afflicted by the negative emotional effects of perceived large differences in performance.

Another prominent feature of compensatory education and philosophy is the emphasis on *earliness*: the notion that early learning will make a big difference later on, and the earlier you can teach a child, the better. Interestingly enough, there is little, if any, evidence in human psychology that compellingly supports this belief, and it is now being seriously questioned by developmental psychologists. Elkind (1969), for example, argues that there is no evidence for the long-term effects of pre-school instruction or enrichment. He suggests the hypothesis that '. . . the longer we delay formal instruction, up to certain limits, the greater the period of plasticity and the higher the ultimate level of achievement'. He adds, 'There is at least as much evidence and theory in support of this hypothesis as there is in favor of the early instruction proposition' (p. 332). Husén (1967), in a cross-national study of mathematics achievement involving twelve different nations, found that there was a negligible correlation (rho $= -0.06$, $p > .05$) between the age of school entry and mathematics achievement at age 13; but there was a strong correlation (rho $= -0.72$, $p < 0.01$) between earliness of school entry and attitudes toward school, i.e., those who had started their schooling earlier had the more negative attitudes toward school by age 13. Schools with even two years' head-start in formal instruction showed no advantage over other schools by the time children were 13. The older children learn faster, and they quickly catch up with those who had two years' head-start. There is nothing in these findings that would suggest that earlier education would have any long-term benefits, and there are indications that the contrary is more likely. This theme has been elaborated upon by Rohwer (1971).

It will be noted that all of the major compensatory attempts, and the means employed, were aimed at improving disadvantaged children's mental abilities and learning capacity so as to have them keep up with the national norms for scholastic progress. The main ability involved in scholastic achievement is intelligence, as measured by IQ tests, and so the aims of compensatory programs have usually been described and assessed in terms of raising the IQ, especially of disadvantaged children. Educationists have searched for the method or combination of methods that would produce the desired result. Along with the disillusionment following the numerous and now well-known failures of these attempts, there grew up a new idea and a new hope among educational researchers: the aptitude × training interaction, or ATI for short. (Also called aptitude × instruction interaction, or AII.) All that ATI means, briefly, is that the best method of teaching for some children is not the best method for others, and the best way to minimize the effects of ability differences in school is to match each child to the kind of instructional method that suits him best in terms of his own aptitudes. If Johnny learns better than Billy by method A and Billy learns better than Johnny by method B, perhaps they will achieve equally if Johnny is taught by method A and Billy by method B. Such, at least, is the hope of ATI researchers, who aim to achieve optimal performance by matching a diversity of instructional methods with the diversity of individuals' aptitudes. The idea is not to wipe out differences in aptitudes (which has more or less proved hopeless) but to take advantage of the differences in the design of instruction. The field is still too new to allow definitive evaluation, and any strong conclusions would be premature. But so far, after several years, nothing has been produced by those who are trying that would arouse great hope. All too often it is found that whatever new instructional technique aids learning for the 'slow learners' usually turns out to do even more for the 'fast learners', thereby increasing the achievement gap. Thus, ATI so far does not appear to be the philosopher's stone that educators have dreamed of. The evidence, such as it is, was reviewed by Bracht (1970), who included only those studies in the ATI field which met certain methodological statistical and criteria to permit rigorous valuation. He found that out of 90 studies that were specifically designed to produce aptitude × training interactions of the kind that would solve the achievement difference between Johnny and Billy in the example above, only five studies showed such an A × T interaction, and in none of these cases was IQ the aptitude involved; the 'aptitudes' in these particular studies were all psychological variables unrelated to intelligence. Where intelligence or IQ was the aptitude involved, useful interactions with instructional variables were not found, that is to say, every form of instruction favored the high IQs, usually to about the same degree. ATI could not overcome the consequences of a low IQ. Bracht's conclusions contain a number of interesting and important points:

'When a variety of treatment stimuli, especially conditions not controlled by the experimenter, are able to influence performance on the dependent variable, it is unlikely that a personological variable can be found to produce a disordinal interaction with the alternative treatments. . . . Success on a combination of heterogeneous treatment tasks is predicted best by measures of general ability [i.e., IQ tests], and the degree of prediction is about equally high for alternative treatments' (p. 636). 'The degree of task complexity may be a major factor in the occurrence of ATI. Although the treatment tasks for most of the 90 studies were classified as controlled, the treatments were generally relatively complex tasks. Conversely, four of the five experiments with disordinal interactions [ATI] were more similar to the basic learning tasks of the research laboratory' (p. 637). 'Despite the large number of comparative experiments with intelligence as a personological variable, no evidence was found to suggest that the IQ score and similar measures of general ability are useful variables for differentiating alternative treatments for subjects in a homogeneous age group. These measures correlate substantially with achievement in most school-related tasks and hence are not likely to correlate differentially with performance in alternative treatments of complex achievment-oriented tasks' (p. 638).

If Bracht's conclusions hold true, then unless we can come up with something radically different from anything that has yet been tried, the prospect of substantially minimizing the overwhelming influence of IQ differences (whether measured or not) on scholastic achievement seems quite dim indeed.

This does not mean that education itself could not be improved; it only means that the aims and criteria for improvement would better be concerned with something other than minimizing performance differences in those aspects of schooling which are most highly related to IQ differences. Exactly what forms such improvements in the educational system should take are only suggested in the most general terms in some of the selections contained in this collection. But explicit consideration of this matter is another large topic in itself, involving not only educational psychology, but also educational philosophy, sociology, economics, and administration. The improvement of education must be informed by the findings of psychological research, but psychology *per se* cannot decide the aims of the educational system or the institutional and administrative arrangements for achieving them. These are societal matters, broadly speaking. But there has been a growing awareness among educators and the general public alike, increasingly substantiated by research findings, that any workable educational system cannot be based on the premise that ability differences can be ignored, or dismissed, or denied as mere artifacts of defective measuring instruments and culture bias.

The ability differences we observe among individuals, social classes, and racial groups, are real – real in the sense that they are not artifacts of the tests used to assess abilities and achievements. Whatever their causes, they are human differences which show up not only on psychological and educational tests, but in practically every human activity in which abstract, conceptual, and symbolic mental activities are called upon. In this sphere, the test results are not discrepant with life performance.

Whether society should accord unequal value and unequal rewards to unequal performance is an arguable issue. A society that truly creates equality of opportunity and promotes a high degree of occupational mobility in accord with individual differences in abilities and drives, but allows very unequal rewards for unequal performance, may find itself in serious trouble. Yet, it may be asked, how much can rewards be equalized without risk to the welfare of the society as a whole? If high abilities are a rare and valued resource, as seems now to be the case throughout the industrialized world, can society afford not to provide strong inducements to attract scarce ability into those pursuits where it is most needed for society's well-being? Many are now questioning whether our culture's system of rewards and punishments is all wrong. Should we try to decrease the range of some kinds of human differences, and if so, which ones and how? Or must we accept them as a part of the reality we must learn to live with, and if so, how can we best do this? Does it call for a radical reorientation of societal values that will somehow take the sting out of differences in the abilities to compete and achieve? These are the type of questions that will loom larger on the horizon as equality of opportunity becomes more and more a reality.

Differential psychology will not remain aloof from such concerns, but meanwhile there is still much cultivation needed in its own garden, which has been rather neglected in psychology during the sovereignty of behaviorist environmentalism of the 1950s and '60s. But differential psychology is beginning to command more interest once again, in part because of developments in the educational scene and in part because of the infusion of questions and methods from the comparatively new field known as behavioral genetics. Behavioral genetics has always rightfully been a necessary branch of differential psychology, for without reference to genetics differential psychology cannot hope to achieve its aim, which is the description and explanation of the causes of behavioral differences. The tools of statistics, measurement, and experimental psychology are all necessary but insufficient.

Observed consistencies and correlations among human behaviors have led to such concepts as traits and abilities, and such concepts aid in the description of individual differences. What is meant when we speak of traits or abilities is that we are dealing with particular classes of behavior that have a high degree of *reliability* (i.e., the individual's behavior is consistent from one time to another under the same circumstances) and *generality* (i.e., the individual's behavior is consistent over a variety of somewhat different circumstances). The measurement and definition of these traits can be just as empirical, just as operational, as anything else in science.

General intelligence is one such class of intercorrelated behaviors. It has become the most embattled of psychological concepts just because of its important educational and social consequences and because individual differences in intelligence are so large and so obvious to the pragmatic man in the street. If intelligence tests had never existed, it would not make the least bit of difference socially. That is why it always seems so fatuous to talk about doing away with IQ tests, as if it would make any real difference. How else to explain the fact that the average correlation between the IQs of marriage partners is almost as high as the correlation between various standard intelligence tests? (Husbands and wives are more alike in IQ than brothers and sisters reared together in the same family.) And how else to explain the fact that when people are asked to rank order various occupations in terms of their own subjective impression of their 'prestige' and 'desirability', they come out, on the average, with a ranking of the occupations that correlates between 0·70 and 0·90 with the rank order of the actual mean IQs found for members of those occupations?

Differential psychologists speak of behavior as having *structure*. It is something more than a mere cumulation of everything one has learned, something more than a history of operant reinforcement contingencies. Structure means there are relatively stable patterns of correlations among many behaviors, and many previously unobserved behaviors may be predicted probabilistically from a knowledge of this structure. Moreover, all behavioral correlations are not merely a product of common learning, i.e., the overlapping of numerous smaller units of behavior with common reinforcement histories, or a result of transfer due to 'identical elements'. There are five main causes of correlations among behaviors in the domain of skills, abilities, aptitudes, etc. These causes are not at all mutually exclusive: (1) dependence of the behavior upon common sensory or motor capacities – this is trivial in most so-called mental tests; (2) part-whole functional dependence, i.e., one behavior may simply be a subunit of some other behavior, such as (*a*) shifting gears smoothly and (*b*) passing a driver's test consisting of driving your car around in city traffic with an examiner present; (3) hierarchical functional dependence, i.e., one behavior is prerequisite to another, or conversely, one is functionally dependent upon the other, as skill in working problems in long division is dependent upon skill in multiplication; (4) genetic correlation among behaviors, apparently due to common assortment of their genetic underpinnings through selection and homogamy, and pleiotropism (one gene having two or more seemingly unrelated phenotypic effects); and (5) environmental correlation among behaviors, due to correlated learning experiences and opportunities (e.g., someone who has learned a good deal about baseball is more apt to have acquired some knowledge also about football than about, say, music or art).

The main task of differential psychology, in addition to discovering, measuring, and mapping the structure of human abilities, is to analyze this structure in terms of these various causal underpinnings. Genetic analysis of the correlations which form the traits that emerge from factor analysis has not even begun. Genetic analysis of human behavior has hardly moved beyond the determination of heritability (i.e., the estimated proportion of individual differences variance attributable to genetic factors). This is but a primitive beginning. Once the heritability of a trait is established, as it has been for a variety of mental abilities including intelligence, the next question concerns the specific genetic *architecture* of the genetic variance, in terms of the components associated with fixed or additive gene effects, assortative mating, dominance, epistasis (gene-gene interactions), and gene-environment interaction and covariance. But such genetical analysis, to be meaningful, must proceed hand-in-hand with behavioral analysis, which consists in part of distinguishing, on the one hand, the experiential and functional basis of the intercorrelations that form the trait in question, from the contribution of genetic correlations, on the other. This is a job for the techniques of experimental psychology as well as of biometrical genetics. Little wonder that the only real progress in this field so far has been limited to the study of comparatively simple behaviors of fruitflies and rats!

The task of scientifically describing and understanding human abilities is formidable indeed. But if one is to do more with a problem than merely to say it is very complex, one must begin by dividing the problem and dealing with very limited parts of it. It could seem almost discouraging, so far may one have to go in this limiting direction in order to find still meaningful behavioral units that will yield to such causal analysis as our present capabilities will permit. Or could it be that this kind of scientific reductionism will have to be superseded by other, as yet unformulated, approaches to the study of human abilities?

The dozen articles in this collection point to a wide variety of problems and frontiers in differential psychology, particularly the psychology of mental abilities, and several articles illustrate how existing knowledge and method in this field are relevant to researching some of today's most important concerns in education.

Readers who wish to delve more thoroughly into the details and

technical aspects of the genetics of mental ability and a consideration of the causes of group differences in educability, topics which
are only introduced in general terms in several of the articles in
the present volume, are referred to my two previous books,
Genetics and Education (1972) and *Educability and Group Differences* (1973).

September, 1972

Arthur R. Jensen

*Institute of Human Learning
University of California*

Hierarchical theories
of mental ability

Three well-established facts, in combination with a new hope, form a central theme in present-day educational psychology. The main stimulus behind this theme is the urgent concern of educators for the educational plight of children called culturally disadvantaged.

The three established facts are: (*a*) there are large individual differences in mental ability; (*b*) these differences are strongly related to level of scholastic performance in today's schools; and (*c*) mental ability is not undimensional, but multidimensional.

The new hope of educational psychology is the possibility of capitalizing on the *interaction* of abilities and methods of instruction. This is now generally called the *aptitude × instruction interaction*, or AII for short. Put simply, AII means that Johnny learns better when taught by Method A than by method B, while Billy learns better when taught by method B than by method A. The crucial question is whether many such interactions can actually be found for school learning. At present AIIs are more a hope than an established fact (Cronbach, 1967; Carroll, 1967).

Why hope for such interactions? Because, if they can be found, it could mean that individual differences in scholastic achievement could be more nearly equalized despite great individual differences in pupils' mental abilities. If an aim of the school is to move pupils from a state of no knowledge, say, in arithmetic, up to a mastery of arithmetic fundamentals, it may be that different pupils could make this intellectual journey most efficiently by taking quite different instructional routes. Taking the same route might lead to greater differences in progress among them, and even to inordinate frustration and final defeat for some. If a dog, a seal, and a robin all had the aim to journey from Southampton to St Ives, they would all do much better to go by different routes and by different means. They would all come out much more equally in the time and effort it takes to achieve their goal than if all three were required to travel by any one means – running, swimming, or flying. Such is the meaning of *interaction*.

Individual differences in scholastic performance have always been with us. But they have recently become accentuated and have led to social pressures on education due to the fact that when individuals are grouped according to various socio-economic and racial characteristics, the groups show different average levels of ability and achievement. The groups that fall below the general average understandably want not only equality of opportunity to achieve scholastically, but equality of achievement as well. If equality of educational opportunity, meaning the same school facilities, curricula, and instruction for all children, should not lead to the attainment of this goal, it has been suggested increasingly of late that highly differential educational approaches for children with different patterns of ability might succeed in more nearly equalizing performance in school, especially in the basic skills. A major socio-economic consequence of this would be a correlated reduction of inequalities in the job market. Such is the hope for exploiting AII for improving the scholastic performance of all children and especially of those who, for whatever reasons, would benefit relatively little from current educational practices. Thorough investigation of the AII's potential for improving education is, therefore, a most important endeavour for educational psychologists.

Where should we look for interactions?

A major problem that confronts researchers who wish to embark on investigations of aptitude × instruction interactions is the great question of which variables to pick in hopes of finding educationally fruitful interactions. There are too many possibilities! The vastness of the prospect can be overwhelming and discouraging at the very outset. To avoid this inhibiting effect on productive research, the investigator needs some basis – empirical or theoretical – of limiting where he will place his bets. For any single researcher, of course, an intensive zeroing-in on a specific class of interactions is absolutely mandatory if he is to move from the armchair to the laboratory. In our present state of ignorance about AII, however, it would seem unwise for the field as a whole to zero-in too narrowly, considering the variety of aptitude and instruction variables that might yield potentially valuable inter-actions. A fairly broad scanning of the possibilities is needed. Yet some rational pattern of search would seem preferable to a com-pletely atheoretical trying-out of just any sets of variables that may strike one's fancy.

Several obvious sources of hunches and hypotheses for AII research can be listed:

PSYCHOLOGY OF SCHOOL SUBJECTS

The lore and the empirical evidence that have accumulated about the methodology of teaching various traditional school subjects would seem to be a possibly rich source of hypotheses for AII research. One can ask, for example, whether different teaching methods have evolved for particular school subjects in different populations and cultures. It seems likely that the predominant form of instruction in any society would bear a stronger relation-ship to the modal learning characteristics of members of the society, and would be somewhat more optimal for that group educationally, than would be most other types of instruction. The danger in this kind of speculation is that it becomes so difficult to separate the educational practices that have truly evolved in a given culture from the educational practices due to historical accidents, from educational systems inappropriately transplanted from one society to another, from far less than optimal practices that were originally dictated by economic necessity and have become traditional, from practices that evolved in accord with the aptitudes of a small minority of the population (e.g., the aristo-cracy or the very well-to-do) and were later generalized to the total population with insufficient modification and therefore with far less than optimal results for the majority (or a large minority) of children, and from traditionalized practices based on long out-moded philosophic and psychologic notions of the past. This jungle of ambiguities probably provides too many speculative hypotheses that could lead the researcher far astray in his search for fruitful AIIs.

This is not to say, however, that *empirical research* on specific teaching methods is not a good source of AII hypotheses. The phonics versus 'look–say' methods of reading instruction, for example, might interact with specific aptitudes. The present literature indicates few AIIs in this realm. But then, AIIs have never been specifically sought in past research on instruction, except with respect to chronological age and gross measures of mental age and IQ. These gross aptitude measures generally show very little interaction with methods of instruction. For various forms of classroom instruction in school subjects, at least, performance is almost equally predictable from measures of mental age or IQ. But this should not be surprising, since IQ tests were expressly designed to predict general scholastic performance over a broad range of educational conditions. Also, since IQ tests are intended to assess innate ability in so far as possible, they have been developed in such a way as actually to *minimize* the IQ's interaction with instructional variables and, in fact, with experiential factors in general. Therefore, IQ differences *per se* are not a likely source of promising AIIs. Indeed, a major aim of AII research is to *reduce* the overall correlation between scholastic performance and IQ. If low IQ children are to be helped to learn more in school, without their having to expend appreciably more individual time and effort than do high IQ children, the question becomes: what abilities that are relatively uncorrelated with IQ can be substituted for IQ in scholastic learning? IQ tests by themselves offer little or no clue to the answer.

SPECIAL EDUCATION

Instructional techniques developed for children with special educational handicaps, such as sensory-motor defects, various aphasias and other organic syndromes, might show interactions with other types of individual differences that are much more prevalent in the general school population. Since organic pathological conditions reflect the functional organization of neurological structures, they may serve as a clue to types or dimensions of individual differences within the 'normal' population. For example, if some proportion of 'normal' children show characteristics mildly resembling those of children with clear-cut receptive aphasia, we can ask if the more normal children would benefit from some adaptation of the instructional methods that have been found to work in cases of more extreme aphasia. Thus, a search of the techniques that have been shown to work for the educationally handicapped might reveal AIIs that would be applicable to broader segments of the population.

EXPERIMENTAL PSYCHOLOGY

Usually the largest source of variance in laboratory experiments on human learning, particularly verbal learning, is the interaction of *subjects × experimental conditions*. Is this a good source of educationally relevant AIIs? There are both advantages and disadvantages to looking here. One advantage not found so generally in educational research is that the independent variables (i.e., experimental conditions) in laboratory experiments on human learning are very precisely specified and one can usually have some confidence that the experiment could be replicated. In short, there are considerably fewer intangibles involved in laboratory experimentation than in studies of classroom learning. But the disadvantages of looking to the literature of laboratory studies of learning are considerable. In the first place, the literature on the experimental psychology of human learning is replete with studies which never looked at subject differences or interactions except as bothersome 'error variance'. In most experiments the true subject × conditions interaction is not distinguishable from error of measurement. Even when the true interaction is clearly separated from measurement error, there is seldom any clue as to the specific nature of the subjects × conditions interaction. That is to say, no subject variables are taken account of by the experimenter, who analyzes only the single dependent variable yielded by the experiment. All we can glean from most studies is the relative magnitude of the subjects × conditions interaction. If it is large, it may be worth investigating in further experiments specially designed for this purpose. Whether one thinks the interaction is worth further investigation will depend also, of course, upon one's psychological judgment of the relevance of the particular experimental variable to instruction in scholastic subjects. The chances are that most of the independent variables traditionally of interest to experimental psychologists will remain irrelevant to scholastic instruction until practicable means are developed for exercising a much higher degree of control over the instructional process, as might be achieved through teaching machines and computer-assisted instruction. Then the interactions found in the experimental psychology of learning might be more directly relevant to instruction. But their relevance to ordinary classroom instruction is most obscure or even entirely non-existent.

A further difficulty is the high probability, as indicated by what evidence we already possess, that most of the subjects × conditions interaction variance in laboratory learning is not correlated with subject variables that can be measured by means of the tests and inventories which have been developed in the field of psychological measurement. It appears that most of this learning variance is *intrinsic* to the learning domain (Jensen, 1967a). The measurement of individual differences in these factors, and identification of their main dimensions, will probably depend upon the development of measurement techniques very much like the laboratory learning procedures for which this class of individual differences is relevant. In other words, only a small fraction of the variance in learning under various conditions is likely to be explained by ability tests, personality inventories, and the like, which were developed outside the learning laboratory and for purposes other than predicting individual differences in performance under various conditions of learning. The discovery of the main dimensions of individual differences in laboratory learning, it appears, will be a Herculean task indeed. Learning in the natural environment (e.g., vocabulary acquisition) is much more predictable from intelligence tests, even of the non-verbal variety, than is most learning under the highly controlled conditions of the laboratory. But the exploitation of AII will depend in large measure upon the fine-grained control of the conditions of learning, and psychometric tests that will predict individual performance under these conditions will have to be quite different from ordinary intelligence tests, which, as was pointed out previously, have been devised to minimize interactions. That is, the typical IQ test would make the same prediction concerning the rank order of individuals' performances under all conditions of instruction. The payoff from AII research would consist presumably of finding some conditions in which the correlation of performance with IQ is very low and yet in which the average level of performance is not appreciably below that attained in other conditions of learning that produce higher correlations with IQ. A special battery of differential aptitude tests would be developed as a basis for assigning subjects to instructional conditions in such a way as to maximize the performance of the group as a whole and at the same time to minimize its variance. As yet, the evidence on AII is much too sparse for us to predict whether this is an attainable goal or the wildest dream. We will find out the limitations of AII only by trying it in many different ways.

HIERARCHICAL CONCEPTIONS OF MENTAL ABILITY

The most valuable AIIs, from a practical standpoint, will be those that involve relatively broad aspects of aptitude and instruction as contrasted with extreme task-specific and individual-specific interactions. By *broad* aspects of aptitude and instruction I mean dimensions or classes of abilities that will account for a substantial proportion of variance in certain types of instruction—methods that are broadly applicable to basic school subjects such as reading and arithmetic.

I am suggesting that a search strategy for AIIs of this type might be oriented most profitably in terms of hierarchical conceptions of mental abilities. Hierarchical models consist of levels and types of mental processes and skills which are likely to interact with instructional variables, broadly defined.

Hierarchical theories of abilities take a number of distinct forms. These are not at all mutually exclusive, but some are more fundamental than others. By 'fundamental' I mean that the hierarchical organization of mental processes implies causal or dependent functional relationships as contrasted with merely correlational and taxonomic relationships. A simple example will help to distinguish between hierarchical relationships that are causal and those that are merely correlational. Of course, all causal relationships are correlational, but the reverse does not hold. Take

B

strength of pull with the right hand, as in lifting a weight. This will be correlated with muscle size in the lower arm and muscle size in the upper arm, among other things. These correlations bear a hierarchical and causal or functional relationship to one another: if the upper arm muscle is weakened through atrophy or injury, the lower arm will be more or less ineffective, regardless of its own muscular condition, and total strength of pull will be poor. On the other hand, if the lower arm muscle is atrophied while the upper arm retains its full power, the total strength of pull will be much less impaired. In other words, the effectiveness of the lower arm is much more dependent upon the strength of the upper arm than is true for the reverse. This is the meaning of a hierarchical functional relationship. Now, if we ask about the relationship of *left* upper arm muscle size to strength of pull with the *right* arm, we will also find a positive correlation. But here the correlation does not represent a functional relationship; there is no dependence of right arm pull on left arm muscles, as shown by the fact that paralysing the left arm muscles has no effect on the strength of right arm pull.

In terms of a *taxonomic* hierarchy, the right and left arms are closely related, for they are anatomically homologous members of the category 'limbs'.

Now we must make a more detailed analysis of the kinds of hierarchical conceptions commonly found in psychology, particularly in the psychology of human abilities.

Types of hierarchical theories

TAXONOMIC SYSTEMS

These are not really theories, but systems of classification for mental tests, learning tasks, psychological processes and the like. As in biologic taxonomy, classification is in terms of manifest distinguishable attributes of the things being classified. A hierarchical taxonomy consists of classes of increasing generality, that is, classes within classes, such as sub-species, species, genus, family, order, class, phyla and kingdom. Just as animals and plants can be classified according to this scheme, so, too, can psychological tests and hypothetical mental processes be hierarchically categorized in terms both of their distinguishing and their common characteristics.

All taxonomic systems are not hierarchical. Guilford's structure-of-intellect model is an example of a non-hierarchical system of classification of mental abilities (Guilford, 1967). (Guilford calls it a 'morphological' model in contrast to hierarchical.) It is the now

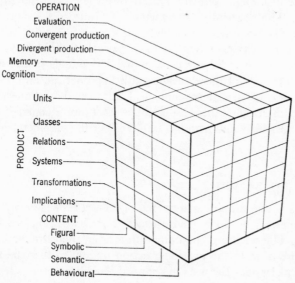

FIGURE 1.1. Guilford's structure-of-intellect model, with three parameters.

familiar 'cube' formed by the three broad parameters: operations, products, and contents, and their various subdivisions, as shown in Figure 1.1.

Such taxonomies based on descriptive characteristics of tests, tasks and processes may be theoretically and empirically useful in our search for sources of individual differences. The independence of the hypothesized sources, however, must be empirically verified. We know that two tests which look very different and might therefore be classified quite differently in terms of their manifest characteristics (e.g., vocabulary and block design) can represent largely the same source of variance (as shown by a very high g loading on both vocabulary and block design). The relationships that exist in a taxonomic model are not necessarily either functional or even correlational. Therefore they may or may not reflect the actual correlational and factorial structure of mental abilities or their functional organization. A good taxonomy, however, should increase the probability of discovering new sources of individual differences, much as the periodic table of elements predicted the existence of certain elements long before they were actually discovered. The descriptive parameters of Guilford's structure-of-intellect, for example, form a 'cube' of $4 \times 5 \times 6 = 120$ cells, each of which represents a hypothetical mental ability, that is, an independent source of variance among individuals in the population. But many of these cells are still hypothetical, awaiting the construction of special psychological tests capable of measuring the hypothesized abilities – abilities that are defined by the various possible combinations (120 in all) of the parameters of the model.

FACTOR HIERARCHIES

A means of determining a hierarchy of mental tests is provided by factor analysis or, to be more exact, certain methods of factor analysis. The resulting hierarchy differs from the taxonomic hierarchy discussed in the previous section mainly in that the factor hierarchy classifies the tests in terms of their latent characteristics or factors rather than in terms purely descriptive of their manifest characteristics. Any congruence between the manifest taxonomy and the latent organization of the tests is, strictly speaking, incidental. Theoretically and methodologically there is no necessary congruence between a purely taxonomic description of tests and a factor model of the tests. In other words, manifest and latent characteristics tend to be correlated, so that tests which look more alike are more highly intercorrelated than tests which look less alike. But there are many exceptions. One of the chief values of factor analysis is that it reveals classifications in terms of latent resemblance among tests, that is, the similarity of tests in terms of their patterns of intercorrelations with other tests. Many patterns which would hardly be imagined from an armchair classification on the basis of manifest characteristics show up in an actual matrix of test intercorrelations. For example, in a manifest taxonomy, tests of reading comprehension and of spelling might be more closely related to one another than either is related to arithmetic reasoning and arithmetic computation, which would be closely related to one another. In terms of the actual pattern of intercorrelations, however, it is often found that the closest relationships are reading comprehension–arithmetic reasoning and spelling–arithmetic computation.

Since different psychological tests have different degrees of generality, that is, they account for greater or lesser proportions of the total variance among persons on a whole battery of tests, we are led to think in terms of a hierarchy of abilities, with some abilities being of broader significance than others. Factor analysis sorts out tests along these lines. A principal components analysis of a test intercorrelation matrix yields a number of components or hypothetical sources of variance of decreasing magnitude, the first component accounting for the largest proportion of variance and each succeeding component accounting for less and less variance, thereby producing the simplest type of hierarchy of sources of variance. Whether or not these components can be given psychologically meaningful descriptions is another matter. Often they cannot, and for this reason other solutions are used, such as rotating the principal axes to approximate Thurstone's criterion of simple structure. (Simple structure maximizes the number of zero or non-significant loadings of tests on each factor, so that as much as possible of the variance of each test is attributable to a single factor.) If the factor axes are not forced to be orthogonal (i.e., zero correlations between the factors) but are allowed to be oblique (i.e., correlated) in order to achieve the best approximation to a simple structure, then one can obtain correlations between the first-order factors. This correlation matrix can in turn be factor analyzed to yield second-order factors (or 'group factors'), and if these are made oblique, the process can be continued to yield third-order factors, and so on. Finally, at some stage in this process, only one factor emerges that accounts for a significant proportion of the co-variance between the factors at the next lower level in generality, and this factor can be called a general factor. The method thus yields a hierarchy of abilities, and one can note where various tests fall out in this hierarchy. The resulting picture depends upon many considerations which are beyond the scope of this discussion. Suffice it to say that no one factorial solution is compelled by nature. Different structures can result from different methods, tests, and populations. Some will provide a more parsimonious description of the ability domain than others; some will make more sense in terms of other theoretical psychological considerations that lie outside factor analysis itself. Thus, factor analysis can never be an end in itself.

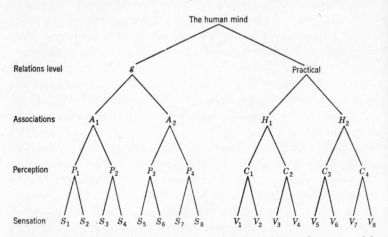

FIGURE 1.2. Burt's hierarchical model for ability factors, with successive dichotomizations at different levels of generality.

It is best regarded only as an adjunct to other lines of investigation for the study of the organization of mental abilities: experimental techniques, quantitative genetic analysis, and developmental and biological approaches that take into consideration the phylogeny and ontogeny of behavior and the relationship of behavior to neurological structures. Factor models can best be evaluated from the standpoint of psychological theory in terms of how well they can be related to data from these other lines of investigation.

Figures 1.2 and 1.3 show two hierarchical factor models. They illustrate the kinds of hierarchical models that can be formulated and tested in terms of factor analysis. For an excellent discussion and evaluation of factor models of ability, the reader is referred to Professor Vernon's *The Structure of Human Abilities* (1950).

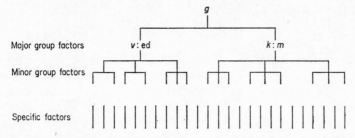

FIGURE 1.3. Vernon's hierarchical model of ability factor. g = general factor, $v : ed$ = verbal–educational aptitude, $k : m$ = spatial–mechanical aptitude.

HIERARCHICAL VERSUS NON-HIERARCHICAL CORRELATIONS

Since factor analysis is based on the matrix of so-called zero-order correlations among a number of tests, factors have essentially the same limitations as zero-order correlations. The most fundamental limitation is that correlation does not necessarily imply causation or functional relationship. Therefore a hierarchical factor model does not guarantee functional relationships between factors at different levels in the hierarchy.

Functional dependence of one ability upon another will, of course, show up as a correlation between the tests, but the correlation alone is not sufficient to establish the functional dependence. One type of correlation, however, may provide a stronger clue to functional dependence than another type. The so-called 'twisted pear' type of correlation may indicate functional dependence, while the bivariate normal correlation has no such implication. For example, there are essentially two ways that variables X and Y can be related: non-hierarchically or hierarchically. A non-hierarchical relationship is implied (but not guaranteed) by the typical bivariate normal correlation scatter diagram. The table below shows this kind of relationship: it implies that X is both necessary-and-sufficient to predict Y.

This says: Low $X \leftrightarrow$ Low Y, and High $X \leftrightarrow$ High Y. The 'twisted pear' (so-called because the actual scatter diagram often has the shape of a silhouetted twisted pear) results in the following

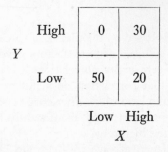

table, which indicates that high scores on X are necessary-but-not-sufficient for high scores on Y, and high scores on Y are sufficient but not necessary for high scores on X. The 'twisted pear' form of correlation is shown below.

	Low	High
High	0	30
Low	50	20

X

This says Low $X \rightarrow$ Low Y, and High $Y \rightarrow$ High X. It is evident that in the 'twisted pear' case X and Y cannot both have normal distributions. One or both must have a skewed distribution. We know that many skewed distributions are merely an artifact of the scale of measurement and that most psychological scales can be made so as to yield a normal distribution of scores in the population. The question therefore arises whether the 'twisted pear' type of relationship is merely an artifact of the scale of measurement. It is a fact that most psychological tests are specially constructed so as to yield a normal distribution of scores in the standardization population. The marginal totals of the contingency table, as shown above, are thus forced to be equal, and the only correlation that can be manifested is of the first variety, described as necessary-and-sufficient. Only if we determine the correlation in some sub-group of the standardization population are we likely to obtain skewed distributions that would permit the emergence of the 'twisted pear' relationship. It is evident that the 'twisted pear' can be said to indicate a hierarchical relationship rather than a measurement artifact only if there is some rational basis for the scale of measurement that would permit the score distribution to be other than normal if such was the actual state of nature. This means having at least an interval scale. If there is no basis for claiming an interval scale, we might as well have the statistical convenience of a normal distribution and make our test to yield scores that assume this form. But if the distribution of scores in the population is normal and there is some rational justification for this distribution, then the non-normality of score distributions in certain sub-groups of the population is justified and the 'twisted pear' relationship can genuinely imply a hierarchical relationship between the variables. The first table above (necessary-and-sufficient) is actually neutral with respect to a hierarchical relationship, since we do not know from the scatter plot alone whether a hierarchical functional relationship actually exists but does not show up because cases in quadrant I have been eliminated, for example, through genetic selection. Suppose, for example, that 100 per cent of the variance in traits X and Y were completely attributable to genetic factors and that assortative mating were such as to cause a very high correlation among spouses for both traits. Then the genes for each trait would be sorted together, so that if a person received the genes for high ability on one characteristic he would receive the genes for high ability on the other, and similarly for low ability. Thus the traits would be highly correlated, yet they could be either functionally independent (non-hierarchical) or could have a hierarchical functional dependence. The latter possibility would be ruled out by finding some sub-population in which zero correlation could be authentically established between the two variables in question. A simple example of a hierarchical dependence which would show up correlationally as a 'twisted pear' is the relationship between pitch discrimination and ability to learn the violin. Poor ability in pitch discrimination insures poor violinistic ability, but good pitch discrimination does not guarantee good violinistic ability; pitch discrimination is thus necessary-but-not-sufficient, and additional aptitudes are needed to become a good violinist. (For further discussion of the psychological significance of the 'twisted pear' the reader is referred to Fisher, 1959, and Storms, 1960).

LEARNING HIERARCHIES

Gagné (1968) has proposed a theory of mental development based on the notion of *cumulative learning*, in which various skills form a *transfer hierarchy*, with some skills being more basic than others in the sense of providing positive transfer to the acquisition of more complex skills in the hierarchy. The model thus views mental ability at any given cross-section in time as a product of cumulative learning. The orderliness of mental development according to this view is brought about by the fact that some skills are prerequisite to the acquisition of others which are so dependent on positive transfer from the earlier acquired skills that it is very unlikely that the more advanced skills would ever be learned in the absence of the simpler sub-skills. This, then, is a true functional hierarchy. It must be tested both in terms of correlations between tests that measure the relevant skills and in terms of experiments that test for amount of transfer from one skill to the acquisition of another.

Gagné clearly believes that this is not only a model for specific kinds of learning, such as mathematics, in which there is an obvious hierarchy of sub-skills, but that it is an adequate model for mental development and the structure of mental abilities in general. He states: 'Intellectual development may be conceived as the building of increasingly complex and interacting structures of learning capabilities. The entities which are learned build upon each other in patterns of great complexity, and thus generate an ever-increasing intellectual competence. Each structure may also build upon itself through self-initiated thinking activity. There is no magic key to this structure – it is simply developed piece by piece. The magic is in learning and memory and transfer' (Gagné, 1968, p. 190). Neurological systems which impose structure on the perceived environment, and the concept of 'readiness' based on neurological maturation, have little or no place in Gagné's formulation. The child is seen as having a rather homogeneous, undifferentiated capability for learning, for recall, and for transfer of previously learned skills to the learning of new skills. 'The child progresses from one point to the next in his development, not because he acquires one or a dozen new associations, but because he learns an ordered set of capabilities which build upon each other in progressive fashion through the processes of differentiation, recall and transfer of learning' (Gagné, 1968, p. 181). A generalized learning hierarchy is shown in Figure 1.4.

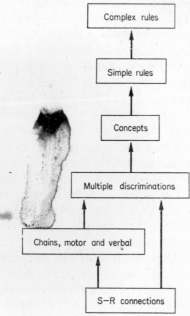

FIGURE 1.4. A general hierarchy for cumulative learning. (From Gagné, 1968.)

It is a well-established fact that at any given age it is much easier to teach some things than others; some skills seem to be acquired almost spontaneously *after* a certain age and it is practically impossible to teach a child to perform certain skills *before* a certain age. Can this be explained entirely in terms of transfer from prerequisite learning? Or must we invoke internal maturational processes dependent upon the autonomous growth of neurological structures, in addition to experiential factors, to explain the great differences in learning capabilities from one age to another? Gagné would probably argue that after the first two or three years of life, at most, the child's neurological capabilities change and develop only as the result of his specific experiences. Individual differences in mental ability are seen as due solely to differences in some undifferentiated basic learning ability plus experiential differences. The structure or organization of mental abilities is thus conceived as entirely imposed on the organism through its encounters with the environment.

Observations of children's vastly different capabilities of copying different simple geometric forms at different ages, for example, would seem to cast considerable doubt on Gagné's theory. A normal child can easily copy a square at age 4, but he has to be 7 before he can copy a diamond. It is practically impossible to teach a 4-year-old to do so. The 7-year-old does so without any teaching. The well-known experiments of Piaget, involving concepts such as conservation of number and volume, show the same phenomenon. Such findings suggest that the learning of particular skills depends upon the maturation of neutral structures. But it is hard to see how such evidence could disprove the Gagné theory. No matter how often we failed to teach 4-year-olds to copy the shape of a diamond, for example, it could always be claimed that we had not hit upon the right method or had not built up the proper hierarchy or prerequisite sub-skills. The Gagné formulation is very likely valid with respect to the acquisition of certain kinds of subject matter, such as mathematics. Gagné's model has been tested on subject matter of this type and there can be little doubt of its validity. '. . . with few exceptions, learners who were able to learn the capabilities higher in the hierarchy also knew how to do the tasks reflected by the simpler rules lower in the hierarchy. Those who had not learned to accomplish a lower-level task generally could not acquire a higher-level capability to which it was related' (Gagné, 1968, p. 183). The crucial question, however, is whether the cumulative learning model is adequate as a general theory of mental development. I doubt very much that it is. If other lines of evidence about cognitive development cannot falsify the theory as a general theory of mental development simply because the theory is not sufficiently spelled out to permit empirical tests of it, this in itself is a defect of the theory which will have to be remedied if the boundaries of its applicability are to be determined.

One of the most important questions about cumulative learning hierarchies is whether there are individual differences in how far up a person can rise in the hierarchy, even assuming all persons are given the same prerequisite experiences. A chimpanzee presumably given the same experiences as a human child never develops beyond a human mental age of 4 or 5 on any kind of test. Why not? There are obviously neurological differences between ape and man involving more than differences in rate of learning. Excluding persons with gross neurological defects, we can similarly ask whether all persons can attain every level in the hierarchy of a subject matter such as mathematics. If the only fundamental individual differences are in learning *rate*, then theoretically even mentally retarded persons in the IQ range from, say, 50 to 70, should be able to obtain Ph.D.s in mathematics, given sufficient time. Other theories would say just the opposite: that individual differences result much less from learning rates than from complexity of neurological organization, and that no matter how thoroughly certain sub-skills or prerequisites are acquired, some individuals will reach a point where they will not be able to move up to the next higher rung of the hierarchy. It is on this issue especially that Gagné's formulation will have to take a stand, one that is empirically testable. There is little satisfaction in being told that a person with an IQ of 70 could become a Bertrand Russell if only he were properly taught over a period of some 100 or 200 years!

NEUROLOGICAL HIERARCHIES

Not only can behavior be conceived hierarchically, but its neurological substrate can also be viewed hierarchically in both structure and function. The central nervous system (CNS) lends itself particularly well to a hierarchical description of its structures and functions. However, no comprehensive or systematic theory or body of data yet exists relating the hierarchies formulated for the behavioral and neurological domains.

Consideration of neurological evidence should provide a good basis for narrowing the range of possible models of mental ability. When there is no empirically compelling basis for choosing between alternative models in terms of behavioral evidence alone, we can ask which model is most compatible with neurological evidence.

Bronson (1965) has pointed out some of the parallels between neural organization and learning processes and mental development. His model emphasizes the hierarchical nature of CNS organization. He postulates a series of three main levels within the nervous system. 'More complex ("higher") levels are seen as a product of the evolution of successively more differentiating neural networks which in part supersede, and in part build upon, the less complex adaptive mechanisms mediated by the phylogenetically older levels. Ontogenetically, the emergence of new behavioral capacities is seen as a function of the sequential maturation of networks within the different levels' (Bronson, 1965, p. 7). The essential scheme, which is depicted in Figure 1.5, is summarized by Bronson as follows: 'Peripheral afferents and efferents (solid lines in Figure 1.5) connect with the CNS at the several levels so that increasingly refined sensory and motor discriminations can be made directly by the successively more differentiating networks. The networks for vertical integration between levels enable the more primitive systems to exercise an upward control for the general programming of patterns of cerebral activation, while higher levels projecting downward effect more highly differentiated overall function through tonic inhibition plus a more selective phasic excitation and inhibition of lower-level systems' (Bronson, 1965, p. 8).

Neurological evidence can add to the interpretation of correlation coefficients which by themselves give no clue as to the underlying basis for the correlation. For example, Jensen (1964) found a perfect correlation between auditory and visual digit span among normal university students. This might suggest that the same neural mechanisms are involved in both forms of memory, except of course, for the neural mechanisms involved in the different receptor channels. However, patients with dominant temporal lobe lesions show an extreme dissociation between auditory and visual digit memory, often performing at a mentally retarded level on auditory digit span while performing completely within the normal range on visual span. This suggests that different mechanisms are involved in auditory and visual memory beyond the receptor mechanisms. Instead of digit span being a single set of underlying processes, as one might infer from the perfect correlation of the two among college students, it is evident from the neurological finding that we are dealing with two distinct sets of processes which are merely highly correlated, but are not functionally interdependent, in the normal population.

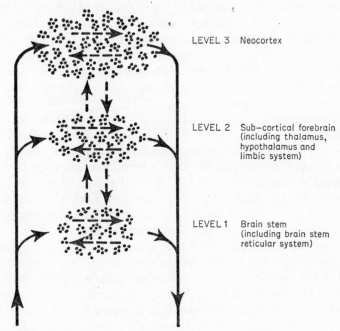

FIGURE 1.5. Basic characteristics of a hierarchical model of central nervous system functioning. (From Bronson, 1965.)

PHYLOGENIC HIERARCHIES

The field of comparative psychology provides ample evidence that we can legitimately speak of the phylogeny of mental abilities. The structural and functional differences in the central nervous systems from the lowest organisms up to the highest in the phylogenetic scale are paralleled by differences in various 'mental' capabilities. The phylogenetic hierarchy in this respect is best characterized in terms of increasing complexity of adaptive capabilities and increasing breadth of transfer of learning as we move from 'lower' to 'higher' organisms.

In general, the lower the demands of a learning task upon complexity of discriminations, number of response alternatives, and transfer from prior experience, the less will be the difference between organisms lower and higher in the phyletic scale. Lashley (1949) noted that '. . . intelligence is usually defined as the capacity to profit by experience, or the capacity to learn . . . [but] under favourable conditions every animal, at least above the level of worms, can form a simple association in a single trial. In this sense the capacity to learn was perfected early and has changed little in the course of evolution' (Lashley, 1949, p. 30).

Experiments by Bitterman (1965) on habit reversal in animals from fish to monkeys show that the intelligence of animals on various rungs of the evolutionary ladder differs not only in degree but also qualitatively. In the habit reversal procedure the animal learns the discrimination A^+ $v.$ B^- and then has to learn the reverse, i.e., A^- $v.$ B^+, and these two conditions are alternated repeatedly. It is one of the most fundamental tests of learning-to-learn, as evinced by the animal's increased speed of learning and 'unlearning' of the habit each time it is reversed. A rat improves markedly from one reversal to the next, a pigeon much less so, and a fish not at all. When extensive portions of the cerebral cortex of the rat are removed, thereby reducing the most prominent feature of the mammalian brain that is absent from the brain of the fish and first appears in the reptilian brain, the intellectual behavior of these decorticated rats is exactly like that of the turtle, an animal with little cortex. Bitterman's conclusions from this extensive work are strictly in line with a hierarchical conception of the evolution and phylogeny of intelligence. He states: 'Thorndike's experiments [on animal learning] led him to deny the existence of intellectual uniqueness anywhere in the evolutionary hierarchy of animals. It was he who set forth the theory that differences from species to species are only differences of degree, and that the evolution of intelligence involves only the improvement of old processes and the development of more neural elements. Our studies of habit reversal and probability learning in the lower animals suggest that brain structures evolved by higher animals do not serve merely to replicate old functions and modes of intellectual adjustment but to mediate new ones (a contradiction of the Thorndike hypothesis). Work with decorticated rats points to the same conclusion' (Bitterman, 1965, pp. 99-100).

Harlow and Harlow (1962) reiterate this theme on the basis of learning and memory experiments performed on rhesus monkeys, chimpanzees, human children and adults. The Harlows conclude: 'In so far as relatively simple intellectual processes are concerned, man is little or no better than many non-human animals. Thus, there is little reason to believe that the human memory is significantly better than that of the chimpanzee' (Harlow and Harlow, 1962, p. 34). The Harlows cite a study of Tinklepaugh, who compared human adults, children and chimpanzees on a very complex memory test. The test involved only memory, not reasoning or problem-solving. 'The young chimpanzees were better than the best human children, who were eight years old, and they were almost as good as the human adults. Since one would expect that the translation of object and position cues into language – an automatic response of older children and adults in a learning situation – would be of some help, one is led to doubt that humans are superior to chimpanzees in basic memory capacity. As we pass from simple to complex intellectual functions, the superiority of man becomes progressively more evident. However, some sub-human animals possess rudimentary capabilities of any and all aspects of thinking that we can measure' (Harlow and Harlow, 1962, pp. 34-5).

Various types of discrimination learning problems (in which sensory acuity *per se* is not at issue) suggest that learning hierarchies in the Gagné sense rise to different levels of complexity in different species and that some levels are unattainable by some species. Harlow (1959) points out that simple object discrimination can be acquired by fish, mice, rats, pigeons, cats, dogs, monkeys, apes and men, the only differences being in rate of acquisition – but all can attain the same final level of performance. However, when we come to a more complex form of discrimination – the so-called oddity problem – the situation completely changes. In the oddity problem three or more objects or patterns are presented; all are the same except for one – the odd item. The animal is rewarded for responding consistently either to the odd or to the non-odd items in each new set that is presented. Harlow states that '. . . no pigeon, rat, cat, or dog has solved the oddity problem' (although they have solved certain simplified versions of it). In fact, the oddity problem is beyond the capacity of the young human child. Adult primates, however, can do it without much difficulty. Still more complex is the combined oddity–non-oddity problem. In this problem the animal must learn to respond to the odd item if the background on which all the items are presented is colored, say green, and responds to the non-odd items if the background is colored red. No animals below primates can ever learn to do the oddity–non-oddity problem, but it is mastered by monkeys and apes without undue difficulty. If we go a step further in complexity and make up a triple-ambiguity problem, in which the selection of the odd or non-odd item depends simultaneously upon two different attributes of the background, such as color and shape (e.g. green *v.* red *and* square *v.* round), the problem is beyond the capabilities of monkeys and of most apes, and it cannot be mastered by many humans or by most humans below a certain age.

Thus the capacity for learning set or learning-to-learn is an example of transfer of learning and, far more than the learning of any single task, is related systematically to phylogeny. Furthermore, there is little correlation between learning rates on simple discrimination problems and performance on more complex tasks. Not only have learning set measurements proven more sensitive and reliable than any other form of learning in studying the phylogeny of behavior, it is also one of the most sensitive methods of studying the ontogeny (individual development) of mental capabilities. Performance on learning-set tasks correlates highly with mental age in young children, when mental age is assessed by standard tests such as the Stanford-Binet.

ONTOGENIC HIERARCHIES

The biologists' generalization that 'ontogeny recapitulates phylogeny' probably holds true for the behavioral as well as of the morphological aspects of development. Cognitive development appears to be hierarchical in the individual's development, with certain capabilities regularly preceding others in their order of appearance. Although no one denies that many important mental processes and skills must be acquired through environmental influences – the acquisition of verbal mediation mechanisms, learning sets, and cumulative learning hierarchies *à la* Gagné – the research evidence is becoming increasingly convincing that the acquisition of hierarchically ordered cognitive processes also depends, not solely upon appropriate inputs from the environment, but upon the maturation of a hierarchically ordered neural substrate. This view holds that certain patterns of neural growth or organization, determined by constitutional factors, must occur before the effects of learning can be manifest in the cognitive processes we identify as intelligence: reasoning ability, abstract and conceptual abilities, the ability to transform the world of the concrete into symbolic representations.

This view does not deny that certain cognitive skills at some level in the developmental hierarchy cannot be specifically trained before their time, so to speak, in the absence of the development of the neural mechanisms normally involved in the acquisition of these skills. But such premature training shows important differences from the learning that occurs almost spontaneously when there is maturational readiness: (*a*) pre-maturational training requires much more time, effort, precision and control of the conditions of learning; (*b*) though the specific skills at which the training is directed may be acquired, they show much narrower transfer, and in a factor analysis of a variety of cognitive tests the specifically acquired skill would probably contribute little if any variance to the *g* factor on which normally most cognitive skills are highly loaded; (*c*) without further specific training or practice, the specially acquired skill shows no continued growth or transfer to other new skills, and may even deteriorate; and (*d*) it does not seem to constitute a 'quantum jump' in the cognitive hierarchy such as to support the acquisition of skills at a higher level.

The Piagetian conservation tests are a good example of a cognitive hierarchy. An even more clear-cut example is the ability simply to copy geometric forms of varying complexity. Ilg and Ames (1964) have presented a set of ten such forms which constitute an almost perfect age scale in terms of the percentage of children who can correctly copy a given form at any particular age level. The ten forms closely approximate a Guttman scale of difficulty. That is, nearly all children who can correctly copy, say, figure number 5 in the scale, can also copy figures 4, 3, 2 and 1; and nearly all those who fail on figure 6 also fail figures 7, 8, 9 and 10. It is exceedingly difficult, if not altogether impossible, to *teach* a child to copy correctly the figures in the scale that lie beyond those he is able to copy easily without any specific training. Performance on this figure copying test is highly correlated with other indices of cognitive development, such as performance on the Piaget tasks and on the Stanford-Binet intelligence test, and with speed and ease of learning school subjects in the primary grades.

Sheldon White (1965) has made an intensive study of developmental changes in children's learning capabilities and has concluded that two main levels of mental development are discernible – the associative and the cognitive. The associative is most in evidence during the pre-school years and the emergence of the cognitive level becomes manifest between the ages of 5 and 7 in the majority of children. White views the associative and cognitive levels as hierarchical, each persisting in adult mental organization as 'layers'. The associative layer is laid down in early development and consists of the capacity for basic aspects of associative learning, discrimination and primary stimulus generalization. The cognitive layer is laid down in later childhood, most markedly between the ages of 5 and 7. During the period many signs of change in the child's mode of cognitive functioning are evident. Between these ages children show a transition from a type of performance in learning situations characteristic of lower animals in similar situations to a type of performance characteristic of adult humans. White (1965) has enumerated some of the many forms of evidence for this transition derived from research on human learning, neurology, and psychometrics:

1. Narrow to broad transposition.
2. Easier non-reversal shifts to easier reversal shifts.
3. Onset of resistance to classical conditioning.
4. Change in the effect of a 'varying-position' condition in discrimination learning.
5. Growth of inference in a problem-solving task.
6. Possible interference of complex hypotheses in discrimination learning.

7. Shift from 'near receptors' (tactual, kinesthetic, etc.) to 'distance receptors' (visual and auditory) in attending to environmental events.
8. Shift from colour to form-dominance in classifying objects.
9. Development of personal left-right sense.
10. Decrease in form, word, and letter reversals.
11. Ability to hold spatial information through disorientation.
12. Change in face-hand test – children under 6 do not indicate awareness of a touch on the hand if the face is touched simultaneously but report only the touch on the face. After about age 6 the child can report both.
13. Increasing predictability of adult IQ.
14. Internalization of speech.
15. Shift from syntagmatic (associations having a meaningful connection but not grammatical likeness) to paradigmatic (associations having the same grammatical form class) word associations.
16. Increased disruptive influence of delayed auditory feedback.
17. Shift of verbalization towards a planning function in the child's activity.
18. Transition from social to abstract reinforcement.
19. A number of transitions involving conservation of number, length, space, volume, etc., shown in Piaget-type studies.

The shifts from the associative level to a predominantly cognitive level of mental functioning can be summarized in terms of four general transitions: (*a*) from direct responses to stimuli to responses produced by mediated stimuli; (*b*) emergence of the ability to induce invariance on the welter of phenomenal variability; (*c*) the capacity to organize past experience to permit inference and prediction; and (*d*) increased sensitivity to information yielded by distance as against near receptors.

The fact that so many diverse forms of cognitive activity change quite rapidly during the years from 5 to 7 in general and probably over a much shorter time-span in individual children suggests the maturation of some common underlying mechanisms. Acquired skills in verbal mediation seem not to be used spontaneously by the child until the neural substrate of the child's cognitive development has reached a certain level of maturity. As White (1968) has said, '. . . the gathering evidence seems more and more to suggest that the child's progressive sophistication in language between five and seven is not the cause, but is rather the correlate of his progressive sophistication in learning'.

Studies at the Center for Research in Human Learning of the University of Minnesota bear out this observation. It is summarized in the Annual Report (June 15, 1967) of the Center as follows: 'The acquisition of symbolic representational abilities in children has been a popular subject of research study in the field of developmental psychology. However, relatively little attention has so far been paid to the factors that determine whether or not the child will, in any given situation, actively call into service and use those symbolic abilities which he has already acquired, i.e., which are already in his cognitive repertoire. Current research by Flavell and his students indicates that age or developmental status is one such fact. There appears to exist a systematic time-lag between the initial developmental attainment of various symbolic representational capacities and their spontaneous utilization by the child as mnemonic aids in recall tasks. The initial study in this area gave clear evidence that kindergarten children do not spontaneously rehearse the names of objects as a strategy for recalling these objects, despite the fact that they have no difficulty in correctly labelling them when later requested to do so. Thus, while capable of representing objects verbally, they have not yet developed a disposition to exercise this capability as a means to particular cognitive ends. A subsequent study . . . demonstrated that first-graders who fail to rehearse the object names in this task recall fewer objects than first-graders who do spontaneously rehearse. However, non-rehearsers of this age can readily be induced to rehearse through brief instruction, and they dramatically improve their recall as a consequence. But, when no longer instructed to rehearse, they quickly abandon this symbolic activity and their recall regresses towards its initial level.' Conceptual learning is clearly of the type that White characterizes as cognitive, as contrasted with associative, and accordingly it develops in most children some time after 5 years of age. In view of this theory, it is especially interesting that the Minnesota researchers failed to find any facilitation as a result of training pre-kindergarten children in certain conceptual abilities. 'This suggests, as many studies now appear to suggest, that the usual learning procedures are not effective unless children are at an age very close to that at which they acquire the concept spontaneously. Simply giving a young child experience with the task does not produce learning of the concept.' In short, it appears that experience is necessary-but-not-sufficient for abstract and conceptual forms of mental activity – those processes we call intelligence.

A HIERARCHY OF COMPLEXITY AND THE QUESTION OF g

In general, mental tests can be ordered along a continuum going from simple to complex. This complexity continuum is not the same as difficulty *per se*. Repeating a series of 10 digits, for example, is a difficult task if judged by the percentage of the population who can do it, but in a more fundamental psychological sense it is a less complex mental task than answering the question: 'In what way are a banana and an orange alike?' An echo chamber or a tape recorder can repeat a 10-digit series, but a relatively complex computer would be required to 'infer' the correct superordinate category, given two subordinates, as in the banana-orange question. The intercorrelations among tests are roughly related to their degree of proximity on the complexity continuum, and tests which are intended to identify g, such as Raven's Progressive Matrices, show increasing correlations with other tasks as one moves along the continuum from simple to complex. In fact, inspection of factor matrices based on a variety of tests at various points on the complexity continuum reveals that the general factor or the first principal component has loadings in the various tasks that are more or less correlated with psychological judgments of the tasks' degree of complexity. It has been noted by Alvord (1969), from his research on transfer in learning hierarchies in the Gagné sense, that a measure of general intelligence becomes increasingly predictive of performance at each successively higher level in the learning hierarchy. The higher correlation of general ability with performance on later tasks suggests that in learning-to-learn the subject behaves as if he 'were gradually overcoming misconceptions and confusions and finding his level' (Alvord, 1969, p. 41).

It is most interesting, however, that when persons are sorted into groups that stand either high or low on some complex measure of ability, such as a test with a high *g* loading, they will be found to differ on nearly all other tests ranging along the complexity continuum, but the differences between the groups will decrease as task complexity decreases. This means, of course, that there is a general ability factor which is manifest in nearly all test behavior that puts any mental demands on the subject whatsoever. Guilford (1964), in examining more than 7,000 correlation coefficients among intellectual measures, found some 80 per cent of them to be significantly greater than zero. Many of the tests involved in his survey measured quite minute factors and most of the analyses were based upon subjects of higher than average IQ; most of them were in training as commissioned officers in the Air Force. This restricted range of talent in a subject pool which has been selected partly on the criterion of above average general intelligence, of course, reduces the *g* variance in the sample and causes fewer significant positive correlations among ability tests. In a sample of the total population it seems likely that hardly any true zero correlations would be found among mental tests of any degree of complexity beyond the level of simple reaction time.

Eysenck (1967) has reviewed evidence that reaction time or response speed to a stimulus situation increases as the number of bits of information in the stimulus situation increases; in fact, response time increases as a linear function of bits of information. Furthermore, it has been found that the *slope* of this function is significantly correlated (negatively) with IQ. A description of the experimental paradigm for determining this will help to make it clear. The subject sits in front of a panel on which there is a single light bulb; directly beneath the bulb is a pushbutton. When the light flashes 'on', the subject pushes the button to turn the light 'off'. The subject's response time is a measure of simple reaction time. When there is only one light/button combination there are zero bits of information conveyed. The subject is required to respond to an increasing number of light/button combinations, responding to the one light that goes 'on' in the increasing array of potential alternatives. The amount of information conveyed increases logarithmically as the number of lights. When zero bits of information are conveyed (one light = simple reaction time) there is no correlation between reaction time and

IQ. With an increasing number of lights, reaction time correlates increasingly with IQ. This relationship was demonstrated experimentally by Roth (1964).

Fox and Taylor (1967) devised a battery of training tests to represent different levels of complexity in terms of Gagné's generalized learning hierarchy. The tasks were specially devised to incorporate the essential features of each level (and subsidiary levels within these) of Gagné's hierarchy: stimulus-response, motor chaining, verbal chaining, multiple discrimination, concepts, principles and problem-solving. Two groups of army recruits were compared on all these tasks. The High AFQT group had scores between 90 and 99 on the Armed Forces Qualification Test (AFQT), an omnibus test of general intelligence; the Low AFQT group had scores between 10 and 21. The performances of these two groups appear to diverge increasingly as they go from the lower to the higher tasks in the hierarchy. What is perhaps most surprising is that there is a significant difference even between the two least complex tasks in the hierarchy; both are at the stimulus-response level, but one involved only simple reaction time, the other complex reaction time. The results are in accord with the finding of Roth, reported above. Fox and Taylor described these two tasks as follows: 'The first two tasks . . . are sequential monitoring tasks which fall at the simplest level of complexity. In fact, they are so simple that no learning is required for performance. These tasks have elements in common with many military jobs. . . . Task 1 (T_1) is a Simple Sequential Monitoring Task. The trainee was told that this "control" panel was part of a communications systems that became overloaded when a red light came on. His task was simply to "reset" the control panel by pressing the lever when a red light appeared. The control panel apparatus was programmed so that white lights flashed intermittently across the panel accompanied by loud clicking noises. After an interval which varied from 15 to 205 seconds, the white lights went out and one of the four red lights came on. The trainee was required to "reset" the panel a total of twenty times over a forty-minute period. The second task (T_2) is a Choice Sequential Monitoring Task and uses the same apparatus as the previous task except for additional response levels. The trainee was to respond to one of the four red lights, labelled A, B, C or D, by pressing the corresponding lever.

All procedures and programming were identical for both tasks.'
The results are shown in Figure 1.6. Note that for both groups
Choice Monitoring resulted in greater response times than Simple
Monitoring and that the difference between the High and Low
AFQT groups increased with the increased complexity of the
task, even at this relatively simple level. This result shows that
subjects who are selected on the basis of performance on a relatively high level test (AFQT) differ even on performance of very
simple tasks; a general ability factor thus extends over an enormous

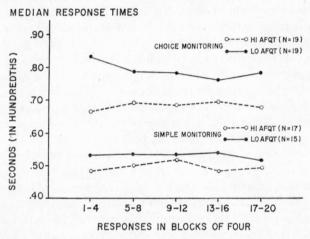

FIGURE 1.6. Response latencies for Hi and Lo AFQT trainees on
simple and choice sequential monitoring tasks. (From Fox and
Taylor, 1967.)

range of complexity and types of performance. One might wonder
if differences in a strictly cognitive task like the AFQT would be
reflected even in types of behavior quite far removed from the
intellectual sphere, and there is some indication that this is the
case, which would make one believe that there exists some very
broad factor of general adaptive capacity that shows up in every
aspect of coping with the environment. Greenberg (1969), for
example, reports studies of men accepted into the armed forces
who score between the 10th and 30th percentile on the AFQT,
with a mean AFQT score at the 14th percentile (as compared with

a mean at the 54th percentile for regular inductees). The study of the response to training by these men was called Project 100,000, since there were 100,000 inductees in this category (technically referred to in the armed forces as Category IV). On a reading ability test regular inductees averaged one year below the number of years of schooling they have completed; the Category IV inductees averaged 4·5 years below the grade level they completed in school. But there are differences also in the non-scholastic sphere. Greenberg notes: 'Training instructions and unit commanders report that Project One Hundred Thousand men, on the whole, have greater difficulty in coping with personal problems – debts, family crises, girl friends – but the machinery exists to counsel and help them' (p. 571).

A two-level theory of mental abilities

My research over the past several years on the intelligence and learning abilities of children called culturally disadvantaged, and the ways in which they differ typically from middle-class children in their intellectual capabilities, has led me to the formulation of a theory of mental ability which will comprehend the phenomena revealed by my investigations. The formulation has also served as a basis for predicting new phenomena concerning the relationship between intelligence, learning ability, and socio-economic status (SES). The theory evolved gradually to accommodate our growing body of psychometric and experimental data, and it is still in a formative stage. In the past two years, however, it has been sufficiently formalized to yield predictions of new phenomena and to be subjected to experimental tests by other investigators. It has also been subjected recently to certain criticisms. One aspect of the theory, at least, is still of doubtful validity, although it has not yet been put to a wholly appropriate test. Since some of the studies that led to the formulation of the theory can be better understood in light of the theory, it will be less to the reader's advantage to present this material in historical sequence than to present it in relation to the key aspects of the theory. To provide an over-view of the theory, it will be outlined first without reference to empirical evidence, which will be filled in later.

THE DIMENSIONALITY OF SOCIAL CLASS DIFFERENCES

The research literature on social class differences in intelligence makes it apparent to me that evidence for social class differences in intelligence cannot be readily systematized or comprehended without positing at least two dimensions along which the differences range. The work of Eells *et al.* (1951) was perhaps the most influential in arriving at this formulation, although Eells himself did not explicitly arrive at the same formulation. Eells pointed out on the basis of his massive data, in which individual test items were analyzed in terms of the percentage of children in different SES groups who could answer the item correctly, that the SES differences were related to (*a*) the cultural content of the test items and to (*b*) the complexity of the items, that is, the degree of abstractness and problem solving involved in the test item. Thus, one dimension along which test items can range is that of cultural loading, by which we mean the differential probability of exposure or opportunity to become familiar with the content of the item from one social class environment to another. Test items involving knowledge of muscial instruments, exotic zoo animals, and fairy tales, for example, can be said to have a high cultural loading. Whole tests differ on this dimension of culture-fairness. I have proposed that a main criterion of culture-fairness of tests be their heritability (i.e., the proportion of variance attributable to genetic factors) in the population in which they are standardized and used (Jensen, 1968c). Eells *et al.* (1951) also noted that the largest social class differences did not show up on the most culturally loaded items, but rather on those items that involved the highest degree of abstraction, conceptual thinking, and problem-solving ability. Often these items had no cultural content to speak of, in the sense of differential exposure of item content in different social classes. Besides, if all of the SES intellectual difference were due to differences between SES groups in cultural experiences, it should be possible to devise intelligence tests that favour low-SES groups over high-SES groups. So far no one has succeeded in doing this. The few attempts have failed to meet a crucial criterion, namely, that the test should still correlate highly with other measures of intelligence. If lower Stanford-Binet IQs in low-SES groups are due to differences in cultural experience, it should be possible to devise a test which correlates with the Stanford-Binet, but which gives low-SES children higher IQs than middle-SES children. In other words, culture bias in tests should be completely reversible. Despite energetic efforts, no one has been able to show that this is in fact possible, which leads me to the conclusion that the culture bias factor in SES intelligence differences is indeed a real effect, but a trivial one as compared with SES differences due to abstractness and complexity of test items. Tests can be devised to minimize the culture factor, but if they are to remain intelligence tests, with the predictive validity in our society that intelligence tests are known to have, they cannot minimize the complexity factor.

Figure 1.7 shows this two-dimensional space, with the hypothetical location of various tests in the space. The horizontal axis is the culture-loading dimension, defined by the theoretical extremes of complete heritability ($h^2 = 1$), in which there is no environmental variance in the test scores, and the other extreme of zero heritability, in which all the variance is attributable to environmental factors. The vertical axis is the complexity dimension, going from conditioning and simple associative learning up to complex conceptual learning and abstract problem solving. Tasks can be found at every point on this continuum; tests do not fall into discrete classes. Another point that needs to be emphasized is that a particular test does not necessarily have an invariant position in this two-dimensional space. Some tasks lend themselves to being learned on an associative level *or* on a conceptual level, and different learners may prefer one or the other approach, so that in one population a test may stand at a different point on the complexity continuum than in another population. Paired-associate learning is not represented in Figure 1.7 simply because it is so ambiguous with respect to the complexity dimension. Some subjects will learn the pairs by rote, others by means of conceptual mnemonic processes, depending upon the age and pattern of abilities of the subjects. Other tasks, like digit span and serial rote learning, are much less flexible in this respect, and nearly always stand low on this continuum. At the other extreme, complex tasks like the Progressive Matrices cannot be solved by simple associative processes and are therefore relatively fixed near the upper end of the continuum.

Although tests range continuously along this dimension, the dimension itself is viewed theoretically as being the result of two different types of mental ability which can be distributed independently in a given population. In other words, the diagram in Figure 1.7 is intended to describe phenotypic test performance and not the underlying genotypic abilities which find expression through these various tests.

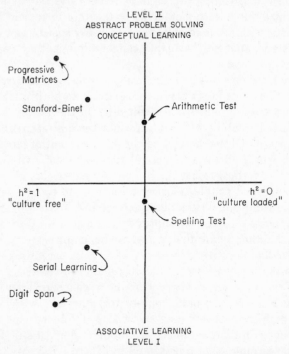

FIGURE 1.7. The two-dimensional space required for comprehending social-class differences in performance on tests of intelligence and learning ability. The locations of the various 'tests' in this space are speculative.

GENOTYPIC ABILITIES: LEVEL I AND LEVEL II

The vertical axis in Figure 1.7 represents the relative admixture in various tests of two fundamental genotypes of ability, which I call

Level I (associative learning ability) and Level II (conceptual learning and problem solving). By 'genotype' I mean simply the physiological substrate of the ability, regardless of whether it is genetically or experientially conditioned.

Level I ability is essentially the capacity to receive or register stimuli, to store them, and to later recognize or recall the material with a high degree of fidelity. I originally called it 'basic learning ability'. It is characterized especially by the lack of any need of elaboration, transformation or manipulation of the input in order to arrive at the output. The input need not be referred to other past learning in order to issue effective output. A tape recorder exemplifies Level I ability. In human performance digit span is one of the clearest examples of Level I ability. Reception and reproduction of the input with high fidelity is all that is required. Reverse digit span would represent a less pure form of Level I ability, since some transformation of the input is required prior to output. Serial rote learning and paired-associate rote learning, especially when the stimulus and response items are relatively meaningless and thereby do not lend themselves very much to verbal mediation or transfer from prior verbal learning, are largely dependent upon Level I ability. Level I is the source of most individual differences variance in performance on rote learning tasks, digit span, and other types of learning and recall which do not depend upon much transformation of the input.

Level II ability, on the other hand, is characterized by transformation and manipulation of the stimulus prior to making the response. It is the set of mechanisms which makes generalization beyond primary stimulus generalization possible. Semantic generalization and concept formation depend upon Level II ability; encoding and decoding of stimuli in terms of past experience, relating new learning to old learning, transfer in terms of concepts and principles, are all examples of Level II. Spearman's characterization of g as the 'eduction of relations and correlates' corresponds to Level II. Most standard intelligence tests, and especially culture-fair tests such as Raven's Progressive Matrices and Cattell's Culture-Fair Tests of g, depend heavily upon Level II ability. Since Level I ability is needed for high fidelity reproduction and is thus exemplified by a tape recorder, Level II ability is needed for transformation and elaboration of stimulus-response elements and what Spearman would call the *fundaments* of learning and is thus exemplified by the intellectual performance of a Newton and a Beethoven, who performed elaborate transformations on clearly circumscribed symbol systems – mathematics and music.

Few if any tests tap either Level I or Level II in a pure form, but some tests depend much more upon one than upon the other. Persons tend to use the abilities they've got, and so we find some subjects approaching what for most subjects is a Level I task as if it were a Level II task. At times this can result in poorer performance on a task. We have had bright college students, for example, approach a task which could be learned only by rote (since it involved only a random pairing and reinforcement of stimulus-response contingencies) as if it were a logical problem-solving task; their attempts to 'break the code' of what was only a random sequence of stimuli actually delayed their mastery of the task, a mastery which average young school children attained considerably faster, since only their Level I ability was brought to bear upon it.

Level I and Level II abilities are seen as largely genetically conditioned. The heritability of high Level II tests, such as the Progressive Matrices, is already clearly established, and there is no reason to suppose that Level I tests would not have equally high heritability (Jensen, 1967b, 1968a, 1968c, 1969a, 1969b). But the exact heritability of Level I and II is not so important, in terms of our theory, as the postulation that the mechanisms of Levels I and II are genotypically independent. They may be correlated in any given population, but since, according to the theory, they are due to genetic factors which can be assorted independently, they need not be correlated. Correlation can come about in two ways: (*a*) through genetic assortment of the two types of ability and (*b*) from a hierarchical functional dependence of Level II upon Level I. But discussion of these points should be postponed until a few more basic issues have been explicated.

FLUID AND CRYSTALLIZED INTELLIGENCE

Cattell (1963) has distinguished between two aspects of intelligence, *fluid* and *crystallized*. Most intelligence tests measure both the fluid and crystallized components of *g*. Fluid intelligence is the capacity for new conceptual learning and problem solving; it is a general 'brightness' and adaptability, relatively independent of education and experience, which can be invested in the particular opportunities for learning encountered by the individual in accord with his motivations and interests. Crystallized intelligence, in contrast, is a precipitate out of experience, consisting of acquired knowledge and developed intellectual skills. The question, then, is where tests of fluid and crystallized intelligence fit into my two-dimensional framework and especially how they are related to Level I and Level II processes. The simplest answer is to say that the two systems are orthogonal, i.e., uncorrelated, with one another, with respect to the Level I–Level II dimension. Crystallized and fluid intelligence cut across both Level I and Level II. Horn (1970) has listed the following tests as representative measures of fluid intelligence: memory span, figural relations, associative memory, induction, letter series, matrices, paired-associates memory for nonsense syllables, and digit span backwards. Measures of crystallized intelligence are: verbal comprehension, vocabulary and general information. It is apparent that tests of fluid and crystallized intelligence can fall at all points on the vertical axis in Figure 1.7. Fluid and crystallized intelligence do, however, correspond rather closely to the horizontal axis in Figure 1.7, the culture-loading dimension. But crystallized intelligence can have very high heritability and therefore would contain little cultural *variance* if the opportunities for learning and acculturation were highly similar for all individuals throughout the population. In brief, Cattell's formulation and mine are not at all in conflict, but are complementary schemata for describing mental test data.

Level I and Level II are viewed as broad categories of abilities which may be further fractionated by factor analysis or related methods. Level I and Level II are ways of conceptualizing two broad sources of variance in a host of mental tests. They in no way contradict or supplant other factors.

HIERARCHICAL DEPENDENCE OF LEVEL II UPON LEVEL I

Level II processes are viewed as functionally dependent upon Level I processes. This hypothesis was formulated as a part of

c

the theory to account for some of our early observations that some children with quite low IQs (i.e., 50 to 75) had quite average or even superior scores on Level I-type tests (simple S–R trial-and-error learning, serial and paired-associate rote learning, and digit span), while the reverse relationship did not appear to exist: children who were very poor on the Level I tests never had high IQs. It also seems to make sense psychologically to suppose that basic learning and short-term memory processes are involved in performance on a complex Level II task, such as the Progressive Matrices, although the complex inductive reasoning strategies called for by the matrices would not be called upon for success in Level I tests such as digit span and serial rote learning. Therefore it was hypothesized that Level II performance depends upon Level I but not vice versa. In other words, Level I is seen as necessary-but-not-sufficient for the manifestation of Level II ability. A person who was very deficient in Level I would never manifest high Level II ability even if his genotype for Level II were in the superior range. On the other hand, an individual's Level I ability could be manifested on many tasks irrespective of his endowment of Level II ability. This kind of functional dependence of Level II upon Level I implies a 'twisted pear' type of correlation between tests that represent each of these levels. Of course, if tests of Level I and Level II were constructed so as to yield a normal distribution of scores in the total population, a bivariate normal scatter-diagram would be forced on the data and the 'twisted pear' would be constrained from appearing. Since there is already good evidence that Level II, as measured by standard intelligence tests, is approximately normally distributed in the population, we would hypothesize that Level I functions have a positively skewed distribution. So far, however, we have no compelling evidence on the shape of the distribution of scores on Level I tests, such as digit span, in the general population. Investigation of the hypothesized functional dependence of Level II upon Level I can probably best be determined from the study of neurological evidence. No thorough study of this nature has yet been attempted. Some evidence indicates that brain damage and ageing which affect Level I processes (short-term memory, etc.) also depress performance on Level II tests such as the Progressive Matrices (Horn, 1970), although the reverse does not seem to hold – Korsakow patients, for example, show defects in conceptual reasoning and problem-solving but have digit spans within the normal range (Talland, 1965). On the other hand, exceptionally high Level I abilities, such as Luria (1968) described in a man who could memorize more than 100 items in a serial or paired-associate list in a single trial, are not necessarily accompanied by a high level of ability in abstract, conceptual reasoning. Luria's subject, in fact, had quite mediocre conceptual abilities. These findings suggest the necessary-but-not-sufficient relationship of Level I to Level II.

DISTRIBUTIONS OF LEVEL I AND LEVEL II AS A FUNCTION OF SOCIO-ECONOMIC STATUS (SES)

The theory postulates that Level I ability is about equally distributed in all SES groups. In short, there is little, if any, correlation between Level I ability and SES. On this point the theory will probably have to be modified slightly, so that there will be a low positive correlation between Level I and SES. To keep the theoretical formulation as simple as possible for the purpose of explication, however, we will posit no SES difference in Level I.

Level II ability is distributed quite differently as a function of SES, there being a positive correlation between Level II and SES. Figure 1.8 shows the hypothetical distributions of Levels I and II in lower-class and middle-class populations.

Why are these abilities said to have different distributions in lower- and middle-class segments of the population? It can be argued that the educational and occupational requirements of our society tend to sort people out much more by their Level II ability than by their Level I ability, and it is occupational status that chiefly determines an individual's SES. Assuming largely genetic determination of individual differences in both Levels I and II, the 'gene flow' would diffuse in both directions with respect to SES. If Level II is dependent upon Level I, then high-SES children who are low on either Level I or II will tend as adults to gravitate to a lower SES level. If their deficiency is at Level I only, they will carry good genes for Level II with them in many cases; if their deficiency is only at Level II, however, they will carry good genes for Level I with them as they gravitate to a lower SES. Moving from lower to higher SES, on the other hand, carries with it good genes for both Level I and Level II. This set of conditions is consistent with two well-established sets of observations. Kushlick (1966, p. 130), in reviewing the research on SES and mental subnormality, notes that cultural-familial retardation (IQs between 50 and 75) is predominantly concen-

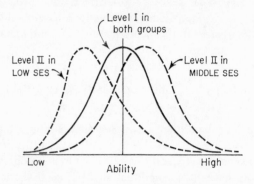

FIGURE 1.8. Hypothetical distributions of Level I (*solid line*) and Level II (*dashed line*) abilities in middle-class and lower-class populations.

trated in the lower social classes. On the basis of a number of surveys made largely in England, Kushlick concludes that mild subnormality in the absence of abnormal neurological signs is virtually confined to the lower social classes. He goes on to say that almost no children of higher social class parents have IQ scores less than 80, unless they have a pathological condition. In short, genes for low intelligence (meaning low Level I and/or low Level II, according to our theory) are largely eliminated from the upper SES segment of the population. (Severe mental deficiency, due to brain damage and mutant gene and chromosomal defects, however, has about equal occurrence in all social strata.) The second important observation that is consistent with our formulation is the fact that it is not nearly as difficult to find gifted (IQs above 130) children in the lower classes as it is to find retarded children in the upper classes. The Scottish National Survey established on a large scale that high intellectual ability is more widely distributed over different social environments than is low mental ability (Maxwell, 1953). This is what we should expect if many genes for high Level II ability gravitated from upper to lower classes as a result of having been combined with poor Level I ability. In reassortment the good Level II genes can combine with good Level I genes to produce a high level of general ability, which will then tend to be upwardly mobile in the SES hierarchy.

LEVEL I–LEVEL II CORRELATION IN LOW AND MIDDLE SES

From the foregoing considerations we can propose a crude model that 'predicts' the form of the correlation scatter diagram between Level I and Level II tests. We begin with the hypothetical distribution of genotypes for Level I and Level II in lower and middle SES. Assume that we divide each of these distributions at the common median for the total population, as follows:

	Low SES	Middle and Upper SES
Level II	0·30 Above	0·80 Above
	0·70 Below	0·20 Below

	Low SES	Middle and Upper SES
Level I	0·40 Above	0·60 Above
	0·60 Below	0·40 Below

Phenotypes on Level I and Level II tests are produced by the joint action of individuals' genotypic standing on each Level. To keep the model simple, we will say that within each social class Level I and Level II genotypes are uncorrelated, so that the proportion of phenotypes that fall above and below the population median can be obtained simply from the product of the independent probabilities of the genotypes. This is shown in the contingency tables below. The entries within the cells represent

	Low SES Level II Below	Low SES Level II Above			Middle and Upper SES Level II Below	Middle and Upper SES Level II Above	
Above	0·28	0·12	0·40	Above	0·12	0·48	0·60
Below	0·42 (0·18)←(0·18)	(0)	0·60	Below	0·08 (0·32)←(0·32)	(0)	0·40
	0·88	0·12			0·52	0·48	

proportions of *genotypic* combinations of Level I and Level II; the marginal totals represent the proportions of phenotypes on Level I and Level II tests. Genotypes in quadrant 4 are shown in parentheses, since their phenotypic performance will be much like that of subjects in quadrant 3, because of the assumed functional dependence of Level II performance on Level I ability. Thus the proportion in quadrant 4 is shown by the arrow as being moved into quadrant 3 in order to arrive at the total proportions of phenotypes. Leaving zero frequency in quadrant 4 is, of course, an overly idealized situation. Because the dependence of Level II performance on Level I is far from exact, there will actually be some subjects remaining in quadrant 4, and we can hypothesize that with increasing age of subjects, from early to late childhood, we should see 'late bloomers' moving from quadrant 3 to quadrant 4, with the growth of Level II functions. These intellectual late bloomers will be children with relatively low Level I ability and relatively high Level II. Thus the incidence of low phenotypic ability would be expected to decrease with increasing age of the subject population, and much more so in the middle than in the lower SES group.

According to this formulation, the correlation scatter-diagrams between Level I and Level II tests would appear somewhat as is shown in exaggerated form in Figure 1.9. The 'twisted pear' is

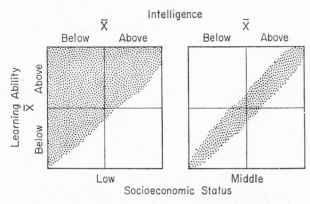

FIGURE 1.9. Schematic illustration of the predicted forms of the correlation scatter-diagram, according to the present model, for the relationship between Level I (e.g., digit span) and Level II (e.g., IQ) abilities in low- and middle-SES groups.

most evident in the low-SES group, with many subjects in quadrant I, i.e., above average in Level I and below average in Level II. The model clearly predicts a much lower correlation between Level I and Level II tests in the low-SES segment of the population than in the middle SES segment. It is an empirical fact that these correlations differ in the way depicted by the model, which was devised to account for the difference in correlations between Level I and Level II in lower- and middle-class groups. The difference in correlations cannot be accounted for by restriction of range in the low-SES group or by differences in test reliability. A theory of intelligence must be able to account for the well-established difference in correlations. The present model does so and is also consistent with much other evidence. At present, however, the model can only be regarded at best as a rather crude first approximation to the model that will hopefully evolve as a result of empirical investigations directed at obtaining the kinds of information needed for refining the model and rigorously testing its basic assumptions.

GROWTH CURVES OF LEVEL I AND LEVEL II ABILITIES

It is hypothesized that Level I and Level II have quite different growth curves, as shown in Figure 1.10. No scale is indicated on

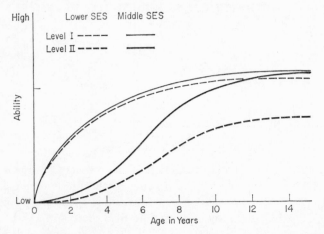

FIGURE 1.10. Hypothetical growth curves for Level I and Level II abilities and middle-SES and low-SES populations.

the *Y*-axis and therefore the exact shape of the growth curves should not be taken too literally. They are merely intended to convey the hypothesis that Level I rises rapidly with age, approaches its asymptomatic level relatively early, and shows little SES difference, as contrasted with Level II, which does not begin to show a rapid rise until 4 or 5 years of age, beyond which the SES groups increasingly diverge and approach quite different asymptotes. The forms of the Level I and Level II curves express some of the developmental characteristics that White (1965) called associative ability (Level I) and cognitive ability (Level II). The hypothesis shown in Figure 1.10 has clear predictive implications for the magnitude of SES differences as a function of age and of type of test.

Empirical evidence

Most of the empirical data relevant to the theory have already been presented elsewhere and are only summarized here. The earlier studies produced the phenomena which the theory has been devised to explain and were not designed as tests of the theory. Later studies, however, have grown out of deductions from the theory and were designed to test specific hypotheses.

INDEPENDENCE OF LEVEL I AND LEVEL II

If Level I phenotypes are defined by scores on digit span and laboratory measures of rote learning, and Level II is defined by scores on standard intelligence tests, particularly those with highest g loading, such as the Progressive Matrices, and by laboratory tasks involving conceptual learning and abstract problem solving, there is ample evidence that these two classes of tasks, Level I and Level II, are factorially distinct abilities. As indicated in our theoretical formulation, they are phenotypically more distinct in lower than in upper SES populations, due to the positive assortment of genotypes and to the hierarchical dependence of Level II upon Level I. In high-SES groups there will be a substantial g loading on both Level I and Level II tests. The fact that very low correlations are found between the two types of tests in some population groups, however, argues for their factorial independence. Zeaman and House (1967) have reviewed the research relating IQ to learning abilities, which shows, in general, that as the learning task becomes more rote, it correlates less with IQ. As learning tasks increase in discriminative and conceptual complexity (not necessarily in difficulty) they are more highly correlated with IQ. Even reverse digit span, since it involves a transformation of the stimulus input, is more highly correlated with g than is forward digit span (Horn, 1970).

c*

TRIPLE INTERACTION OF IQ, LEARNING ABILITY AND
SES

The early studies focused on the interaction of IQ, learning
ability and SES. The basic design of these studies was a 2×2
analysis of variance, with Low $v.$ High IQ on one dimension and
Low $v.$ High (or Middle) SES on the other. In three of the studies
(Jensen, 1961, 1963; Rapier, 1966) the low IQ subjects were in
special classes for the educable mentally retarded. This particular experimental design has been criticized by Humphreys
and Dachler (1969a, 1969b) on the grounds that it is 'pseudo-
orthogonal', i.e., it treats IQ and SES as if they were uncorrelated
in the population by having equal Ns in the four cells of the 2×2
analysis of variance. Unless the results are manipulated by weighting the cell means proportionally to the frequencies of the groups
in the population, the results of the analysis can be said to be
biased, that is, they cannot be generalized to the total population.
Jensen (1969d) argued in turn that the pseudo-orthogonal design
served legitimately to disclose the existence of an interaction
between IQ, learning ability and SES and could now be followed
up by correlational studies in representative population samples
to establish the magnitudes of these intercorrelations.

The essential features of the data of these early studies are
shown in Figure 1.11. The low-SES groups in the studies summarized in Figure 1.11 have been either white children (Rapier,
1968), Mexican-American children (Jensen, 1968), or Negro
children (Jensen and Rohwer, 1968). The findings are essentially
the same regardless of race, though it should be noted that in
selecting groups of children who are high or low on SES and
above or below average in IQ, our samples represent different
proportions of each racial population. The groups labelled high-
SES in these studies were in all cases white middle- or upper-
middle-class children.

Figure 1.11 shows a marked interaction between SES, IQ and
learning ability of the type measured by tasks of free recall, serial
learning, paired-associates learning and memory for digit series.
Low-SES children in the IQ range from 60 to 80 perform significantly better in these learning tasks than do middle-class children
in the same range of IQ. Low-SES children who are above average

in IQ, on the other hand, do not show learning performance that is significantly different from that of middle-class children of similar IQ.

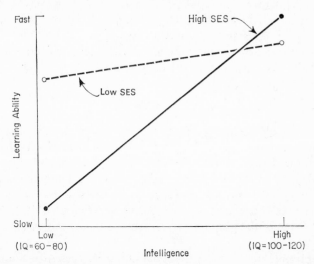

FIGURE 1.11. Summary graph of a number of studies showing relationship between learning ability (free recall, serial and paired-associate learning) and IQ as a function of socio-economic status (SES).

The theory has been made to predict this interaction, so it should not be surprising that these data fit the theory. Since the formulation of the theory, however, this interaction has been predicted in new data. Durning (1968) designed a study specifically to test several hypotheses derived from the theory. She obtained data on 5,539 Navy recruits ('. . . approximately the total input for a period of six weeks to the Naval Training Center, San Diego'); 95 per cent of them were between 18 and 23 years of age, with an average of 11·9 years of schooling. They were given a battery of standard selection tests, including the Armed Forces Qualification Test (AFQT), and a special auditory digit memory test, with a reliability of 0·89. Durning predicted, in accord with my theory, that Negro recruits who scored low on the selection tests would obtain higher digit memory scores than non-Negro recruits with low scores on the selection tests. She compared Negroes and non-Negroes in Category IV (AFQT scores between the 10th and 30th percentiles), and concluded: 'Negro CAT-IVs as a group scored significantly higher on the Memory for Numbers Test than non-Negro CAT-IVs, though the Negroes were lower on most of the standard selection tests' (Durning, 1968, p. 21). CAT-IV recruits, especially Negroes, come largely from low-SES and culturally disadvantaged backgrounds.

SES DIFFERENCES ON LEVEL I AND LEVEL II

In every study we have performed it has been found that low-SES and middle-SES groups differ much less on Level I tests than on Level II. Jensen (1963) found some low-SES children with Stanford-Binet IQs in the range from 50 to 75, who on a Level I test (trial-and-error selective learning) exceeded the mean performance of children of the same age classed as 'gifted' (IQs above 135). None of the gifted, however, scored below average children (IQs 90-110).

Rohwer (1967) tested pre-school children, ages 4 to 6, on the Peabody Picture Vocabulary Test and on serial and paired-associate learning, using picture pairs. In this study the low-SES children ($N = 100$) were Negro, the middle-SES children ($N = 100$) were white. Although these groups differed in IQ by 18 points, they showed no significant difference in either serial or paired associate learning ability. The groups also did not differ significantly on the digit span sub-test of the Wechsler Intelligence Scale for Children, the digit span tests of the Stanford-Binet, or on a more elaborate digit memory test devised by Jensen.

Groups of normal children selected at random from regular classes in grades K (kindergarten and Headstart classes), 1, 3 and 6 were given a paired-associates test devised by Rohwer, using picture pairs presented by means of a motion picture projector. The children were sampled from populations of low and middle SES. These groups differ by 15 to 20 points in IQ. Included in the study was a group of 48 institutionalized familially retarded young adults; they were tested to obtain evidence that the paired-associate learning test indeed taps an important aspect of mental ability, and it was hypothesized that institutionalized retardates would be deficient in Level I as well as Level II ability (Jensen and Rohwer, 1968). Figure 1.12 shows the results, which indicate that the learning test shows a significant age trend but no significant SES difference. Furthermore, the adult retardate group is lower than any other group in the study and significantly lower than all the other groups combined. Comparison of the learning perform-

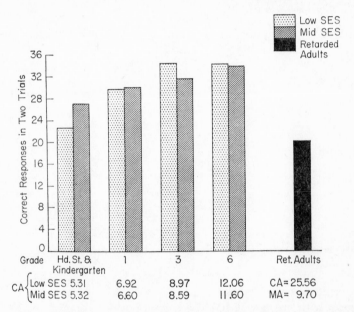

FIGURE 1.12. Comparisons of low- and middle-SES groups of children at various grades in school with institutionalized retarded adults on paired-associate learning consisting of twenty-four picture pairs presented two times at a rate of 4 seconds per pair. $N = 48$ in each of the nine groups.

ance of the adult retardates and the middle-SES third-graders is especially interesting, since the two groups have approximately the same mental age (9·7 *v.* 9·6). It is clear that the paired-associate learning is more highly related to IQ than to mental age.

In another study, Rohwer (1969) administered the Peabody Picture Vocabulary Test (PPVT), Raven's Colored Progressive Matrices, and a paired-associates learning test to a total of 288 children drawn in equal numbers ($N = 48$ per group) from Kindergarten, 1st and 3rd grades in two kinds of schools – ones serving a low-SES Negro area and ones serving an upper-middle-class white residential area. The results are shown in Figure 1.13;

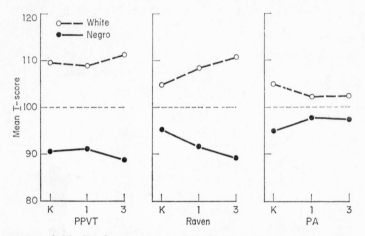

FIGURE 1.13. Performance on the Peabody Picture Vocabulary Test, Raven's Colored Progressive Matrices, and a picture paired-associates learning test in T scores. (From Rohwer, 1969.)

to facilitate comparisons the raw test scores were converted to T scores with a mean of 100 and a standard deviation of 15. Note that, in accord with our theory, the Negro-white or low-SES $v.$ high-SES difference is much smaller for the Level I (paired-associate) test than for either the PPVT or the Raven, which are both Level II tests. The Raven Matrices is presumably less culturally loaded than the PPVT. Also note that in accord with our hypothesis that SES groups diverge on Level II with increasing age (shown in Figure 1.10), the Negro and white groups show an increasing difference with advancing school grade on the two Level II tests, especially on the Raven. Just the reverse appears to be true for the paired-associates test.

Guinagh (1969) tested low-SES Negro ($N = 105$), low-SES white ($N = 84$), and middle-SES white ($N = 79$) third-graders on Raven's Colored Progressive Matrices and a digit span test.

The low and middle SES groups, though differing very significantly on the Progressive Matrices, did not differ significantly on digit span.

Some idea of the discrepancy between digit span (Level I) and Progressive Matrices (Level II) as a function of SES is seen in comparing the thirty *lowest*-scoring children in a white, middle-SES school (i.e., the lowest 6·1 per cent of children in grades 4, 5 and 6) with the thirty *highest*-scoring children on digit span in a Negro, low-SES school (the upper 7·9 per cent of grades 4, 5 and 6). The mean digit span test scores (expressed as per cent of maximum possible score) were 65·3 for the low-SES group and 38·7 for the middle-SES group. The corresponding Progressive Matrices scores (expressed as per cent of maximum possible score) were 64·7 and 72·6, respectively (Jensen, 1968b).

Scholastic tests which involve more rote learning than reasoning also correlate less highly with indices of pupils' SES. For example, Project TALENT data on a 10 per cent sample of male twelfth-graders ($N = 2,946$) show multiple correlation between a number of SES indices and Level II-type scholastic tests of 0·53 (Information), 0·44 (English), 0·46 (Mathematics), 0·41 (Mechanical Reasoning) as compared with only 0·24 for Memory for Words ('the ability to memorize foreign words corresponding to common English words') (Flanagan and Cooley, 1966, p. E-8).

CORRELATIONS BETWEEN LEVEL I AND LEVEL II IN LOW AND MIDDLE SES GROUPS

We have found substantial correlations between Level I tests (serial and paired-associate learning, free recall and memory span) and IQ or MA (mental age) in middle-class children, but very low correlations in low-SES groups, as would be predicted from the forms of the scatter-diagrams hypothesized in Figure 1.9.

In a study of white children, ages 8 to 13, Rapier (1966) found that the average correlation (Pearson r) between IQ (PPVT) and serial and paired-associate learning tasks was 0·44 for the middle-SES ($N = 40$) and 0·14 for the low-SES group ($N = 40$). Corrected for attenuation, these correlations are 0·60 and 0·19, respectively.

The correlation between PPVT and paired-associate learning

(with age partialled out) in pre-school children, ages 4 to 6, was 0·10 in the low-SES group ($N = 100$) and 0·51 in the middle-SES group ($N = 100$) (Rohwer, 1967). In this study the low-SES children were Negro, the middle-SES children were white. In serial learning, the correlations with mental age (chronological age partialled out) were 0·10 and 0·36 for the low- and middle-SES groups, respectively. The multiple correlation between PPVT mental age and fourteen predictor variables (1 serial learning test, 4 paired-associate tests, 8 digit series of 2 to 9 digits, and chronological age) was 0·54 in the low-SES group and 0·71 in the middle-SES group.

In a study of children from grades 4 to 6 in an all-Negro school in a low-SES neighborhood and an all-white school in an upper-middle-class neighborhood, the non-parametric correlation (phi coefficient) between digit span and Progressive Matrices was 0·33 for the low-SES ($N = 60$) and 0·73 for the upper-middle SES ($N = 60$) (Jensen, 1968b). The importance of this finding lies in the *difference* between these correlations rather than in their absolute magnitudes, since they are based on extreme groups and thus are not to be regarded as estimates of population parameters.

Guinagh (1969) obtained the following correlations (corrected for attenuation) between digit span and Progressive Matrices among third-graders: 0·29 for low-SES Negro ($N = 105$), 0·13 for low-SES white ($N = 84$), and 0·43 for middle-SES white ($N = 79$). An interesting finding of Guinagh's study was that low-IQ/low-SES Negro children with low digit span scores showed no significant improvement on Progressive Matrices after a specific instructional programme on this type of problem-solving, while low-IQ/low-SES Negro children with high digit span scores showed a significant gain on matrices performance after instruction, with the gains measured against no-instruction matched control groups.

Durning (1968), analyzing data on 5,539 U.S. Naval recruits, determined the correlation between the Armed Forces Qualification Test (AFQT) (a test of general intelligence and scholastic skills) and a digit memory test. The correlation (corrected for restriction of range) for Category IV recruits (AFQT scores between the 10th and 30th percentiles) was 0·21; for non-CAT-IVs it was 0·40, a difference significant beyond the 0·01 level.

SES DIFFERENCES WITHIN DIGIT SPAN PERFORMANCE

Jensen (1968b) found that low- and high-SES children encode digit series by different mental processes, even though they differ little if at all in their capacity for recall of auditory digit series.

Different encoding processes are revealed by scoring digit recall in different ways. We have used three methods: (*a*) *Span* – the longest series recalled perfectly on 50 per cent of trials; this is the measure used in the Binet and Wechsler tests. (*b*) *Position* – the number of digits recalled in the correct absolute position. (*c*) *Sequence* – the number of digits correct in adjacent sequence, regardless of absolute position.

Table 1.1 compares the digit recall performance of children from low- and upper-middle-class backgrounds. The low-SES children were predominantly Negro; in all cases the parents were receiving public welfare assistance. The upper-middle-SES group were white children in private nursery schools. The mean ages of the low- and high-SES groups were 52 and 50 months, respectively, and all the children were between 3 and 5 years of age. The intercorrelations between all the variables shown in Table 1.1 (plus sixteen other variables not directly relevant to the present discussion) were factor analyzed (technically, a varimax rotation of the first five principal components, approximating orthogonal simple structure); only the factor identified as 'intelligence' in this analysis is shown in Table 1.1.

First of all, we see in Table 1.1 that although the low- and high-SES groups differ in mental age by 16 months (equivalent to an IQ difference of 19 points), they show no appreciable differences in means or standard deviations in the digit memory tests, scored either by position or by sequence.

The loadings on the 'intelligence' factor (so identified because it is the only factor to emerge in the analysis on which PPVT mental age has a significant loading) indicate that digit span performance involves different mental processes or patterns of ability in the two SES groups. Note that digit span has very substantial loadings on the intelligence factor in the high-SES group and that the loadings are highest in the region of the subjects' average memory span (4 to 5 digits). There are no comparable loadings on the corresponding variables for the low-SES group. The low-SES group, how-

TABLE 1.1. Means, standard deviations, and correlations with intelligence factor in low and high socio-economic groups ($N = 100$ in each group)

Variable	MEAN Lo-SES		Hi-SES		STANDARD DEVIATION Lo-SES		Hi-SES		FACTOR LOADINGS Lo-SES		Hi-SES	
	Pos.	Seq.	Pos.	Seq.	Pos.	Seq.	Pos.	Seq.	Pos.	Seq.	Pos.	Seq.
Mental age (mos.)	48·41		64·46		22·67		19·16		0·504		0·512	
Binet digit span	3·72		3·63		1·05		1·07		0·047		0·482	
WISC digit span	3·99		4·12		1·02		1·12		0·073		0·613	
Digit series 2	1·99	1·99	1·99	1·99	0·05	0·05	0·09	0·05	0·032	0·032	0·023	0·023
3	2·82	2·85	2·88	2·91	0·40	0·31	0·38	0·29	0·138	0·181	0·214	0·210
4	3·06	3·20	3·02	3·13	1·13	0·88	1·15	0·95	0·023	0·010	0·877	0·870
5	2·00	2·46	1·83	2·42	1·32	0·98	1·58	1·21	0·157	0·156	0·563	0·511
6	1·02	2·01	1·05	1·95	1·03	0·83	1·03	0·90	0·340	0·478	0·372	0·273
7	0·54	1·53	0·56	1·63	0·65	0·63	0·84	0·88	0·325	0·534	0·072	0·017
8	0·41	1·66	0·38	1·46	0·49	0·71	0·60	0·65	0·138	0·698	0·057	0·020
9	0·26	1·71	0·28	1·71	0·37	0·83	0·49	0·91	0·148	0·760	0·133	0·194

ever, shows significant loadings on the intelligence factor on digit series that greatly exceed their memory span and only for sequence scoring. We know that when the number of digits presented exceeds the subject's memory span, he resorts to a simpler strategy of merely associating adjacent digits with little regard for absolute position or other more complex organizing relationships within the series. This change in the encoding process has been found in university students when presented with supraspan series of 12 to 15 digits (Jensen, 1965). This particular form of associative learning is the only component of the low-SES group's digit recall performance that has any significant correlation with their intelligence test performance, and since this component has no appreciable relationship with the intelligence factor in the high-SES group, it suggests that the intelligence test itself is measuring different mental processes in the two groups. Table 1.2 shows the

TABLE 1.2. Correlation between position and sequence scoring of digit series test

| | SERIES LENGTH | | | | | | | |
SES	2	3	4	5	6	7	8	9
High	1·00	0·98	0·93	0·93	0·85	0·60	0·47	0·39
Low	1·00	0·95	0·91	0·90	0·83	0·29	0·16	−0·01

correlation between position and sequence scores in the high- and low-SES groups. Note that the correlations diminish rapidly in the series that exceed the subjects' average memory span, and that the decrease is much more pronounced in the low-SES group. The SES differences in correlations for series lengths 7, 8 and 9 are all significant beyond the 0·05 level.

Of the various Level I tests that have been used so far, paired-associates appears to be the least 'pure' measure. The test materials, method of administration (e.g., pacing interval), and age of the subjects seem to determine to some extent whether it behaves as a Level I or a Level II test. Apparently, under certain conditions, subjects can bring to bear upon learning paired-associates whichever of their abilities is strongest, and thus PA learning can tap either Level I or Level II under appropriate conditions. In one study, Rohwer (1968) found correlations between Progressive Matrices and paired-associates learning of 0·44 in a low-SES group (grades 1, 2 and 3 combined) and of 0·41 in a middle-SES group. (When age is partialled out of these correlations, they become 0·26 and 0·05, respectively.)

EVIDENCE FOR THE 'TWISTED PEAR' CORRELATION

As indicated by Figure 1.9, the theory calls for a 'twisted pear' correlation scatter-diagram in low-SES groups; it would also imply a lesser degree of 'twisted pear' in the total population. So far, we have no definitive evidence on this point. Jensen (1963) found a much greater variance of learning scores on a trial-and-error selective learning task among children of low IQ than among children of average and superior IQ, which is consistent with the 'twisted pear' formulation. However, evidence of a 'twisted pear' has not appeared in two investigations in which it was specifically sought. Guinagh (1969) correlated Progressive Matrices and digit span in low- and middle-SES groups and concluded '. . . the scatter-diagrams give no evidence for Jensen's hypothesis that high BLA [basic learning ability as measured in this study by digit span] is necessary for high IQ [measured by Progressive Matrices].' This leaves the question of how to account for the large difference in correlations between digit span and matrices in low- and middle-SES groups (0·13 *v.* 0·43, after correction for attenuation). If there is not a 'twisted pear', why do the correlations differ? At present, no theory accounts for this finding. Durning (1968) also failed to find evidence of a 'twisted pear' in her naval recruit data. The scatter-diagram for the correlation between AFQT and digit memory, based on 5,539 recruits, showed an almost perfectly linear regression of digit memory scores on AFQT; there was no greater variance on digit memory for low scorers on the AFQT than for high scorers. This definitely contradicts the theoretical prediction. Durning concluded: 'Basic learning ability as measured by digit span was not found to bear the "necessary-but-not-sufficient" relationship to general intelligence . . . the hierarchical relationship between Level I and Level II which [Jensen] observed may be evident only in children' (Durning

1968, p. 61). Another explanation might be the fact that both the AFQT and the digit memory test were so considered as to yield normal score distributions in the navy population, which would force a bivariate normal scatter-diagram. Unfortunately, there was no index by which one could classify recruits as to SES, for the correlation between AFQT and digit memory in lower and upper SES groups could have helped to clarify this issue. At present, it must be concluded that the precise form of the correlation scatter-diagram between Level I and Level II tests is not established. Data on over 6,000 school children are now available which will provide a definitive answer to this question, but it has not yet been analyzed.

GROWTH FUNCTIONS OF LEVEL I AND LEVEL II

The hypothesis of increasing divergence of low- and high-SES groups on Level II as compared with Level I ability (shown in Figure 1.10) has been investigated in two studies explicitly designed for this purpose. Both studies made use of the technique of free recall, a Level I form of learning. The same kind of test can be made a Level II measure by presenting items for recall which can be categorized into several general classes, such as animals, food, furniture, vehicles, etc. Although the items in the categorized list are presented to the subject in a random order on each trial, subjects tend to recall the items in clusters which correspond to the superordinate categories. This clustering tendency, and the associated improvement in recall as a result of it, is clearly a Level II process, since it involves conceptual transformation of the random input prior to recall. Two predictions, therefore, can be made from the theory: (a) low- and high-SES groups will show a greater difference on the free recall of categorized lists (FR_c) than on uncategorized lists (FR_u), and (b) the difference between low- and high-SES groups on FR_c will increase with age of the subjects. An ancillary hypothesis essential to the argument that FR_c is a measure of Level II is that in an analysis of co-variance that controls for IQ, the effect of SES will be more or less eliminated.

Glasman (1968) tested these predictions. She used several twenty-item lists of four categories each, with five items per category. The categories were: animals, foods, furniture, musical instruments, jobs, eating utensils, clothing and vehicles. The items consisted of models, toys, or other three-dimensional representations of real objects. The twenty items were presented singly for 3 seconds each, in a random order, for five trials. After every trial subjects were allowed 2 minutes to verbally recall the items in any order; the subject's output was tape-recorded. There were 32 *S*s in each of the four groups formed by the 2×2 design: kindergarten *v*. 5th grade and low-SES *v*. high-SES. The low-SES group was composed of Negro children from a school in a poor neighborhood; the high-SES group was drawn from an all-white school in an upper-middle-class neighborhood. Thus race and SES were confounded in this study. The mean IQs (PPVT) of the groups were 90 for low-SES and 120 for high-SES. The grade levels were matched on IQ. The main results of the study are shown in Figures 1.14 and 1.15. The measure of clustering (Figure 1.15) is the one most commonly used in studies of clustering and is described by Bousfield and Bousfield (1966). A cluster is defined as a sequence of two responses from the same category which are immediately adjacent. The Bousfield formula corrects this value by subtracting the expected value for a random sequence of the items recalled. The results shown in Figures 1.14 and 1.15 clearly bear out the theoretical predictions. At grade 5 the low-SES and high-SES groups differ by approximately one standard deviation, both in recall and in clustering. The Grades × SES interaction is statistically significant beyond the 0·05 level for recall and beyond the 0·001 level for clustering.

Since FR_c is essentially a Level II process, it should be correlated with mental age (MA) about equally in both low- and high-SES groups. This is what Glasman found. Correlation between MA and amount of *recall* was 0·62 for low-SES and 0·72 for high-SES; the correlation between MA and the amount of *clustering* was 0·76 for low-SES and 0·77 for high-SES. The correlations are much higher for fifth-graders than for kindergarteners, who show very little clustering and are presumably still operating in this task by a Level I process. (The correlation of MA and recall is 0·06 at kindergarten and 0·59 at grade 5; the correlation between MA and clustering is 0·02 at kindergarten and 0·68 at grade 5.) FR_c performance is so strongly related to MA that when the data

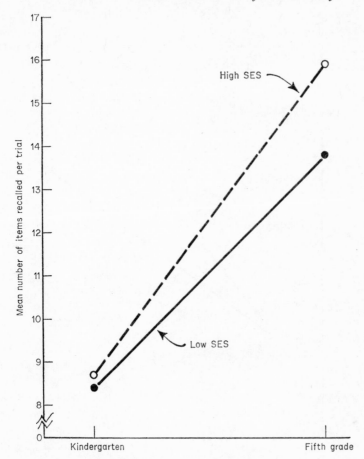

FIGURE 1.14. Free recall of categorized lists as a function of grade (age) and socio-economic status. (From Glasman, 1968.)

of Figures 1.14 and 1.15 were subjected to an analysis of covariance, with MA as the control variable, all the main effects and the interactions were completely wiped out.

Although Glasman's study demonstrated age and social-class differences in the free recall of *categorized* lists, it was not designed to study age and SES differences in performance on the free recall of categorized *versus* non-categorized lists. A non-categorized list

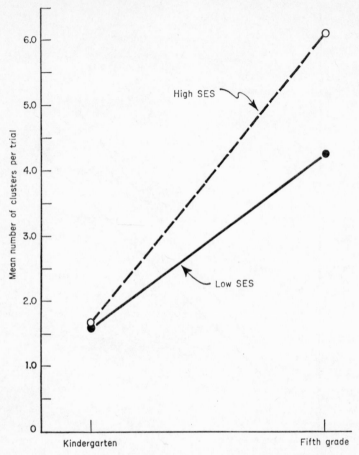

FIGURE 1.15. Amount of clustering in free recall of categorized lists as a function of grade (age) and socioeconomic status. (From Glasman, 1968.)

is made up of unrelated or remotely associated items which cannot be readily grouped according to supraordinate categories. Subjective organization of the items in the list is likely to consist of pairs of items related on the basis of primary generalization, clan association or functional relationship. A non-categorized list therefore lends itself less than a categorized list to evoking Level

II processes. Consequently, subjects differing in Level II ability (but not in Level I) should show less difference in FR_u than in FR_c.

Jensen and Frederiksen (1973) tested this prediction directly. The low-SES and high-SES groups were drawn from essentially the same populations as those in the Glasman study, i.e., lower-class Negro and middle- to upper-middle-class white children.

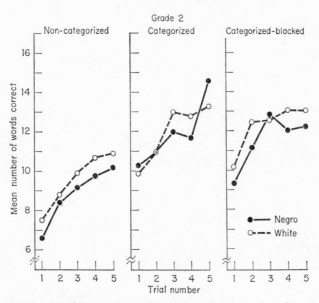

FIGURE 1.16. Free recall performance of lower-class Negro and middle-class white second-grade children.

The age factor was again investigated by comparing grades 2 and 4. Sets of twenty objects were used for the non-categorized and categorized lists; the four categories of the latter were: clothing, tableware, furniture and animals. Forty Ss received the non-categorized list, consisting of twenty common but unrelated objects, including one object from each of the four categories of the categorized lists. Forty Ss received the categorized list with the items presented in a random order, and another forty Ss had the same categorized lists with the items presented in a 'blocked' fashion, i.e., all items within a given category are presented in immediate sequence – a procedure which prompts clustering and facilitates recall. Five trials of presentation followed by free recall were given in all conditions. The results, in terms of amount of recall, are shown in Figures 1.16 and 1.17. For the categorized lists, the results were essentially the same as those of the Glasman experiment: grade 4 was superior to grade 2 under all conditions,

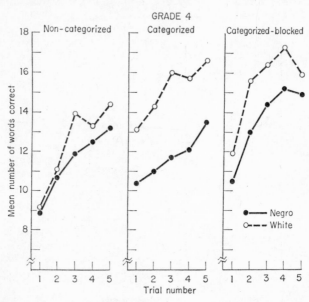

FIGURE 1.17. Free recall performance of lower-class Negro and middle-class white fourth-grade children.

and the SES differences were greater at grade 4 than at grade 2. Whereas at kindergarten there was no difference between SES groups, a difference in free recall clearly emerges by grade 2, in favor of the high-SES group. At grade 4 there is a large inter-action between SES level and FR_u *v.* FR_c for both random and blocked lists, although the blocked condition reduces the SES difference by boosting the recall performance of the low-SES group. In other words, when the input is already categorized and therefore no transformation of the input is called for, the output is facilitated in the low-SES group. The high-SES group, on the other hand, spontaneously transforms the random input into clustered (i.e., categorized) output and obtains approximately the same facilitation as when the input is already blocked into categories. Recall of the non-categorized list showed a relatively small difference in favor of the high-SES group at both second and fourth grades. Also, for the non-categorized list there is no significant interaction between SES and grades – the SES difference is nearly the same at grades 2 and 4. This is in marked contrast to the categorized lists, which show a large SES × Grades interaction.

All of these findings on free recall are highly consistent with our theory that social class differences in ability involve mainly Level II processes rather than Level I.

Practical validity of Level I tests

If Level I and Level II are two broad classes of abilities, we might return to the opening concern of this paper – the aptitude × instruction interaction (AII) – and ask if the Level I–Level II distinction has practical value, or at least practical implications, in terms of AII. The fact that we have discovered a class of mental abilities (Level I) on which social class differences are much less than those found on IQ tests raises the question of whether it is possible to devise instruction in basic scholastic skills in such a way as to be less dependent upon Level II abilities and more fully utilize the Level I abilities which children called disadvantaged possess to a relatively greater degree. Can instruction geared to Level I ability improve the scholastic performance of the majority of low-SES children who now perform relatively poorly in school? School success is highly predictable from standard IQ tests. Is this true mainly because instruction is aimed so strongly at Level II ability? Is it necessary that a child who is low on Level II ability, but high on Level I, fail to acquire the basic skills in school? Children who are above the general average on Level I abilities, but below the average on Level II performance, usually appear bright and capable of normal learning and achievement in many situations, although they invariably have inordinate difficulties in school work under the traditional methods of classroom instruction. Many such children who are classed as mentally retarded in school later become socially and economically adequate persons when they leave the academic situation. On the other hand, children who are much below average on Level I, and consequently on Level II as well, appear to be much more handicapped in the world of work. One shortcoming of traditional IQ tests is that they make both types of children look much alike. We therefore need tests that will reliably assess *both* Level I and Level II separately. Even more important is the need for research on more effective utilization of Level I ability in scholastic instruction. It seems sensible that instruction should be based upon a pupil's strengths rather than upon his weaknesses, and we have found that many children lacking strength in Level II possess strength in Level I. At present we do not know how to teach to Level I ability. Although Level I is manifested in rote learning, it is not advocated that simple notions of rote learning be the model for instruction. Instructional techniques that can utilize the abilities that are manifested in rote learning are needed, but this does not necessarily imply that the instruction consist of rote learning *per se*. We also need to find out to what extent Level II abilities can be acquired or stimulated by appropriate instruction to children who possess good Level I ability but are relatively low on Level II as assessed by IQ tests. Guinagh's (1969) finding that low-SES Negro children with low IQs, but who had above average digit span (Level I), were able to improve in matrices performance after appropriate instruction seems extremely important. It should be followed up intensively.

The only study of the practical predictive validity of a Level I test (digit memory) is Durning's (1968) investigation of naval recruits. Durning correlated a battery of standard selection tests, as well as a digit memory test, with a measure of recruits' response to the first eight weeks of basic training. This measure was obtained by means of an objective paper-and-pencil test called the Recruit Final Achievement Test (RFAT). RFAT items cover basic seamanship, military courtesy and conduct, first-aid and safety, and other topics included in the eight weeks of recruit training. Durning states: 'The fact that the RFAT is essentially an academic criterion is one of the major limitations of the present study, for the digit span test was chosen as a promising predictor of more practical, less scholastic criteria.' Omnibus aptitude tests, such as the General Classification Test and the AFQT, correlated with the RFAT criterion in the range of 0·55 to 0·71. The verbal tests had the higher validities. Digit span correlated significantly with RFAT ($r = 0.30$, $p < 0.001$). This is not an impressive correlation, but it should be remembered that the RFAT as well as the class instruction in the subjects assessed by the RFAT were academically oriented. Durning concluded that '... though the Memory for Numbers Test was not an efficient predictor of RFAT, it nonetheless may have promise as a predictor of more practical, less academic measures of success in the Navy.' Navy psychologists have since been analyzing these data further and are finding that for certain job categories within the Navy, the Memory for Numbers Test is a better predictor of success than the more academically oriented tests in the selection battery.

The theory presented here provides a broad base for the discovery of AIIs that will possibly prove fruitful for improving the education of many children who under present methods of instruction seem to derive little educational benefit from schooling. Present-day schooling is highly geared to conceptual modes of learning, and this is suitable for children of average and superior Level II ability. But many children whose weakness is in conceptual ability are frustrated by schooling and therefore learn far less than would seem to be warranted by their good Level I learning ability. A certainly important avenue of exploration is the extent to which school subjects can be taught by techniques which depend mostly upon Level I ability and very little upon Level II. After all, much of the work of the world depends largely on Level I ability, and it seems reasonable to believe that many persons can acquire basic scholastic and occupational skills and become employable and productive members of society by making the most of their Level I ability.

The culturally disadvantaged: psychological and educational aspects

The literature on children called culturally disadvantaged that has recently proliferated is likely to give the impression to those who have not surveyed it in detail that much scientifically verified knowledge is now at hand as a sound basis for large-scale ameliorative action promising highly predictable and optimal results.

This is an incorrect impression. Although substantial knowledge about disadvantaged children, particularly of a demographic nature, is now available, the literature dealing with the psychological aspects of the problem is better viewed as a source of program for research and theoretical formulation. It is important to keep this in mind, not to discourage action programs, which are obviously needed immediately, but to insure that such action programs are conceived of and conducted as research and not as the application of knowledge already established by research. This means that school programs for the disadvantaged should be conducted, as far as possible, in the manner of scientific experimentation, which is to say with great attention to control and description of the 'input' variables (what we do with the children, their parents, their environments, etc.) and the 'output' variables (how the children respond). As in any investigation which attempts to evaluate the effects of an experimental variable, there should be appropriate control groups. Finally, there should be careful description of the population's social, economic, racial, family, and individual psychological characteristics.

The aim of this report is to indicate some of the main trends of thought and research on the psychology of disadvantaged children, to comment particularly on the research findings and hypotheses which seem to have the most direct implication for ameliorative action, and to point out a few of the most crucial gaps in our current knowledge and the controversies issuing from them.

Description and assessment of the culturally retarded

Descriptions of the disadvantaged have usually consisted of both environmental and personal characteristics. There is seldom any attempt to separate the causal, or background, factors from the supposedly resultant behavioral characteristics, of which the most important to the educator is the low educability of the disadvantaged child. In fact, low or mediocre intelligence (as assessed by standard intelligence tests) and particularly poor school achievement, are often included in the definition and identification of the 'culturally deprived', along with such criteria as low socioeconomic status and culturally impoverished home environment. The relatively rare slum child with a high IQ and superior school achievement is often not regarded as being culturally disadvantaged, while low-IQ, low-achieving pupils from what may appear to be very similar home backgrounds are characterized as disadvantaged and their poor school performance is attributed largely to this condition.

The question raised by this type of definition is not without important practical implications. If we assume that the low-IQ children actually have the potential both for higher intelligence and for normal progress in school, but have merely been 'depressed' by an unfavorable environment, we must ask if average or above-average culturally disadvantaged children are similarly depressed. A slum child with an IQ of 115 might thus have the intellectual potential of the middle-class child with an IQ of 130 or 140, and he might be able to realize this potential more fully if he were provided with the right kind of cultural stimulation at some stage of his development. Thus, in looking for potential college material among low socio-economic status children, we might pin our greatest hopes on those already of at least average ability, despite a poor environment, and simply regard most low 'socio-economic status' children (whose IQs are in the 'dull' range of intelligence, that is, from 75 to 95), though capable of benefiting educationally from intervention programs such as Headstart, as more or less destined for intellectual and occupational mediocrity. This wide-spread belief gives rise to various plans for watered-down, less intellectual, and less academic educational programs tailored to the apparent limitations of a large proportion (at least one-half to two-thirds) of low socio-economic status children. This is a harmful and unjust set of beliefs, if acted upon, since some evidence now makes it reasonable (though surprising) to hypothesize that a greater absolute amount of educational potential may exist among the low socio-economic status children who, under present circumstances, obtain IQs in the range of 70 to 90 than among those whose measured IQs are in the above-average range from about 100 to 120. To state this proposition even more paradoxically, we can hypothesize that there is a greater chance of finding a potential IQ of 130, or 140, or 150 among the groups whose measured IQs are 70 to 90 than among the group whose IQs are 100 to 120, providing we are dealing with a population regarded by the usual criteria as predominantly culturally disadvantaged. All the evidence, which is massive, indicates conclusively that such a prediction with respect to children from middle-class families would be utterly ridiculous. With respect to low socio-economic status children (especially, in the U.S.A., Negroes; and possibly, in Britain, children of immigrant groups), however, it is a hypothesis worth investigating. No evidence as yet contradicts the hypothesis, and some evidence makes it seem reasonable, and, in fact, suggested this seemingly paradoxical idea in the first place (Jensen, 1963). But before we can elaborate on this line of thought, some supporting background information must be provided.

Differential diagnosis of cultural retardation

In principle, intellectual and educational retardation can and must be clearly distinguished from what we will here refer to as primary retardation. Primary and cultural retardation are not at all mutually exclusive; one may exist without the other, or they may exist in independently varying degrees simultaneously. There is substantial evidence of some degree of correlation, albeit quite low, between primary and cultural retardation in the total population (Burt and Howard, 1956; Tyler, 1965).

Primary retardation can be subdivided into three main types, all having an essentially biological causation: (1) an inevitable consequence of what geneticists call the multifactorial or poly-genic inheritance of intelligence; (2) a result of a single, major gene defect; and (3) a result of brain damage. Factors 1 and 3 and factors 2 and 3 are not mutually exclusive, but may occur singly or together. Factor 2, however, always overrides factor 1, so that when factor 2 is involved, factor 1 is of almost no importance.

POLYGENIC INHERITANCE

Intelligence is inherited in much the same fashion as height (Burt, 1955, 1958, 1966; Burt and Howard, 1956; Huntley, 1966; Pearson, 1903). It is the result of a large number of genes each having a small additive effect. Because of random assortment of these genes, the total additive effect will be normally distributed in the popula-tion. Thus, the hereditary mechanism (in effect a random lottery) that results in one person's being bright, results in another's being dull, and the person who is dull or mentally retarded for this reason is, biologically speaking, no more abnormal or pathological than the average or bright person or the short or tall person. He is simply a part of normal variation. Being at the very low end of the distribution may be a personal misfortune from an educa-tional standpoint, but it is not an abnormality in a medical or psychological sense and is presumably not biologically or environ-mentally remediable. (In this respect dullness and brightness are genetically quite analogous to shortness and tallness of stature.) Persons at the low end of the distribution of intelligence need educational treatment somewhat different from that afforded average and bright persons. The majority of dull children in our schools who do not show neurological signs of organic impair-ment are of this type, regardless of their race or social class. For these children, education must be modified in accordance with their intellectual limitations, which is not to say that an appro-priate education is not just as important for them as for the bright child. It must simply be a different kind of education, with different goals. The great misfortune of culturally disadvantaged children is that many are treated educationally (and they often perform

D

accordingly) as if they were at the lower end of the genetic distribution of intelligence when, in fact, they may be in the middle or even at the upper end of the distribution. Failure to distinguish between hereditary retardation and cultural retardation, as well as being a social injustice, results in a waste of educational potential and talent. The consequences are especially damaging to the social progress of minority groups, and the costs are borne by our whole society. The discrimination between cultural and genetic retardation in the culturally disadvantaged is a difficult diagnostic problem which does not even arise in middle-class children, with exceedingly rare exceptions, since retardation in this group is almost always of the primary type. There are, of course, gradations of cultural retardation, just as there are gradations of primary retardation. But it is unlikely that the degree of cultural retardation is a simple linear function of the degree of environmental impoverishment. There is evidence that the environment may act as a threshold variable in such a way that a quite severe degree of environmental deprivation must exist in order to produce cultural retardation in a child of normal genetic potential. This idea is explicated more fully in a later section of this paper.

MAJOR GENE DEFECT

Practically all severe forms of mental deficiency, where the IQ is below 50, are the results either of severe brain damage or of major gene defects (Ellis, 1963, p. 276). Examples of major gene defects are Mongolism, phenylketonuria, and amaurotic idiocy. Genetically these intellectual defects are analogous to dwarfism in the trait of stature. They are caused by Mendelian inheritance of a single gene or by a mutant gene, which for all practical purposes may be regarded as completely overriding the normal polygenic determinants of intelligence. The resulting severe degree of mental defect, which is generally easy to diagnose in the first days or weeks of life, is not of concern in the present discussion except to distinguish it from retardation which constitutes a part of normal variation.

BRAIN DAMAGE

Brain damage, especially prenatal and perinatal, is a continuous variable; that is, its effects can range from the negligible to the disastrous, and the effects can be manifest at all levels of genetic potential. Thus, a child who would have grown up to have an adult IQ of, say, 150 may, as a result of the brain damage incurred by anoxia at birth, have an actual IQ of 140. The literature on the subject suggests that brain damage to a degree that makes a difference in measurable mental ability is sufficiently rare not to constitute an appreciable source of variation in intellectual ability in the total population. An upper-limit estimate would be about 5 per cent of the total variance of measured intelligence, which means that, on the average, brain damage lowers the IQ only slightly more than three IQ points (Corah, *et al.*, 1965; Eichenwald, 1966; Graham, *et al.*, 1962; Pasamanick and Knobloch, 1966). Of course, the effects of brain damage in individual cases may be intellectually devastating. There is also evidence that brain damage has a higher incidence in low socio-economic status groups in which the mother's nutrition, prenatal care, and obstetrical practices are substandard (Osler and Cooke, 1965). All possible efforts should, of course, be made to minimize these conditions in order to decrease the chances of brain damage, but these ameliorative efforts should prove considerably easier than combating the causal agents of *cultural* retardation *per se*.

All three types of primary retardation have three major effects in common: they result in below-average measured intelligence (IQ), in below-average educability in school subjects, and in a slow rate of what we shall refer to as basic learning ability. Cultural retardation, on the other hand, is distinguishable from primary retardation, at least in principle, on this third factor – basic learning ability. While cultural deprivation results in lowered IQ and lowered school achievement, it does not, except in extremely rare cases, result in lowered basic learning ability. This is a theoretically and practically important distinction, because it means that in trying to improve the educability of the culturally disadvantaged, we are trying not to make over genetically poor material but to allow sound innate learning potential to manifest itself. But now, to present further our thesis, we must clarify the special meaning we have given the terms *intelligence*, *basic learning ability*, and *educability*.

Intelligence, learning ability and educability

Standard intelligence tests, such as the Stanford-Binet and the Wechsler, are measures of specific knowledge and problem-solving skills which have been acquired by the testee at some time prior to the test situation. Mental age is determined directly from the amount of such knowledge and skill. By taking into account the amount of time the individual has had to acquire this knowledge, that is, his chronological age, we obtain a measure of learning rate expressed as the IQ. The validity of the IQ as a measure of learning ability, therefore, depends to a large extent upon equal opportunity for exposure to knowledge and skills that the test calls upon. Since intelligence tests were originally devised to predict school performance, they call upon knowledge and cognitive skills similar to the kinds of learning required in school – skills which are more or less prerequisite for school learning and which have considerable transfer value in the classroom.

Now, if IQ is a measure of learning rate, we should expect that learning tasks of the type used by experimental psychologists to study learning should show substantial positive correlations with IQ. This, in fact, is exactly what our research has found (e.g., Jensen, 1965). But here is the interesting thing: the correlation between IQ and learning ability, as measured directly in a controlled laboratory learning task, is much higher among middle-class children than among lower-class children (Jensen, 1961, 1963; Rapier, 1966). Furthermore, in comparing level of performance (i.e., speed of learning) as a function of IQ level and of social-class (lower *v.* middle), we have found in several studies that low-IQ (60-85) lower-class children are, on the average, markedly superior in learning ability to low-IQ middle-class children. In the IQ range above 100, on the other hand, there are not significant differences in learning ability between lower- and middle-class children matched for IQ. This suggests that once the IQ has exceeded a certain level (somewhere in the neighbourhood of 100 to 110), it gives a fairly accurate assessment of learning ability regardless of social-class level. In the lower IQ range (which, incidentally, contains the modal performance of lower-class children), the IQ test grossly underestimates learning ability among lower-class children. We are speaking here, of course, only of averages, for a certain proportion of lower-class low-IQ children are slow learners on the laboratory tasks just as are middle-class low-IQ children. The middle-class low-IQ groups seem to be made up almost completely of slow learners. But the lower-class low-IQ group contains all levels of learning ability. The probability of finding a very fast learner (i.e., learning speed comparable to that of 'gifted' middle-class children) seems to be greater in the low-IQ low socio-economic status than in the average IQ range of either social-class group. This suggests that the IQ is almost totally unpredictive of learning ability in the low-IQ range for low socio-economic status children. It should be noted that the majority of low socio-economic status children are in the below-average IQ range. This is especially true for Negroes in the U.S.A. On a national average only about 12 per cent of Negroes exceed the median IQ of the white population (McGurk, 1956; Tyler, 1965; Shuey, 1966).

In view of what has been said above, it might seem puzzling that the IQ is substantially correlated (correlations between 0·50 and 0·70) with school achievement regardless of social class. Ability for school learning may be referred to as *educability*. Educability is much more complexly determined than intelligence or learning ability. For one thing, it depends not only upon learning ability of the type measured in the laboratory, in which transfer from prior learning is relatively unimportant, but also upon a fund of prior knowledge, skills, and acquired cognitive habits, much of which is tapped by intelligence tests. But educability also involves much more than these intellectual abilities, as indicated by the fact that intelligence tests do not account for more than about 50 per cent of the variance in school achievement. A host of other factors must be taken into account to 'explain' the remaining variance. These are usually described under labels, such as attitudes, motivation, work habits, regularity of school attendance, parental interest, and help in school work.

Another point of interest and educational implication lies in a comparison of the heritabilities of intelligence and of educability. Despite the popular denigration of the genetic study of intelligence in educational circles in recent years, it is entirely possible to estimate the relative contributions of heredity and environment to the total variation in intelligence in a given population. The numerous studies done in this field over the past fifty years show a great consistence (Erlenmeyer-Kimling and Jarvik, 1963). They indicate that in Caucasian populations above the poverty line (and this is an important qualification), some 80 to 90 per cent of the variability in measured intelligence can be attributable to genetic factors and about 5 to 10 per cent to social environmental factors (Burt, 1958). (The remaining variance is divided between biological environmental factors and error of measurement.) The genetic component in school achievement or educability, on the other hand, is much less than for intelligence, accounting for only 40 to 50 per cent of the total variance (Burt, 1958; Jensen, 1967). Family influences largely account for the remaining variance. One of the obvious tasks of educational psychology and sociology is the analysis and isolation of these environmental influences on educability, so that they may be provided by one means or another when they are lacking in the child's natural environment. But before these environmental factors are discussed, a few other points need to be made concerning the inheritance of intelligence and the distribution of intelligence in the total population.

Environment as a threshold variable

By virtue of a largely fortuitous set of conditions, the Stanford-Binet intelligence test, when used on a white American population, which for the most part excludes the lowest segment of the socio-economic status continuum, yields a distribution of IQs which conforms almost exactly to the so-called normal or Gaussian distribution. This is the distribution one would expect on the basis of polygenic inheritance of intelligence (Burt, 1957, 1963). In this same population, estimates of the genetic component in the variance of intelligence range between 80 and 90 per cent (Burt, 1958). Even the seemingly rather large environmental variations within this bulk of the American population apparently contribute very little to the variance in intelligence, as measured by an excellently constructed test such as the Stanford-Binet.

However, if the Stanford-Binet is administered to a large and truly representative sample of the total population (or to the *entire* population of school children, as was done in Scotland in 1947), we find that the distribution of IQs departs in a very systematic way from the normal Gaussian distribution. There is a bulge (i.e., excess frequency) in the lower half of the distribution, especially in the IQ range from about 65 to 90 (Burt, 1957, 1963). This suggests the presence of some non-genetic influence which hinders intellectual development. (Another possible explanation is the differential fertility of dull and bright persons, there being a negative correlation of about $-0\cdot2$ between intelligence and family size, which would result in there being a slight preponderance of low IQs. This theory is seriously undermined by the fact that by far the best explanation for the negative correlation between family size and IQ involves strictly environmental causation; there is no equally reasonable genetic interpretation of this correlation.) An American study shows that if low socio-economic status subjects are removed from the distribution, and especially if Negroes are removed, the distribution again closely approximates the normal (Kennedy, Van de Riet, and White, 1963). There is always a slight bulge, however, at the very lowest end of the distribution, below an IQ of 50, due to major gene defects and brain damage (Zigler, 1967).

These facts taken together are consistent with the hypothesis that the environment influences the development of intelligence as a threshold variable. (Actually it is best thought of as a number of thresholds.) That is to say, once certain kinds of environmental influences are present to a probably rather minimal degree, the individual's genetic potential for the development of intelligence will be more or less fully realized, and variations in the extent of these influences beyond this minimal threshold level will take only a slight contribution to the variance in measured intelligence. The situation is analogous to diet and physical stature. Once the diet is up to a certain minimal standard of adequacy with respect to vitamins, minerals, and proteins, the addition of more of these elements to the diet will not make any appreciable difference in physique; if they are present in the required minimal amounts, it will make no difference whether the person lives on beans and hamburger or on Oysters Rockefeller and pheasant-under-glass – the genes will entirely determine variations in stature. The case for intelligence seems much the same.

Another line of evidence is quite consistent with this threshold hypothesis, namely the studies concerned with upward changes in the IQ as a result of rather drastic environmental changes, either from 'natural' causes or by means of experimental manipulation of the environment. Environmental changes or manipulations seem to affect to any marked degree only those children whose social environments are quite wretched and clearly below what is presumably the environmental threshold for the normal development of genetic intellectual potential. Thus, when children are removed as infants from very poor homes, in which the natural parents have subnormal IQs, and are placed in foster homes, in which the foster parents are of average or superior intelligence, the children will grow up to obtain IQs that may be from 10 to 30 points higher than would be predicted if they had been reared by their natural parents, and their educational attainments will be even higher (Skodak and Skeels, 1966). (Of course, due allowance is made here for statistical regression.) It is only when there is a great discrepancy between the early environmental background of the natural parents and the environment provided for their children by the superior foster parents that we find evidence of a substantial boost in the children's IQs. It is simply a case of innate intellectual potential receiving the nurturance needed for its full development. It is also instructive to note that even though the IQs of foster parents may span a fairly wide range, the IQs of foster children are not correlated in the least with those of their foster parents (Honzik, 1957). Again, once the threshold of adequate environment is attained (the adoption agencies see that this is nearly always the case in foster homes), practically all the variability in the children's IQs will be determined by genetic factors.

Social class and intelligence

It has been hypothesized that the bulge in the lower half of IQs is due to the proportion of the population reared under conditions which are below the threshold of those environmental influences necessary for the full development of genetic intellectual potential. Thus, presumably, if these environmental lacks were eliminated, the bulge in the distribution of IQs would be smoothed out and the distribution would more nearly approximate to the Gaussian curve required by genetic theory. The portion of the population which contributed to the bulge would become redistributed at various higher points along the IQ scale; some would make only very slight gains, while others would make considerable gains in IQ. It would be difficult to estimate precisely the average expected gain, but it is likely to be somewhere between 10 and 20 IQ points.

Differences in mean IQ among various social classes and occupational levels are, of course, a well-established fact. But it is commonly believed that *all* of the socio-economic status differences are due to environmental factors and none to differences in genetic potential. Though the evidence on this point is quite complex, and therefore cannot be presented in this brief paper, it suggests the conclusion that social classes probably differ in innate potential (Burt, 1961; Burt and Howard, 1956). Perhaps as much as half of the between-classes variance in IQ is genetically determined. Several lines of evidence lead to this conclusion. One of the most striking is the phenomenon of regression to the population mean, which can be most satisfactorily accounted for in terms of genetic mechanisms. Even though low socio-economic status parents provide a poor environment for their children, their children, on the average, have higher intelligence than the parents; and though high socio-economic status parents provide a good environment for their children – often better than the environment they themselves grew up in – their children, on the average, have *lower* IQs than the parents (Burt, 1961; Jensen, 1968). This would be almost paradoxical from an environmentalist point of view, while it is completely in accord with genetic expectations. Also, it should be pointed out that the greater the equality of opportunity in a society and the fewer the restraints on social mobility, the greater will become the genetic differences between social classes. The educational and occupational hierarchies act as an intellectual screening device. Genetic differences between social classes could be minimized only by means of imposing rigid and impermeable class and caste boundaries that would rule out social mobility for many generations. This obviously is the very antithesis of a democratic society which, strange as it may seem at first glance, actually tends to maximize genetic differences and minimize environmental differences as a basis of social and economic rewards.

D*

Racial differences in intelligence

The above statements concerning socio-economic status differences in innate potential cannot be applied to differences between racial groups when there are greater barriers to social and occupational mobility in one racial group than in another, as is clearly the case for Negroes and Mexicans as compared with Caucasians of European origin in the U.S.A. There are probably socio-economic status differences in innate intellectual potential *within* any particular racial group, but these innate differences would be diminished to the extent that intellectually irrelevant genetic factors, such as lightness of skin color and other caucasoid features, are important as determinants of social and occupational mobility. Therefore, the fact that Negroes and Mexicans are disproportionately represented in the lower end of the socio-economic-status scale cannot be interpreted as evidence of poor genetic potential. For we know that there have been, and are still, powerful racial barriers to social mobility. Innate potential should be much more highly correlated with socio-economic status among whites than among Negroes or other easily distinguishable minorities, who are discriminated against on the basis of intellectually irrelevant characteristics.

The Negro population in the U.S.A. as a whole has an average IQ about 15 to 20 points below the average for the white population, and the variance of Negro intelligence is less than 60 per cent than in the white population (Kennedy, Van de Riet, and White, 1963; Tyler, 1965). The Negro population (11 per cent of the total U.S. population) is thus largely bunched up in that lower part of the IQ distribution where we find the bulge or departure from the so-called normal distribution. Since we know that the Negro population for the most part has suffered socio-economic and cultural disadvantages for generations past, it seems a reasonable hypothesis that their low-average IQ is due to environmental rather than to genetic factors. A much larger proportion of Negroes (and Mexicans) than of white probably grow up under conditions that may be *below* the environmental threshold required for the realization of genetic potential. It also appears that the economic condition of the Negro, which has markedly improved over the past two generations, does not bear a close relationship to the really crucial environmental threshold variables. It has been pointed out that the rise of the Negro IQ since World War I has not been nearly commensurate with the improvement of the Negroes' economic condition (McGurk, 1956). But the important environmental threshold variables, mainly interpersonal and psychological in nature, seems to be only incidentally correlated with economic status. Except in the most extreme cases, economic factors in themselves seem to have little causal potency as determinants of IQ and educability.

Environmental influences on intelligence and educability

It remains now to identify those environmental factors presently thought to be the most potent influences in the development of intellectual and educational potential. In recent years there has been a shifting of emphasis by psychologists working in this area. The trend has been away from rather crude socio-economic variables towards more subtle intrafamily and interpersonal psychological variables. This shift in emphasis is given cogency by the fact that crude socio-economic variables, such as income, occupation, and neighborhood, do not correlate as highly with intelligence and educability as do ratings of more psychological variables, such as whether the parents read to the children during the pre-school years, whether the family eats together, whether children are brought into the conversation at the dinner table, and other features of parent-child interaction, especially involving verbal behavior. The usual socio-economic variables found to correlate with IQ and educability have shown correlations in the range from 0·30 to 0·50. At most, only about 30 per cent of the variance in intelligence can be predicted from a composite of various indices of socio-economic status. Most variables that index socio-economic status, however, are better thought of as incidental correlates of IQ rather than as causal factors. The quality of the parent-child relationship, on the other hand, may be thought of as causal correlation, even though one cannot overlook the high probability that the quality of the parent-child interaction is influenced to a not inconsiderable degree by the genetic potential of both the parents and their children.

What are some of the environmental variables most highly

associated with the development of intelligence? Wolf (cited in Bloom, 1964, pp. 78-9) found that ratings on 13 process variables, describing the interactions between parents and children, would yield a multiple correlation with intelligence of +0·76. These variables may be classified as follows:

(a) Press for Achievement Motivation
    1. Nature of intellectual expectations of child
    2. Nature of intellectual aspirations for child
    3. Amount of information about child's intellectual development
    4. Nature of rewards for intellectual development

(b) Press for Language Development
    5. Emphasis on use of language in a variety of situations
    6. Opportunities provided for enlarging vocabulary
    7. Emphasis on correctness of usage
    8. Quality of language models available

(c) Provision for General Learning
    9. Opportunities provided for learning in the home
    10. Opportunities provided for learning outside the home (excluding school)
    11. Availability of learning supplies
    12. Availability of books (including reference works) periodicals and library facilities
    13. Nature and amount of assistance provided to facilitate learning in a variety of situations

Specific experiential deficiences of the culturally disadvantaged

More specifically, in terms of educational potential, what are presently thought to be the most crucial psychological deficiencies of the culturally disadvantaged can be grouped into three main categories: perceptual and attentional abilities, verbal and cognitive abilities, and orectic or motivational factors. A knowledge of the exact nature and etiology of deficiencies in these areas is, of course, highly germane to methods of prevention and remediation.

We have not mentioned motor abilities in connection with the disadvantaged, but because of current practices in some school programs for the culturally disadvantaged, the topic deserves a few words. Retarded motor development, poor muscular co-ordination, balance, and the like, are known to be characteristic of mental retardation of the primary type, particularly of retardation associated with brain damage. There is no evidence [in fact, there is evidence to the contrary (Bayley, 1965)] that a greater proportion of culturally disadvantaged children are retarded in motor development or are in any way deficient in this sphere than the proportion in the total population. Yet in some kinder-gartens and primary grades we find culturally disadvantaged children being required to engage in various tasks intended to develop or improve motor co-ordination, such as 'rail walking' – balancing on the narrow edge of a two-by-four. Though such exercises may be found helpful for primary retardates, there is no reason to believe they are anything but a waste of school time for culturally disadvantaged children, unless these children also show definite signs of primary retardation or motor deficiency. This is one example of the mistaken notion, which unfortunately is rife in the field of education of the disadvantaged, that the educational methods suitable for primary retardates and slow learners are also the most effective methods for the culturally disadvantaged.

PERCEPTUAL ABILITIES

From the rather meagre research now available, it appears that low socio-economic status children come to kindergarten or first grade with less well developed visual and auditory discrimination abilities (Jensen, 1966). The deficiency is not great in an absolute sense, but it is generally thought to hinder learning to read. Exer-cises in perceptual skills have been developed which apparently overcome these deficiencies fairly readily. Since ability to dis-criminate differences among shapes and sounds is an important prerequisite skill to school learning, these abilities should be assessed in kindergarten and compared with middle-class norms, and appropriate remedial training applied where deficiencies exist. Special tests, norms, and remedial techniques have still to be developed for this purpose, though some techniques already have been developed for experimental use. These remedial techniques can usually be played as games by small groups of children with the teacher, and the perceptual training can readily be combined with the much needed training in language skills.

ATTENTIONAL ABILITY

Anyone who has observed culturally disadvantaged children in the classroom, particularly in the primary grades, notes as one of the most outstanding deficiencies these children's inability to sustain attention. This deficiency is not so conspicuous in kindergarten but becomes clearly manifest in the first grade, as soon as reading is introduced and other structured cognitive demands are made upon the child. I have noticed this attentional lack in culturally disadvantaged children in my own observations in classrooms, and it has also been described to me by numerous teachers of the disadvantaged. The recent literature makes little reference to attention, but some of the phenomena discussed here under this heading have come to be identified with the concept of motivation. An excellent discussion of attention, as the term is used here, and of its importance to educability is found in Sir Cyril Burt's *The Backward Child* (1937, pp. 479-85). Attentional ability presumably is innate but may be strengthened through reinforcement in infancy and early childhood. It develops differentially in various kinds of situations and is reinforced through the parent-child relationship. Typically, the disadvantaged child's attention is poorly developed with respect to the teacher's speech and whatever things the teacher tries to make the focus of the child's attention. These particular attentional abilities are developed in middle-class children from an early age, probably through certain features of the parent-child relationship (reading to the child, mutual play accompanied by relevant speech, etc.) which are presumably relatively lacking in lower-class parent-child relationships. These activities are mutually reinforcing to the parent and child: attentional behavior on the child's part reinforces the parent's interaction with him, and the parent's interaction with the child further reinforces and shapes the child's attention. This shaping of attention in middle-class children is probably not only greater in sheer amount than in lower-class children but is related to activities that more nearly resemble those of the school and of the pupil-teacher relationship.

Thus, attention is less well developed in the low socio-economic status child at the time he enters school. In addition, I have observed a secondary phenomenon: there is an actual deterioration of the child's attentional ability, usually beginning in the first grade (Jensen, 1968). Some children begin actively to resist focusing attention on teacher-oriented tasks and activities. Normal attentional behavior gives way to a kind of seemingly aimless and disruptive hyperactivity. This is an almost universal observation by teachers of the disadvantaged, especially disadvantaged Negro children. This behavior can be likened to some extent to the phenomenon referred to by Pavlov as 'experimental neurosis'. In Pavlov's conditioning laboratory, dogs which were forced to learn discriminations beyond their capabilities became disturbed and resisted further attempts at training, even on much simpler tasks; they developed aversion to the entire laboratory setting and at times even lost previously conditioned habits. Though the analogy with culturally disadvantaged first-graders may seem far-fetched, it does suggest the possibility that the gap in difficulty between the tasks required of the disadvantaged child in the kindergarten and those encountered in the first grade might be too great in many schools. If the child cannot meet the tasks set by the teacher with *successful* performance (not merely receiving indiscriminate approval by the teacher for any quality of performance), the child gradually develops aversion to the school-learning situation. His attention is, as teachers are heard to say, 'turned off', and distractability and aimless hyperactivity ensue. The gap between preschool or kindergarten and first or second grade is not yet being bridged satisfactorily for the culturally disadvantaged child. The steps in the learning requirements are too big. For the middle-class child the transition from home to school is clearly a much less radical change from the activities and demands of the home.

LANGUAGE DEFICIENCIES

By far the greatest and most handicapping deficiencies of the culturally disadvantaged child are found in the realm of language. But the term language is here used in a much broader and psychologically more profound sense than is generally appreciated by teachers of English, speech therapists, and the like. The immediately obvious aspects of the language of the culturally disadvantaged – the lack of genteel English, incorrect grammar, poor pronunciation, use of slang, etc. – are psychologically the most superficial and the least important from the standpoint of intellectual development. This is not to minimize the social, economic, and occupational advantages of good oral and written English. It is simply important to realize that the language deficiencies of lower-class children have a much more detrimental psychological effect than the obvious social disadvantages of their language habits. Because the eschewal of certain lower-class language habits by the middle-class is perceived by some persons as undemocratic snobbery, there has grown up another utterly erroneous notion that lower-class language is just as good as any other kind of language, in the same sense the English, French and German, though obviously different from one another, are all equally good languages, as far as one can tell. Thus, social class differences in language habits are viewed as desirable or undesirable only according to one's acquired tastes, values and standards, and – to paraphrase the argument – who is to say that middle-class values are any better than lower-class values? This line of thinking can be quite discredited in terms of our growing understanding of the functions of language. Language not only serves a social function as a means of interpersonal communication but is also of crucial importance as a tool of thought. It is in this latter function that lower-class language deficiencies are most crippling psychologically.

General language characteristics

With respect to language functions, Metfessel (in Frost and Hawkes, 1966, p. 46) has listed the following general characteristics of culturally disadvantaged children:

1. Culturally disadvantaged children understand more language than they use. Even so, by second grade the comprehension vocabulary of such children is only approximately one-third that of normal children, while by sixth grade it is about one half.

2. Culturally disadvantaged children can use a great many words with fair precision, but not those words representative of the school culture. It has been estimated that something less than half the words known by middle-class pre-schoolers are known to slum children. Even such common name words as *sink, chimney, honey, beef* and *sandwich* are learned by culturally disadvantaged children one or two years later than other children.

3. Culturally disadvantaged children frequently are handicapped in language development because they do not have the concept that objects have names, and that the same objects may have different names.

4. Culturally disadvantaged kindergarten children use fewer words with less variety to express themselves than do kindergarten children of higher socio-economic status.

5. Culturally disadvantaged children use a smaller proportion of mature sentence structures, such as compound, complex, and more elaborate constructions. This is not limited to the non-English-speaking child, but occurs among most children who come from a disadvantaged background.

6. Culturally disadvantaged children learn less from what they hear than do middle-class children. Part of this deficiency has been attributed to the fact that disadvantaged children come from a milieu in which radio, television, and the sounds of many people living together in crowded quarters create a high noise level, which the child eventually learns to shut out psychologically, so that verbal stimuli generally become less salient.

7. Culturally disadvantaged children are less likely to perceive the symbolic and conceptual aspects of their environment; the verbal means of abstraction and analysis are relatively undeveloped.

8. Culturally disadvantaged children frequently end the reading habit before it is begun; the cycle of mastery which demands that successful experiences generate more motivation to read, which in turn generates higher levels of skill sufficient to prevent discouragement, and so on, often never gets under way. These children, of course, have poor adult models for reading behavior.

In general, it has been found that throughout the entire sequence of language development, from the earliest stages of speech in the first two years of life, there is retardation among culturally disadvantaged children (Bereiter and Engelmann, 1966; Jensen, in press; McCarthy, 1946, pp. 557-9). Furthermore, this retardation should not be thought of entirely as the disadvantaged child's merely lagging behind the middle-class child, with the same level of development merely being attained somewhat later. The characteristics of the language habits that are being acquired and the kinds of functions the language serves in the child's experience, actually shape his intellectual development, especially the development of the ability for abstraction and conceptual learning. Poor development of this ability places a low ceiling on educational attainment.

The most detailed analysis of social class differences in language characteristics, important to the development of cognitive abilities, has been made by Basil Bernstein (Bernstein, 1961). Except for minor details, his findings and conclusions seem to be applicable to social-class differences in the American culture as well as in the British, since social class differences in language behavior of the type that concerns him are probably even more pronounced here than in England. It is especially important that Bernstein's type of socio-linguistic analysis be applied to some of the various American low socio-economic status subcultural groups.

In characterizing social class differences in language behavior, Bernstein distinguishes two main forms of language, which he refers to as *public* and *formal*. In formal language, the variations of form and syntax are much less predictable for any one individual, and the formal possibilities for sentence organizations are used to clarify meaning and make it explicit. In *public* language, on the other hand, the speaker operates in a mode which individual selection and permutation are grossly restricted. In formal language the speaker can make highly individual selection and permutation. Formal language, therefore, can fit the speaker's purposes with much greater subtlety and precision and does not depend to any marked degree upon inflection, gestures, facial expressions, and a presupposed prior mutual understanding of the main gist of the communication, as expressed in the highly frequent use of the phrase 'you know what I mean' in lower-class speech. While middle-class persons can understand and use public as well as formal language, lower-class persons are more or less restricted to public language. Public language is almost completely limited to the single function of social intercourse within a community of tacit common understandings and values. It is not designed for expository functions, for detailed representation of past events or future plans, or for manipulating aspects of one's experience abstractly and symbolically. In public language, the quantity of speech is not reduced, but the variety of functions which speech can serve is limited. This becomes especially important in the realm of private or internal speech, where the person must use language to recall, review, structure, or otherwise mentally manipulate his past or his anticipated experiences, aims, plans, problems, and so on. Bernstein lists the following characteristics of public language:

1. Short, grammatically simple, often unfinished sentences with a poor syntactical form stressing the active voice.
2. Simple and repetitive use of conjunctives (so, then, because).
3. Little use of subordinate clauses to break down the initial categories of the dominant subject.
4. Inability to hold a formal subject through a speech sentence; thus, a dislocated informational content is facilitated.
5. Rigid and limited use of adjectives and adverbs.
6. Infrequent use of impersonal pronouns as subjects of conditional clauses.
7. Frequent use of statements where the reason and conclusion are confounded to produce a categoric statement.
8. A large number of statements/phrases which signal a requirement for the previous speech sequence to be reinforced: 'Wouldn't it?' 'You see?', 'You know?', etc. This process is termed 'sympathetic circularity'.
9. Individual selection from a group of idiomatic phrases or sequences will frequently occur.
10. *The individual qualification is implicit in the sentence organization: it is a language of implicit meaning.*

In contrast, the following are characteristics of formal language:

1. Accurate grammatical order and syntax regulate what is said.

2. Logical modifications and stress are mediated through a grammatically complex sentence construction, especially through the use of a range of conjunctions and subordinate clauses.
3. Frequent use of prepositions which indicate logical relationships as well as prepositions which indicate temporal and spatial contiguity.
4. Frequent use of the personal pronoun 'I'.
5. A discriminative selection from a range of adjectives and adverbs.
6. Individual qualification is verbally mediated through the structure and relationships within and between sentences.
7. Expressive symbolism discriminates between meanings within speech sequences, rather than reinforcing dominant words or phrases, or accompanying the sequence in a diffuse, generalized manner.
8. It is a language use which points to the possibilities inherent in a complex conceptual hierarchy for the organizing of experience.

Robert Hess, of the University of Chicago, has found considerable evidence of these two modes of language behavior in the parent-child interactions of lower-class and middle-class Americans observed in situations in which the mother is required to instruct her child in learning a simple task (Hess and Shipman, 1965). The language of the lower-class mother does not provide the child with cues and aids to learning to the same extent as the language of the middle-class mother. Since children tend largely to internalize the language of their home environment, mainly that of the parents, the low socio-economic status child acquires an inferior set of verbal techniques to apply on his own in learning and problem-solving situations.

Verbal mediation of cognitive functions

From the standpoint of the development of intelligence, the most important aspect of language is its relationship to a variety of processes listed under the general heading of *verbal mediation* (Jensen, 1966).

We have hypothesized, and some supporting evidence is already available, that one of the crucial psychological differences between low and middle socio-economic status children is in the spontaneity of verbal mediation, especially in ostensibly non-verbal learning or problem-solving situations. In short, low socio-economic status children are much less likely than middle socio-economic status children to talk to themselves as an aid to 'thinking'. On ostensibly non-verbal tests and learning tasks, which nevertheless require private verbal mediation, culturally disadvantaged children perform especially poorly. This is the main reason that so-called non-verbal intelligence tests are not by any means 'culture free' or 'culture fair'.

Several main processes of verbal mediation, that is, covert language, can be identified.

1. LABELING

In middle-class children the habit of labeling, or naming objects and events in the environment, becomes automatic and unconscious. It is practically impossible to look at, say, a chair or a book, or any object, without these stimuli eliciting a verbal (usually covert) response of naming. Perception and verbalization are more or less unified, so that one cannot see a chair without thinking 'chair', at least when the chair is the focus of one's attention. At first, in very young children, this naming tendency is overt; it gradually becomes covert. Most middle-class children enter school with this particular form of verbal equipment already fairly well developed. Lower socio-economic status children do not. Apparently the conditions under which the lower-class child spends his pre-school years are insufficient to instil the habit of naming or labeling. Experimental evidence has shown conclusively that verbal labeling greatly facilitates learning, retention, and problem solving. Furthermore, this type of verbal mediation is learned in a particular environment; it is not an innate aspect of learning ability. It is a form of behavior which must become habitual and automatic in children, if they are to develop their educational potential.

2. THE ASSOCIATIVE NETWORK

Words in context acquire associations. These verbal associations have other associations, and so on, to form an elaborate, ramifying verbal associative network. This network is thought to act, more or less automatically and unconsciously, as a broad source of transfer for conceptual learning and retention. It is the psychological background or 'net' which enmeshes the child's experiences in the classroom. Word association experiments on children indicate that low socio-economic status children have a less rich associative network. Even the words they know and use have, in this sense, less associative meaning to them, and the associations are not as structured in terms of hierarchical characteristics that facilitate categorization, conceptual analysis, and the like. The quality of the child's verbal environment is the chief determinant of the richness and structure of his associative network. All children who can speak have an associative network, but the network of associations of culturally disadvantaged children is more like that of middle-class children who are two or three years younger (Entwisle, 1966).

3. ABSTRACTION AND CATEGORIZATION

Conceptual learning, which includes much of school learning, involves the ability to abstract and to categorize things in terms of various abstracted qualities. For example, plates, wheels, doughnuts, and pennies, have in common the abstract property of being *round*. Young middle-class children and old culturally disadvantaged children are not likely to perceive anything in common among these disparate objects; in short, the objects as stimuli do not arouse abstract associations, and consequently the number of ways the objects can be grouped will be limited or entirely idiosyncratic, depending upon the child's particular experiences with the objects, such as the fact that his mother may have served him *doughnuts* on a *plate*. The ability to disassemble what is registered by the senses into various conceptual attributes is an important ingredient of educability, and it is greatly facilitated by, if not wholly dependent upon, verbal behavior, either overt or covert.

4. SYNTACTICAL MNEMONIC ELABORATION

The ability to respond to one's experiences on the verbal level in a way that makes use of the structuring and ordering properties inherent in the syntactical aspects of language, greatly facilitates learning, comprehension, retention and retrieval of, and reasoning involving various kinds of experience, both verbal and non-verbal. Language imposes its structure upon raw experience and structures and organizes it in ways that the subject is able to recall for use at a later time. This ability is limited for the person who either has not acquired or does not habitually use the logical and structural properties contained in formal language.

Compensatory education for the disadvantaged

The most radical, yet probably most successful, of the pre-school programs for the culturally disadvantaged is being conducted at the University of Illinois by Carl Bereiter and Siegfried Engelmann (Bereiter, 1965; Bereiter and Engelmann, 1966). It focuses intensively on training disadvantaged children to use the language in ways that facilitate learning and thinking.

The Bereiter program is based on the premise that it would be practically impossible to make up every environmental disadvantage that slum children have experienced, and that we must therefore concentrate all our efforts only on those which are most crucial to the development of educability in a normal school setting. These crucial skills, Bereiter maintains, are concerned with the use of language as a tool of thought. His program consists of drilling the kinds of language habits we have described into children by methods that produce high motivation, unanimous participation, and maximal concentration and effort on the child's part, with a minimal waste of time. The specific techniques have been described in greater detail elsewhere, and Bereiter and Engelmann have a book on their methods for use by pre-school teachers of the disadvantaged (Bereiter and Engelmann, 1966).

Bereiter correctly maintains that disadvantaged children must learn at not a normal but a superior rate in order to compete successfully with middle-class children. Otherwise they will never catch up to grade-level.

The Bereiter program attempts through direct and intensive training to remedy lacks in the following types of language skills, which Bereiter and his colleagues believe to be most crucial to early academic learning. The list is far from exhaustive, consisting only of the most basic language tools.

1. Ability to use both affirmative and 'not' statements in reply to the question, 'What is this?': 'This is a ball. This is not a book'.
2. Ability to handle polar opposites ('If it is not..., it must be..') for at least four concept pairs; e.g., big-little, up-down, long-short, fat-skinny.
3. Ability to use the following prepositions correctly in statements describing arrangements of objects: *on, in, under, over, between*. Example: 'Where is the pencil?' 'The pencil is under the book.'
4. Ability to name positive and negative instances for at least four classes, such as tools, weapons, pieces of furniture, wild animals, farm animals, and vehicles. Example: 'Tell me something that is a weapon.' 'A gun is a weapon.' 'Tell me something that is not a weapon.' 'A cow is not a weapon.'
5. Ability to perform simple 'if-then' deductions. Example: The child is presented a diagram containing big squares and little squares. All the big squares are red, but the little squares are of various other colours. 'If the square is big, what do you know about it?' 'It's red.' (This use of *if* should not be confused with the antecedent-consequent use that appears in such expressions as, 'If you do that again, I'm going to hit you', which the child may already be able to understand.)
6. Ability to use 'not' in deductions: 'If the square is little, what else can you say about it?' 'It is not red.'
7. Ability to use *or* in simple deductions: 'If the square is little, then it is not red. What else can you say about it?' 'It's blue or yellow.'

OTHER INTERVENTION PROGRAMS

Other systematically developed intervention programs for culturally disadvantaged pre-schoolers are more or less typified by those of Martin Deutsch in New York City, and Susan Gray in Nashville, Tennessee (George Peabody College). These programs cover a broader spectrum of activities and experiences than the Bereiter program, though the emphasis is still on stimulating cognitive development. It is generally agreed that the traditional middle-class nursery curriculum, with its emphasis on personal-social adjustment, in inappropriate and inadequate as a means of pulling lower-class children up to the developmental level of his middle-class age-mates. The Deutsch and Gray programs are described in articles by these investigators (Deutsch, 1962; Gray and Klaus, 1965.

Unfortunately, as of this date, the evidence regarding the efficacy of any of these programs is still meagre. It is insufficient merely to report gains in IQ, especially when this is based on retest with the same instrument or an equivalent form of the test, and when there is a high probability that much of the gain in test scores is the result of highly specific transfer from materials and training in the nursery program that closely resemble those used in the test. For example, the writer has noticed that in one pre-school program, some of the nursery materials consisted of some of the identical equipment used in the Stanford-Binet IQ test, and IQ gains resulting from children's spending several weeks in the program were based on pre- and post-training with the Stanford-Binet! Such unwitting self-deception must be guarded against in evaluating the effects of pre-school programs.

The most important evidence for the efficacy of such programs, of course, will be based on the child's performance in the elementary grades, especially his progress in reading. Probably the most significant predictor of satisfactory progress in the educational program, as it now exists in the public schools, is reading ability. If a child can surmount the reading hurdle successfully, the prognosis for satisfactory educational progress is generally good. It is also at this early point in the educative process – the introduction of reading – that so many culturally disadvantaged children meet a stumbling block, and head down the demoralizing path of educational retardation. Pre-school programs for the disadvantaged should concentrate, as does Bereiter's, on the development of cognitive skills basic to reading. In many cases this will probably require a greater attention to the development of perceptual-discriminative skills than is found in the Bereiter program.

The motivational aspects of reading and reading-readiness are much less clear, but most teachers who are experienced with the disadvantaged believe there are social-class differences among children's attitudes towards reading that affect their desire to learn to read. The best guess is that this motivational component of reading has its origin in early parent-child interaction in reading situations. Social-class differences in this respect apparently are enormous. Can anything be done about it?

This brings us to the question of parent involvement in intervention programs. Unfortunately, it has been the common experience that low socio-economic status parents are difficult to change with respect to child-rearing practices. If these parents are not reached long before their children are 4 or 5 years of age, much valuable time is lost in terms of the development of the child's educational potential. The child will come to Headstart or to kindergarten without ever having looked at a book, without ever having been read to, and without ever having seen an older child or adult engaged in the act of reading. Some unknown, but possibly large proportion of the determinants of reading failure among low socio-economic status children may be attributable directly to this set of conditions. Since it is unlikely that the majority of mothers of the most severely disadvantaged children can be reached by any feasible means that could create lasting changes in their mode of child-rearing, we should look elsewhere for practicable means of bringing appropriate influences to bear on culturally disadvantaged children early in their development.

One possible approach would be to require junior and senior high school girls to work with culturally disadvantaged children between 6 months and 4 years of age. It would be regarded as a practical course in the psychology of motherhood for all school girls, especially those from a low socio-economic status background, extending from about the 8th or 9th grade through the 12th. Each girl would spend at least an hour a day with a child, either in a nursery or in the child's own home. Instruction and supervision would, of course, accompany the girls' activities in working with young children. Much of the activity would consist of types of play thought to promote cognitive development. Children would, for example, be read to regularly from about one year of age. There should be sufficient consistency of the relationship between the child and the student for emotional rapport to develop. In many cases, of course, low socio-economic status high school girls will have to be taught and coached in detail about how to interact with infants and children in ways that promote cognitive development. They must be made to realize that these activities are probably the major hope for realizing the educational potential of low socio-economic status children. An experiment essentially very much like this was carried out on a small scale by Skeels and Dye (1939) some twenty-five years ago, with extremely encouraging results, substantiated by follow-ups over a twenty-five-year period (Skeels, 1966). Such a program on a large scale would, of course, constitute a major educational undertaking, involving considerable expenditure of funds for additional personnel, facilities, and efforts to gain widespread public acceptance. It could first be tried experimentally on a modest scale to test its feasibility.

Finally, it must be emphasized that all educators who have worked with the disadvantaged are agreed that pre-school intervention without adequate follow-up in the first years of elementary school is inadequate, because the culturally disadvantaged child does not go home after school, as does the middle-class child, to what is essentially a tutorial situation. Middle-class parents take a greater interest in their children's school work and offer them more help than do low socio-economic status parents. The educational system should make some provision for the lower-class child's opportunity for a tutorial relationship with an older child or an adult, at least throughout the elementary grades.

We are gradually having to face the fact that, in order to break the cycle of poverty and cultural deprivation, the public school will have to assume for culturally disadvantaged children more of the responsibilities of good child-rearing – responsibilities universally regarded among the middle-class as belonging wholly to the child's own parents. The brutal fact is that for culturally disadvantaged children, these responsibilities are not being met, for whatever reason. Whether or not the public school system should intervene where educationally important environmental lacks exist is, of course, strictly speaking, not a psychological or scientific question, but one of social policy.

Understanding readiness

Recent research papers in child development and educational psychology reflect a renewal of interest in readiness among educational researchers. There is a new awareness of the importance of the really old notion of readiness and of the need to re-examine the diverse phenomena associated with this concept in light of recent theory and research in child development, individual differences, and the psychology of learning and instruction. The fact that empirical researchers in psychology and education are again seriously approaching the problems of readiness, now with more sophisticated theories and research methodologies than were available in the former heyday of the concept, is an important trend in the right direction.

A generation ago, readiness in a biological-maturational sense was of greater interest to educational psychologists and was regarded more seriously than it has been in the past decade, which has been dominated largely by conceptions derived from theoretical positions of extreme environmentalism and behavioristic learning theory. In its most extreme form, this view holds that the degree of readiness for learning at any given age is merely the product of the amount and nature of the learner's previous experience. Readiness is viewed as the amount of previous learning that can transfer to new learning.

There can be no doubt about the *fact* of readiness; that is, the common observation that certain kinds of learning take place much more readily at one age than at another. No one disputes this. Disagreements arise only when we try to *explain* readiness. The theoretical explanation of readiness is important, of course, because much of what we do about readiness in educational practice will depend upon our conception of its nature.

For the sake of conceptual clarity, one can state two distinct theories of readiness. One theory can be called the *growth-readiness* view of mental development. It is associated with such eminent psychologists as G. Stanley Hall and Arnold Gesell, and it holds that certain organized patterns of growth of neural structures must occur before certain experiential factors can effectively contribute to development. The rate of intellectual development is seen as due primarily to internal physiological mechanisms and their orderly, sequential growth, rather than to inputs from the environment.

The contrasting viewpoint emphasizes learning as the major causal factor in development. The simplest, most extreme statement of this position is simply that humans, like all mammals, possess the neural structures for the formation of associations between the sensory inputs from receptors and the output mechanism of the effectors. This is, in short, the capacity for acquiring stimulus-response connections or habits. The sets of habits which we identify as intelligent behavior are seen as being built up through the acquisition of habits and chains of habits which interact to produce complex behavior. Thus mental development is viewed as the learning of an ordered set of capabilities in some hierarchical or progressive fashion, making for increasing skills in stimulus differentiation, recall of previously learned responses, and generalization and transfer of learning. In recent years this viewpoint has been most notably developed by Gagné (1965, 1968), who refers to it as the *cumulative learning* model of mental development.

Probably everyone who has attended to the relevant evidence in this field would agree that *both* the *growth-readiness* and the *cumulative learning* theories are necessary for comprehending all the facts of the matter. These two aspects are not at all mutually exclusive but work hand in hand to produce the phenomenon we observe as cognitive development. There is little doubt that the physical maturation of the brain, particularly the cerebral cortex, underlies the development of particular cognitive abilities. The developmental sequence of these abilities or, more exactly, of the readiness to acquire them through interaction with the environment, is especially evident between birth and 7 or 8 years of age. In fact, we know that not all of the brain's potential neural connections are physiologically functionable until at least 7 or 8 years of age in the vast majority of children.

The orderly sequence of maturation of neural structures is such that the capability for certain kinds of learning and performance falls along an age scale. Standard intelligence tests, such as the Stanford-Binet, yield scores in terms of mental age and attempt to index the child's level of mental maturity. These standard indices, especially in childhood, unquestionably measure a composite of factors associated with both neurophysiological maturation and cumulative learning; there are more specialized tests which clearly measure more of one of these factors than of the others. Acquiring the names of objects – learning common nouns, for example – is highly dependent upon experience once the child begins to talk; the child's vocabulary of common nouns at a given age may thus be conceived of as cumulative learning. The ability to copy geometric forms of increasing complexity, however, seems to depend more upon maturational than upon experiential factors. For example, many children who can easily copy a circle or a square cannot copy a diamond, but the reverse is not true. There is a sequence or hierarchy in the emergence of some abilities. The average 5-year-old can easily copy a square. But he must be 6 before he can easily copy a square containing a single diagonal and he must be 7 before he can copy a diamond. Intensive training in the specific act of copying a diamond is surprisingly difficult and generally ineffective in the average 5-year-old. At 7, no training is necessary.

Everyone will agree, too, that these sequential stages of capability are not abrupt steps but that these are transitional stages from one to another. Some transitions are relatively rapid, so that in the pre-school years an age difference of just a few months can make for quite striking differences in the child's learning capability for certain tasks.

In learning, as in perception, often the whole equals more than the sum of the parts. It is in the child's progressing ability to *integrate* the component sub-skills that the phenomenon called readiness is most apparent. Prior acquisition of the sub-skills is usually necessary but often not sufficient for learning a particular skill requiring the integration of the sub-skills. It is the integrative process, the development of a higher-order 'master plan', that depends most upon the maturation of brain structures. The physical and mental *sub-skills* for drawing a diamond are clearly possessed by the 5-year-old child. The abstract concept of a diamond, however, is still beyond him, and he therefore cannot integrate his sub-skills into the total performance of copying the figure of a diamond. He lacks the necessary program, the master plan, so to speak. If anyone doubts this, let him first try to teach a typical 5-year-old to copy a diamond, and then to teach a 7-year-old. It is a highly instructive experience to the teacher and provides a most tangible demonstration of the meaning of readiness.

A task with more clearly defined sub-skills lends itself even more readily to a demonstration of the interactive effects of mental maturation and cumulative learning. Learning to play chess is a good example. I was able to observe the simultaneous roles of maturation and cumulative learning quite clearly while trying to teach my daughter to play chess when she was 5 years of age. At the time, I was especially interested in Gagné's formulation of cumulative learning in terms of learning hierarchies – the idea that each new step in learning is dependent upon the prior acquisition of certain sub-skills, and that learning takes place most efficiently when we insure that all relevant sub-skills have been mastered prior to the next-to-be-learned skill in the learning hierarchy. The notion of a hierarchy of skills seems clearly applicable to the teaching and learning of chess, and I proceeded carefully to teach my 5-year-old daughter the game of chess with this hierarchical model in mind.

First, I had her learn to group the chess pieces into their two main categories, white and black. At 5 this was so easy for her that it hardly needed to be taught, as shown by the fact that she would spontaneously sort out the shuffled pieces in terms of their color when putting them away in the two compartments of the chess set's wooden storage box. If she had been only 4 years old, it might have been necessary to spend some time teaching her to categorize the items on the basis of color, but by 5 she had already acquired some concept of classes of objects that look alike in terms of some attribute – in this case, color. The next step was to learn the names of the six chess pieces, an example of paired-associates learning. Mastery of this was attained within a few trials and was accomplished with evident pleasure at having learned something new.

The next day's lesson consisted of learning the proper placement of the pieces on the chess board. This was learned, also with evident pleasure, in one brief session, but there was a slight retention loss before the next day, and further practice in placing the pieces was needed to bring this performance up to mastery. Then, one by one, the rules for moving each of the pieces were learned – another instance of paired-associate learning, but this time requiring practice with each piece in a number of different positions so that the general principle of each piece's movement could be acquired. This aspect of the learning also progressed quickly and easily. It seemed like fun to my daughter, and she appeared 'motivated' and eager to learn more in the next lesson. Her learning had proceeded so smoothly and easily up to this point that I almost became convinced that if each step in the learning of the sub-skills of chess were carried to mastery and if interest and motivation persisted, each subsequent step would prove as easy as the preceding one. This was conspicuously not the case.

After the sub-skills of chess had been learned and the object of the game was explained and demonstrated repeatedly, we tried to play the game of chess, using all that had been learned up to that point. But a game did not emerge; good moves were reinforced by praise, illegal moves were prohibited and had to be taken back, poor moves resulted in the loss of a piece, and half the time bad moves were not made to result in a loss, in order to avoid too much discouragement. Further coaching resulted in no discernible improvement, there was no co-ordination or plan in the movement of pieces such that an actual chess game would result, and learning seemed to come to a standstill. Moreover, at this stage interest and motivation took such a slump that even some of the earlier acquired, simple component skills deteriorated. Further lessons led to boredom, inattentiveness, restlessness, and finally complete rejection of the whole enterprise. To continue would have required extreme coercion on my part, so we quit the lessons completely. A few weeks later we tried checkers, which she learned easily. It was sufficiently less complex than chess, and she had no trouble playing a reasonably good game. Learning and improvement in performance in checkers was a smooth, continuous process, and at no point did my daughter show signs of 'turning off'. Checkers became her favorite game for a time, and she often coaxed me and others to play with her.

What was the difference between chess and checkers? I doubt that I was a better teacher of checkers than of chess; I doubt that my daughter was more motivated to learn checkers than chess or that checkers was in some way more 'relevant' to her than chess. I believe it was a difference in the complexity of checkers and chess and of the level of complexity that my child at age 5 could cognitively integrate into the total act of playing a game of checkers or chess.

A most instructive part of this experience to me was the rapidity of motivational slump and psychological 'turn-off' when instruction persisted beyond the level of readiness. The same phenomenon must occur in the learning of school subjects as well as in the present chess example. I doubt also that what I observed could be explained entirely in terms of my having used inappropriate teaching methods at the final stage of the chess instruction.

Exactly one year later, when my daughter turned 6, I again got out the chess set. By this time she had lost most of her negative reaction to it, and we ran through the component skills again; relearning was rapid. The only source of difficulty was some negative transfer from checkers; she now had to learn that chess pieces do not take other pieces by jumping over them but, rather, by displacing them on the same square. I believe she would have relearned faster had she never practised checkers. But it was a trivial difficulty. What was interesting was that this time, though my instructional technique was no different from that used before, there was no hitch in the learning, and a smooth, easy transition was made from the learning of the sub-skills to learning to integrate them into playing a real game of chess. Simultaneously, there was a growing interest and motivation, and my daughter's skill in the game itself showed continuous improvement with practice. For many weeks thereafter, the first thing I heard from my daughter every night when I arrived home from the office was, 'Daddy, let's play chess!'

This is a clear example of learning readiness in both of its aspects – the need to have already acquired the component sub-

E

skills underlying the next level in the learning hierarchy and the need to have reached the level of cognitive development necessary for the integration of the sub-skills into a functional whole. Learning is a normal biological function. Children do not have to be cajoled, persuaded, coerced, manipulated, or tricked into learning. Given the opportunity and the appropriate conditions, including readiness, children simply learn. The most effective reinforcement for learning or the behaviors that promote learning (such as attention, effort, persistence, and self-direction) is the child's own perception of his increasing mastery of the skill he is trying to acquire. When this perception is lacking, learning bogs down, and external reinforcements or rewards are usually inadequate to maintain cognitive learning. The child's *efforts* are rewarded, but not the cognitive processes that lead to further mastery; and the end result is frustration and turning off in the particular learning situation. This reaction can become an attitude that generalizes to many similar learning situations; for example, school learning in general.

An important aspect of readiness is the child's ability to perceive discrepancies and approximations in his own behavior in relation to a good model or plan. It is becoming increasingly clear from the research on cognitive development that the child's capacity for plans increases with age and is underpinned by genetically coded neurophysiological developments. Any complex integrative activity – playing chess, reading with comprehension, doing arithmetic thought-problems – depends upon the development of these plans or cognitive structures. The child adapts his behavior to the model or plan and the self-perception of successive approximations provides the reinforcement (reward) that shapes behavior in the desired direction. This is the essence of cognitive learning. Though several years ago I believed that the child's learning of language was the chief instrument of his cognitive learning abilities and that these abilities were almost entirely dependent upon his use of language and his acquisition of habits of verbal mediation, my reading of more recent research in this field inclines me to reject this view. The evidence leads me to closer agreement with the position expressed by Sheldon White that '. . . the gathering evidence seems more and more to suggest that the child's progressive sophistication in language between five and seven is not the cause, but is rather the correlate of, his progressive sophistication in learning' (White, 1968, p. 3).

The relativity of readiness

The age for readiness for some particular learning is rarely confined to a single point on a developmental scale for any given child. Readiness cannot be determined independently of the method of instruction. A child can evince readiness for learning to read, for example, at age 3 by one method of instruction and not until age 6 by another method. The materials and methods that will work at 3 will work at 6, but the reverse may not be true. For example, most 3-year-olds would not learn to read in the typical first grade classroom nor with the size of type typically used to print first-grade primers, nor by a phonic method. Individual instruction, using very large, poster-sized type, and a 'look-say' method will permit many 3-year-olds to learn to read, although such reading at 3 is probably a quite different process psychologically than reading at 6. In other words, what appears superficially as the same behavior may be acquired by different means and involve different psychological processes at different developmental stages. The often superficial nature of the resemblance of the two behaviors can be observed in the extent and nature of the transfer of learning. The 3-year-old who learns to read 'leg', for example, will be at a loss when the new word 'peg' is presented, and it will take as long to learn 'peg' as it would to learn 'can'. For the 6-year-old, reading need not be so much a form of audio-visual paired-associate rote learning as it is a form of problem-solving using phonetic mediators. Therefore there will be a high degree of transfer from 'leg' to 'peg'.

Little is known about the extent to which the readiness factor can be minimized in learning by manipulating instructional techniques. Experiments on such tasks as copying a series of geometric figures of increasing complexity suggest that, at least in this realm, performance is far more dependent upon maturational factors than upon any variations that different instructional techniques can produce. Differences in instructional techniques in most forms of school learning may well be of maximum importance at the threshold of readiness, although beyond this threshold a variety of techniques may be relatively indistinguishable in their effectiveness.

Ignoring readiness

What happens when we ignore the readiness of children who are of approximately the same chronological age but different readiness levels and attempt to teach all the children the same thing in the same way? Obviously we will observe marked individual differences in the speed and thoroughness with which the children learn, and we may be inclined to increase our efforts and persistence in teaching the slower learners in order to help them catch up to the others, or at least to try to achieve the same degree of mastery of the subject as attained by the faster children, even if it takes somewhat longer.

Aside from the accentuation of individual differences in the classroom, are there likely to be other effects of ignoring readiness with possibly greater psychological consequences than those of merely making more visible individual differences in scholastic performance? We do not have any firmly established answers to this question. However, recent animal research on readiness factors in learning and some of my own observations of certain classes in which many children appear not to be learning much of anything at all, despite heroic efforts of the teachers, lead me to hypothesize that ignoring readiness can have adverse psychological effects beyond merely not learning what is being taught at the time it is being taught.

These adverse effects seem to take two main forms: (1) The child may learn the subject matter or skill by means of the cognitive structures he already possesses; but because these structures are less optimal than more advanced structures in the sequence of cognitive development, the learning is much less efficient and results in the acquisition of knowledge and skills with lesser capability of transfer to later learning. The increasing breadth of transfer of learning is a chief characteristic of the sequence of cognitive development. (2) The second adverse effect of ignoring readiness by persisting in instruction beyond the child's present capability is to cause the phenomenon referred to earlier in the chess example as 'turning off'. This amounts to an increasing inhibition of the very behaviors that promote learning, and I believe it can become so extreme that it may eventually prevent the child from learning even those things for which he is *not* lacking in readiness.

'Learning to learn', or what psychologists call the acquisition of learning sets, is of greater educational importance, and requires more complex cognitive structures, than the learning of any specific associations or facts. All animals are capable of forming new associations between stimuli and responses, but only higher mammals are capable of learning-set acquisition to any appreciable degree, and this capability is not easily demonstrated below the level of primates. Much research on learning sets has been conducted with monkeys and apes. This research clearly shows that learning to learn, more than any specific learning, is dependent upon maturational factors. Since a high degree of control can be maintained over the experiences of monkeys in the laboratory, it is possible to assess the relative importance of maturational and experiential variables for different kinds of learning and to study the consequences of forcing certain types of learning before the maturational factors are optimal for that particular learning.

Research on primates leaves no doubt that learning ability increases with age up to adulthood and that the asymptote of capability for various types of learning comes at later and later ages as the complexity of the learning task increases. The 5-day-old monkey, for example, forms conditioned reflexes as rapidly as the adult monkey. The speed of learning object-discriminations, on the other hand, does not reach its maximum until about 150 days of age. When monkeys are given a *succession* of object discrimination problems, each involving different visual discriminations, the monkeys' learning speed gradually increases from one problem to the next. The first problems may require 100 to 200 trials to learn a single discrimination; but after the animal has learned to learn by being given a sequence of many different object discrimination problems, these discriminations may be learned in only one or two trials. In other words, the animal is said to have acquired a learning set for object discriminations and in this type of learning is capable of close to 100 per cent efficiency; that is, learning in the fewest possible trials.

It is known that the speed with which learning sets are acquired depends upon the monkey's age; that is to say, its maturational readiness for learning set formation or interproblem learning. Young monkeys (60 to 90 days old) show much less readiness for learning set formation than older monkeys (150 to 300 days old), as reflected in the great differences in learning rates. The most interesting finding, however, is that the monkeys trained at the earlier, preoptimal age for learning set formation apparently do *not* eventually catch up with the older monkeys, even when they finally reach the same age as that at which the older monkeys were trained with much greater ease. In other words, the early training not only was less efficient, but it resulted in these young monkeys' attaining an asymptote at a lower level of proficiency than that attained by older monkeys with much less training. The too-early training resulted in a low ceiling for the subsequent development of this particular ability.

Harlow, who conducted these experiments, concluded

These data suggest that the capacity of the two younger groups to form discrimination learning sets may have been impaired by their early, intensive learning-set training, initiated before they possessed any effective learning-set capability. Certainly, their performance from 260 days onward is inferior to that of the earlier groups with less experience but matched for age. The problem which these data illustrate has received little attention among experimental psychologists. [And, we might add, educational psychologists.] There is a tendency to think of learning or training as intrinsically good and necessarily valuable to the organism. It is entirely possible, however, that training can either be helpful or harmful, depending upon the nature of the training and the organism's stage of development (Harlow, 1959, p. 472).

For the neonatal and infant rhesus monkey each learning task is specific unto itself, and the animal's intellectual repertoire is composed of multiple, separate, and isolated learning experiences. With increasing age, problem isolation changes to problem generalization, and this fundamental reorganization of the monkey's intellectual world apparently begins in its second year of life. From here on, we can no longer specify the monkey's learning ability for any problem merely in terms of maturational age and individual differences. The variable of kind and amount of prior experience must now be given proper value (Harlow, 1959, pp. 477-78).

The shift in cognitive style in the second year of life in the rhesus monkey, described by Harlow, seems to have its counterpart in the human child between 5 and 7 years of age – the age at which children universally begin their formal schooling. Sheldon H. White (1965) has adduced a diversity of data in support of his hypothesis that adult mental organization is hierarchical, consisting of two main 'layers': an associative layer laid down early in development and following conventional associative principles and a cognitive layer laid down in later childhood. The formation of the cognitive layer is most marked between the ages of 5 and 7. Between these ages children show a transition from a type of performance in learning situations characteristic of lower animals in similar situations to a type of performance characteristic of adult humans. Thus, it is during this period of most rapid qualitative changes in cognitive processes that consideration of readiness factors of the maturational type is of most importance. The period is better thought of as extending from age 5 to ages 8 or 9, to include more or less the full range of individual differences in making this cognitive transition. Tests such as the Stanford-Binet, the Piagetian developmental tests, and the types of tests and indices described by Ilg and Ames (1964) are the best means now available for assessing readiness for cognitive learning in this age range.

As I mentioned before, the second major type of difficulty that can result when readiness is ignored is what I previously called 'turning off'; that is to say, the extinction or inhibition of those forms of behavior which are essential aspects of learning – attention, self-directed effort, rehearsal, and active involvement. Signs of discouragement, waning interest, boredom, and the like are merely surface indicators of the inhibition of learning.

The psychological mechanism by which turning off comes about is well known in laboratory research on learning and was first described in detail by Pavlov under the names 'experimental extinction' and 'conditioned inhibition'. It is a reasonable hypothesis that these processes operate in school when certain analogous conditions prevail in the learning situation. The essential condition is responding without reinforcement or with very inconsistent reinforcement. In animal learning, reinforcement or reward must be external; it is dispensed by the experimenter, usually as bits of food, to strengthen the responses defined as correct by the experimenter. Withholding reinforcement results in decrement or extinction of the response in question, and the stimuli that are present while this extinction process in underway become conditioned inhibitors; that is, the mere presence of these stimuli can come to inhibit the class of responses with which they were associated during extinction.

In humans, reinforcement can be external or internal, so to speak. External reinforcement in the pupil-teacher relationship generally involves both approval and praise by the teacher and 'informative feedback' from the teacher as to the correctness or incorrectness of the child's responses. But more important in human cognitive learning is internal reinforcement resulting from the learner's self-perception of his own behavior and its approximation to self-perceived goals. Behavior is sustained and shaped by reinforcement or feedback. If there are no internalized standards or structures as a basis for feedback concerning the approximation of one's performance to the standard, then reinforcement must be external. A simple, clear-cut example is the comparison of a beginning student on the violin and a professional musician. The former must have a teacher to provide immediate feedback on the correctness or incorrectness of performance; the standard is in the teacher's head, so to speak, and not the pupil's. When the professional practices a new piece, on the other hand, his activities are reinforced by his successive approximations to his own internalized standards, which have been acquired through years of musical training, and the subtleties of which can only be referred to as musical talent.

Human cognitive learning (as contrasted with rote learning and motor learning) depends in large part on such internalized regulation of the learning process. The source of self-informative feedback is highly dependent on readiness, the capacity for plans or models to which the child's performance can achieve successive approximations. There is a difference in readiness, for example, between the child who reads by naming symbols (words) he has rote-learned and the child who perceives reading as making an effort to extract meaning from the printed words. Much of the activity of the latter child is self-instructional. Children who do not engage in self-instructional activity do not make normal progress in school. Forced practice in the absence of internal reinforcements, I suggest, can lead to extinction of the behavior being practiced.

Readiness in the cognitive sphere is largely the ability to conceptualize the learning task, to grasp the aim of one's efforts long before achieving mastery of the task. The relative ineffectiveness of shaping one's behavior to external requirements as compared with internal requirements is perhaps seen most dramatically in the child's efforts to copy geometric figures of varying difficulty. Unless the child can internalize a conceptual representation of the figure, he cannot copy it, even though the model is directly before him. Partly for this reason, as well as for its correlations with school readiness, the Ilg and Ames figure copying test is probably one of the most convincing and valuable measures of cognitive development in the pre-school years and throughout the primary grades (Ilg and Ames, 1964).

Conclusion

Many school learning problems could be circumvented if more attention were paid to readiness in the primary grades, when children's learning is most easily turned off through extinction due to inadequate readiness. The risks of delaying instruction too long seem much less than the possible disadvantages of forcing instruction on a child who is still far from his optimal readiness for the subject of instruction.

We need much more experimentation on readiness; that is, trying the same instructional procedures over a much wider range than is ever the case in traditional schools. It may well be that some sizeable proportion of children in our schools will, for example, be better readers at age 12 if they began reading instruction at age 8 than if they began at age 6, and this may apply to the learning of most scholastic skills. The high rate of reading failures and other deficiencies in basic scholastic skills found among high school graduates in groups called disadvantaged can

E*

hardly be explained in terms of deficiencies in basic learning abilities. It would seem necessary to invoke turn-off mechanisms at some early stage of their schooling to account for some of their marked educational deficiencies. Experimental programs of primary education that pay special attention to readiness factors in learning and actually *delay* formal instruction (meanwhile inculcating pre-requisite experiential factors) until readiness is clearly in evidence are needed to test this hypothesis for its practical effectiveness in improving the ultimate educational achievements especially of children called disadvantaged. It is among this group that turning off in school is most evident.

I suggest that more of the factors which cause turning off are found within the school than outside the school and that among the prime causal factors is an inadequate recognition of the importance of readiness, both in terms of cognitive maturation and cumulative learning. Compared with the potential benefits of such experiments as suggested here in terms of the readiness concept, the risks seem almost trivial. It appears that considerably more bold and daring educational innovations are called for if we are to improve the outcomes of schooling for the majority of children called disadvantaged. The present large-scale programs of compensatory education, which so far have failed to yield appreciable scholastic gains among the disadvantaged, are psychologically and educationally probably still much too conservative. A variety of much more radical educational experiments, with the outcomes properly assessed, would seem to be indicated. At least a few such experiments should give extreme emphasis to readiness factors and to the avoidance of turn-off in school learning.

The role of verbal mediation in mental development[1]

The nature of mental development

The importance of current theory and research pertaining to verbal mediation is highlighted mainly by two factors: (*a*) conceptions of the nature of mental development, and (*b*) social concern with the educational problems of children called culturally disadvantaged.'

Historically and currently, ideas about mental development may be characterized in terms of the relative degree of emphasis given to (*a*) growth or developmental factors, and to (*b*) learning or experiential factors.

Until about the last decade, child psychology, pre-school education, and primary education were dominated by a developmental or growth-oriented approach to the study of changes in mental ability as a function of age. The same developmental factors were invoked to explain individual differences and even social class and ethnic group differences in scholastic achievement and in performance on mental tests. This *growth-readiness* view of mental development, associated with such eminent psychologists as G. Stanley Hall and Arnold Gesell, holds that certain organized patterns of growth of neural structures must occur before certain

[1] This paper was written under contract with the National Institute of Child Health and Human Development, National Institutes of Health, for inclusion in a Task Force report titled *Perspectives On Human Deprivation: Biological, Psychological, and Sociological*.

131

experiential factors can effectively contribute to development. Rate of intellectual development is seen as related primarily to internal biological mechanisms and their orderly, sequential growth, rather than to inputs from the environment.

The opposite viewpoint emphasizes learning as a major causal factor in development. The most elemental and radical statement of this position is simply that humans, like all mammals, possess the neural structures for the formation of associations between the sensory inputs from receptors and the output mechanisms of the effectors – in short, the capacity for acquiring S-R habits. The sets of habits which we identify as intelligent behavior are seen as being built up through the acquisition of habits and chains of habits which interact to produce complex behavior. Mental development is thus viewed as the learning of an ordered set of capabilities in some hierarchical or progressive fashion, making for increasing skills in stimulus differentiation, recall of previous learned responses, and generalization and transfer of learning. In recent years this viewpoint has been most vigorously espoused by Robert M. Gagné (1965). He refers to it as the *cumulative learning* model of mental development.

My own view of these contrasting theories is that when each is stated in an extreme form, they serve as a useful set of co-ordinates in terms of which what is probably the true nature of mental development may be represented. One can represent the importance of developmental factors on the X axis and the importance of experiential factors on the Y axis. Various types of performance can be represented by their locations in this space, and for many types of performance the location will depend upon the age of the individual. For example, developmental factors may be relatively important in vocabulary acquisition in early childhood, while experiential factors may be of much greater importance for vocabulary acquisition in teenagers. Also, vocabulary acquisition in early childhood may depend less on developmental factors than, say, ability to copy geometric forms of varying complexity (1964). As will be pointed out shortly, there is increasing reason to believe that both the growth and cumulative learning models are necessary to comprehend all the results of recent research. It is when we attempt to force either of the two extreme interpretations on the data that we must either strain credulity or severely restrict the range of phenomena that can be explained.

THE RECENT IMPORTANCE OF MEDIATION THEORY AND RESEARCH

In recent years the cumulative learning model seems to be most in tune with hopes for improving the educability of children from poor families, now called the culturally disadvantaged. The *growth-readiness* model has perhaps seemed too pessimistic to many educators and social scientists concerned with this problem. Those aspects of behavioristic learning theory which come closest to dealing with what we think of as the mental processes involved in intelligence have been seized upon as a means for explaining social-class differences in manifest intelligence and scholastic perform-ance. Also, since the learning model makes explicit the processes that characterize intelligence, it offers the possibility that these may be changed through behavioral techniques to the advantage of many children whose chances of succeeding in school would ordinarily be poor.

Mediation theory was developed by behavior theorists speci-fically to comprehend those forms of behavior classed as 'thinking', the abstract attitude, etc. Disadvantaged children are especially characterized by deficiencies in those behaviors for which medi-ation processes are invoked as explanatory concepts. It is apparent that cognitive proficiency depends upon covert, self-initiated intellectual processes, and the only formulations of these processes which seem to present distinct possibilities for manipulating them by strictly behavioral means have been the S-R mediation theories. We know little or nothing about manipulating the rate of cognitive development on the biological level. Behavior theories of mediation based on the acquisition of verbal mediators through S-R associ-ations, on the other hand, offer both a means of explaining mental development and of influencing its course through environmental intervention. Hence the attraction of this approach for those who wish to change behavior, and particularly for those who seek to improve the intellectual capabilities of disadvantaged children. The guiding hypotheses of such workers is that the main disadvantage of the 'disadvantaged child' is inadequate exposure to the particular stimulus inputs which, for most children, are responsible for the learned forms of behavior we call 'intelligence'.

FORMULATION OF THE PRINCIPAL RESEARCH PROBLEM

The enthusiasm for seeking behavioral means for improving intelligence and educability has probably led to a too exclusive emphasis on those aspects of cognitive behavior that can be experimentally manipulated by the traditional techniques of the experimental psychology of conditioning and learning. Some theorists have cast nearly all aspects of mental development into a rather simple learning-theory framework. For a time, the idea of developmental factors – the growth of neural structures independently of experience, although perhaps requiring specific experiences for their activation – was eclipsed by an almost exclusive emphasis on the importance of learning *per se*.

There is now a growing disillusionment with an exclusive learning approach to cognitive development. Since it would be undesirable for the pendulum to swing to the other extreme, the problem should be reformulated as that of determining the relative importance of developmental and learning factors and their interaction for various cognitive skills. There is evidence that some of the cognitive skills needed for educability (i.e., the ability to learn school subjects under ordinary conditions of classroom instruction) are normally acquired through experience afforded by a good home environment, and they can be learned under special conditions by children whose environment has failed to provide the appropriate experiences. On the other hand, there are other cognitive skills, also an essential part of 'intelligence' and educability, which cannot be explained easily without reference to developmental factors, the maturation of brain structures, and the like, and which are relatively unsusceptible to training. One of the key problems is to determine the extent to which some cognitive behaviors achieved through special training merely *simulate* the same behaviors achieved through development (i.e., when there is no evidence of direct training) and the extent to which the trained behavior is actually the same as that achieved by 'growth' rather than by specific training.

Recent history of research on mediation processes

RUSSIAN WORK

Although the concept of verbal mediation may be traced in its various forms back to antiquity, it was probably not until Pavlov that the concept emerged from philosophical discourse into the realm of experimental science. The philosopher Cassirer stated the notion in the most general terms: 'Man has, as it were, discovered a new method of adapting himself to his environment. Between the receptor system and the effector system, which are to be found in all animal species, we find in man a third link which we may describe as the symbolic system' (1953, p. 43).

Pavlov translated this idea into a form permitting experimental investigation. He referred to speech (and other symbolic behavior) as a second signaling system, as distinguished from the first signaling system consisting of responses conditioned to the impingement of physical stimuli on the sensorium. It was apparent that as individuals grow from early childhood to adulthood, their overt responses to stimuli are increasingly mediated through the second signal system.

The stages through which this development occurs have been intensively studied by students of Pavlov and by later Russian psychologists, most notably A. R. Luria (1961). Both developmental and learning factors are clearly evident in Luria's research on the verbal control of motor responses in children. There is a rather definite progression between the ages of $1\frac{1}{2}$ to 6 years in the capability of subjugating motor responses to verbal control. At first, external commands act like any other conditioned stimuli as signals for some overt behavior. This stage is followed by the semantic meaning of utterances evoking or inhibiting responses, such that, for example, a child conditioned to press a bulb on the command 'Press!' can be inhibited from pressing by the new command 'Don't press!' At an earlier age the command 'Don't press!' since it contained the signal 'press', would cause the child to press the bulb. Luria views this transition as a developmental process and not as solely the result of cumulative learning. It is not until much later that the child's own speech is capable of regulating his overt behavior, somewhere between $4\frac{1}{2}$ and 6 years of age.

It is the internalization of speech and its capability of governing behavior that Russian psychologists, such as Luria (1961) and Vygotsky (1962), see as the basis for abstract and symbolic thought. The child's speech becomes not only an instrument of expression and social interaction but an instrument for the self-regulation of behavior and for increased control over the environment – through self-initiated planning, recall of past relevant experiences in new problem situations, self-instruction and rehearsal of newly acquired experience, and fantasies that lend coherence and continuity to play activities. The overt aspects of speech diminish as the child grows older and they become manifest from time to time when the child faces a new or difficult problem. Even as adults, we begin 'thinking out loud' when confronted with complex problems.

The recent Russian research on the developmental characteristics of the second signal system and some of the American research in this line have been reviewed by Thomas F. Hartman (1965). The techniques developed by the Russians are powerful tools for exploring covert thought processes. The technique consists essentially of conditioning various autonomic responses, such as GSR, to either non-verbal (objects or pictures) or verbal stimuli (words, phrases, and sentences) and measuring the amount of semantic generalization or transfer of the conditioned response to other related verbal stimuli. Probably no more refined technique has been devised for studying the development of meaning, concepts, semantic equivalence, and covert verbal processes involved in problem solving.

AMERICAN RESEARCH ON MEDIATION

The idea of verbal mediation as covert *behavior* was an essential part of John B. Watson's behaviorism (1914). Watson's formulation of thinking as subvocal speech, obeying simple laws of S-R association, was the precursor of later attempts at more detailed behavioristic accounts of thinking.

Clark L. Hull postulated the existence of 'pure stimulus acts' to account for behavior in animals and men which did not follow directly from the stimuli to which the behavior had been originally conditioned and which could not be accounted for in terms of primary stimulus generalization (1930).

In Hull's system 'pure stimulus acts' are responses which serve only as cues or self-produced stimuli to which other responses can be conditioned. They make for generalization or transfer of responses beyond the confines of primary stimulus generalization, which is limited to relatively small variations of the physical stimulus situation.

This Hullian notion that behavior itself serves a stimulus or cue function to which still other responses may be conditioned was greatly elaborated upon in the 1940s and '50s by Cofer (1942), and Osgood (1953). The most sophisticated and far-reaching extension of this earlier work is the cumulative learning model of Gagné, which has been most succinctly explicated in an article in the *Psychological Review* (1968). In this article Gagné makes a case for interpreting the development of complex and abstract behavior entirely in terms of learning, including such cognitive activities as conservation of volume, which, following Piaget, most developmental psychologists have regarded as depending largely on biologically determined developmental factors.

Types of mediation processes

In studies of human learning, mediation nearly always refers to *verbal* mediation. In the most general terms mediation refers to all mental processes that intervene between stimuli and responses when the relationship between these two sets of events cannot be attributed to simple associative processes. In most cases the intervening processes are conceived of as covert verbal responses to external stimulus situations; the verbalizations act in turn as stimuli for other responses.

Most mediational processes may be classified according to their effects into one of two broad categories – (*a*) those that make for stimulus *reduction* or *selection*, and (*b*) those that consist of stimulus *elaboration*.

Learning is facilitated in complex stimulus situations when the learner pays attention to only limited aspects of the stimuli and ignores those aspects which are irrelevant to mastery of the responses to be learned, the concept to be attained, or the problem to be solved. Learning or problem situations can elicit previously acquired mediators or 'sets' in the learner which permit him to reduce the problem to its essentials. This is a form of mediation in that the subject is not responding to the entire stimulus complex, but rather to his self-initiated restructuring or abstraction of it. It is the difference between acquiring an S-R association and an S-r-s-R association, where the mediating links, r-s-R, have been previously acquired by the subject.

On the other hand, in relating *simple* stimulus situations, such as learning paired-associates, it is to the learner's advantage to *elaborate* on the stimulus elements, as by recalling other associations to these elements, thereby imbedding them in a larger associative framework, investing them with meaning, etc.

Most, but perhaps not all, forms of verbal mediation depend upon an active, self-initiated, conscious process in the learner. Relatively passive or automatic responding in the learning situation is generally incompatible with mediational processes, which depend upon the subject's activity, usually covert verbalization.

A number of different mediation phenomena and paradigms have been subjected to experimental study. The most prominent phenomena are listed below. They all share in common the important fact that they are forms of verbal mediation which occur 'naturally' (that is, they are not just experimentally contrived), and yet they also lend themselves to being manipulated experimentally. Most important is the fact that these forms of mediation can be learned or at least enhanced by training and practice, and all are known to facilitate learning, concept formation, and problem solving.

LABELING

Labeling or assigning names to things is perhaps the simplest instance of the 'elaboration paradox' – that is, the fact that in some situations it is easier to learn more than less. A classic demonstration of the phenomenon is that by Marjorie Honzik Pyles (1932). She found that children learned much more quickly to respond to (i.e., pick up) the rewarded three-dimensional nonsense form among a number of such forms if children first learned nonsense syllable names for the objects. This may seem paradoxical, since it involves learning *two* things – the 'names' of the objects *and* which object contained the reward. Yet children who were instructed to learn the names of the objects learned the main point of the task – to find the reward – more quickly than children who were not instructed to learn names for the objects. Older children tend to assign names to the objects spontaneously, and if this is made easier by using familiar objects rather than nonsense shapes, learning to pick up the object that conceals a reward is greatly facilitated.

A number of studies have shown that free recall of a number of familiar objects or pictures presented only once is facilitated in pre-school children and in primary grade disadvantaged children if the children name the items while they are being presented. Older children (beyond 6 years of age) show little or no increase in amount recalled when they are told to name the items on presentation. Presumably the majority of children beyond 6 years of age spontaneously make some overt or covert naming response to the items, so that being instructed to do so adds little to the facilitation of recall.

One of the important differences we find between middle-class children and culturally disadvantaged children is not in their ability to name things but in the strength of their tendency to do so spontaneously without being asked, in situations in which learning is markedly facilitated by naming the items to be recalled or the elements of the problem to be solved.

In a study comparing trial-and-error selective learning in gifted, average, and retarded school children, Jensen (1963a) found that gifted and average children were quite active verbally during learning, while retarded (IQs 50 to 75) children showed little evidence of spontaneous verbal activity. However, when the retarded children were instructed to verbalize in relevant ways (e.g., naming the stimuli), their learning rate was often markedly facilitated.

Flavell, Beach, and Chinsky (1966) noted these verbalization tendencies in children learning discrimination and transfer problems, by noting speech, lip movements, etc. It was found that children who failed to learn did not produce verbal mediators at the appropriate points during learning trials.

MEDIATED AND SEMANTIC GENERALIZATION

Mediated generalization is the learned equivalence of stimulus elements that are physically unrelated: i.e., they do not lie on the same stimulus dimension, as in the case of primary stimulus generalization. This form of mediation has been most intensively studied by Russian psychologists by means of classical conditioning techniques, in which transfer of usually autonomic conditioned responses (e.g., the galvanic skin response) from objects to words or from one word (or phrase or sentence) to another is measured.

Mediated generalization, especially semantic generalization, is of interest in that it indicates that certain subject-generated stimuli (covert verbal responses) are elicited by the external stimulus situation and become conditioned to it as well. More interesting is the fact that there are gradients of semantic generalization, as well as of primary stimulus generalization. For example, if a galvanic skin response (GSR) is conditioned to a blue light, the word 'blue' will also elicit the conditioned response (CR), and to a lesser degree the word 'sky' will elicit the CR, as will other semantic associates of the word 'blue'.

Semantic generalization is of special interest to developmental psychologists because young children do not show it and its appearance and increasing strength in the age range from 5 to 7 are indicative of the development of the verbal mediational system, a system which is of great importance to school learning. Children with higher IQs (and higher mental age) show a greater tendency for mediated generalization than lower IQ children (Bailer, 1961).

Mediated generalization is also the basis for categorizing, an important intellectual ability on which great emphasis is placed in early childhood programs aimed at facilitating cognitive development.

FAR TRANSPOSITION

In the transposition paradigm the subject learns a discrimination between two stimuli which have values at two different points on some stimulus dimension (e.g., size or brightness). After the discrimination is learned, two new stimuli are presented, representing different points on the stimulus continuum, and the nature of the subject's transfer is noted.

In *near* transposition the subject learns the discrimination $1 - v$. $2 +$ (1 is unrewarded and 2 is rewarded stimulus; the numbers represent values on some stimulus continuum), then is given stimuli $2\ v.\ 4$. In *far* transposition, the learned discrimination $1 - v.\ 2 +$ is followed by, say $4\ v.\ 8$.

In far transposition, rats, monkeys, and young children generally respond to value 4 as the positive stimulus in the transfer situation, while older children and adults will choose value 8. (Results for near transposition are usually ambiguous, so that discussion is limited here to far transposition.) The predicted response would be made to value 4 if the subject's transfer were based only on primary stimulus generalization. Response to value 8 is interpreted as an instance of verbally mediated transfer. That is, the subject had not learned to associate a response to the physical stimulus, but to his verbal representation of some aspect of its relationship to the negative stimulus – e.g., 'the larger (or brighter) is correct'. In short, the physical stimulus elicits some verbal response and it is this verbal response (mediator), supplied by the subject himself, to which the overt response (selecting one or another stimulus object) becomes conditioned.

Classic experiments support this interpretation of transposition as verbally mediated transfer which overrides primary stimulus generalization, and they show a positive relationship between this phenomenon and age, intelligence, tendency to verbalize in the learning situation, and ability to state the basis for mediated transfer (Kuenne, 1946; Stevenson *et al.*, 1955).

REVERSAL-NON-REVERSAL SHIFT

The reversal and non-reversal shift paradigm has been used extensively by Howard and Tracy Kendler to study the development of verbal mediation as a function of age (e.g., 1962). The paradigm is based on the subject's learning discriminations between two sets of stimuli which differ simultaneously on two stimulus dimensions, such as size and brightness. The learned discrimination involves only one dimension, the other being irrelevant. After the discrimination has been learned up to some criterion, the discrimination task is changed in either one of the two ways: (*a*) the positive (rewarded) stimuli on the previously relevant dimension are made consistently negative (unrewarded) and the previously negative instances are made consistently positive – this is the *reversal* shift; or (*b*) the previously irrelevant stimulus dimension is made the basis for the discrimination and the previously relevant dimension becomes irrelevant – this is the *non-reversal* shift.

The Kendlers and others have reported age differences in the relative difficulty of learning the reversal and non-reversal shift discriminations. Younger children (under 6) do better on the non-reversal shift than on the reversal; older children (over 6) do better on the reversal than on the non-reversal shift. The performance of the younger children is in this respect characteristic of lower animals. At kindergarten age children are divided about 50-50 in superiority of the reversal shift.

The change in case of learning reversal or non-reversal is interpreted in terms of mediated *versus* non-mediated learning, and the Kendlers have shown that instructions to verbalize relevant or irrelevant dimensions of the discrimination influence performance markedly and in ways that are consistent with the Kendler's mediation interpretation of the phenomenon (1962). Much of the recent theoretical development of mediation theory has involved extensive research on the reversal-non-reversal shift difference (Wolff, 1967).

EXPERIMENTALLY ACQUIRED MEDIATION

Experimental psychologists in verbal learning have studied mediation by providing conditions under which subjects learn verbal mediators and then obtain measures of transfer to new learning. Much of this work has been reviewed by Jenkins (1963).

The most common paradigm is that of three-stage mediated association in paired-associate (PA) learning. The subject learns a list of PAs designated as A-B, then learns list B-C, and then A-C. The A-C list can be learned in the same way that A-B was learned, or it can be learned by mediation through the A-B, B-C common link that B provides between A and C. The degree of facilitation afforded by the use of the mediator is assessed against the control condition of A-B, D-C, A-C.

An appreciable degree of facilitation due to mediation is generally found. In view of this, therefore, it is of considerable interest that four-stage mediation is almost never found, even when the conditions for it are made ideal and when the same kinds of subjects show a high degree of mediated facilitation in the three-stage paradigm. (The four-stage paradigm consists of A-B, B-C, C-D, A-D, with the speed of learning A-D measured against an appropriate non-mediated control condition.)

Lee and Jensen (1968) hypothesized that the reason for the sharp discontinuity between the facilitation yielded by the three- and four-stage paradigms was due to the need for subjects to perform one other mediational act for the mediation paradigm to become effective in facilitating learning. That additional act is for the subject to perceive or become aware of the nature of the paradigm: that is, to 'see' the connections between A-B, B-C, and A-C and B is the common link. This is relatively easy to see in the three-stage paradigm (as testimony of the subject shows) and very difficult in the four-stage paradigm. An experiment was designed to test the hypothesis that 'awareness' of the paradigm and a conscious effort by the subject to use this knowledge in learning the A-C list is necessary for mediated facilitation to occur (Lee and Jensen, 1968). The hypothesis was borne out by the experiment. The finding indicates that mediation, at least of the type found in this experiment, does not occur passively just as a result of having previously acquired the necessary primary associations on which mediation is based. The subject must perform still another mediating act ('awareness' or verbalizing to himself the nature of the paradigm and the conscious effort to use this information) in order for the other elements needed for mediation to be manifested as facilitation of learning. Some subjects gain this awareness spontaneously. Others can be made aware by instructions, and their performance is facilitated. Still others can be made aware and yet do not use the possibility for mediation and consequently do not show facilitation. There appear to be individual differences not only in the spontaneity of mediation, but in the ability to use mediators even when they are explicitly provided for the subject.

EXTRAEXPERIENTIALLY ACQUIRED MEDIATORS:
IMPLICIT CHAINING PARADIGM

The phenomenon of apparent implicit verbal chaining as a facilitator of PA learning was first demonstrated in an experiment by Russell and Storms (1955). Their experiment showed that verbal mediators that are never explicitly introduced into the learning situation, but which had been acquired at some previous time, can facilitate PA learning. It is still not certain whether such mediation can take place without the subject's awareness of using a mediational process, although Russell and Storms believed that the process was unconscious and automatic. It appears that previously formed associations were capable of mediating and facilitating PA learning of list A-D in the following paradigm: A-B, B-C, C-D, A-D. The subject learns A-B pairs, then A-D pairs. The B-C and C-D pairs are never brought into the situation; but the whole sequence above is constructed in such a way that B-C and C-D are high frequency associates in word association norms. That is, there is high probability that these associations already exist in the subject, who thus can 'use' these connections to mediate the learning of the A-D list.

A real problem is why the four-stage paradigm is so unsuccessful when all the elements have to be acquired in the laboratory and why it works in the Russell and Storms situation in which the mediating links (B-C, C-D) have been acquired in the subject's natural environment. The facilitating effect is weak, in any case. Its chief theoretical significance is that it shows the influence of previously acquired verbal associations on the learning of new associations which are not explicitly or directly related to the new associations. It suggests that a person's richness of verbal associations may provide a general enhancing and facilitating basis for new learning and thus may constitute a part of what we mean by 'intelligence' and 'learning ability'.

Consistent with this notion is the finding that simple PA learning is faster in subjects who can give more free associations per minute to nonsense syllables than for subjects who have difficulty producing free associations (Mandler and Huttenlocker, 1956).

ASSOCIATIVE CLUSTERING

This phenomenon is observed when a list of words which can be classified into several categories (e.g., professions, vegetables, animals, clothing, etc.) are presented in a random order, and subjects are then asked to recall as many of the words as possible (Bousfield, 1953). It is generally found that the words are recalled as 'clusters' corresponding to the categories and that subjects are able to recall more words when clustering is possible than when it is not, as in the case of lists of unrelated words.

The occurrence of associative clustering means (*a*) that the input has been actively reorganized by the subject before it is recalled, and (*b*) that the reorganization is verbally mediated by superordinate category labels which are apparently elicited by the presentation of the single instances of the categories. This implies a hierarchical arrangement of the verbal associative network, an important requirement for categorization, concept attainment, and related skills that are closely identified with cognitive development and intelligence.

VERBAL SELF-REINFORCEMENT

If all the immediate environmental consequences of the human learner's responses were biologically rewarding or non-rewarding, learning could proceed without the need for secondary reinforcement. In human learners the secondary reinforcement usually takes the form of an overt or covert verbal response, which I shall designate a verbal confirmatory response, V_c. It is a form of self-initiated feedback which tells the learner he is or is not on the right track in his attempt to learn something or to solve a problem. In other words, the immediate results of the subject's response (e.g., getting the 'right' or 'wrong' answer), if it is not a primary reinforcer, must elicit some mediated reinforcer which will shape the learner's performance much as do primary reinforcers. The subject utters to himself 'Good', 'Correct', 'Right', 'Wrong', etc.

So-called 'informative feedback' in the learning situation seems to be powerless as a reinforcer unless it simultaneously elicits some verbal acknowledgement of its meaning in the subject. And there is some evidence that low socio-economic status children are relatively deficient in this type of verbal confirming response as compared with middle-class children (Terrell, 1959; Terrell *et al.*, 1959).

In a trial-and-error selective learning task in which the responses (pressing one of a number of pushbuttons) had to be paired with colored geometric forms projected on a screen and the informative feedback indicating correct responses was a green light going 'on' for one second, Jensen (1963a) found that the learning rate of some educationally retarded children could be markedly improved when they were instructed to say aloud 'good!' or 'right!' whenever their button-pushing response caused the green light to go 'on'. Some showed absolutely no learning at all until they began making this verbal response to the informative feedback. It was found that average and, especially, 'gifted' (IQ over 135) children make the V_c spontaneously in this situation without having to be explicitly instructed to do so. Some children in the retarded group needed a good deal of practice and urging by the experimenter before the V_c became more or less habitual.

Merely being told at the beginning of a session that the green light means 'right' is apparently without any appreciable reinforcing effect unless the subject says aloud or to himself 'right' (or some equivalent thereof) each time he sees the green light.

Why some children do this so spontaneously – even if they are not told that the green light means anything – and why some children have such a high threshold for spontaneous verbal utterance in what outwardly appears to be a non-verbal problem situation is the key question. In social and verbal contexts one type of child is as verbal as the other. In fact, many of the non-verbalizers in the problem situation are highly verbal in a social context, if by verbal one means sheer amount of speech production accompanying social interactions.

It is worth entertaining the hypothesis that acquiring strong habits of verbalizing elements in certain learning situations can be a powerful facilitator of learning. The facilitating effects of such verbalization have already been demonstrated in situations where the verbalization helps to reduce the seeming complexity of the input and to focus the subject's attention on the most relevant aspects. It is not yet known how broadly such verbalization training will transfer.

SYNTACTICAL MEDIATION AND MNEMONIC ELABORATION

This form of verbal mediation was first described by Jensen and Rohwer (Jensen, 1965b; Jensen and Rohwer, 1963a and b, 1965). It has since been extensively studied by Rohwer and his co-workers (Rohwer, 1968; Rohwer and Lynch, 1968; Rohwer *et al.*, 1967 and 1968). Syntactical mediation, which Rohwer regards as just a special case of a whole class of mediators he calls *mnemonic elaboration*, is by far the most powerful mediational process we have worked with in terms of its facilitating effects on associative learning.

The basic paradigm is simple. The subject is presented with a list of paired-associates to learn by the standard method of anticipation. (The paired items are usually words or pictures of familiar objects.) On the first presentation of the pairs (our studies used from eight to 24 pairs), the subject is instructed to make up a simple sentence which relates the two items in each pair, or, in some experiments, the experimenter says aloud a sentence which serves this purpose. This is done *only* on the first presentation trial. It is found that subjects learning under such conditions learn the list in fewer trials than a control group which has been instructed only to *name* the two items in each pair on their first presentation.

An example of a syntactical mediator for the pair HAT-CHAIR is 'The HAT is on the CHAIR'.

The amount of facilitation of learning achieved by syntactical mediation depends upon the age and intelligence of the learner. In general, the amount of facilitation decreases from about age 7 to age 17, presumably because with increasing age an increasing proportion of children spontaneously provide their own mediation. They report this on questioning. Second-grade children learn as fast as twelfth-graders (matched for IQ) when they are told to form syntactical mediators. Twelfth-graders show no appreciable gain in performance. Retarded adults (IQs 40-60), however, can learn a list of paired associates approximately five times as fast under mediation instructions (Jensen, 1965b). Kindergarten children (ages 5-6), however, seem to benefit little if at all. This absence of facilitation below about age 6 raises the question whether children of this age are developmentally incapable of deriving benefit from this form of elaboration or if they simply have difficulty in carrying out the elaboration instructions to generate sentences under the constraints of the PA task. Many do, in fact, generate what would be adequate sentences for facilitation in slightly older age groups. The fact that learning is not facilitated in the younger children is consistent with other findings to the effect that under 6 years of age the child's verbalizations have little influence on his learning and problem-solving behavior.

Rohwer has further investigated the degree of facilitation of learning as a function of the linguistic form classes of the elaborations employed by the subject or manipulated by the experimenter's instructions. For example, conjunctions, prepositions, and verbs differ in their potency as mediators, conjunctions being least effective and verbs the most. A series of studies by Rohwer designed to pinpoint the locus of syntactical mediation, leads to the following conclusions:

(*a*) The difference in facilitatory power between conjunctions, prepositions, and verbs is not attributable to the fact that the degree of formal intralist similarity is lower in a list of verb strings than in a list of conjunction or preposition strings.

(*b*) The form-class effect is not attributable to the greater degree of semantic constraint exerted on subsequent string components by verb than by conjunction connectives.

(*c*) Normal sentences facilitate the learning of the constituent noun pairs, whereas anomalous sentences (i.e., abnormal syntax) do not.

(*d*) As connectives, verbs implying relatively little overt action facilitate learning as much as verbs implying considerable overt action.

(*e*) Even though matched for number and identity of words, sentences in which two nouns are connected by a conjunction produce less efficient learning than sentences in which the nouns are connected by a verb.

(*f*) The presence or absence of adjective modifiers appears to have no effect on the learning of noun pairs presented in sentences.

(*g*) The principal locus of the effect of sentence elaboration appears to be at the time of input rather than at the time of retrieval.

(*h*) Entire verb strings or sentences are easier to learn than entire conjunction strings or phrases when matched for number of words to be recalled.

Another form of mnemonic elaboration being studied by Rohwer is pictorial in nature. Pairs of objects are shown in motion pictures; the objects briefly interact with one another (e.g., a ball rolls toward a candle and knocks it over). The rate of learning such picture pairs (one object is shown and the subject must name the other object that had been paired with it) is assessed against a control condition in which the same pairs of objects are shown in still pictures for the same duration.

Rohwer was led to this procedure by the hypothesis that verbal-mediation of paired associate learnings may act through the verbal evocation of imagery. If so, it may be the variations in properties of the evoked images that determine learning efficiency directly, rather than properties of the verbal units that constitute the nominal learning materials in the usual PA task. Consequently, Rohwer has been investigating the degree of equivalence of verbal and pictorial mediation of paired-associate learning.

The rated capability of words for evoking representational images determines a substantial proportion of the variance in difficulty of learning of verbal paired-associates, even when these are controlled for frequency, meaningfulness, and pronounceability.

For elementary school children, a list of paired associates is easier to learn when the items are shown pictorially than when represented verbally by their names. Acquisition is most efficient when the two objects in each pair are shown in some action episode (e.g., a ball dropping into a glass), less efficient when the two are static but in a particular spatial juxtaposition (e.g., a ball in a glass), and least efficient when static and represented independently (e.g., a ball and a glass, merely side by side). These relationships hold up over the age range from 6 to 12.

One may wonder whether individual differences in rate of PA learning are related to individual differences in verbalization *per se* or in differences in the degree to which verbalization evokes images or otherwise causes some kind of 'associative arousal' which speeds learning.

LEARNING SET FORMATION

Learning sets ('learning-how-to-learn') are forms of mediated transfer which may or may not depend upon verbal or symbolic processes. It is known that there is a phylogenetic gradient for speed of acquiring learning sets, and there are individual differences within species. Zeaman and House, for example, report a higher relationship between measured intelligence and rate of acquisition of learning sets than between intelligence and simple learning (1967).

Learning set formation apparently involves higher-order processes than conditioning or simple associative learning. Harlow's error factor theory (1959) accounts for learning set formation in terms of the extinction or inhibition of irrelevant response tendencies for certain classes of problems. At the human level additional mechanisms probably also play a part. The most important of these are attentional and problem-solving strategies which subjects learn to summon when confronted with problem situations they can classify, such classification being, in part, the mediational stimulus for evoking the appropriate strategy.

The theory of knowledge acquisition as learning which is mediated by positive transfer from a hierarchy of subordinate learning sets has been espoused chiefly by Gagné (1965, 1968). The importance of his theory is that it focuses attention on task analysis – the discovery of the set of sub-skills that are necessary prerequisites for the acquisition of new skills or knowledge. It specifies the conditions of prior learning necessary for transfer to some new learning. Learning difficulties at 'higher' levels of knowledge acquisition are interpreted as due to a failure (for whatever reason) to learn certain subordinate skills. This basic premise of the Gagné model is questioned in a later section of this paper.

CROSS-MODAL TRANSFER

Cross-modal transfer is not yet well understood. But it has implications for mediation theories, and measures of cross-modal transfer may provide an important index of mental development.

The procedure for measuring cross-modal transfer consists of presenting a stimulus in one sensory modality and having the subject identify it in a recognition multiple-choice test in a different modality. The most commonly used modalities are visual and haptic. The subject, for example, puts his hand behind a screen and feels an object of a particular shape, then is shown several different objects (or pictorial representations of several objects) and is asked to point out the one which he had handled. The importance of the subject's ability to transfer the knowledge gained in one modality to recognition in another is the fact that there is no direct connection or neural isomorphism between the sensory 'information' from the two modalities. The sensory information must arouse a central mediating process which represents the object in some abstract way and reference to which permits recognition of the object in some other sense modality. Lower animals, including the great apes, are apparently incapable of learning cross-modal transfer. It is unique to man, as far as we know. It is absent in young children and the capability for it does not develop much before other forms of mediation processes are manifest, between ages 5 and 7. Also, temporal lobe damage impairs haptic-visual transfer in adults; the same patients have inordinate difficulties with other learning tasks thought to involve mediational processes in normal subjects.

CURRENT RESEARCH PROBLEMS

As was pointed out in the first section of this paper, much of the current interest in verbal mediation processes has been stimulated by the facts that (*a*) these processes seem to be the stuff of which abstract and conceptual intelligence is made, (*b*) these aspects of intelligence play a crucial role in educability: that is, the ability to achieve scholastically under ordinary conditions of instruction, and (*c*) a segment of our population called culturally disadvantaged does poorly in school and on the average scores low on measures of abstract intelligence.

Consequently, there has been great emphasis in recent years on stimulating, training, and developing educationally relevant cognitive processes in children whose deficiencies in these processes are hypothesized to be due to certain cultural or environmental lacks during the preschool years. This environmental interpretation of poor scholastic performance and slow rate and low asymptote of cognitive development is not proved and still has the status of a working hypothesis.

A number of independent current research findings are beginning to suggest that the views of acquired mediational skills or of a cumulative learning model à la Gagné as the basis for abstract intelligence, and of cultural enrichment or even specific training as a means of inculcating or enhancing the desired cognitive process in disadvantaged children, will have to be supplemented and modified by taking into greater account biological development factors.

A view that seems consistent with all the research evidence in this area is that the verbal mediation mechanisms, learning sets, and cumulative learning hierarchies, as described in the previous section, are all involved in cognitive development and are of crucial importance for school learning. Also, it is evident that these processes must be acquired through environmental influences. But the evidence is becoming increasingly convincing that the acquisition of hierarchically ordered cognitive processes also depends, not solely on appropriate inputs from the environment, but upon the maturation of a hierarchically ordered neural substrate. This view holds that certain patterns of neural growth or organization, determined by constitutional factors, must occur before the effects of learning can be manifest in the cognitive processes we identify as intelligence – reasoning ability, abstract and conceptual abilities, the ability to transform the world of the concrete into symbolic representations.

This view does not deny that certain cognitive skills at some level in the developmental hierarchy cannot be specifically trained in the absence of the development of the neural mechanisms normally involved in the acquisition of these skills. But there are differences: (*a*) the training requires much more time, effort, precision and control of the conditions of learning; (*b*) though the specific skill may be acquired, it shows much narrower transfer and in a factor analysis of a variety of cognitive tests the specifically acquired skill would probably contribute little if any variance to the *g* factor on which normally most cognitive skills are highly loaded; (*c*) without further specific training or practice, the specially acquired skill shows no continued growth or transfer to other new skills, and may even deteriorate; and (*d*) it does not seem to constitute a 'quantum jump' in the cognitive hierarchy such as to support the acquisition of skills at a higher level.

HIERARCHICAL ARRANGEMENT OF LEARNING PROCESSES

Sheldon H. White (1965) put forth an argument, supported by a diversity of data, that adult mental organization is hierarchical, consisting of two main 'layers': (*a*) an associative level laid down early in development and following conventional associative principles, and (*b*) a 'cognitive layer' laid down in later childhood. The formation of the cognitive layer either begins or is most marked between the ages of 5 and 7, a period during which many signs of a change in mode of cognitive functioning are evident. Between these ages children show a transition from a type of performance in learning situations characteristic of lower animals in similar situations to a type of performance characteristic of adult humans. Some of the experimental paradigms which reveal this transition and are discussed in detail by White are the following:

1. Narrow to broad transposition.
2. Easier non-reversal shifts to easier reversal shifts.
3. Onset of resistance to classical conditioning.
4. Change in the effect of a 'varying-position' condition in discrimination learning.
5. Growth of inference in a problem-solving task.
6. Possible interference of complex hypotheses in discrimination learning.
7. Shift from 'near receptors' (tactual, kinesthetic, etc.) to 'distance receptors' (visual and auditory) in attending to environmental events.
8. Shift from color to form-dominance in classifying objects.
9. Development of personal left-right sense.
10. Decrease in form, word, and letter reversals.
11. Ability to hold spatial information through disorientation.
12. Change in face-hand test – children under 6 do not indicate awareness of a touch on the hand if the face is touched simultaneously but report only the touch on the face. After about age 6 the child can report both.

F

13. Increasing predictability of adult IQ.
14. Internalization of speech.
15. Shift from syntagmatic (associations having a meaningful connection but not grammatical likeness) to paradigmatic (associations having the same grammatical form class) word associations.
16. Increased disruptive influence of delayed auditory feedback.
17. Shift of verbalization toward a planning function in the child's activity.
18. Transition from social to abstract reinforcement.
19. A number of transitions involving conservation of number, length, space, volume, etc., shown in Piaget-type studies.

The fact that so many diverse forms of cognitive behavior change rather rapidly during the years from 5 to 7 in general and probably over a much shorter time-span in individual children suggests the maturation of some common underlying mechanisms. To Sheldon White's list of behaviors may be added increased susceptibility to certain perceptual illusions (e.g., the spiral after-effect) and the fact that the ability to copy certain geometric figures conforms to an almost perfectly unidimensional age scale: e.g., the ten figures in Ilg and Ames' *School Readiness* (1964).

The shifts from the associative level to a predominantly cognitive level of mental functioning can be summarized in terms of four general transitions: (*a*) from direct responses to stimuli to responses produced by mediated stimuli; (*b*) emergence of the ability to induce invariance on the welter of phenomenal variability; (*c*) the capacity to organize past experience to permit inference and prediction; and (*d*) increased sensitivity to information yielded by distance as against near receptors.

An important question is: can these cognitive functions be trained in children who do not manifest them normally?

TRAINING COGNITIVE SKILLS

Within the normal range of environmental variation on just about any index of any dimension of the socio-cultural environment one wishes to consider, it seems obvious that other factors are also needed to account for differences in the rate and asymptote of mental development. A verbally rich environment is certainly not sufficient to produce superior intelligence, and it may not even be a necessary condition, since some intellectually superior children come from impoverished homes; and an impoverished environment is certainly neither necessary nor sufficient to cause mental retardation, since some retardates (IQs under 75) come from good homes and the majority of children reared in the poorest circumstances are not mentally retarded. The evidence clearly indicates that a major share of the variance in mental abilities must be attributable to genetically determined biological factors in development and a minor share to experiential inputs for the majority (say, 95 per cent) of the population (Erlenmeyer-Kimling and Jarvik, 1963; Jensen, 1969a).

The crucial question concerning the culturally disadvantaged is the extent to which their environmental disadvantages are responsible for their generally lower scholastic achievement and their performance on mental ability tests. To the extent that their deficiencies are not just cultural but also involve biological developmental factors, something different from merely providing the amenities of middle-class culture will be needed in order to improve the educability of such children. Thus, the real problem of the disadvantaged may be not whether an ordinary middle-class type of environment will boost their intellectual performance up to the general average, but whether one can improve their cognitive structures by special forms of training and cumulative learning experiences which may be quite different from what is needed for normal mental development by most children.

The meager gains in intelligence and scholastic performance made by general enrichment pre-school programs suggests that something more and something different than providing the usual accouterments of middle-class nursery education, even in intensified form, is necessary.

Almost any enrichment experience, including ordinary kindergarten, causes a slight boost in IQ (5 to 10 points) in the majority of disadvantaged children (Jensen, 1969a). This is clearly due to the fact that the test had a certain small cultural loading and the child's cultural-information lacks are quickly made up by the school environment. But the rapid initial rate of gain does not persist, and by the second or third year of school, children called disadvantaged average about one standard deviation below the general population average in just about all areas of measurable intellectual and scholastic performance. This one standard deviation deficit persists quite uniformly throughout the school years, right up to the twelfth grade. There is no compelling evidence for a 'cumulative deficit'. The achievement gap is consistently close to one standard deviation throughout all the school years (Coleman, 1966).

The pre-school programs which show some promise of improving the educability of disadvantaged children, but which have not yet been adequately evaluated for long-term (more than one year) effects, have one characteristic in common: the intensiveness and specificity of training. The Bereiter-Engelmann program at the University of Illinois and University of Toronto and the tutorial language program of Marion Blank at the Albert Einstein College of Medicine, Yeshiva University, are good examples of this approach. Certain specific lacks in cognitive skills are identified and are then explicitly trained.

Blank and Solomon express the common observation made by most workers in the field that the behavior of children called culturally or socially disadvantaged 'reflects a lack of a symbolic system by which to organize the plentiful stimulation surrounding them' (1968, p. 379). Blank and Solomon have analyzed the 'abstract attitude' into the behavioral components and specific skills of which it seems to be comprised and which presumably can be taught by one-to-one tutorial techniques.

The specific skills that are taught in the Blank program are (*a*) Selective attention, (*b*) Categories of exclusion, (*c*) Imagery of future events, (*d*) Relevant inner verbalization, (*e*) Separation of the word from its referent, (*f*) Models for cause and effect reasoning, (*g*) Ability to categorize, (*h*) Awareness of possessing language, (*i*) Sustained sequential thinking.

Nursery school children in a deprived area in New York City were individually tutored five days (15 -20 minutes per day) a week over a four-month period. The average Stanford-Binet IQ gain was close to one standard deviation and ranged from 4 to 28 points. Untutored control groups showed average gains of less than three IQ points. The IQ changes were accompanied by other signs of improved adjustment to the school setting.

Studies such as this should be conducted on a larger scale, with more representative samples of the disadvantaged population, and with a follow-up of at least two years. Also, the breadth of transfer of such training should be assessed by using a variety of tests and behavioral criteria. Blank and Solomon found, for example, that a non-verbal intelligence test (Leiter Scale) showed smaller gains than the highly verbal Stanford-Binet. There are other indications in the literature that the magnitude of gains is positively correlated with the amount of cultural loading of the test. It is easy to show gains after training on the Peabody Picture Vocabulary Test and difficult to show them on Raven's Progressive Matrices.

Rohwer (1967, 1968; and Lynch, 1968; *et al.*, 1967a and b; 1968) has trained disadvantaged kindergarten children in the use of verbal and imagery mediation in paired-associate learning. A systematic training program extending over several months produced complex and ambiguous results which are difficult to interpret. Disadvantaged children benefited from the training in the visual modality but not in the auditory (PAs were presented in both forms). That is, mediation training in both visual and auditory modalities showed learning rate gains only in the visual mode for the disadvantaged. A 'control' group of middle-class kindergartners showed larger gains than the disadvantaged as a result of the same training, and the gains were manifested in both visual and auditory modalities. This finding is in line with the general impression of many teachers of the disadvantaged that they are poor auditory learners.

They differ, however, from totally deaf children in one very important way: they never catch up. Deaf children are retarded in school learning and various cognitive functions associated with verbalization. However, from early childhood to late adolescence deaf children gradually catch up and, on the average, finally attain a normal level of intellectual functioning. A major study comparing cognitive processes in deaf and hearing adolescents and adults found no differences between the deaf and the hearing by adulthood; such indices as dissociation between words and referents, verbalization adequacy, and level of verbalization were not different for deaf and hearing adult subjects. The investigators concluded that differences found between deaf and hearing children 'fall along a normal developmental line and were amenable to the effects of increased age and experience and education' (Kates *et al.*, 1962, p. 32). Such findings may lead one to wonder if the cognitive deficit of the disadvantaged can be adequately explained in terms of inadequate verbal stimulation. Verbal stimulation is increased in the school situation and yet the majority of disadvantaged children do not maintain gains in verbal intelligence which permit them to reach the same asymptote as the average level of the general population.

If general social-cultural deprivation is at fault, then one has to explain why some extremely deprived groups perform better in school and on tests than some less deprived groups. For example, on the 12 environmental indices used in the Coleman study of *Equality of Educational Opportunity* (1966), American Indians rate as far below Negroes as Negroes rate below whites, and yet on all the scholastic measures used by Coleman, American Indians performed significantly better than Negroes. Apparently school performance is not related to the quality of the environment in any simple, monotonic way.

ASSOCIATIVE CLUSTERING IN FREE RECALL

As was pointed out in a previous section, the phenomenon of associative clustering in verbal free recall is one of the clearest forms of evidence of conceptual, hierarchical processes. For clustering to occur, the subject must actively organize the stimulus input according to certain self-providing superordinate categories.

Two studies of this phenomenon as a function of age and socio-economic status (confounded with race, since the low-SES group was Negro, the middle-SES group was white) have been made by Glasman (1968) and Jensen and Frederiksen (1973). Though the two studies were carried out in different school systems and with slight procedural variations, they are in close agreement in their results. First of all, in *random* lists of words which are made up so as not to lend themselves to categorization, there is no significant difference between low- and middle-SES groups in amount of recall over five recall trials. In categorized lists (20 words that fall into four categories), on the other hand, middle-SES show better recall than do low-SES children. The degree of clustering in recall increases over the five trials and the amount of recall is highly correlated with degree of clustering – this is true over trials and over subjects. Clustering and amount of recall increase with age. At the kindergarten level the two SES samples do not differ, whereas by fifth grade the middle-class group is substantially superior. Although the low-SES group's output order of recall more closely approximates the input order than is the case for the middle-SES groups, there is evidence that both groups organize the random input in some fashion, but the principles of organization are apparently quite different. The clustering by the middle-class group clearly is correlated with amount of recall. The main research problems now are (*a*) to determine the degree to which disadvantaged and non-disadvantaged children organize items for free recall with different kinds of principles, (*b*) whether the differences in types of organization is responsible for discrepancies in free recall performance, and (*c*) whether it is possible to improve free recall through training in categorization.

Examination of recall protocols from our free recall studies shows that low-SES children produce many two-item clusters according to some functional rather than conceptual relationships. For example, *table* and *bed* are not likely to be clustered (both furniture), while *shoe* (clothing) and *bed* may be a cluster because 'you take off your shoes when you go to bed'. In interviews with children as to the basis for their clusters in recall, many more such idiosyncratic pair-wise clusters are found in the low-SES group. It suggests a deficiency in hierarchical organization of the verbal associative network.

Since the SES differences in clustering tendency and amount of recall *increases* with age from kindergarten to fifth grade (the total range we have studied), one may wonder why the common school experience for both groups does not produce a convergence rather than a divergence in their clustering tendency and recall ability. This finding forces the question as to what extent clustering, and hierarchical and conceptual modes of learning in general, involve developmental, as well as experimental factors.

PSYCHOMETRIZING PIAGET CONSERVATION TESTS

Piaget's various conservation demonstrations would seem to involve some sort of mediation process, though its nature remains obscure. The resistance of conservation to specific training is one of its most remarkable properties and strongly suggests that the sequence of development described by Piaget is largely controlled by developmental rather than by experimental factors, although the latter may well be a necessary but not sufficient ingredient. Factor analyses of performance on a variety of Piaget conservation tests along with various standard psychometric tests, such as the Stanford-Binet and Raven's Progressive Matrices, show that the Piaget tests contain a high g loading and introduce no source of variance not found in other developmental tests like the Stanford-Binet (1965). Also, Piaget conservation tests show about the same social class and race differences as are found with standard IQ tests. If one argues that such differences are due to cultural bias in traditional IQ tests, can it be that the Piaget tasks are equally culturally biased? If so, of what, precisely, does the bias consist? Apparently it is in the capacity for some kind of mediational arousal in the case of a nominally non-verbal problem. Yet supplying verbal mediators to non-conserving children does not alter their performance.

There is an interesting doctoral dissertation on this problem, by De Lemos (1966), who studied Piaget conservation problems in Australian aborigines and found marked significant differences in the age of attaining conservation between groups of pure aborigines and those who had one Caucasian grandparent, even though there was no indication of any environmental difference or mode of upbringing between the pure and the mixed aborigines. Many of the pure aborigines never reach the stage of conservation of volume even by adulthood.

THE AGE-SCALE PROPERTIES OF FIGURE COPYING

Various geometric forms can be scaled according to the age at which, say, 50 per cent of children can accurately *copy* the figure. It is possible to make up such scales which seem to be quite invariant in rank order of difficulty across diverse segments of the population. Another striking feature of such scales is the rather discrete quality of the 'quantum jumps' that exist from one item in the scale to the next, and the very few reversals of rank order of difficulty even for single subjects. The copying test consists of ten geometric figures of increasing difficulty. The increasing difficulty of the figures may correspond to some developmental process. Dexterity, drawing ability, etc. are not important factors. A child who can copy any particular figure in the normal manner can do it also with his nondominant hand or with pencil between his toes. It is essentially a conceptual, not a manual, ability that is manifested in this performance.

In brief training sessions with individual subjects we find that it is practically impossible to teach children to copy the figures in the scale beyond the last one in the series they were able to copy without help. The child often acts quite amazed, chagrined, and frustrated by his failure to copy, say, a diamond, even after the experimenter has repeatedly shown him how to do it. The problem is not perceptual, because the child has no difficulty in recognizing the deficiency of his own performance.

Dr David R. Olson, while at Harvard's Center for Cognitive Studies, performed an elaborate series of experiments on children's ability to copy one such figure – a square or rectangle containing one diagonal (1970). Whereas most 3- and 4-year-old children are able to copy a square, they have to be 5 or 6 before they can copy a square containing a diagonal.

Olson performed experiments which ruled out motor or perceptual inabilities as the basis of the difference between 4- and 6-year-olds. He concluded that the difficulty for the 4-year-old was a *conceptual* difficulty. He then attempted to teach the skill of copying the diagonal to 3- and 4-year-olds who could not do so originally. The training involved a number of methods, such as making the diagonal with rods – first with one rod which simply had to be placed in the right position, etc., and then with peg boards, and checkers. Children were also taught to verbalize definitions of diagonal and other aspects of the figure. The verbalization training was the only technique that facilitated performance, but even this was not uniformly successful. It seemed to work for some children and not for others, as if some were closer to 'readiness' than others. This interpretation is supported by the fact that 4-year-olds were able to profit from verbalization while 3-year-olds did not, although originally both were equally unable to copy the diagonal. The ease and spontaneity of the children who can copy the diagonal the first time they try and the great

F*

difficulty of teaching such performance to children who cannot do it right off leads Olson to say, 'The recalcitrance of the problem of the diagonal strongly suggests a large maturational component in the development of this system.'

FAILURE IN MEDIATION AROUSAL

Some children fail to show signs of verbal mediation in situations where it is facilitating, even though they seem to have all the necessary component behaviors. For example, in our experiments on clustering we find children who do not cluster items in categorized lists and yet who recognize the categories and can clarify the items when told to do so. We find children whose performance in recall of objects is facilitated when they are told to name the objects, but who do not use this technique unless they are told to do so. We have instructed subjects in ways to mediate and facilitate paired-associate learning. Though the technique is part of the subject's repertoire, in that it is fully functional when he is told to use it, he does not use it *spontaneously*. It is as if this is not his 'natural' mode of approach to a learning task. This is not true of all children, but seems to be most characteristic among those called disadvantaged. Why some children evince such resistence to verbalizing in effective ways in non-social problem situations remains a mystery. Some of these children appear highly fluent in conversation. Their verbal production, however, seems to have little or no functional value when they are privately confronted with a problem. In short, their language does not serve as a tool of thought. One of the major goals of research should be to try to discover methods of instruction that might give language this particular power for these children.

RELATIONSHIP BETWEEN LEARNING ABILITIES AND INTELLIGENCE

The writer's chief research effort at present involves the study of the relationship between performance in a variety of learning tasks typically used in the experimental psychology of human learning and psychometric intelligence (1968). Special attention has been directed to the experimental analysis of learning abilities in children called culturally disadvantaged.

The major finding that has emerged from this research so far is highly relevant to the understanding of the intellectual performance of children called disadvantaged. The basic finding is already well established, although in its details, its theoretical interpretation, and its possible implications for instruction and educational policy, it still needs much more research and thought.

The basic finding is this: children from a low socio-economic background who have measured IQs in the below-average range from 60 to 80 perform in general much better on a variety of associative learning tasks than do middle-class children in the same range of IQ. On the other hand, low-SES children who are above average in IQ do not show learning performance that is significantly different from the performance of middle-class children of the same IQ. This finding holds in Caucasian, Negro, and Mexican-American groups. Most of the research, along with a theoretical interpretation, is summarized elsewhere (1969a).

The theoretical interpretation proposed to comprehend these findings is that there is a continuum of ability to perform on mental tests, going from simple associative rote learning to conceptual problem solving. This continuum of test complexity taps two functionally dependent but genotypically independent types of mental process: associative learning ability, called Level I, and conceptual or abstract reasoning ability, called Level II. Level I processes are best measured by tests of digit span and serial and paired-associative rote learning. Level II processes are best measured at present by non-verbal intelligence tests highly loaded on the g factor, such as Raven's Progressive Matrices and Cattell's Culture-Fair Tests. Level II processes are hierarchically related to Level I. That is to say, Level I ability is necessary but not sufficient for the manifestation of Level II ability. For example, short-term memory is necessary for solving the Progressive Matrices problems, but the processes of abstraction and symbolic manipulation needed for the Matrices are not necessary for digit memory. Level I ability appears to be distributed about the same in lower-class and in middle-class populations, while Level II ability is distributed about a higher mean in middle-class than in lower-class groups. These hypotheses taken together are so far adequate to account for our data. In brief, the three hypotheses are (*a*) the genetic independence of the processes called Level I and Level II, (*b*) the functional hierarchical dependence of Level II upon Level I, and (*c*) the differential distributions of Level I and Level II genotypes in upper and lower social classes.

One of the key questions that needs to be answered is the origin of Level II ability. Is it wholly acquired? Or does it depend upon inherited neural mechanisms which mature at a later age than the mechanisms involved in associative learning? Many psychologists and educators have been acting on the assumption that the 'higher' cognitive processes are a result of the cumulative effects of learning, particularly of verbal mediation strategies and the like. This assumption must now be questioned anew.

A number of different research approaches will help to determine the relative roles of developmental and experiential factors in cognitive functioning.

1. The relationship between various physical growth indices and measures of mental development needs to be studied *within* and *between* various SES and racial groups. Within Caucasian groups we know that a fairly substantial multiple correlation exists between a number of indices of physical maturation and performance on various mental tests. Does the same multiple regression equation predict, say, mental age, in other racial groups to the same degree as in Caucasian groups? In short, are the correlations between various indices of maturation, both physical and mental, the same for different social class and ethnic groups?

2. What is the normative distribution of various developmental indices in large representative samples of various segments of our population? How much consistency in status on developmental tests is there among various groups?

3. How well do the rather simple polygenic models that so closely fit the patterns of correlations among blood relations so well for, say, height and fingerprint ridge counts also fit developmental indices? We need methodologically and genetically sophisticated heritability studies of most of the measures we use in developmental research.

4. We need highly focused and long-range attempts to train specific cognitive abilities in children who are *high* in associative learning ability (Level I) and poor in conceptual ability

(Level II). One important factor that has vitiated much of the enrichment and cognitive training research is that no distinction has been made between Level I and Level II and the S's initial status on Level I. A group of lower-class children all with rather low Stanford-Binet IQs, is made up of children who stand at all points on the continuum of Level I learning ability. Those who are low in Level I have little potential for any kind of learning – they are much like middle-class retarded children. Cognitive training should be focused on children with average or superior associative learning ability and short-term memory. Probably more than half of the children called disadvantaged fall into this category. The problem, then, is to see if these children with good associative learning ability can, through intensive, highly focused training, acquire Level II abilities – that is, those abstract cognitive modes of processing information that characterize *g*.

Such research should be aimed, in part, at determining whether *g* can actually be built in through training or if the resultant behavior is only a kind of *simulation* of Level II functions by means of training that really involves only Level I associative ability. Measuring the breadth of transfer of the trained cognitive skills, as compared with control groups who have the skills 'naturally', and determining the factorial structure of the trained skills are probably the best methods of investigating this problem.

For the purposes of ordinary school education, merely *simulated* Level II ability may be adequate, so we should not belittle the importance of training cognitive skills even in children who may have some deficiency in the brain mechanisms which normally subserve these functions.

Present-day schooling is highly geared to *conceptual* modes of learning and many children whose weakness is in conceptual ability, even though they may be superior associative learners, are frustrated by schooling and therefore learn far less than is warranted by their good Level I learning ability. An important avenue of exploration is the extent to which school subjects can be taught by techniques which depend only on Level I and not upon Level II ability. Much of the work of the world, after all, depends only on Level I ability and it may be that many persons can become functionally educated, employable and productive by making the most of their Level I ability.

Summary

Various types of verbal and symbolic mediational processes which facilitate learning and comprise much of what is meant by 'intelligence' are viewed in terms of both maturation and learning. The relative roles of developmental and experiential factors in the growth of complex cognitive abilities are discussed with reference to recent research on verbal mediation, and current research gaps and directions for future research in this field are indicated. The chief practical significance of research on verbal mediation is that it suggests some of the mechanisms by means of which instructional techniques might inculcate or train cognitive skills that facilitate learning and problem solving. A hierarchical theory of cognitive development is proposed to explain social-class differences in mediational processes and to suggest further research directed at discovering techniques for strengthening cognitive mediational processes in children typically called disadvantaged.

Another look
at culture-fair testing

It is galling, but not wholly unrewarding, to be misquoted in a popular magazine. I had the experience when *Life* (March 31, 1967) ran a feature article on 'early learning' and incorrectly stated that I had invented a culture-free test of intelligence. The results of this misunderstanding were instructive to me and provided much of the stimulus for writing the present paper.

In the several weeks following the appearance of the *Life* article, I had to send out more than two hundred copies of a form letter in answer to inquiries about the culture-free test erroneously attributed to me. I had not invented any culture-free test, I explained, and all I had were some not at all unusual experimental techniques for studying the learning abilities of children, including children called 'culturally disadvantaged'.

This spate of mail (and several long-distance phone calls) gave me some interesting insights into the passionate aspects of intelligence testing. Only a few of the letters were from persons writing as parents, and still fewer were from psychologists. Most were from public school people – teachers, counselors, principals, heads of school research bureaus, and administrators of special education, and the like. Some wanted further information, but mostly they wanted copies of the 'test' – a few ordered hundreds of 'copies' and sent billing numbers without even asking the price. Others were skeptical, saying they had tried everything on the market without finding a test that wiped out status or race differences but would be delighted to find any test that could really do so. One schoolman said he was in 'hot water' because the tests being used in his school district discriminated among groups as well as among individuals,

167

and there were public spirited persons in the community who were quite upset by this. Somewhat more ominous to me was that the sincere expression of what might very well prove to be a false hope was accompanied in some letters by derogatory, hostile censure of conventional standardized tests – a brand of outrage which almost makes one wonder if the writers believe there are some mean, hateful persons somewhere who can be blamed for deliberately making up culturally unfair, biased tests to discriminate against children of the poor. It gave me mixed feelings to be praised for helping to combat this evil conspiracy!

Let me say right off that I fully agree with my correspondents that many of the problems of public education which give rise to their worries about testing are real indeed, and much must be done to solve them. But I doubt that a culture-free test – even if we had one – could do any more than highlight the problem. Of course, this in itself might be of value. As far as I can tell, problems are never resolved by tests; but tests can help to define and evaluate the problems – and I mean the crucial problems that now confront public education in its struggle to be of tangible benefit to all children in all segments of the population.

In so far as the role of culture-free tests may be involved in this endeavor, this article is my *present* answer to many of these misguided but nonetheless informative letters from readers of *Life*. I emphasize 'present', because this is my answer as of May, 1968 – not guaranteed to be perfectly correlated with my views on the subject six months or a year from now, although I would surely expect a substantial positive correlation, for we are not totally without bearings in this field. The current pace of relevant research, however, is such that anyone who hopes to view these issues constructively and creatively must assiduously eschew a doctrinaire stance.

An old issue

The issue of cultural bias or status bias in intelligence tests is as old as intelligence testing itself. Alfred Binet in 1905 made a clear distinction between the kinds of judgment, adaptability, and general problem-solving ability he called intelligence and attempted to measure by means of his mental age scales, on the one hand,

and, on the other, the kinds of information acquired in schools or in a cultured home. Despite his efforts to come as close as possible to assessing the child's innate endowment of general intelligence by means of his scales, he consistently found systematic differences between various social status groups. The first formal study of this social aspect of intellectual assessment was published by Binet just five years after the appearance of the first edition of his now famous intelligence test, which became the prototype of nearly all subsequent individual tests of intelligence (1916). Binet reported evidence from France and Belgium that children of professional workers did better on his new intelligence tests, on the average, than did children in working-class neighborhoods. Since then, the question of social-class bias in tests versus real social-class differences in intelligence has been an issue of dispute among psychologists, sociologists, and educators. Innumerable investigations have been made in the United States, in Europe, and in Asia, of the relationship of social status to performance on intelligence tests. These investigations have used a wide variety of intelligence tests and many different methods of measuring social status. Without a single exception, the studies show a positive correlation between intelligence test scores and social status; half of the studies yield correlations between 0·25 and 0·50, with a central tendency in the region of 0·35 to 0·40. When children selected from the total population are grouped into social status categories, the mean IQs of the groups differ by as much as one to two standard deviations (15 or 30 IQ points), depending on the method of status classification. The fact of social class differences in measured intelligence is thus about as solid a fact as any that we have in psychology, and apparently it has long since ceased being a point of dispute. Most of this evidence has been reviewed by Kenneth Eells *et al.* (1951).

There is an even greater number of studies of racial differences in measured intelligence, most of them involving comparisons of Negroes and Caucasians. The results of the more than 380 studies of Negro intelligence up to 1965, comprehensively reviewed by Audrey Shuey (1966), are highly consistent in showing mean Negro-Caucasian IQ differences of between 10 to 20 points and an average median overlap (i.e., the percentage of Negroes exceeding the Caucasian median) of 12 per cent. In most, if not all, of these estimates racial classification is confounded with socio-economic status (SES); when the racial groups are roughly 'matched' on the usual SES factors, the mean IQ difference is diminished to about 10 points. The logic and validity of such 'matching' is, of course, highly questionable, since it involves comparing quite different proportions of the two populations, and, furthermore, SES is not strictly a *causal* variable in relation to IQ. But more on this point later – here I am just sketching the raw empirical findings without trying to explain them. They are the generally agreed upon results of testing with the kinds of instruments we call intelligence tests. Whether the results are 'fair' or not is the point at issue.

Status-fair versus culture-fair tests

What we shall be talking about here are social status differences within the same national culture. In this context the terms 'culture-free', 'culture-fair', or 'culture-controlled' as applied to most such tests of intelligence are really misnomers. We should be using the preferable terms 'status-free' or 'status-fair' instead. I wish to avoid extending the discussion in the present paper to the slippery problem of the cross-cultural assessment of mental abilities in primitive cultures or other essentially anthropological uses of tests for which the designation 'culture-fair' may constitute a legitimate use of this term. Cross-cultural testing is a complex problem in its own right, and part of what I have to say may be relevant to it, but it should be clear now that our chief concern is with test results as related to social status and ethnic background factors within a single national culture. The much more difficult subject of true cross-cultural testing will probably remain hopelessly problematical so long as the nature of the environmental differences between widely disparate cultural groups cannot be conceptualized in a generally agreed upon fashion with reference to common dimensions on which differences range. In the absence of such schemata there is the risk of perceiving and describing environments *post hoc* in terms of performance on particular tests, which is putting the cart before the horse. Thus, we shall stick to the more mundane task of looking at status-fair tests, and shall bypass the usual polemics in the area of cross-cultural testing, like debating how Einstein would rate on an aborigine's 'IQ' test consisting of throwing boomerangs and tracking wallabies.

Why intelligence tests are like they are

It should not be forgotten that intelligence tests as we now know them evolved in close conjunction with the educational curricula and instructional methods of Europe and North America. Schooling was not simply invented in a single stroke. It has a long evolutionary history and still heavily bears the imprint of its origins in predominantly aristocratic and upper-class European society. Not only did the content of education help to shape this society, but, even more, the nature of the society shaped the content of education and the methods of instruction for imparting it. If the educational needs and goals of this upper segment of society had been different, and if their modal pattern of abilities – both innate abilities and those acquired in these peculiar environmental circumstances – were different, it seems a safe conjecture that the evolution of educational content and practices and consequently the character of public education in modern times would be quite different from what it is. And our intelligence tests – assuming we had them under these different conditions – would most likely also have taken on a different character.

The particular direction taken by education at its origins in Western European cultures emphasized a host of conditions which will largely characterize modern education: beginning formal instruction at the same age for all children – universally between 5 and 6 years of age; instruction in groups; keeping the same age groups together in a lock-step fashion at least throughout the first several years of schooling; learning under instructional conditions of relative teacher activity and pupil passivity – a showing-seeing and telling-listening relationship between teacher and pupil. This approach capitalized on the attentiveness and obedience of children in a telling-listening relationship with an adult. These habits were thoroughly inculcated in the children by their parents long before the children entered school. Of even more fundamental importance is that the success of this method of schooling depended heavily upon the child's possession of certain abilities, both innate and acquired: an attention span long enough to encompass the teacher's utterances and demonstrations; verbal comprehension – extracting meaning from verbal forms; ability to grasp the relationship between things or events and their symbolic representations; and, largely because of the overtly passive nature of the pupil's role, the demand for *covert* activity on the pupil's part – to repeat things to himself, to voluntarily focus his attention where it is called for; when confronted with new tasks to be learned or problems to be solved, to talk to himself in relevant ways for self-direction, for self-provided cues, for active scanning of memory stores for pertinent bits of information – in short, the capacity overtly to inhibit large-muscle activity and covertly to respond to the instructional inputs. Physical activity had to give way to mental activity – an active processing of the instructional input, not just a passive reception. To succeed, pupils had to learn not only the manifest educational content and skills explicitly imparted by the teacher, but they also had to acquire the skills of self-instruction without which group instruction by the teacher leads to little actual learning.

The interesting and important fact is that the system worked. It worked satisfactorily for the majority of children who were exposed to it, not because it was a gift of God or an inspired invention of man but for the simple reason that the class of children whom it served had largely shaped it to their capabilities. Thus, school methods were not *designed*. They were not *imposed*. They *evolved*. This evolution was shaped by the predominantly bookish educational content valued by the well-to-do classes of Europe and by the particular learning capabilities of their children. If the system had not worked to the satisfaction of the majority whom it served, or proved unduly frustrating to the teachers and pupils, it seems safe to say it would have evolved in a different direction.

The extension of public education over the years to an increasingly broader segment of the population, toward the goal of universal education through the twelfth grade or even beyond, has caused pressures to be exerted to change the rather highly crystallized (some would say fossilized) structure of the educational system. The system now, in fact, does appear to impose itself – often with consequent frustration and defeat – on many in our population whose cultural and racial forebears played no part in the evolution of the system.

Returning now to the subject of intelligence tests, my contention is that our definitions of intelligence and our methods of measuring it have been significantly shaped by the schools and the historical and geographical factors involved in their development. Intelligence tests, as we all know, were originally made to be able to rank-order children in terms of their probable success in profiting from the traditional curriculum under the traditional methods of school instruction. They were not intended to measure the typical *outcomes* of such instruction, but to assess, by means relatively independent of scholastic performance, the probable scholastic attainments of children given more or less the same standard instruction in school.

Tests were made to perform this function very well indeed, and despite many auxiliary advances in test theory and test construction, the high predictive power of intelligence tests for scholastic performance has remained essentially unchanged for decades.

Psychologists became interested in intelligence as more than just scholastic ability and devised tests which could rank persons along a supposedly broader 'bright-dull' continuum, differences which are intuitively, though roughly, recognized by nearly all persons who thoughtfully observe other persons – at play, at school, and at work. Various terms designating roughly agreed upon differences along such a continuum have been used throughout recorded history and probably longer. Without specifying precisely what the behaviors consist of, this 'brightness' continuum along which persons range is recognized by all teachers, employers, and parents (especially if they have more than one child). Intelligence tests were intended by their makers as a means for objectifying, quantifying, and sharpening these subjective judgments.

From the very beginning, differences in what came to be called intelligence were regarded as largely inborn, and it was the inborn aspect of intelligence that psychologists were mainly attempting to assess by means of their new tests.

Whether tests were made to correspond to subjective judgments of relative brightness or to predict performance, they looked much alike and were, in fact, much alike in whatever it was they measured, as shown by their high intercorrelations. Tests that failed to correlate highly also failed to meet the external criteria of intelligence.

Spearman's concept of a *general factor* of intelligence, accounting for the substantial correlations among all tests and criteria that were independently agreed upon in general as representing samples of intelligent behavior, was practically inevitable. It is difficult and rare to find ability tests of any degree of complexity that do not show substantial positive intercorrelations when administered to a cross-section of the population. When the intercorrelations among a dozen or more different tests of mental ability (like the vocabulary, general information, memory span, block designs, figure copying, mazes, and other subtests of the Wechsler and Binet scales) are subjected to a factor analysis or principal components analysis, typically 50 per cent, and often more, of the individual differences variance in subtest scores is attributable to a general factor common to all the subtests. Henceforth, when we speak of intelligence, we will have in mind mainly this general factor, g. Thus we need not tie the concept of intelligence to any particular test or method of measurement, but shall use the term to refer to the general factor (g) common to practically all tests of complex mental abilities.

Fluid and crystallized intelligence

Raymond B. Cattell (1963) has made an important conceptually and empirically justified distinction between what he calls *fluid* general intelligence (g_f) and crystallized general intelligence (g_c). Fluid intelligence is a basic, general 'brightness' that can be marshalled for new learning and novel problem solving and adaptibility; it is relatively independent of education and experience but it can be invested in the particular opportunities for learning afforded by the individual's life circumstances, motivations and interests. Tests of fluid intelligence are essentially like those intended to minimize the importance of cultural and educational attainments. Examples are Cattell's *Culture Fair Tests* and Raven's *Progressive Matrices Test*. Crystallized intelligence (g_c), on the other hand, consists of acquired knowledge and intellectual skills. Since the original acquisition of such knowledge and skills depends upon fluid intelligence, there will usually be a substantial correlation between measures of g_f and g_c, and thus within a common culture there will be a super general factor common to both g_f and g_c. John L. Horn has characterized crystallized intelligence as 'a precipitate out of experience. It results when fluid intelligence is "mixed" with what can be called "the intelligence of the culture". Crystallized intelligence increases with a person's experiences and with the education that provides new methods and perspectives for dealing with that experience' (1967). This distinction between fluid and crystallized intelligence parallels closely one of the major distinctions between 'culture-free' and 'culture-loaded' tests, although not all attempts to minimize cultural loading in tests are based on this distinction.

Intelligence A, B, and C

An important set of distinctions that seems essential to any discussion of culture-free or status-fair testing is Donald O. Hebb's well-known distinction between intelligence A and B and the further refinement, added by Philip Vernon, of intelligence C.

Intelligence A refers to the individual's *genotype* as regards mental ability; it is the genetic code or 'blueprint', established at the moment of conception by the uniting complements of genes received from each parent, which genetically conditions the internal biological factors involved in the individual's mental development. Intelligence A is, of course, not directly observable or measurable. It is only inferable on a probabilistic basis from evidence on the heritability of intelligence.

Intelligence B refers to the individual's *phenotype* for mental ability, that is, the actual manifest mental ability resulting from the interaction of genetic and environmental influences. It should be emphasized that the term 'environment' really means *non-genetic* and includes much more than just those influences arising from cultural, social, and interpersonal factors. It includes also a host of prenatal, perinatal, and postnatal factors related to the nutrition and physical health of the mother and the child. Intelligence B is in part directly assessable by means of various psychological tests, observation of the individual's actual achievements, and so forth. It is the sum total of the individual's mental abilities, which are not measurable by any one test and in their totality probably not by any combination of presently existing tests.

This brings us to *intelligence C*, that aspect of mental ability which is actually measured by a particular intelligence test, since no single test draws upon the entire domain of mental abilities. When we speak of a person's score on a typical test of intelligence, such as the Stanford-Binet or the Wechsler, both of which are highly loaded with the *g* factor, we are referring to intelligence C. Each test measures a somewhat different constellation of abilities, as shown by the less than perfect intercorrelations among tests even after correction for unreliability of measurement.

Purposes of testing

Another preliminary consideration in our discussion of status-free tests is one's purpose in assessing abilities.

Prediction of Scholastic Performance. If one is interested only in predicting the individual's scholastic performance under certain relatively unchanging conditions of instruction, the question of the status-fairness of the test is of no real concern. All one attempts to do in this situation is to maximize the validity of the test for predicting the criterion, say, students' grade point averages. If the test's validity can be increased by including culturally and educationally loaded items, it is probably because these kinds of knowledge play a part in performance on the criterion. If the regression equation for predicting the criterion can be made more powerful by including items of background information of the subjects (e.g., previous school grades, sex, socio-economic status of parents, race, scores on interest and personality inventories), so much the better. That is, if all we want is to maximize prediction of success or failure in a given academic setting. Whether this is a worthy goal is another issue entirely. It is not a technical matter but one of educational and social policy.

However, if a test is used for selection and it predicts well for group A and has low predictive validity for group B, the test can be said to be unfair to group B. It may be unfair because of its cultural bias, but this is not the main point. It is really unfair because it selects or predicts with less precision in group B than in group A. If removing culture-loaded items from the test improves validity for group B without lowering it for group A, this is well and good. If overall prediction is improved by giving each group entirely different tests, while both groups are measured on the same criterion, this is well and good. The necessary safeguard to fairness in any selection program is continually to examine validity coefficients of the selection tests within every significant identifiable sub-group in the population which competes in the selection process.

In terms of the foregoing criteria, there has been little, if any, indication that the standard scholastic aptitude tests used in selection for higher education – the major sphere in which tests play a role in selection – are unfair in terms of differential validity across social-class and racial lines within the United States. (This generalization does not extend to the selection of foreign students, for certain groups of whom the standard tests do not have the same predictive properties as they have for American students.) The Educational Testing Service, for example, studied the *Preliminary Scholastic Aptitude Test* (PSAT) and the *Scholastic Aptitude Test* (SAT), (among the most widely used tests for college selection), to determine whether they were biased in such a way as to deny Negro students equal opportunity in admission to three integrated colleges (1968). Cleary, Two criteria of test bias were examined: (*a*) individual item biases, and (*b*) the total score's predictive validity for grade point average (GPA). If the rank order of item difficulty were different for Negroes and whites or, in terms of analysis of variance, if there were an 'item × race' interaction or an 'item × social-class within race' interaction, this would constitute evidence of item bias for race or socio-economic status (SES). No significant race or SES bias was found. The 'item × race' and 'item × SES within race' interactions made the smallest contributions to the total variance. As for the predictive validity of total scores for GPA, it was found that in two of the three colleges studied, the validity coefficients were essentially the same for Negro and white students; it made little difference whether predictor scores for Negroes or whites were plugged into the common regression equation or the equation for any sub-group. In short, the same test scores predicted GPA equally accurately in all groups. In one of the three colleges the Negro students' GPA was slightly overpredicted by the use of the common regression line, a bias which increased Negro applicants' chances of being accepted in that college.

Studies of test bias in selection in Negro colleges in the South, by Professor Julian C. Stanley of the Johns Hopkins University, have revealed that a kind of pseudo-bias exists when the SAT test is used in these colleges (1967). The predictive validity of the SAT is markedly lower in the Negro colleges than in white or integrated colleges because the test is too difficult, causing the distribution of scores to be markedly skewed, with a piling up of scores at the lower end of the scale and consequently a severe restriction of variance. When an easier test – the *Secondary School Admissions Test* (SSAT) – was used, so that the distribution of scores was approximately normal, the predictive validities were just as high as those achieved by the SAT in white colleges. In other words, for the purpose of predicting academic performance, the evidence indicates that our tests work as well for Negroes as for whites, provided the difficulty level of the test is such as to avoid ceiling or floor effects which seriously skew the distribution of scores or restrict the variance.

Employment Selection. It is probably in this realm more than in any other that test practices can be improved to reduce SES and race bias. In every situation where psychological tests are used for personnel selection or promotion, care must be taken to insure that the tests are truly valid for the actual job to be performed. If there is a negligible correlation between the test and actual work performance criteria, the test, no matter how good it may be on other grounds, is worse than a random lottery to the extent that it may deny equal opportunity for employment in terms of socio-cultural factors with which the test is correlated but which are irrelevant to performance on the job. The problem is underlined by the fact that most intelligence and aptitude tests correlate as highly with social-class factors as with job performance. If a test is shown to select differentially among social-class or racial groups of applicants for a particular occupation, the test may be considered unfairly discriminatory if the correlation between the test and the criterion is not significantly lowered when the variables of social-class or race are partialed out of the correlation. In other words, when race or social classes are correlated with the test but are not independently correlated with the criterion, the test may be regarded as biased. Note that this criterion of bias does not necessarily imply that various groups should obtain the same scores on an unbiased test, nor does it say that social background factors should not be correlated with the criterion. It simply says that if the social background factors are irrelevant to the criterion performance, they should not surreptitiously creep into selection via tests that are correlated with both the criterion and the social status factors.

The risk of such bias is emphasized by the known surprisingly low correlations between a wide variety of intelligence tests and actual proficiency on the job. Such correlations average about 0·20 to 0·25, and thus predict only 4 or 5 per cent of the variance in work proficiency (Ghiselli, 1955). Intelligence correlates more highly with occupational status, however, since intelligence is highly correlated with educational attainment, which in turn is a major determiner of eligibility for various occupations. Speed and ease of training show correlations with mental tests of around 0·50, which is four or five times the predictive power that the same tests have in relation to job proficiency *after* training. From the standpoint of sheer economy of job training, tests can therefore make a substantial contribution. The same criteria for ruling out test bias as described above should, of course, be applied also to the use of tests in selection for training. Furthermore, the economy of job training should be viewed in the broad perspective of the long-term economy of increasing productive employment in previously undereducated or underskilled persons. In this endeavor the speed or ease with which persons can be trained for a specific job may be a far less important criterion in the long run than the final level of their performance on the job. Here previous scholastic performance or scores on tests which are predictive of school achievement may be quite irrelevant. And where some selection for job training is necessitated by a great disparity between the number of job opportunities and the number of applicants, tests quite different from those now generally in use may prove just as predictive without introducing socially biasing factors that are irrelevant to success in training or job performance. One type of such test, called 'a direct learning test', is described later on. The *Porteus Maze Tests* are also promising in this respect (Cooper *et al.*, 1967).

Diagnosis of School Learning Problems. An intelligence test is just one among a number of techniques used by school psychologists for assessing the learning and adjustment problems of children whose progress in their school work is markedly deviant from that of their age mates. Intellectual assessment of such children should be based upon more than a single instrument in order to take into consideration a greater variety of cognitive functions than are exposed by any one test. A diversity of tests is needed to discover the child's cognitive strengths as well as his deficiencies. This is important for all children who perform scholastically below the normal range (more than one standard deviation below grade level) and it is especially important for children from an educationally disadvantaged background, since there is evidence of less uniformity among these children in their individual profiles of abilities. Any single test of ability is therefore apt to be less generally representative of low-SES children's capabilities for profiting from education than is the case for middle-class children. It is also likely that there is a greater diversity and unevenness among the various cognitive capabilities of children viewed as 'slow learners' in school than of 'average' or 'fast' learners. A relatively uniform but merely slowed and watered down version of the regular instructional program is not what so-called 'slow learners' need. They need a greater diversity of course content and instructional approaches than are necessary for the average run of children. But this goal becomes feasible only if there is some rational and empirically valid basis for assessing individual differences in patterns of abilities and for relating these to differential educational treatments. We know that children who are grouped together on the basis of scores on any one test are still extremely heterogeneous in a variety of other abilities, and this is especially true of those children in the bottom half of the distribution. When grouping based on a single test or a narrow criterion of scholastic achievement cuts across the full socio-economic spectrum in the population as well, the heterogeneity of capability within groups is made even greater. I have become reasonably convinced by our own research at Berkeley that the pattern of abilities of the majority of lower-class children who become identified as 'slow learners' in school is quite different from that of the majority of middle-class children with the same designation. This difference appears to be more fundamental than the kinds of differences that would be wiped out if we had perfectly culture-free or culture-fair intelligence tests. Consequently, I suspect that the instructional requirements of the two groups referred to would be quite different if the school hopes to provide optimal educational advantages for both. The socio-economic factor, it should be emphasized, is not the primary basis of this distinction. It is the ability patterns that matter; the fact that these may be correlated with SES is incidental, and it should not be construed to mean that children would be given different educational treatment *because* of their SES background. One major aspect of this difference in ability patterns is described in a later section.

Discovering Abilities. One of the important functions of tests is the discovery of abilities in children that may ordinarily escape notice by teachers. The discovery and development of abilities in socio-economically heterogeneous schools and in educationally disadvantaged groups calls not only for status-fair tests of general intelligence but for a broad coverage of other abilities which may not be highly correlated with g but which may nevertheless be developed to the educational and social advantage of the child. Tests of g which are free of obvious cultural content, like Raven's *Progressive Matrices* (1952), Cattell's *Culture-Fair Tests* (1959), and the *Domino* test (Gough and Domino, 1963), should be used much more widely in schools that serve the educationally disadvantaged in order to spot those children with potentially strong academic aptitude. One important criterion of a school's excellence is the level of scholastic performance attained by its pupils from disadvantaged backgrounds who score above the general average on culture-fair tests of g such as those just mentioned. Poor scholastic performance despite high scores on these tests, in the absence of other severely disabling conditions, is a strong indication that the child's abilities are going to waste where formal education is concerned. Every urban school should assess its population by means of such tests and lavish special attention on the scholastic progress of those children from relatively poor backgrounds who score above the general average. They will have the basic intellectual equipment to compete successfully with children from any other strata of society, but they may need to be given extra encouragement and more individual help, especially in the first years of school, if they are to make the most of their ability. For many of these children, the school or some allied community agency will have to provide the motivational and tutorial supports to scholastic achievement that are normally provided for most middle-class children by their educationally oriented parents.

What about those who get low scores on these relatively culture-fair tests of *g*? Are they doomed to failure in school? No. But to profit maximally from school they may need a different instructional program from that which is suitable for those who are relatively high on *g*. There are other educationally important abilities that are not highly correlated with *g* and are not assessed by means of the tests mentioned so far, but which, with appropriate instructional techniques, may be utilized to achieve mastery of the traditional school subject matter. It is probably only when *all* children are indiscriminately taught by methods which depend heavily upon *g* – a heritage from the days when education was intended for only a select few – that a substantial proportion of children called disadvantaged fail ever to master even the subject matter of the elementary grades.

One of the worst examples I ever saw of needlessly infusing verbal-academic criteria of success in an essentially non-academic course was in my wood shop course in junior high school. A week before the end of the term the teacher announced that the course grade would be based entirely on a written test of our knowledge of the full names of each of the more than 150 wood-working tools in the shop! I would be surprised if there were better than zero correlation between the grades in the course and the actual wood-working skills and interests displayed by the students. How often do such essentially irrelevant criteria work against the less academically inclined children in our schools?

Comparisons of Schools and School Systems. Statewide and nationwide testing programs supposedly permit a comparative assessment of different regions of the country or state and of different neighborhoods and schools within a single school system. Because these group tests are usually administered by the teachers in each classroom under quite variable conditions, the test scores have an unknown but probably large degree of error variance. Although the errors may tend to cancel out in large samples to give reasonably stable means, the usefulness of the data for correlational analysis is greatly impaired. Small random samples of the school population tested under highly controlled, uniform conditions by expert testers with no vested interest in the performance of a particular school would actually yield much more satisfactory data from a statistical and psychometric standpoint. Test score means and standard deviations *per se* are the least revealing aspect of the differences among schools and school systems, for the means and standard deviations are largely a function of the particular segments of the population served by the school. More important in comparing schools or educational practices is the regression of scholastic achievement on intelligence test scores. And for this purpose status-fair tests of intelligence are the most desirable, since they are less loaded on scholastic content and should remain relatively stable across a variety of educational treatments. In a statewide testing program, the mean achievement scores of various schools and districts by themselves tell us practically nothing. The regression of achievement scores on culture-free or status-free intelligence measures, on the other hand, tell us how successful different schools are in translating their raw material – the pupils' intelligence – into scholastic achievement. Other community and pupil status variables may also be entered into the regression equation for predicting test scores. Schools that depart markedly in either direction from the common regression line could profitably be subjected to a thorough study.

Means of achieving status-fair tests

Nearly all attempts to devise culture-free or status-free tests have resorted to the principle of reducing test content to the lowest common denominator of experiences encountered in the various cultures or social strata across which the test is intended to give a 'fair' assessment of individuals' intelligence. In practice, the attempts to make tests that sample the common elements from a wide range of cultural, social, and educational backgrounds have taken a number of forms. Each has its advantages and disadvantages.

Common Information. The least satisfactory method of attempting status-fairness of tests is by seeking items of information that are common across various status groups. Information tests consisting of questions like 'Who was the first President of the United States?', 'Whose picture is on a penny?', and so on, make poor test items mainly for two reasons: (*a*) they do not get at complex mental processes, and (*b*) they cannot be steeply graded in difficulty level without introducing items of information to which there is a relatively low probability of exposure, in which case social status and educational differences become practically impossible to avoid. The same thing holds true for vocabulary tests, including picture vocabulary. Consider these three items from the information subtest of the old *Wechsler-Bellevue Intelligence Scale*. They vary markedly in 'difficulty' level (indicated by the percentage of the population giving the right answer): 'Who is the President of the United States?', 'Who wrote Hamlet?', 'Who wrote Faust?'. Knowledge of the answers to all three questions involves the same kind and degree of mental ability. The difficulty levels differ only because of frequency of exposure. Such items based on information and vocabulary are rightly regarded as more culturally loaded than items which vary in difficulty because of the complexity of the mental processes involved. One can think of this in terms of the kinds of computer programs that would be required to handle the test items. One and the same simple program could handle 'Who wrote Faust?' and 'Who is President of the United States?', but the same would not be true for the easy and the difficult items of Raven's *Progressive Matrices Test*, which would call for programs differing markedly in complexity.

Thus, in examining classes of test items for their potential value in constructing status-fair tests, one should distinguish between *intrinsic* and *incidental* correlates of intelligence. Scores on information and vocabulary tests do, in fact, correlate substantially with *g* in a culturally more or less homogeneous segment of the population, since amount of information acquired under fairly equal exposure reflects learning capacity. But such items are here regarded as *incidental* correlates of mental ability, since the mental processes of acquisition are themselves not involved in response to the test question. One can go a step further, as Harrison Gough (1953) has done, and devise a thoroughly incidental test of intelligence which contains not a single item calling for the use of any mental ability (other than the ability to read the questions and mark the true-false answers). All 52 items in Gough's test are 'personality' questions, such as 'I have often been frightened in the middle of the night' (keyed *False*) and 'I gossip a little at times' (keyed *True*). Yet this 'test' correlates about 0·50 with conventional IQ measures in a high school population. This non-intellectual intelligence test is so obviously culturally loaded that it may serve a useful function in evaluating the culture-fairness of other tests. If the Gough test reflects the culture-laden values, attitudes, and interests associated with measured intelligence, it would be interesting to compare different social status and racial groups on conventional IQ tests, controlling with scores on the Gough test. In other words, what is the correlation between SES and IQ after their correlation with Gough scores is partialed out? It would also be interesting to know how the Gough variance is distributed in a factor analysis of a variety of tests of mental ability, and to compare the factor scores of different sub-populations on factors with high and low loadings on the Gough test. One would expect the factor with low loadings on the Gough to be more status-fair.

The distinction between intrinsic mental test items and incidental-correlate items parallels E. L. Thorndike's distinction between *altitude* and *breadth* of intelligence. General information and vocabulary tests mainly get at intellectual breadth; tests involving problem solving get at altitude. Since the breadth factor depends so much on amount and range of exposure, as well as the person's interests and values, status-fair tests have generally tried to minimize the breadth factor. In the general population, breadth and altitude measures are both highly correlated with *g*, but test content reflecting breadth is more influenced by environment and training. It is on breadth tests, like the *Peabody Picture Vocabulary Test*, for example, that it is easiest to show IQ gains in programs such as Headstart. Although measures of breadth and altitude are usually highly correlated, there is a real psychological distinction between the two. Any moderately endowed person may, for example, learn to play chess, checkers, dominoes, bridge, and many other games moderately well and the person who can play ten games at this level is not necessarily more able than the person who can play only one or two; they probably differ mainly in the amount of time they have devoted to learning

G

the games. But only a few persons can ever become chess masters even by concentrating all their effort on chess alone. Similarly, given sufficient time, almost anyone can learn to play a dozen different musical instruments, but most persons cannot achieve a virtuoso level even on a single instrument, given any amount of time, training, and drive. The altitude factor thus seems much more dependent on innate endowment than the breadth factor. In the strictly intellectual realm this distinction parallels Cattell's distinction between fluid (altitude) and crystallized (breadth) intelligence (Cattell, 1963).

In his first attempts to increase the culture fairness of tests, Cattell made use of items testing word knowledge, but he used all quite familiar (high frequency) words to which we could expect that almost everyone had been more or less equally exposed. He manipulated the difficulty of the items by requiring subjects to make increasingly difficult choice or discriminations between the meanings of highly familiar words. This, of course, introduces the altitude component, but it would now be argued by most students of social-class differences that subtleties of word meanings and fine shades of distinction in the use of language are more highly valued and given more attention and emphasis in high status homes. Cattell wisely gave up this method in his later versions of culture-fair tests.

A classic example of attempting to make a test that used presumably status-common content to measure the altitude of the problem-solving aspect of intelligence was the *Davis-Eells Games*, now defunct because it proved to have less satisfactory reliability and validity for its stated purposes than conventional tests of intelligence. The *Davis-Eells Games* consisted of cartoon pictures of persons engaged in activities familiar and recognizable to everyone in our society. The examiner asked questions about the pictures in simple language. One item, for example, shows a series of pictures of a boy trying to climb over a high fence by several different methods, only one of which appears very practicable. The subject has to pick out the picture he thinks shows the best method of scaling the fence.

Today an informational test based on television programs would probably have greater universality than any other source of content. A recent study of low-SES inner-city Negro boys in

Washington, D.C. failed to identify content areas of interest to this disadvantaged group that would set them off from middle-class groups (Orr and Graham, 1968). The source of this common core of interest areas seems mostly attributable to television, which now apparently is equally spread throughout the entire SES range.

Eliminating Status-Biasing Factors. In addition to avoiding content of a scholastic or specific cultural nature, construction of status-fair tests have tried eliminating or minimizing the role of factors such as reading, language, and speed. Dependence on reading skill is a strongly biasing factor in group tests when they are used in educationally heterogenous populations. To avoid this bias Orr and Graham (1968) have devised a *Listening Comprehension Test* to identify educational potential among disadvantaged junior high school students who had failed to develop reading and writing skills commensurate with their grade level. It was thought that these students would also show better comprehension on auditory measures than on visual measures. The test devised by Orr and Graham drew on a common core of interests in sports, TV, and comic books. The authors note that interest in these subjects is shared across economic strata among 8th grade boys. They also comment that on the basis of interviews intended to sample interest content areas in the disadvantaged population, 'It did not appear possible to construct a test that would be entirely specific to disadvantaged subjects of Negro ethnic background.' The common core of content served as the basis of orally administered (on a tape recorder) test items that required students to draw conclusions, to make inferences, to learn, remember, and follow directions. To increase understanding, the audio tape was narrated by a native of the disadvantaged neighborhood who spoke with a Washington Negro accent. They found a correlation of 0·60 between the Listening Test and total score on a conventional scholastic aptitude test (SCAT). The Listening Test had negligible correlations with an economic index within the disadvantaged population. The test statistics however, were not compared with a middle-class group or other ethnic groups. In such group comparisons, this test, with its emphasis on sports and entertainment and narrated in a Negro accent, if it has any bias at all, would seem to favor low-SES Negroes. If such a test were to be used for making status and ethnic comparisons, it should be factor analyzed within each group along with a number of other tests of g to determine whether it has the same g saturation in both groups. The test may still be useful even if it were not a test of g in certain subpopulations, but the interpretation of the scores would depend on knowledge of their factorial composition. The test's satisfactory reliability (0·85 to 0·89), the existence of equivalent forms, and the correlation with scholastic performance (0·45) surely recommend it for further investigation. What needs most to be determined is whether the *uniqueness* of the test (that part of its total variance which is not shared by other ability tests) consists of any educationally relevant variance.

Spatial-Quantitative Relations. If one eliminates reading, language, scholastic content and pictorial representation of real objects, what is left from which to make up intelligence test items? About all that is left, and forms the basis for what are probably the most satisfactory culture-free and status-free tests, are spatial and quantitative concepts. Spatial tests make use of elementary topological properties and relationships which are common features of all environments. The basic forms of spatial percepts are common to all cultures and are largely uninfluenced by material aspects of the culture. Thus the basis for test items can be found in such universal topological concepts as 'inside-outside', 'up-down', 'above-below', 'left-right', 'behind-in front', 'in-out', 'full-empty' and such space-form percepts as 'straight-curved', 'smooth-jagged', and so forth. Add to these such elementary quantitative concepts as 'many-few', 'increase-decrease', 'large-small', etc., and one has virtually all the basic elements with which to make a Raven's *Progressive Matrices*, Cattell's *Culture-Fair Tests*, and the *Domino Test* (Gough and Domino, 1963). These three tests generally show higher loadings of g, when factor analyzed with other measures of intelligence, than any other tests. This shows that it is possible to measure general intelligence with a high degree of reliability simply by means of the elemental topological quantitative properties mentioned above. They are one of the few forms of test content which can cross many language and cultural differences which are often barriers to the use of conventional tests. Kidd and Rivoire (1965) have analyzed the items in tests such as the Cattell and Raven from the standpoint of their topological properties and point out that most of the concepts employed appear in the pottery, baskets, carvings, face paintings, body paintings, blankets, and clothing of a majority of primitive societies.

Gough and McGurk (1967) have made up what they call a group *Test of Perceptual Acuity*, consisting largely of visual illusions and discriminations. Although the test reliably measures individual differences in perceptual functions which show an age-gradient, nothing has been reported concerning the relationship of these measures to other cognitive abilities.

Another test in the same vein but which has been shown to correlate satisfactorily with conventional intelligence tests is the *Johns Hopkins Perceptual Test* devised by Leon Rosenberg (1966). It is still in a developmental stage and its factorial content has not been explored.

Control of extrinsic factors in taking tests

Test performance can be influenced by extrinsic factors that may be associated with social status but are not central to the psychological functions the test attempts to measure. Personality factors, motivation, 'test anxiety', 'test sophistication' and other test-taking attitudes, 'personal tempo', 'clerical' skills, and susceptibility to distraction all come under this category of extrinsic contributors to individual and group differences in intelligence, aptitude, and achievement tests. The contribution to variance of many of these factors can be reduced by improving testing procedures, wording instructions to make them perfectly clear to all subjects, using simplified forms of the test for preliminary practice, and the like. Answer sheets and other 'clerical' aspects of test taking can be minimized by eliminating complexities in the mechanics of test taking and by giving subjects training and practice on the mechanics.

In our research we have found that low-SES children are relatively more distracted in a classroom testing situation than when they are tested individually and there is thus a greater discrepancy between group and individual test scores for low-SES than for middle-class children. Testing procedures can probably be devised which will minimize this gap.

But improvements in testing procedures alone will not eliminate all variance due to extrinsic factors. Further steps are necessary. Personality scores and other relevant measures may be entered into prediction equations along with the intelligence test scores. We have found, for example, that college students who obtain high scores on extraversion in the *Eysenck Personality Inventory* rush through untimed tests faster than more introverted subjects and thereby obtain slightly lower scores. In one study, extraversion scores correlated -0.45 with time spent on Raven's *Progressive Matrices* when college subjects were allowed more time than needed and could quit when they thought they had done their best on this test. Extraversion correlated -0.13 with total number correct (Jensen, 1965a).

Timed tests introduce a speed factor, part of which may be irrelevant to what the test intends to measure. There is evidence of at least two kinds of speed factors (Line and Kaplan, 1932). One is an intellectual factor involving speed and efficiency of mental operations in problem solving. This is an important component of intelligence and enters into complex problem solving. The other speed factor is essentially non-cognitive. Although its effects are spread throughout all difficulty levels of a test, it shows up in relatively pure form in the easiest items. As an extreme example, suppose a 100-item test is made up of 50 very easy problems followed by 50 very difficult problems. Subjects will differ in the time they need to get through the easy items and to begin working on the difficult items, and consequently they will have unequal amounts of time for the difficult items. The chief source of variance on the easy items is not intellectual ability but is essentially a non-cognitive speed factor. I call it a 'speed and persistence' factor, since it involves the ability not only to work fast but also to avoid taking rest pauses. Subjects who are low in this trait are at a disadvantage in time tests. A group of mathematics graduate students given a timed test consisting of several hundred simple addition problems, for example, will show reliable individual differences in their total time scores, but the scores will reflect nothing of their mathematical ability. It will represent a pure speed and persistence factor. The same factor enters into timed tests at all levels from kindergarten through graduate school.

We are attempting to assess the importance of this factor in group testing in elementary schools across a wide range of socio-economic levels by measuring speed and persistence independently of intelligence and using the speed scores as a control variable in making group comparisons. It should be possible to determine how much of the variance in social status differences on intelligence tests is due to the non-cognitive speed and persistence factor. It is measured by having subjects mark Xs in 150 boxes, given 1·5 minutes. The procedure is given twice, first under instructions that make no mention of speed and second with instructions to work as fast as possible in order to do much better than the first time.

Listening attention is another factor that plays an important role in group administered tests at the elementary level. We have devised a 'Listening-Attention' test which helps to separate the variance due to this factor from the more strictly cognitive factors we wish to measure with intelligence tests. To separate listening attention from memory span for digits, for example, children are given a test which shows whether they can listen to digits on a tape recorder and simultaneously check those digits that they hear on a special answer sheet. The task makes no memory demands but shows whether the subject can hear, understand, and pay attention to digits read on a tape recorder. If the child cannot do this, his score on a test of auditory digit span cannot be regarded as a valid test of his auditory memory span.

By thus sorting out the sources of variance in social class differences in intelligence test scores we can arrive at more status-fair conclusions and uses of the tests, and we can better determine the kinds of instructional procedures most likely to improve the performance of the educationally disadvantaged.

Improving subtests with status-fair potential

Various subtests of omnibus intelligence tests such as the Stanford-Binet and Wechsler show different degrees of discrimination between status groups, yet they may have approximately equal correlations with total IQ. This is presumptive but not conclusive evidence that the subtests differ in status-fairness. Digit span correlates almost as highly with total IQ as vocabulary in the normative population, when both are corrected for attenuation. We have found, however, that digit span has a much lower correlation with total IQ in Negroes of low socio-economic status (Jensen, 1968c). A possible interpretation of this finding is that digit span is one of the more status-fair subtests in the Stanford-Binet and Wechsler. The usefulness of the digit span test, however, is impaired by its relatively low reliability due to the brevity of the test as it is usually presented in omnibus batteries. We have lengthened the digit span test, added procedural variations (e.g., immediate *v.* delayed recall and single *v.* multiple repetitions of the same digit series), and standardized administration by presenting the digits by tape recorder at a metronomic one-second rate. Reliabilities are over 0·90. Social status differences are much smaller than for other tests. Whether the test still measures the intellective *g* factor of mental ability in low status groups, however, is now seriously open to question (Jensen, 1968c). It appears that digit span gets at an important component of mental ability, but it is different from *g*. Its substantial loading on *g* in factor analyses of the Stanford-Binet and Wechsler in the white and predominantly middle-class normative groups may be explained by the hypothesis that memory span is a component of mental ability which is necessary but not sufficient for the development of *g*. The *g* factor is indexed mainly by tests involving complex reasoning.

Another subtest with apparently little status bias but a very substantial *g* loading is *Block Design*. Its reliability is in the 0·80s for various age groups and could be made still higher if the test were lengthened and more difficult items were added. The Kohs block design test improves on the Wechsler in these respects. The high *g* saturation of the test, despite its non-verbal and non-scholastic character, suggests its great potential as a status-fair measure of intelligence. The test involves a speed factor and could be improved by providing a means of assessing non-cognitive speed. Performance time on a series of very easy block designs could be used for this purpose. Time scores on more difficult designs could be 'regressed' on time scores for the easy designs in order to get an estimate of intelligence relatively uncontaminated by the non-cognitive speed factor.

The *Porteus Maze* test is another example of a more elaborate form of one of the Wechsler subscales in the children's form. The

Porteus Maze test has been shown to discriminate between behaviorally retarded and non-retarded Negro adolescents all of whom had Wechsler and Stanford-Binet IQs in the retarded range (Cooper *et al.*, 1967). The maze test distinguished those regarding whom the following eight questions could be answered in the affirmative:

Is he socially alert? Is he socially effective? Is his general activity level high? Is he mentioned more often? Is his vocational ability high? Does he have sports ability? Is his physical appearance good? Is his social judgment accurate?

This study indicates that the Porteus test measures a socially important dimension of behavior which is relatively undetected by conventional tests of intelligence in an educationally disadvantaged population.

A bias in age-graded scales

The vocabulary and digit span subtests are not given at every age level in the Stanford-Binet. The same thing is true for other subtests as well; they are staggered over the age scale. This raises a question of whether the particular selection of subtests in one age grouping are equated with those of another age grouping in their status-fair properties.

If the age groupings differ in the status-fairness of their subtests, the biasing effect could be exaggerated well beyond the bias in the individual items, because of the way age scales are administered. That is, the testing is discontinued when the child fails all the subtests in one age category. A preponderance of status-biased items concentrated at one age level could therefore prevent many subjects from even having a chance at the less biased items at the next age level. In this respect the Wechsler tests, which are not construed in accord with the age-scale notion, are superior to the Stanford-Binet. In the Wechsler the subject has an equal chance at every type of item, so that the single effects of status-biased items are not magnified in their effect on the total score. We do not know how large a status bias this factor causes in Stanford-Binet scores, but it should be investigated and, if it is found to be significant, some change in the Stanford-Binet testing procedures would be called for. An index of status discrimination

G*

could be obtained for every item in the test and the age groupings of the items could be rearranged, if necessary, to yield the same average discrimination index at each age level.

Physiological indices of intelligence

Is there a possibility of bypassing cultural factors in tests altogether by measuring the brain or its neurological efficiency directly? So far no one has found any single brain measurement or combination of measurements that correlates sufficiently with behavioral criteria of mental ability to be of practical use. Even if high correlations between electrophysiological brain measurements and intelligence test scores were found, however, we would still have to establish by means of factor analysis that the physiological measure was loaded on the g factor in all the various social class or racial groups for whom the test is intended to be 'fair'.

From the laboratory of Dr John P. Ertl, director of the center for cybernetic studies at the University of Ottawa, there is now some evidence of a common factor in IQ and the rapidity of evoked potentials in brain wave patterns as recorded by the electro-encephalograph (EEG) (1966). While the subject's brain waves are being recorded in a darkened room, a bright light is flashed in the subject's eyes for a fraction of a second. The stimulus is registered as an 'evoked potential' – a spike – in the subject's brain waves. The brief period of time between the flash of light and the peak of the evoked potential which follows it has been found to correlate with IQ. But so far the only reliable discriminations that have been reported are between children differing as widely in IQ as retarded and gifted children. Technical improvements, however, may lead to substantial correlations with psychometric measures of g and we would have a culture-free method for studying individual and group differences in the brain processes that underlie intelligent behavior. If status differences are associated with nutritional or other biological factors that affect the brain's development early in life, these factors would be reflected also in electrophysiological measurements. No one claims a test that can 'read through' environmental factors that have direct biological influences on mental growth. As pointed out previously, we cannot directly measure Intelligence A (the individual's genotype). But physiological techniques may ultimately permit measurement of Intelligence B free of all environmental factors but those of a strictly biological nature.

Definitions and criteria of status-fairness

The literature on culture-free and culture-fair testing reveals an almost total confusion and misconception concerning the definition of 'fairness', and the criteria by which it is to be recognized. One author of a culture-fair test stated as the criterion of fairness: '. . . a test is culture-fair if the obtained scores are demonstrated to be free of the influence of socio-economic differences between subjects'. In other words, the degree of culture-fairness is judged in terms of the degree of reduction in SES variance in obtained scores. When tests designed to be culture-fair, such as the *Davis-Eells Games*, the *Davis-Hess Individual Test of Intelligence*, and the *Cattell Culture-Fair Tests*, are shown still to differentiate between social status groups, as they do, this is claimed as evidence that the tests are not 'fair' and that the authors have failed in their purpose. It is a fact that no tests of intelligence have yet been derived which consistently wipe out social class and racial differences.

Does this mean that the tests are culturally biased? To claim the absence or reduction of group differences as the criterion of fairness is to beg the question completely. It is a wholly inappropriate criterion. A culture-fair or status-fair test should, in principle, be capable of showing status differences where such differences are not due solely to cultural factors but to genetic factors as well. The notion that culture-fair tests should wipe out SES differences is based on the implicit assumption that high- and low-SES groups do not differ in their genetic potential for the development of intelligence. Such an assumption is not only unwarranted by the evidence but is in fact contradicted by the preponderance of the relevant evidence. This evidence cannot be reviewed in detail here. It consists of highly consistent findings from diverse studies of the inheritance of intelligence: identical twins separated in the first year of life and reared in widely differing social classes still show greater resemblance in IQ than unrelated children reared together or even than siblings or fraternal twins (who have half their genes in common) reared together (Jensen, 1970c); the IQs of children adopted in infancy show a much lower correlation with the socio-economic and educational level of the adopting parents than do the IQs of children reared by their own parents (Honzik, 1957); the IQs of children reared in an orphanage from infancy and who have never known their true parents show approximately the same correlation with their true father's occupational status as is found for children reared by their own parents (Lawrence, 1931); the correlations between the IQs of children adopted in infancy and the educational level of their true mothers is close to that of children reared by their own mothers ($r = 0.44$), while the correlation between children and their adopting parents is close to zero (Honzik, 1957); children of low- and high-SES show, on the average, an amount of regression from the parental IQ toward the mean of the general population that is predicted by a polygenetic model (Leahy, 1935); when full siblings (who, on the average, have half their genes in common) differ significantly in intelligence, those who are above the family average tend to move up the SES scale and those who are below the family average tend to move down (Young and Gibson, 1963). In view of these lines of evidence, it would be surprising to find a test that claimed to wipe out SES differences in measured intelligence; one would question whether the test was actually measuring intelligence – an issue that could be checked by factor analyzing the test along with other standard tests and noting its g loading.

Anastasi (1964) has stated that a test is not culture-fair 'when it fails to control relevant cultural parameters'. This is an extremely slippery criterion. It is always applied in a *post hoc* manner. If what is thought to be a relevant cultural parameter is controlled and the test still discriminates between status groups, a new relevant cultural parameter is then invoked as an explanation for the difference. Anastasi, for example, points to findings which challenge the belief that non-verbal tests are more culture-fair than verbal tests. When American Negroes perform less well than other groups on a highly verbal test like the Stanford-Binet, the explanation is that their language background is different or impoverished in the kinds of words or syntax common to white middle-class society. Then, according to Anastasi, it was found that Negroes generally perform more poorly on tests involving concrete objects, numerical problems, and spatial relations than on most verbal tests. 'One explanation proposed for these differences,' Anastasi continues, 'centers around problem-solving attitudes. Insofar as the social environment of the American Negro has traditionally encouraged attitudes of passive compliance rather than active exploration, it would be more conducive to rote verbal learning than to perceptual manipulation of stimuli and problem solving.' This may or may not be true. The point is that since an unlimited number of 'cultural parameters' can be hypothesized that would have to be controlled to make a test 'fair' by Anastasi's criterion, and since presumably the only criterion that all relevant factors have been controlled is the absence of group differences (the presence of any difference would always be seen as the result of another cultural parameter that was not controlled), I regard Anastasi's definition of culture-fairness as quite meaningless and useless from an objective, operational standpoint. Obviously, some other criterion of culture-fairness or status-fairness is needed.

What are some other possible criteria by which we might judge the status-fairness of a test?

We have already mentioned the criterion of predictive validity. If a test had different predictive validities for different groups in the population and these differences cannot be attributed to differences in variance on the test or the criterion, it is likely that the test is biased in favor of some groups and not others.

Another indicator of a test's loading on environmental influences is its correlation with environmental ratings or other indices of relevant environmental factors. Other things being equal, the test with lower environmental correlations is probably more status-fair than tests with higher environmental correlations. It is an especially strong indication of culture-fairness if the mean test scores of a number of widely different cultural groups are not monotonically related to mean environmental ratings for the groups, when the environments are rated on a scale of experiential and educational similarity to that of the population on which the test was standardized. Probably the most powerful test of environmental influence on test scores can be achieved by determining the multiple correlation between the scores and indices of a large number of environmental factors.

The effects of training and practice on test scores may also reflect the test's susceptibility to environmental influence. Performance on all tests shows practice effects, but some tests show more than others. Although high susceptibility to improvement with practice does not rule out the test's lack of bias, high resistance to practice gains strongly suggests that the test is getting more at internally regulated developmental processes than at environmental attainments. Tests on which gains in score resulting from practice rapidly reach asymptote, and which show little transfer across equivalent forms, and which leave little or no residue in measurements obtained with the same tests or equivalent forms a few months later, can probably be regarded as more status-fair than tests which do not show these properties to as high a degree. Seventy-eight practice sessions on a variety of memory span tasks spread over a period of four and a half months, for example, showed a significant gain in young children in relation to an un-practiced matched group, but after another four and a half months without additional practice both groups performed the same. Then both groups were given 22 days of intensive training on memory span tasks; at the end both groups were approximately equal. There was no evidence of any permanent effect of the 78 days of practice (Gates and Taylor, 1925). Thus it seems highly unlikely that memory span tests manifest any appreciable status bias. Raven's *Progressive Matrices* appears to have a similar resistance to training, as shown by recent, as yet unpublished, research by Paul Jacobs of the Educational Testing Service. Transfer of training on the matrices is surprisingly small, even when there is high similarity between the training items and the test items.

Copying geometric figures of varying difficulty also seems to get at developmental rather than experiential aspects of mental ability (Ilg and Ames, 1964). There is an age scale for ability to copy such figures, going from a circle to a cube drawn in perspective. My experience in testing children on these figures and in trying to teach children how to copy figures that are beyond their developmental level makes me believe that this type of ability is highly resistant to specific training. It is interesting to observe a 5-year-old who can copy a circle, a cross, a square, and a triangle as perfectly as any adult, and then cannot begin to copy a diamond. Instead, the child will usually draw an ellipse with little arrow points on the top, bottom, and sides. Training and practice, using imitation, verbal instructions, tracing, and the like, do not improve the child's performance. Wait a year or so, and the child will copy the diamond without any difficulty. Piaget's conservation problems evince this same resistance to specific training. Piaget tasks have been found to have very substantial loadings on the *g* factor when analyzed with conventional psychometric tests (Vernon, 1965).

Probably the major pitfall for most attempts to devise status-fair tests results from uncritical acceptance of the following common criteria of fairness: (*a*) the test score means and variances should be the same in high and low status groups, and (*b*) the test should correlate highly with conventional tests of intelligence in the high status group. We have found a number of tests that meet these criteria, the best example being digit span (Jensen, 1968c). But these two criteria are insufficient. They do not tell us whether the test measures the same intelligence in the low status group as in the high status group. My own research has shown that digit span and various types of associative learning do not measure much of the variance in intelligence in low status groups. Even though scores on conventional tests may be depressed by a poor environment, subjects should remain in about the same rank order of ability on both status-fair and conventional tests. When there is almost no correlation between the two kinds of tests, it is highly doubtful that they are measuring the same psychological processes. A principal components analysis or factor analysis of a status-fair test can help to answer this question. Since there is no necessary connection between the means of various tests in a population and their intercorrelations, a requirement of a status-fair test should be that it show essentially the same factorial composition in a low status as in a high status group. The test's *g* saturation, especially, should be by far its largest component, if the test is claimed to measure intelligence, and it should be of about the same magnitude in both lower and upper status groups. As stated before, it is not at all necessary that the test yield the same means across low and high status groups. So far no culture-fair intelligence test yet devised that meets the criterion of measuring *g* in both high and low status groups fails to show significant social class and racial differences (e.g., Ludlow (1956)). As already pointed out, the 'fairness' of these tests is not disproved by the findings of status group differences. How then can their fairness be judged? Are there any objective criteria we can apply?

Criteria derived from quantitative genetics

I propose the following definition of status-fairness of a test: a test is status-fair to the degree that its correlation with 'Intelligence A' in the population in which the test is used approaches unity. In other words, the higher the correlation between phenotype and genotype, the higher is the 'fairness' of the test. If the genotype-phenotype correlation is perfect, after correction for attenuation, the test can be said to measure innate ability. The phenotype-genotype correlation for individual tests like the Stanford-Binet is approximately 0·9 in the normative Caucasian population. This figure is actually the square root of the heritability of intelligence test scores. The heritability of intelligence as measured by conventional tests has been estimated by the methods of quantitative genetics in a large number of studies in Europe and North America. The average value of these heritability estimates is about 0·80 (Jensen, 1967a), which means that about 80 per cent of the true-score variance on intelligence tests is attributable to genetic factors and about 20 per cent is attributable to non-genetic factors. 'Non-genetic' includes all environmental influences – physical, biological, and social – acting on the individual from the moment of conception.

The Concept of Heritability. The equation for the total population variance of the phenotypes (i.e., actual measurements) for a given characteristic can be specified as follows:

$$V_P = \underbrace{(V_G + V_{AM}) + V_D + V_i}_{V_H \atop \text{Heredity}} + \underbrace{V_E + 2\,\text{Cov}_{HE} + V_I}_{V_E \atop \text{Environment}} + \underset{\text{Error}}{V_e} \quad (1)$$

where: V_P = phenotypic variance.

V_G = genic (or additive) variance.

V_{AM} = variance due to assortative mating.

  $V_{AM} = 0$ under random mating (panmixia).

V_D = dominance deviation variance.

V_i = epistasis (interaction among genes at 2 or more loci).

V_E = environmental variance.

Cov_{HE} = covariance of heredity and environment.

V_I = true statistical interaction of genetic and environmental factors.

V_e = error of measurement (unreliability).

Each of these variance components can be further partitioned into a Between-Families component and a Within-Families component. The Between-Families component in the case of the genetic variance is that proportion of the variance which relatives have in common by virtue of common ancestry; the Within-Families component is that proportion of the variance which they do not share in common, since relatives receive a random selection of genes from their ancestral pool. In the case of environmental variance, the Between-Families component in the variance is shared in common by virtue of the individuals' being *reared* in the same family setting; the Within-Families component is the variance not shared in common by individuals reared in the same family, since environmental variations occur within the family setting.

The estimation of heritability by any one of several known methods is an attempt to estimate the proportion of phenotypic variance attributable to genetic factors. Not every heritability formula takes into account all the components shown in Equation 1. What geneticists refer to as heritability in the 'narrow' sense (or 'strict' sense) is:

$$H_N = \frac{V_B + V_{AM}}{V_G - V_e} \qquad (2)$$

Heritability in the 'broad' sense is:

$$H_B = \frac{V_G + V_{AM} + V_D + V_i}{V_P - V_e} \qquad (3)$$

Other kinds of H are, of course, possible, with values ranging between H_N and H_B, depending on the components included in the numerator. The variance due to the correlation between heredity and environment and to the statistical interaction of genetic and environmental factors do not get included in these fundamental definitions of heritability. The interaction of heredity and environment could be included with the genetic components. The technical definitions of heritability, however, put the genetic environmental interaction on the side of environment and in this sense may be regarded as 'conservative'.

In practice, some formulas intended to estimate H tend to give an underestimate because of the heredity-environment interaction. Loehlin (1971) has shown that the generalized heritability formula (Equation 4 below) proposed by Jensen (1967a) is unaffected by the genetic-environmental interaction. However, the correlation between genotype and environmental influences causes some degree of under-estimation of H by the Jensen formula, as it does with every other formula designed for extracting heritability estimates from twin data. Fortunately, empirical estimates in the case of intelligence test scores have shown that the covariance of

TABLE 5.1. Analysis of variance for intelligence test scores (Burt, 1958)

Source of Variance	Per cent
Genetic:	
Genic (additive)	40·5
Dominance and Epistasis	16·7
Assortative mating	19·9
Environmental:	
Covariance of H and E	10·6
Random (including V_I)	5·9
Unreliability (test error)	6·4
Total	100·0

genotype and environment and the genetic-environmental interaction constitute a very minor proportion of the total variance. One of the best estimates of these components shown in Equation 1 was made by Sir Cyril Burt (1958) from many different kinship correlations in large samples of the London schools population. The results are shown in Table 5.1.

The variance components that account for the correlation between different degrees of kinship, reared apart or reared together, are shown in Table 5.2. The intraclass correlation between members of any particular relationship is:

$$r_i = \frac{\text{sum of components in common}}{\text{total variance}}$$

TABLE 5.2. Variance components in various kinships

Relationship	Reared	Components* in Common				Components not in Common					
		A	D	Ep	EBF	A	D	Ep	EBF	EWF	e
MZ twins	Together	1	1	1	1	0	0	0	0	1	1
MZ twins	Apart	1	1	1	0	0	0	0	1	1	1
DZ twins (sibs)	Together	1/2	1/4	<1/4	1	1/2	3/4	>3/4	0	1	1
DZ twins (sibs)	Apart	1/2	1/4	<1/4	0	1/2	3/4	>3/4	1	1	1
Half-sibs	Together	1/4	0	<1/16	1	3/4	1	>15/16	0	1	1
Half-sibs	Apart	1/4	0	<1/16	0	3/4	1	>15/16	1	1	1
Parent-child	'Together'	1/2	0	<1/4	?>0	1/2	1	>3/4	?<1	1	1
Parent-foster child	'Together'	0	0	0	?>0	1	1	1	?<1	1	1
Unrelated children	Together	0	0	0	1	1	1	1	0	1	1
Unrelated children	Apart	0	0	0	0	1	1	1	0	1	1

* A = Additive.   D = Dominance.   Ep = Epistasis.   EBF = Between-Families environment.   EWF = Within-Families environment.   e = error.

The total variance, of course, consists of the sum of all the variance components (in common and not in common) shown in Table 5.2. If we wished to include the interaction and covariance terms of Equation 1 in Table 5.2, they would go on the side of 'components not in common' in every case. Thus, they would always lower the intraclass correlation between relatives.

Table 5.2 should highlight the fact that heritability estimates based on comparison of identical or monozygotic (MZ) twins with fraternal or dizygotic (DZ) twins give values of H that are actually somewhat inflated in proportion to the degree that dominance and epistasis are important sources of trait variance. MZ twins have *all* of the genetic components in common; DZ twins have something less than half in common overall. The method for estimating the dominance variance is also apparent in Table 5.2: compare DZ twins or sibs, who have one-quarter of their dominance variance in common, with half-sibs or parent-child relationships, which have none of the dominance in common. Examination of the entries in Table 5.2 will reveal which comparisons will yield estimates of other variance components. The same components can often be estimated by comparing different sets of relationships, which provides evidence of the consistency of estimates in the population under consideration.

One of the most valuable relationships from the standpoint of heritability analysis is half-siblings. (I have not been able to find studies of half-siblings reported anywhere in the literature of human genetics.) For one thing, a comparison of half-siblings (of the same mother) and full siblings probably yields the best single estimate we can get of the dominance variance. More important, however, is the fact that half-siblings can give us some information about the effects of individual differences among mothers in the quality of the prenatal environment they provide. A comparison of the correlations between half-sibs having the same mother with those having different mothers should give an indication of the amount of environmental variance attributable to maternal differences in prenatal environment. It is hard to see why the necessary data should be hard to obtain in a society with as high a rate of divorce and remarriage as ours. There must be many half-siblings in the population. Double first cousins could also be used in such comparisons, since they are genetically as much alike as half-sibs but, of course, always have different mothers. Unfortunately, double first cousins are rare in human populations.

Estimation of narrow heritability (H_N)

The proportion of variance due to additive genic effects is important to know if one is interested in the rate of change from one generation to the next under selective breeding. It is only the additive component that 'breeds true'. Sir Ronald Fisher referred to this component as 'the essential genotype'. It is estimated by H_N – heritability in the narrow sense. The value of H_N cannot be determined by the twin method, however. Comparison of parent-child with half-sibs would seem to be the easiest method of estimating H_N. (This estimate would include something less than one-quarter of the epistatic variance, which can be considered as negligible.) The appropriate correlations are simply entered into Jensen's generalized formula (Equation 4). Another estimate of H_N is given directly by the mid-parent – mid-child correlation. H_N, in fact, can be defined theoretically as the correlation between the mid-parent (i.e., mean of the parents) and the mean of an infinite number of their offspring. This offspring mean rapidly asymptotes, so a correlation based on a large sample of average-size families gives a fair estimate. The one attempt I have found to estimate H_N for Stanford-Binet IQ in this fashion is by Jones (1954.) The mid-parent–mid-child raw correlation was 0·693. Corrected for attenuation (i.e., test unreliability) this gives a value of $H_N = 0·72$.

A final reason for cross-checking heritability estimates by various methods is the large sampling error of estimate obtained by any one set of data, especially when the sample size is not large, as is typically the case in twin studies. There may also be systematic biasing factors in one set of kinship correlations that do not exist in correlations for some other degree of kinship. This is why I am impressed by the Erlenmeyer-Kimling and Jarvik (1963) survey of 52 studies of the correlation of relatives for tested intellectual abilities, using a wide variety of intelligence tests and involving some 30,000 correlational pairings obtained from eight countries in four continents. The median values of these correlations probably constitute the best estimates we have of kinship correlations for intelligence. They are shown in Table 5.3, which also includes the expected values if only genetic factors were involved and no assumptions were introduced about assortive mating, selective placement of foster children, and so forth. The expected values are those given by the simplest possible polygenic model. We can obtain three independent estimates of heritability from Table 5.3. (Because the correlations have not been corrected

TABLE 5.3. Correlations for intellectual ability obtained and expected among relatives on the basis of Mendelian inheritance

Correlations between	Number of Studies	Median Correlation, r Obtained*	Expected
Unrelated persons, reared apart	4	−0·01	0
Unrelated persons, reared together	5	+0·23	0
Foster parent-child	3	+0·20	0
Parent-child	12	+0·50	+0·50
Siblings, reared apart	2	+0·42	+0·50
Siblings, reared together	35	+0·49	+0·50
Fraternal twins, opposite sex	9	+0·53	+0·50
Fraternal twins, same sex	11	+0·53	+0·50
Identical twins, reared apart	4	+0·75	+1·00
Identical twins, reared together	14	+0·87	+1·00

* Erlenmeyer-Kimling and Jarvik, 1963.

for attenuation, the values of H in every case are slightly underestimated by about 5 per cent.) The correlation between identical twins reared apart gives one estimate of $H = 0.75$. The comparison of correlations for MZ and DZ twins (reared together), using Jensen's formula (Equation 4) gives a value of $H = 0.75$. Still another estimate consists of 1 minus the difference between correlation of unrelated children reared together, and from this we obtain $H = 0.77$. These independent estimates are highly consistent and if the correlations were corrected for attenuation the H values would average very close to 0.80.

A Generalized Heritability Formula. In 1967 I proposed a generalized heritability formula which can be used to derive heritability estimates from any two sets of kinship correlations where one degree of kinship is closer than the other, e.g., identical (MZ) *v.* fraternal (DZ) twins, sibs *v.* half-sibs, sibs *v.* cousins, and sibs *v.* unrelated children (Jensen, 1967a). In all cases the two groups should consist of pairs either reared together or reared apart; that is to say, both groups must either share or not share the Between-Families environmental component (Table 5.2). When possible, all correlations should be corrected for attenuation, or H will be underestimated. The proposed generalized formula is:

$$H = \frac{r_{AB} - r_{CD}}{\rho_{AB} - \rho_{CD}} \tag{4}$$

where: r_{AB} is the obtained correlation (corrected for test unreliability) between pairs of individuals of a particular degree of kinship.

r_{CD} is the correlation between pairs of individuals whose degree of kinship is less than that of group AB.

ρ_{AB} is the theoretical genetic correlation (i.e., proportion of genes in common) between pairs A and B.

ρ_{CD} is the theoretical genetic correlation between pairs C and D.

With random mating, the theoretical genetic correlations, ρ, between relatives is 1 for identical twins; 0·50 for fraternal twins, siblings, and parent-child; 0·25 for half-siblings, grandparent-grandchild, and double first cousins; 0·125 for first cousins; and 0 for unrelated persons. The values of ρ under a known degree of assortative mating (i.e., parental correlation on the trait in question) can be determined from formulas given elsewhere (see Crow and Felsenstein, 1968; Jensen, 1967a).

When applied to twin data (MZ and DZ reared together), this formulation can be used to obtain estimates of the proportions of Between-Families and Within-Families environmental variance. The proportion of Between-Families variance is:

$$E_B = \frac{r_{DZ} - \rho_s r_{MZ}}{1 - \rho_s} \tag{5}$$

where ρ_s is the genetic correlation between siblings (it is 0·50 under random mating and 0·55 when the parental genetic correlation is 0·25, a conservative estimate). The proportion of Within-Families environmental variance is:

$$E_W = 1 - H - E = 1 - r_{MZ}. \tag{6}$$

Formulation of Correlation Between Persons. An interesting derivation from Equation 4 yields a conceptualization of the correlation between any set of paired individuals, where A is the first in the pair and B is the second:

$$r_{AB} = \rho_G H + \rho_E E_B \tag{7}$$

ρ_G is the theoretical genetic correlation between members of the pair and ρ_E is a parameter for the correlation between their environments. ρ_E is generally assumed to be 1 when the individuals are reared together and 0 when they are reared apart. If there are direct, independent estimates of the degree of environmental similarity, there would, of course, be a basis for substituting other values of ρ_E that lie somewhere between 0 and 1.

Estimating the Mean of a Population from Theoretical Genetic Parameters. If the mean of a population on a given trait can be closely estimated, without being directly estimated from a random sample of the population, by making use of genetic parameters, this would constitute evidence for the genetic determination of the trait. Continuously distributed physical traits that are highly determined by polygenic inheritance, such as stature, head circumference, and fingerprint ridges show a highly precise degree of regression 'to the mean' of the population – for offspring, siblings, and other degrees of kinship, the amount of regression being directly proportional to the remoteness of kinship. The genetically expected value (EX) of a characteristic for a relative (R) of a 'target' person (T) can be expressed as:

$$EX_R = \rho_G(X_T - M_P) + M_P \tag{8}$$

where: EX_R = the expected value of the relative of the target person.

X_T = value of target person.

M_P = mean value for the population from which T and R are drawn.

ρ_G = the theoretical genetic correlation between T and R. (Under the assumptions of random mating, no dominance, epistasis, or genetic-environment interaction, these values are 1 for MZ twins, 0·50 for parent-child, DZ twins and full siblings, 0·25 for half-siblings and double first cousins, and 0, for unrelated persons.)

From this equation it should be possible to estimate M_P by measuring a target group (T) and measuring their relatives, even if the target group is a highly select sample, such as children in gifted classes or classes for the educable mentally retarded. It should little matter how the target group is selected, so long as they are not pathological. The expected value of the population mean (EM_P) is obtained by transposing Equation 8:

$$EM_P = \frac{\Sigma[(X_R - \rho_G X_T)/(1 - \rho_G)]}{N} \qquad (9)$$

where: EM_P = expected mean of population.

X_T = value of target person, T.

X_R = value of relative, R, of target person.

N = number of T-R pairs.

If T and R are siblings, $\rho_G = 0·50$ under the simplest assumptions, and Equation 9 can be simplified:

$$EM_P = \frac{\Sigma(2X_S - X_T)}{N} \qquad (10)$$

where: X_S = the value of the sibling of T.

The discrepancy between EM_P as obtained by Equations 9 or 10 and M_P as obtained from a random sample of the population provides an indication of the degree to which the population distribution of scores can be accounted for by assuming a simple polygenic model. We can work this procedure in reverse, and estimate ρ_G simply by selecting subjects at random from a defined population and computing the correlation between relatives and seeing how discrepant the obtained values of r are from the theoretical ρ_G for any given degree of kinship. The data summarized by Erlenmeyer-Kimling and Jarvik (1963), shown in Table 5.3, are the median values of such correlations from a large number of studies. The discrepancies between obtained and expected values are, of course, assumed to be due to the influence of non-genetic factors. (The discrepancies, however, are slightly reduced if the expected values are derived from a more complex genetic model (Burt, 1966).) The considerable consistency of the degree to which environmental factors (excluding prenatal effects) cause discrepancies between correlations among relatives is shown by plotting the median values of all the correlations reported in the literature for various kinships reared together and reared apart, as shown in Figure 5.1.

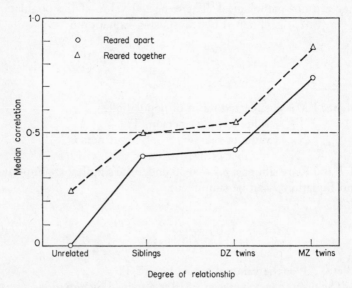

FIGURE 5.1. Median values of all correlations reported in the literature for the indicated kinships (Erlenmeyer-Kimling and Jarvik, 1963)

Checks on the Obtained Correlations for Different Kinships. At times there may be some doubt about the reported kinship of relatives in the population under study. This is probably extremely rare in the case of twins, but may constitute a serious source of error for siblings and half-siblings, especially in populations with high rates of illegitimacy and multiple paternities within the same nominal family unit. Correlations can be checked and corrected, however, in terms of 'baseline' correlations based on physical characteristics of known high heritability. Perhaps the most ideal measurement for this purpose is fingerprint ridge count, which Sir Ronald Fisher originally suggested could be used as a 'sheet anchor' for assessing other kinship correlations. Fingerprint ridges may be measured with a high degree of reliability and the quantitative values when used in kinship correlations correspond perfectly to a simple additive genetic model without assortative mating. The correlations between relatives come as close to the theoretical values as reliability of measurement and sampling error permit (Holt, 1961). For large samples ($N = 100$), the obtained correlations (corrected for attenuation) show a virtually perfect fit to the theoretical values. This only means, of course, that the heritability of fingerprints is 100 per cent. Since fingerprints may not always be available or obtainable, correlations for other highly heritable physical traits may serve the purpose nearly as well. Head circumference and standing height, standardized for chronological age, have heritabilities only slightly lower than fingerprints (Huntly, 1966). Correlations (corrected for attenuation) between relatives on the trait under study can be further 'corrected' simply by dividing them by the correlations (corrected for attenuation) on a highly heritable physical trait in the same sample. Given the precision of fingerprint correlations and a fairly large sample size, it should be possible quite accurately to estimate the proportion of half-sibs in a group of all nominal siblings which actually contain some proportion of half-sibs. If one wanted to go even further in 'purifying' the sample, a number of independent genetic polymorphisms could be used in a discriminant function analysis to exclude, with a specified probability of error, individual pairs of subjects from the sample as not belonging to the particular kinship classification in question. This is essentially the same method as used for determining the zygosity of twins.

Sibling Correlations Alone. Can sibling correlations alone provide us with any information at all concerning the heritability of test scores? I believe they can, but only in a one-sided fashion. If the correlation is close to the genetically expected value, we can say it is consistent with a genetic model and the heritability of the test in question may be high. But this is not proved by a sibling correlation alone, because a correlation of 0·50 could arise also from strictly environmental factors without any genetic determination whatsoever. If, on the other hand, the correlation significantly departs in *either* direction from the theoretical genetic value, we can be quite sure that the trait variance has a significant environmental component. This information can be used for roughly classifying measurements of various psychological characteristics for their degree of environmental determination in the population on which they are obtained. For example, psychological tests range along a continuum of the absolute deviation of the sibling correlation from the theoretical genetic value. This use of sibling correlations is proposed only as a less than optimal substitute for heritability estimates which require correlations in at least two kinship groups.

Heritability and Psychometrics. Characteristics of psychological and educational tests such as the mean, standard deviation, reliability, validity, and factorial composition are unquestionably important parameters of psychological tests and have a long tradition of being the main questions asked about any test. The heritability of the test in the normative populations (or various sub-populations) should be added to this list. We should know more about the degree to which score variance on particular tests is attributable to genetic and environmental sources within the population in which the test is used. The heritability of a test is, of course, not a constant value; it can vary from one age group to another, from one sub-population to another, and from one generation to another in the same population. It is an interesting index in the case of ability and achievement tests in that it tells us a good deal about equality of environmental conditions for mental development in the population. With increasing improvement and equalization of the environmental conditions needed for children's optimal mental development, including greater equality of educational opportunity, there should be an increase in the heritability of intelligence and scholastic achievement scores. Greater increases in H should be expected in sub-populations whose environmental conditions are upgraded and equalized most. Because of much potentially valuable information about population changes that can be gotten from heritability estimates, I would urge that large-scale assessment programs make a point of obtaining various kinship correlations, especially for twins and siblings, that can be used in heritability formulas. For this reason I urged the National Assessment Program, which proposes to test a representative sample of over 150,000 of the U.S. population on a kind of general intelligence and educational achievement test, to obtain test results on MZ and DZ twins, a large number of which should turn up in a sample of 150,000 persons. The heritability of the test in different socio-economic and racial sub-groups of the population could be determined from these data and would provide a basis for assessing future changes in an important population parameter, in addition to the changes in means and variances. My suggestion along these lines to the Director and Advisory Board of the National Assessment Program unfortunately was rejected. At present the only large-scale testing programs I know of that have systematically collected twin data in this country are the National Merit Scholarship Corporation and the American Institute of Research in the Project TALENT study. The Scandinavian countries are far ahead of us in this sphere; they have established national twin registries, in which are kept records on every pair of twins in the entire population. Such a data bank is of great potential value to researchers in the fields of medicine, psychology, sociology, and criminology, to name a few. We would do well to follow suit. We are especially lacking such data in our minority populations.

Heritability as a Criterion of the Status-Fairness of Ability Tests. The inventors and developers of intelligence tests – men such as Galton, Binet, Spearman, Burt, Thorndike, and Terman – clearly intended that their tests assess as clearly as possible the individual's innate brightness or mental capacity. If this is what a test attempts to do, then clearly the appropriate criterion for judging the test's 'fairness' is the *heritability* of the test scores in the population in which the test is used. The quite high values of H for tests such as the Stanford-Binet attests to the success of the test-maker's aim to measure innate ability. The square root of the heritability, $(\sqrt{H})$, represents the correlation between phenotype and genotype, and, as pointed out before, this is of the order of 0·9 for our best standard intelligence tests. However, I would be hesitant to generalize this statement beyond the Caucasian population of the United States and Great Britain, since nearly all the major heritability studies have been performed in these populations. At present there are no really adequate data on the heritability of intelligence tests in the American Negro population. In my own work so far I have not gone beyond obtaining IQ correlations between a large number of Negro sibling pairs. The intraclass correlation for siblings ($N = 380$) was 0·46 (0·50 when corrected for attenuation) for a group-administered intelligence test. The fact that this value does not differ significantly from the sibling correlation for Caucasians would lead me to predict that heritability estimates obtained in the Negro population probably will not differ markedly from the values of H typically found in the Caucasian population. But this is far from certain, as I have indicated elsewhere (Jensen, 1970a), and the facts should be determined directly by means of full-fledged heritability studies. Values of H may well differ for Negroes and Caucasians from one test to another. The 'fairness' of various tests in each population is indexed by the test's H value in that population. It is quite conceivable that tests having the same *predictive* validity in two populations may have quite different H values in those populations. Though two tests may give the same degree of prediction of success in college, in the Armed Services, or in industry, if the tests differ in H, their results may lead to differences in just who gets screened out in the selection procedure. This is why I believe H should be determined especially on tests used in selection procedures wherever there is concern about eliminating unfair discrimination and an effort is made to insure equality of opportunity. I believe we should estimate the H of current widely used tests and develop methodologies for maximizing or minimizing H values, so that tests with very high and very low H values can be made for use wherever tests of high or low heritability seem most appropriate. We know nothing of the predictive validities of tests intended for various purposes such as academic and personnel selection, as a function of their H values.

Heritability and Group Comparisons. Can heritability estimates tell us anything about whether group differences are attributable to genetic or environmental factors or to some specifiable proportion for each source of between-groups variance? My conclusion is that heritability by itself cannot answer this question, but that heritability estimates combined with other data and certain assumptions, which may or may not be tenable, may provide some reduction in uncertainty concerning the nature-nurture controversy with respect to social class and race differences in abilities.

If the heritability of a trait is 100 per cent in both groups A and B, and if A and B are reared in environments that 'overlap' each other on factors relevant to the development of the trait, then it would probably be safe to say that a mean difference between groups A and B is due to a difference in genotypes. When heritability is considerably less than 100 per cent, as in the case of measures of intelligence and other important psychological characteristics, the answer to the questions of group differences becomes considerably more speculative. If H is less than 100 per cent but is the same in groups A and B, and if groups A and B are reared under conditions which on the average are indistinguishable, then, too, it would probably be safe to say that a mean difference between groups A and B is due to genetic factors.

What can we say, however, when the environment is *not* the same for A and B? Assume that we can rate or measure environments on some scale that is relevant to the development of the trait in question, say, intelligence as measured by our typical tests. If groups A and B show no overlap in their distributions of environmental ratings, then I believe nothing can be said about their genotypes if the group with the lower mean intelligence also has the poorer environment. If the group with the lower mean intelligence has the better environment, however, one could then claim this as evidence that the groups differ genetically.

In most cases, however, the group with the lower mean also has poorer environmental conditions. Can heritability estimates throw any light on group comparisons in this situation? I believe it can if there is substantial overlap between the relevant environmental conditions of the groups being compared; the environments need not be equal in the two populations, but they must overlap. Then we can take the following tack, which I put forth at this point only for discussion and criticism. If it is inadequate it may at least help to suggest a better method. If $M_A < M_B$ and

$H_A = H_B$, and if we hypothesize that groups A and B do *not* differ genetically on the trait in question, we must conclude that there is a constant environmental decrement for each member of group A. Thus, if individuals from groups A and B are matched by pairs on the test scores (i.e., $M_A = M_B$), then the genetic value of group A would have to be higher than the genetic value of B. If we then compare these matched groups on a different measure of the same trait, but one which has higher heritability in both groups, group A should exceed group B, $(M_B < M_A)$. On the other hand, if we used still another test of the same trait which had lower heritability in both groups, we should expect the reverse, that is, $M_B > M_A$. (Of course, in each case correction would be made for regression due to measurement error.)

This, then, illustrates the rationale of one method by which heritability estimates may serve to reduce the heredity-environment uncertainty. The method can, of course, be made more general in practice. As a beginning, for example, one could estimate the heritabilities of a variety of mental abilities tests in the population sub-groups one wishes to compare. We would expect a considerable range of values of H for the various tests, and there could be different values of H for any one test in the two population groups, A and B. The next step would be graphically to plot separately for each group the median overlap (i.e., the percentage of subjects in group A who exceed the median of group B) between groups A and B on the various tests as a function of the test's heritability. (Median overlap is on the ordinate; heritability is on the abscissa.) If the median overlap between A and B increases with an increase in H, it would favor the hypothesis that the difference between groups A and B is mainly the result of differences in environmental factors. If median overlap decreased with increases in H, on the other hand, it presumably would be indicative of a genetic difference between the groups. I will leave it to the statisticians to work out the optimal test of the statistical significance of the slopes of these plots relating median overlap to the H values of different tests. I imagine the statistical problems are not insurmountable, since confidence limits can be established both for H and for median overlap. It seems fairly certain that a large sample size would be needed to make this type of analysis statistically worthwhile.

I think we might learn important things if analyses of this type were made. To go far out in search of any data that even begins to resemble the requirements for such an analysis, I note some of the data in the well-known Coleman Report (1966). Other studies have shown that intelligence tests, especially non-verbal tests, have generally higher heritabilities than scholastic achievement tests and highly verbal tests of intelligence (Jensen, 1967a), at least in British and American populations. The Coleman study did not attempt to determine the heritability of its psychological and educational tests. But it came up with some interesting findings which could be better understood if we did have heritability estimates on the tests in the various population categories used in the Coleman study. For example, it was found that Southern Negro children scored higher on verbal and scholastic achievement tests, relative to the non-verbal intelligence test, while Negroes in the North and West scored lower on the verbal and scholastic tests relative to the non-verbal test. Negroes in the rural South showed the largest discrepancy between the non-verbal and achievement tests, with higher scores on the scholastic achievement tests. What is the meaning of these findings? I submit we would be closer to knowing the answer if we knew the heritabilities of these various tests in the different subpopulations.

The Achievement of More Refined Genetic Models. So long as we depend only upon omnibus-type psychological tests on which the individual's score represents a conglomerate of mental processes, skills, response tendencies, and their interactions with procedural factors in psychological testing – all with unknown weightings in the composite score – we will not be able to advance our understanding of the inheritance of mental abilities beyond the crudest and simplest models of polygenic inheritance. In order to advance further our knowledge of human behavioral genetics, especially as regards individual differences in mental abilities, I believe we will have to make more highly analytical studies of the psychological components of particular abilities. I have suggested one approach to this problem elsewhere (Jensen, 1965a). Memory span (digit span), for example, is a subtest in many omnibus tests of intelligence such as the Stanford-Binet and the Wechsler. Corrected for attenuation, it correlates 0·75 with both Stanford-Binet and Wechsler total scores (minus digit span). It has a loading of 0·80

H

on the *g* factor in these tests. It can therefore be regarded as an important test of mental ability. In my laboratory we are taking digit span apart through a combination of experimental analysis and factor analysis. First of all, it is gratifying to find that individual differences in digit span are highly reliable and stable in young adults. It is possible to obtain measurements of individual differences that are as reliable as measures of physical characteristics such as height and weight. Furthermore, it is apparent that digit span is not a unitary ability. It has a number of subcomponents on which there are reliable individual differences. I plan to go on fractionating digit span ability until just about all conceivable reliable sources of individual differences have been exhausted. How many dimensions of 'ability' will ultimately be found to constitute what we call 'memory span' is still anyone's guess. I put 'ability' in quotes, because the components of digit span ability may not even resemble *abilities* as we ordinarily use this term. When digit span (to use only one example) is thus fractionated into reliably measurable factors or components, will these components better lend themselves to quantitative genetic analysis than the more conglomerate score or than conventional intelligence test scores? May not the components – the 'atoms' of ability, so to speak – be controlled by fewer genes and by more specific environmental factors? If so, it would seem that such experimental analysis of abilities, hand in hand with quantitative genetic analysis, should make possible greater progress in understanding the nature and nurture of mental abilities than we have known heretofore.

Extending the spectrum of measured abilities

What if it turns out that tests of *g* which do in fact meet acceptable criteria of status-fairness still show mean differences between various social class and racial groups? And what if such tests have the same predictive power for all groups in the present educational system? How could such a state of affairs be reconciled with our ideals and hopes for equality of educational and occupational opportunity for all persons in all segments of the population?

The answer will come, I believe, by putting *g* in its proper place. It now carries much more weight in school than it ever has in life outside of school. And much of its importance in the world of occupations is derived from their often unwarranted dependence upon formal educational attainments as selection criteria.

The educational system operates in such a way as to maximize the importance of g as a source of variance in scholastic attainment. Yet g is only one aspect, perhaps not even a major aspect, of mental ability. Throughout the preceding discussions I have used the terms 'intelligence' and 'mental ability'. I have not used them interchangeably. By 'intelligence' I have referred to that aspect of ability that is tapped by tests heavily loaded on g – the capacity for abstract reasoning, or 'the eduction of relations and correlates', to use Spearman's original definition. By 'mental ability' I refer to the full spectrum of abilities, of which g is only a part. If tests are 'unfair', it is more likely to be because of their limited sampling of the total spectrum of abilities than because of culturally biased content. Even if our intelligence tests meet all the usual criteria of fairness, they could still be unfair in the sense that they fail to tap other abilities that could be just as important as g for educational and occupational achievement.

It is possible to design instruction in school subjects (or almost anything else) in such a way as to maximize the importance of g and minimize the importance of all other abilities. We know it is possible because it is what we are doing all the time in school. In such a situation intelligence tests heavily loaded on g will inevitably have high predictive validity. But does this mean that g is the most essential ability for learning under any and all conditions of instruction? I seriously doubt it.

It seems to me that the *sine qua non* of educability under any conditions is not g, but learning ability – the ability to acquire information and skills by one means or another. What I call basic learning ability is, in the final analysis, the most fundamental source of individual differences. It is not the same as g. While it is rare to find children high on measures of g who do not also perform well on measures of basic learning ability, we find many children, especially among groups called disadvantaged, who score low on tests of g but whose performance on direct learning tests is average or above in relation to middle-class norms.

It is a common observation of many teachers of children called disadvantaged that those in the IQ range from 60 to 80 seem much brighter than their IQs would suggest on the basis of experience with middle-class children of the same IQ. Usually the brightness shows up, however, only in non-scholastic activities. We have found in our research that although this brightness is not tapped by any standard IQ tests, it can be tapped by direct learning tests. Most of these children are capable of learning with an ease and speed far beyond what one would predict on the basis of their conventional IQs. The two main reasons that they do not perform better scholastically than would be expected from their IQs are (*a*) the instruction is geared to their weakest abilities and not their strongest, and (*b*) after the first year or two in the classroom they become 'turned off' for scholastic activities because of lack of the reinforcement that comes from success in learning.

At least part of the answer will consist of discovering abilities other than *g* that can be brought into play by appropriate instructional techniques to achieve useful and realistic educational goals, which includes the 3 Rs and other traditional forms of scholastic attainment in addition to more specific occupational knowledge and skills. Thus, the true meaning of culture-fair or status-fair testing, it seems to me, is to assess as broad a spectrum of abilities as possible and to design instruction so as to capitalize on existing strengths. For many children in our school population we should strive to *lower* the correlation between conventional IQs and scholastic attainment and boost the correlation between direct learning measures and scholastic attainment.

Our research on learning abilities in disadvantaged children shows that their strength exists in their fundamental ability to learn, whether they are high *g* or low *g*. If they are high *g*, they can learn in the traditional classroom. If they are low *g*, they fail in the traditional classroom. But most of those in the latter group have shown that they can learn just as well as any other children when given learning tasks in our laboratory.

On learning tasks involving memory span, serial learning, paired-associate learning, trial-and-error selective learning, and free recall of certain kinds of informational input, we find highly reliable individual differences in performance but no significant differences in the distribution of scores as a function of social class or racial background. Some of this research has been described elsewhere (Jensen, 1968a, b and c; Jensen and Rohwer, 1970). To summarize briefly, we have found that children of low-SES whose IQs are in the range below 90 on standard intelligence tests are quite different from middle-class children of the same IQs in associative learning ability. Low-SES children of relatively low measured IQ are generally markedly superior to their middle-class counterparts in IQ tests involving free recall, serial learning, paired-associate learning, and digit span. Low-SES children of average IQ or above, on the other hand, do not differ from their middle-class counterparts in these associative learning abilities. This interaction among IQ, associative learning ability, and socio-economic status has been found in children sampled from Caucasian, Mexican-American, and Negro populations.

My current attempts to conceptualize these findings in a theoretical model that will suggest further hypotheses and empirical investigations is based on the notion of a hierarchy of mental abilities going from associative learning to conceptual thinking, in which the development of lower levels in the hierarchy is necessary but not sufficient for the development of the more complex levels involving symbolic or abstract thinking, conceptual learning, semantic generalization, and the use of language as a 'tool of thought' in learning and problem solving. A crucial question concerns the extent to which the development of these complex abilities are determined by the nature of environmental inputs. The fact that the best tests of these abilities, such as the *Progressive Matrices*, have quite high heritability suggests that the development of these complex mental abilities depends upon the development of innate neural structures, so that appropriate environmental influences may be necessary but not sufficient for their manifestation in performance. As for associative learning ability, which may be a necessary but not sufficient substrata in the development of conceptual abilities, there is no reason to believe that it is not at least as heritable as psychometric intelligence, although there is little direct evidence on the heritability of associative learning ability in humans. It is likely that both types of ability, associative and conceptual, are highly determined by genetic factors. The important point is that individual differences in associative learning ability *per se* apparently are not differentially distributed according to socio-economic background.

But such exploration of learning ability has only begun, and it is possible that instructional techniques can be developed that will mobilize various learning capacities in the classroom to achieve much the same educational goals that have traditionally depended in such large measure on a limited pattern of cognitive processes, generally characterized by *g*. Perhaps more thought and effort should go into discovering ways of radically making over our educational methods to accord with the full variety and range of children's innate patterns of mental abilities. The long-term rewards from such efforts, I believe, will be greater than any derived from massive efforts to shape all children to the requirements of an instructional system which inordinately emphasizes one type of ability at the expense of all others. The ideal of equality of educational opportunity should mean the opportunity for every child to put his *best* foot forward on the path to achieving his educational and occupational goals.

Selection of minority students in higher education

The boom in higher education

In the past decade the United States has seen a fantastic boom in higher education. Nothing like it has ever happened in any other country or in any other period of history. Unfortunately, but not surprisingly, it would be fallacious to equate the quantity of increase in college attendance with the quality of the product. College attendance, if not graduation, is now viewed by most middle-class parents as an essential ingredient for their children's getting ahead in the world, and the pressure on today's high school graduates to 'go on to college' is enormous. Increasing numbers of youths are forced to college not by aptitudes for and interests in academic studies, but in pursuit of the educational union cards that so many view as the *sine qua non* of the good life in our education-conscious society. In the past fifteen years American colleges have increased in enrollment from about 3 million to 7·1 million. Some 40 per cent of American youths now continue their formal education beyond high school.

A currently conspicuous element of the general insistence on a college education is the demand for equal opportunity for educationally disadvantaged minority groups, especially the black population, which historically has had much less than a fair share of social, economic, and educational opportunity. The present demand that minority groups have equal opportunities throughout the educational ladder, from pre-school and kindergarten through college and graduate training, is one that, if realized, would benefit the whole society. No effort should be spared in pursuit of this

223

goal. Indeed, vigorous efforts are already underway at all levels of education.

The drive for equal educational opportunities has highlighted certain problems which become most conspicuous and troublesome in the sphere of higher education. It is not that colleges create the problems. They are essentially the same educational problems of the disadvantaged that already exist in the first grade in school; they are only greatly magnified at the college level. Before proceeding further, however, it will help to focus the following discussion if we divide the educational problems of the disadvantaged into two main categories, which we will label simply as *extrinsic* and *intrinsic*.

Extrinsic and intrinsic problems in minority education

The *extrinsic* problems are those barriers to equal opportunity in education, employment, housing, and the like, that are a direct result of racial prejudice and discrimination, and economic disadvantage. Unfortunately these factors still exist, more so in some regions than in others, though they are clearly diminishing. Fortunately, they can be combatted by changing people's attitudes regarding racial discrimination, and through legislation. Since it is more feasible to enact and enforce laws than to change attitudes, citizens and their representatives in government must exercise unrelenting pressure for enacting and enforcing laws that help to wipe out all forms of discrimination and unequal opportunity connected with individuals' race or national origin. Also, public subsidy of higher education for all interested and qualified economically disadvantaged persons should become the general rule. In principle, these problems classified as extrinsic should be the easiest for society to solve. I believe and perceive that the majority of citizens are making steady progress toward the desired goal of true equality of opportunity through goodwill and a sense of justice.

But there still remains the other category of problems I have labeled *intrinsic*. Blacks and other disadvantaged minorities understandably want not only equality of opportunity, but equality of performance as well. The problems associated with this legitimate aspiration unfortunately are not so simple as to be attributable to any lack of goodwill or good intentions on the part of anyone. These are real problems, difficult problems, that loom before all those who are working for equality of educational opportunity for all citizens. The extrinsic factors referred to above seem almost trivial by comparison with the problems that remain even after the barriers of social discrimination in educational treatment are removed. At present, in most of the nation, the problems of minority selection and performance in higher education are almost entirely of the intrinsic variety. By intrinsic, I do not mean irremediable, or that we can point to some group of persons, least of all to the minority persons themselves, who are 'to blame' for the problem. By intrinsic I mean only that the problems are not of the kind that can be solved merely by legislation or by a change of attitudes or policies on the part of educators and college admission boards. While the extrinsic problems may be of considerable legal and political interest, they are of only minor interest from a psychological standpoint, since the intrinsic problems would still exist even if we could eliminate the extrinsic problems overnight. Indeed, as the extrinsic problems of racial discrimination and economic disadvantage are diminished, the remaining intrinsic problems become even more starkly apparent. It is with these intrinsic problems, especially with their psychological aspects, that the present article is concerned. It aims to describe the problem as clearly as our present information permits and to try to gain some understanding of the problem in terms of psychological and educational research.

The aspiration of minorities for college education

Proportionally fewer blacks than whites graduate from high school; still fewer blacks go on to college; and still fewer blacks attend predominantly white colleges, to say nothing of the more selective and prestigious colleges and universities. Alexander Astin, director of research for the American Council on Education, has summarized the situation:

> Among the 1·5 million new freshmen who entered college in 1968, between 6 and 7 per cent were black. Even though many colleges have gone to considerable effort recently to recruit more black students, the proportion has changed only slightly since

H*

1966. In short, the representation of blacks among new college students is far below their representation in the college-age population (about 12 per cent) and shows little evidence of increasing. Furthermore, those blacks who do attend college are not distributed evenly among the various types of institutions. Nearly half of all black freshmen, for example, attend predominantly Negro colleges, while more than half of all the institutions in the country enroll freshmen in classes in which blacks make up less than 2 per cent (1969).

The problem, then, is that there continues to be virtually *de facto* segregation in American colleges, despite recent efforts of leading institutions to recruit larger numbers of minority students. The problem is even more acute at the graduate level and in admissions to professional schools, such as law and medicine, because of the large proportion enrolled as freshmen who fail to complete their undergraduate education.

The pressure to recruit more blacks into college is an understandable corollary of the yearning of Americans in general for educational prestige and of the nation's commitment to improving the lot of blacks and other historically disadvantaged groups in our population. Higher education is viewed as a prime instrument in this endeavor. Not only higher education, but the prestigious higher education associated with highly selective big name institutions is seen by many as necessary for the social, economic, and political advancement of the black population.

Sir Arthur Lewis, a professor of economics at Princeton University and a distinguished member of the black community, has clearly expressed this educational goal of black Americans:

> While we are 11 percent of the population, we have only two percent of the jobs at the top, four percent of the jobs in the middle, and are forced into as much as 27 percent of the jobs at the bottom. Clearly, our minimum objective must be to capture 11 percent of the jobs in the middle, and of the jobs at the top.
>
> The road to the top in the great American corporations and other institutions is through education. Scientists, engineers, lawyers, financial administrators, Presidential advisers – all these are recruited from the university. Indeed nearly all of the

top people come from a select number of colleges – from some 50 or 60 of the country's 1647 degree-granting institutions. The breakthrough of the Afro-American into these colleges is therefore absolutely fundamental to the larger economic strategy of black power.

... I am talking about the university partly because it has become so controversial, and partly because if we conquer the top it will make much easier the conquering of the middle – both in our own minds, and in other people's minds.

What can the good white college do for its black students that black colleges like Howard or Lincoln or Fisk cannot do? It can give our people the kind of cachet that is looked for by people who fill the top jobs in the large corporations and other institutions which do the greater part of the country's business. To put it in unpopular language, it can train them to become top members of The Establishment.

. . . .

... Any kind of America that you can visualize, whether capitalist, communist, fascist or any other kind of *ist*, is going to consist of large institutions like General Motors under one name or another. It will have people at the top, middle and bottom. And the problem of the black will essentially be the same whether he is going to be mostly in the bottom jobs, or whether he will also get his 11-percent share of the top and middle. And his chance at the top is going to depend on getting the same kind of technical training that the whites get as their gateway to the top (Lewis, 1969).

This, then, is the understandable and worthy aspiration not only of blacks but of all who wish to right the wrongs of inequality of opportunity, of social and economic disadvantage. The chief problem in realizing this aspiration has not been a lack of willingness and support by colleges, least of all those in the top league. The problem has been that there have not been nearly enough blacks who are even minimally qualified by interest and academic preparation for a reasonable chance of success in first-rate colleges. Highly competitive recruiting by colleges across the country has not been able to fill the desired quotas recently established for minority students in our leading institutions, public and private.

So far short have these efforts fallen that some educators are advocating the abandonment of the usual standards for college admission in terms of academic preparation as indicated by high school records and college entrance examinations. Dr O. B. Parker, of Virginia Commonwealth University, for example, has urged that state colleges must educate as many 'high risk' black students as they can recruit, even those whose high school records are totally unpromising. He insisted, 'Any institution, no matter how prestigious, that isn't reflecting this fact is not doing an adequate job'. Is the difficulty of finding enough blacks who are promising college material really so great as to force the recruitment of such 'high risk' students in order to achieve a greater proportion of blacks on college campuses?

The probable supply of college qualified blacks

Qualification for college work is not an entirely arbitrary criterion but is dependent upon the standards and degree of selectivity that the college has traditionally maintained. It is well known that colleges' academic standards differ greatly, as expressed in the common phrase among college admissions officers and high school counselors, 'there's a college for every level of ability'. This is not quite true, but it is true that American colleges span a range of academic standards that will accommodate at least 60 per cent of high school graduates. On the other hand, only the top 10 to 15 per cent of youths, in academic aptitude and scholastic preparation, can reasonably be expected to succeed in the nation's more selective colleges. Few high school graduates of *any* ethnic group or socio-economic level are adequately qualified to succeed in Harvard, Princeton, or MIT.

A student has the best chance of profiting from a college in which the general level of the student body's abilities and preparation is not too disparate from his own. A useful index of developed academic aptitudes and skills highly predictive of performance in college is the well-known Scholastic Aptitude Test or SAT. It has two main parts – the Verbal, called SAT-V, and the Quantitative, called SAT-Q. The SAT-V is the most frequently used and the most predictive for most college curricula; the SAT-Q has its greatest predictive validity for students in the physical sciences and engineering. The SAT is standardized on a nation-wide basis, so that the scores have approximately the same meaning no matter where or when the test was taken. Nationwide, high school graduates who aspire to go to college and who take the SAT as a basis for selection or admission, have an average score of 500. The test has a standard deviation of 100 points; this means that 16 per cent obtain scores below 400, 16 per cent obtain scores above 600, and 68 per cent obtain scores between 400 and 600. Most students who score 500 on the SAT-V have IQs between 115 and 120. Thus, the SAT-V average of 500 is slightly more than one standard deviation above the mean for the general population. Most selective colleges use some combination of high school grades, recommendations, and SAT (or equivalent) scores as the basis for selection and admission. Since SAT scores are not the only criterion, one usually cannot identify any specific score which is the selection cut-off for a particular college or group of colleges of a given category, such as Ivy League colleges. In practice, however, most selective colleges do not admit students whose scores are much below a SAT-V of 500. Harvard's range may go as low as 500, for example, because many other criteria are used. But the average will be at least 100 to 200 points above this lower boundary. The average score of entering freshmen at Berkeley is close to 600. The top 50 or 60 most selective private and public colleges and universities – the ones presumably referred to in the previously quoted statement by Sir Arthur Lewis – would nearly all fall in a similar range. In other words, they are admitting the top 10 to 15 per cent of high school graduates in scholastic aptitude and preparation for college work.

What proportion of black students would meet the same criteria? Surveys by the College Entrance Examination Board estimate that not more than 15 per cent and perhaps as few as 10 per cent of Negro high school seniors score above 400 on the SAT-V, and only 1 or 2 per cent score 500 or more. On the basis of the College Board Statistics, Professor Julian C. Stanley, of Johns Hopkins University, has estimated the total *number* of black high school graduates who could be admitted by the usual criteria to a Johns Hopkins-level college, which may be regarded as fairly representative of the nation's selective colleges. Stanley states that to succeed academically at Hopkins an entering student needs at least upper-20 per cent ability on College Board tests *and* demon-strated ability to earn good grades in high school. (Grades are indicative not only of ability but of interest, motivation, applica-tion and other non-intellectual characteristics that enter into scholastic achievement.) Stanley (1969) asks,

> Firstly, how many Hopkins-level black male high school gradu-ates become available each year? A few rough calculations will quickly give us an approximate figure. If 3,500,000 babies are born in the United States during a given year, 6% of them are black males, half of those black males graduate from high school, 2% of those graduates score 500 or more on SAT-V, and half of those have high enough grades, we find the number to be 1,050.

Stanley estimates that if both males and females were included, the yearly number of available candidates would be about 3,000, a figure more than double that for men alone, since 'black women seem academically abler, on the average than black men, and more persistent and successful in school'. (This sex difference is discussed in detail in a later section.) Thus, if Stanley's estimate of 3,000 available black students per year who meet the usual entrance criteria for selective colleges is reasonably accurate there simply are not enough qualified blacks to 'go round' to all the selective colleges now competing for increased enrollment of black students. But this is only the most visible aspect of the problem, that small part of the iceberg that troubles those college admissions boards desiring more than a 'token' 1 or 2 per cent of black students on their campuses. For without special recruiting and special standards, the percentage of blacks on most college campuses is rarely more than 1 to 2 per cent of the total student enrollment. In 1964, under the usual admissions procedures, for example, Berkeley enrolled only 1·1 per cent blacks, although public schools in the vicinity had nearly 40 per cent black students.

It is doubtful whether predominantly Negro colleges are promis-ing recruiting grounds for selective white colleges. Too few of their students are in the range of developed scholastic abilities as assessed by the SAT or similar tests to have a reasonable chance of succeeding in the top white colleges. Stanley, for example, compared the SAT-V scores over an eight-year period (1957-65) of the three predominantly Negro co-educational state colleges in

Georgia with the three predominantly non-Negro state colleges in Georgia that in 1964-65 had the *lowest* SAT-V averages of all the state colleges. Stanley (1967) found,

> The median for Negro males (SAT-V = 254·0) was at the 1·1th percentile of the white male distribution (median SAT-V = 399·9), indicating that 98·9 percent of the white males exceeded the median of the Negro males. The median of the Negro females (258·0) was at the 1·0th percentile of the white female distribution (median = 419·3): 99 percent of the white females exceeded the median of the Negro females.

Stanley concludes,

> It would appear, then, that if these predominantly Negro state colleges in Georgia were abolished, the bulk of individuals formerly destined for them might not, even disregarding direct racial prejudice, be acceptable to admission officers of most of the least selective four-year predominantly non-Negro state colleges in Georgia. The situation would probably not be much better in the four Georgia state junior colleges, for which the *lowest* SAT-V mean of either sex in 1964-65 was 359·2; compare this with 275·8, the *highest* mean for either sex in any of the three predominantly Negro colleges.

The five or six elite predominantly Negro colleges in the United States, of course, have considerably higher SAT-V averages than the Georgia state colleges mentioned by Stanley. Freshmen in the elite Negro colleges have a SAT-V average close to 400. But there are probably few, if any, predominantly Negro colleges in which the mean SAT-V score of enrolled beginning freshman is as high as 450. The vast majority of students, regardless of their race or socio-economic level, with SAT-V scores below 500 would experience inordinate difficulties academically in the nation's top 50 or so selective colleges and few indeed could be expected to persist to graduation.

Reasons for the dearth of college qualified blacks

Before considering the validity of the traditional college selection criteria, particularly entrance examinations such as the SAT, let us accept them for the time being at their face value in order to attempt to understand why their use results in the scarcity of black students for recruitment by selective colleges wishing to apply their standard admission criteria to all prospective students.

The College Entrance Examination Board's Scholastic Aptitude Test (SAT) is the most typical and most widely used college entrance examination. It is essentially a high-level test of verbal and quantitative comprehension and reasoning. It differs from most tests of general intelligence in that it samples from the total spectrum of human mental abilities a narrower range of mental abilities and that it depends to a somewhat greater extent on certain developed scholastic skills, such as reading and arithmetic. The particular abilities tapped by the SAT are those most relevant to the academic demands of the typical college curriculum. SAT scores are undoubtedly highly correlated with tests of general intelligence and with omnibus aptitude-achievement tests such as the Armed Forces Qualification Test. The SAT verbal score (SAT-V) is based on a number of subtests comprising vocabulary, antonyms, sentence completion, analogies, and reading comprehension. The quantitative score is based on verbally presented problems in arithmetical reasoning; in principle a student who has had first-year high school algebra should be able to do all the problems, the difficulty of which is based more on level of reasoning than on material covered in advanced mathematics courses. The SAT-V is the most frequently used for college selection and has the higher correlation with freshman grades. The scaled scores on each test range from 200 to 800, with a mean of 500 and a standard deviation of 100 for the total population of high school seniors competing for admission to college. For high school seniors in general, according to the 1968-69 *College Board Score Reports*, the mean SAT-V for boys is 390 and for girls 393. The standard deviation for high school seniors in general is estimated to be 132, as compared with 100 for students seeking college admission. If we assume that high school seniors have an average IQ of 105 on a general intelligence test like the Stanford-Binet or the Wechsler Adult Intelligence Scale, with a standard deviation of 15, it can be estimated that a SAT-V score of 500 (the national average of students competing for college admission and the lower-bound of the more selective colleges) corresponds to an IQ of 117.

Now let us look at the distribution of IQs in the general population. A fairly close approximation of the actual distribution is shown in Figure 6.1.

In this IQ distribution only about 13 per cent of the general population equals or exceeds an IQ of 117; and assuming a mean IQ of 105 for high school graduates, about 20 per cent of them fall above IQ 117. This is the group that, by definition, the

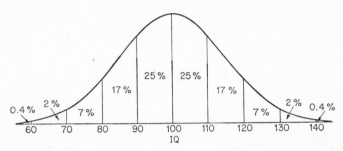

FIGURE 6.1. The theoretical or Gaussian distribution of IQs, showing the expected percentages of the population in each IQ range. Except at the extremes (below 70 and above 130) these percentages are very close to actual population values. (The percentage figures total slightly more than 100 per cent because of rounding.)

selective colleges aim to recruit – the upper one-fifth of high school graduates.

The form of the IQ distribution for the black population is somewhat less certain. The largest single normative study of Stanford-Binet IQs, by Kennedy, Van De Riet, and White, is based on school children in five Southeastern states (1963). The distribution is shown in Figure 6.2 in comparison with the white norms for the Stanford-Binet. While these data probably give a reasonably accurate picture of the *form* of the IQ distribution for Negroes, the mean IQ of 80·7 is undoubtedly biased toward the low side as a result of using a Southern sample. A survey of all studies of American Negro intelligence, drawing on samples from all parts of the United States, places the mean IQ closer to 85, with a standard deviation of about 13 (as compared to 15 or 16 for whites) (Shuey, 1966). On the basis of these generally accepted figures, it is estimated that there are approximately 0·7 per cent of Negroes with IQs at or above 117. The average IQ of Negro high school graduates, nationwide, is about 90. Given this mean, there would be approximately 2 per cent of Negro high school graduates who score above IQ 117. These figures are in close

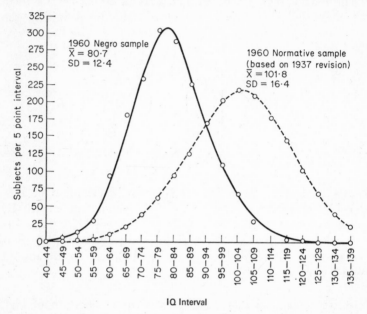

FIGURE 6.2. Stanford-Binet IQ distribution of Negro children in five Southeastern states and the white children in the 1960 normative sample. From Kennedy, Van De Riet and White, a Normative Sample of Intelligence and Achievement of Negro Elementary School Children in the Southeastern United States. *Monogr. Soc. Res. Child Devel.* 1963, **28**, No. 6.

agreement with the actual percentage enrollment of blacks in selective colleges, which, until very recently, has been between 1 and 2 per cent, more or less depending on regional variations. In summary, for colleges with a selection cut-off of 500 on the SAT-V, 20 per cent of white high school graduates as contrasted with 2 per cent of black graduates would be eligible for admission, a per capita ratio of 10 to 1.

This large ratio is attributable to a combination of two factors: the average black-white difference in IQ (about 15 points or 1 standard deviation), and the fact that the form of the distribution of IQs (and of SAT scores) for both blacks and whites approximates the so-called normal, bell-shaped curve shown in Figure 6.1. Because of the features of the normal distribution, even a relatively small difference between the averages of two populations can make for very large differences in the proportions of each population that fall above (or below) some given selection cut-off score. Figure 6.3 illustrates this effect for two hypothetical populations which differ by only 8 IQ points, their means being 92 and

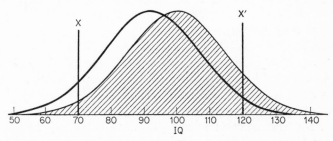

FIGURE 6.3. Two normal distributions of IQs with means at 92 and 100. The cut-offs X and X′ illustrate the effects of a mean difference of 8 points on the proportions of each distribution that fall in the lower and upper 'tails' of the distributions.

100. When the selection cut-off (X′) is 120, percentages of the two populations that will 'pass' are 9·18 *v.* 3·07, or a ratio of about 3 to 1. At the other end of the scale a cut-off (X) at IQ 70, generally regarded as the borderline of mental deficiency, results in the percentages falling below 70 of 7·08 *v.* 2·28. Thus, an average IQ difference of only 8 points can have quite impressive consequences in terms of population distributions, while a difference of 8 IQ points is trivial in comparing any two individuals. The average difference between full siblings reared together in the same family is about 12 IQ points, a difference which is of little concern to most parents. And the average difference between spouses is about 10 IQ points. Thus, these average differences of 15 IQ points between blacks and whites, which reduces to about 10 or

11 points when the racial means are compared within broad
socio-economic classes, is of major consequence not because a
difference of 15 IQ points between any two individuals is important in any significant social sense, but because *as populations*
blacks and whites are so disproportionately represented in any
selection procedure in which the cut-off is much above the white
population mean. Even if the cut-off were at IQ 100, the percentage
of whites and blacks exceeding this score would be 50 *v.* 12,
respectively, a per capita ratio of more than 4 to 1. These ratios
are seen not only in screening applicants for college but in Civil
Service examinations, personnel selection in business and industry,
and in the armed forces.

The supply of black high school graduates who during their
high school years have taken the traditional prerequisites for
college work is relatively a much smaller percentage than of white
students. The ratio of students in academic to non-academic
curricula is approximately 3 to 1 for whites and 1 to 2 for blacks.
Thus there is a severe reduction in the pool of eligible blacks in
terms of academic preparation when high school records are used
as part of the selection criteria, as is commonly the case. It is
doubtful, however, that merely increasing the percentage of black
students in academic curricula in high school would have any
marked effect on the overall level of blacks' scores on aptitude
and achievement tests. There is ample evidence that at present,
on the average, black high school seniors who were in academic
programs obtain scores on tests of scholastic aptitude and scholastic
achievement (e.g., reading, writing, science, mathematics, and
social studies) at about the same level as white students who were
in *non*-academic programs.

SEX DIFFERENCES

It is a fact of considerable social importance that among blacks
there appears to be more academically able females than males.
The evidence for this comes from diverse sources. For example,
studies based on both sexes show the median overlap of blacks
and whites on intelligence tests to be about 12 per cent; that is to
say, 12 per cent of blacks exceed the white median. (By definition,
50 per cent of whites exceed the white median.) The Armed

Forces Qualification Test (AFQT), administered to nearly the entire male population between ages 18 and 26, shows a black-white median overlap of only 8 per cent. From these figures it is a reasonable inference that the black-white median overlap for females would be 15 or 16 per cent. This corresponds to a sex difference among blacks of 5 or 6 IQ points. Inference from these data, however, seems slightly to overestimate the sex difference. I have reviewed the evidence on sex differences in intelligence as assessed by a variety of tests administered to some 18,000 white and 15,000 black school children and find that the average difference between boys and girls corresponds to about 3 or 4 IQ points for blacks and 2 or 3 points for whites. Thus, the sex difference is not peculiar to blacks, but is found in both races. It may be slightly smaller in the white population only because many test makers in standardizing the test try to equalize the scores of males and females by eliminating test items that markedly discriminate and by balancing the remaining items so as to minimize any sex difference. Tests which were not made to minimize sex differences usually favor girls. The two consistent exceptions are tests of quantitative and spatial-mechanical ability (Jensen, 1971).

The cause of the sex difference is not definitely known. We do know that males have a higher rate of infant mortality, are much more susceptible to contracting all communicable diseases, and are psychologically less well buffered against environmental influences, either good or bad. Boys' IQs show higher correlations with environmental factors. Since a disproportionate number of blacks as compared with whites grow up under poor conditions and are therefore subjected to more physical and psychological stresses in the course of their early development, this could account for the slightly greater sex difference among blacks than among whites. There is no need to postulate particular psychological or sociological conditions peculiar to black culture, such as the so-called matriarchical family pattern, to account for the sex difference in IQ and scholastic achievement, which is barely larger than that found for whites.

The only compelling hypothesis concerning the basic cause of the sex difference was advanced by the geneticist Curt Stern, who suggested that the lower vitality of the male is due to the fact that the male has only one X chromosome, while the female has two. If one of the X chromosomes carries recessive genes of lower viability, its effects are usually overruled by dominant genes at the same loci on the other X chromosome. But the male has XY instead of XX, and Y chromosome has very few gene loci and thus cannot counteract the undesirable recessive genes on the X chromosome. It is probably for this reason also that the incidence of various birth defects is so much greater in boys than in girls, and it definitely accounts for the greater incidence in boys of so-called sex-linked defects such as hemophilia and color blindness (Stern, 1949).

As far as individuals are concerned, sex differences in abilities are practically trivial, as is also the fact that races seem to differ slightly in the magnitude of this small average sex difference. Why, then, was it stated at the beginning of this section that the sex difference is of considerable social significance for blacks?

Again, it is because of the consequences of this seemingly small difference when we deal with whole populations and their ratios of representation above various selection cut-offs, whether the selection cut-offs are based on tests, school performance, or job performance. The higher the selection cut-off, as long as it is related to mental abilities, the greater will be the disparity in the ratio of males to females. Thus, we read in what is now called the *Moynihan Report* that among blacks,

> The disparity in educational attainment of male and female youth age 16 to 21 who were out of school in February 1963, is striking. Among the nonwhite males, 66·3 percent were not high school graduates, compared with 55·0 percent of the females. A similar difference existed at the college level, with 4·5 percent of the males having completed 1 to 3 years of college compared with 7·3 percent of the females.
>
> . . . .
>
> In 1960, 39 percent of all white persons 25 years of age and over who had completed 4 or more years of college were women. Fifty-three percent of the nonwhites who had attained this level were women.
>
> . . . .
>
> There is much evidence that Negro females are better students than their male counterparts.

Daniel Thompson of Dillard University . . . writes:

As low as is the aspirational level among lower class Negro girls, it is consistently higher than among the boys. For example, I have examined the honor rolls in Negro high schools for about 10 years. As a rule, from 75 to 90 percent of all Negro honor students are girls.

Dr. Thompson reports that 70 percent of all applications for the National Achievement Scholarship Program financed by the Ford Foundation for outstanding Negro high school graduates are girls, despite special efforts by high school principals to submit the names of boys.

The finalists for this new program for outstanding Negro students were recently announced. Based on an inspection of the names, only about 43 percent of all the 639 finalists were male. (However, in the regular National Merit Scholarship program, males received 67 percent of the 1964 scholarship awards.)

Moynihan goes on to note that these disparities are carried over to the area of employment and income.

Negro males represent 1·1 percent of all male professionals, whereas Negro females represent roughly 6 percent of all female professionals. Again, in technician occupations, Negro males represent 2·1 percent of all male technicians while Negro females represent roughly 10 percent of all female technicians. It would appear, therefore, that there are proportionately 4 times as many Negro females in significant white collar jobs than Negro males.

It is most interesting that every one of these male/female percentage disparities is completely consistent with a male-female ability difference of 0·1 to 0·3 of a standard deviation, which is equivalent to 1·5 to 4·5 IQ points. In other words, the figures that Moynihan presents on the ratio of the sexes for different educational and occupational attainments is just what we would predict on the basis of an average IQ difference between males and females of between 1·5 and 4·5 points, which is the magnitude of the differences we actually find. The main reason that the sex difference is made to appear so much more prominent for blacks than for whites is that these selection cut-offs are in all cases at least one standard deviation (equivalent to 15 IQ points) higher in relation to the black mean than in relation to the white mean. For example, a cut-off at IQ 115 is only one standard deviation above the white mean and 16 per cent of whites exceed this score; but the same cut-off is about two standard deviations above the mean of the black distribution, and only about 2 per cent of the blacks would exceed this score, making the per capita ratio of 8 whites to 1 black. If black males and females differ by one-fourth

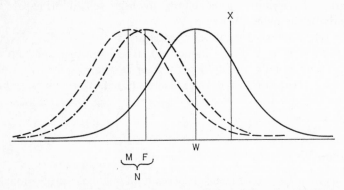

FIGURE 6.4. Normal curves for male (M) and female (F) Negroes (N) and for whites (W) (both sexes combined) to illustrate how a relatively small average sex difference can result in markedly different proportions of males and females that fall above any given selection cut-off (X).

of a standard deviation, or about 4 IQ points, the ratio of females to males with IQs aboue 115 will be roughly 2 to 1. This statistical phenomenon is illustrated in Figure 6.4.

As can be seen in Figure 6.4, the relatively small male-female (M-F) difference for Negroes (N) results in quite large differences in the proportions under the male and female curves beyond the selection cut-off (X), and the higher the cut-off the greater will be the ratio of females to males. We see just the opposite effect at the low end of the ability scale. Thus, one of the largest studies ever conducted on the incidence of mental retardation (defined as IQs under 70), showed a sex ratio of 1·68 males to 1 female for whites and only 1·31 males to 1 female for blacks (Lemkau and Imre, 1966). This is just another facet of the same basic phenomenon (with its opposite effect) that we see in selecting persons at the upper end of the ability spectrum.

There is one other aspect of sex differences which tends to counteract the mean difference to some extent when the selection cut-off is high enough. This is a difference in the amount of variance or dispersion of scores, which is reflected by the standard deviation of the distribution. Males have a slightly larger standard deviation (or spread of scores) than females, which means there are slightly more very high and very low scores among males than among females. This is shown in an exaggerated form in the two distributions in Figure 6.5; both have the same means but different

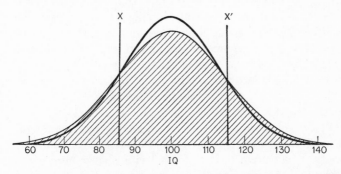

FIGURE 6.5. Two distributions that have the same mean but differ in variance (spread). Note that even though the averages of the groups are the same, one group has a larger proportion at the high and low ends of the scale.

standard deviations. This sex difference in dispersion of IQs is a well-known phenomenon in the white population, but less is known about it in the black.

In the white population, above some point (probably about two standard deviations above the mean, i.e., above IQ 130) the percentage of males begins increasingly to exceed that of females. Thus, for example, when Terman sought a large number of 'gifted' children (IQs above 140) for his famous longitudinal study, he found a ratio of 12 boys to 10 girls in his final sample of 1,528 gifted children (Terman, 1925-59). Why this phenomenon seen in the white population does not result in a larger proportion of black males than females above selection cut-offs that are more than two or three standard deviations above the black mean is not known. The question merits investigation.

A WORD ABOUT INTELLIGENCE TESTS

Before attempting to say anything about the causes of the racial difference in IQs or other psychometric indices of mental ability, a few words about the nature of intelligence measurement are in order. One of the easiest ways of brushing aside any attempt to understand the observed differences between socially recognized racial groups in performance on intelligence tests is to claim that the tests do not really measure intelligence or at least that they are invalid for the group that comes out with the lower average. These misguided arguments are simply the result of their proponents' misunderstanding of what most psychologists actually mean by intelligence and what they claim for intelligence tests.

I have discussed the nature of intelligence and intelligence testing much more extensively elsewhere (Jensen, 1969a). The gist of what I have tried to convey is that intelligence is one significant attribute of a person's behavior that distinguishes him within his society. From prehistoric times it has probably been a common observation that persons differ in brightness, in speed of learning, in ability to solve problems, to invent new solutions, and so on. Parents, teachers, and employers are able roughly to rank children and adults in terms of a subjective impression of brightness or capability, and there is a fairly high agreement among different observers in the rank order they assign in the same groups of children. It is helpful to think of the subjective perception of intelligence as analogous to the subjective perception of temperature, which is also an attribute. Before the invention of the thermometer, temperature was a matter of subjective judgment. The invention of the thermometer made it possible to objectify the attribute of temperature, to quantify it, and to measure it with a high degree of reliability. With some important qualifications, the situation is similar in the case of intelligence tests. The most essential difference is that intelligence, unlike temperature, is multidimensional rather than unidimensional. That is to say, there are different varieties of intelligence, so that persons do not maintain the same rank order of ability in every situation or test that we may regard as indicative of intelligence. It so happens that from among the total spectrum of human behaviors that can be regarded as indicative of some kind of 'mental ability' in the broadest sense, we have focused on one part of this spectrum in our psychological concept of intelligence. We have emphasized the abilities characterized as conceptual learning, abstract or symbolic reasoning, and abstract or verbal problem solving. These abilities were most emphasized in the composition of intelligence tests because these were the abilities most relevant to the traditional school curriculum and because the first practical intelligence tests were devised to predict scholastic performance. When tests were devised to predict occupational performance, they naturally had a good deal in common with the tests devised for scholastic prediction, since the educational system is intimately related to the occupational demands of a given society. Much the same abilities and skills that are important in schooling, therefore, are also important occupationally. Thus, we find that in industrialized countries practically all intelligence tests, scholastic aptitude tests, military classification tests, vocational aptitude tests, and the like, are quite similar in composition and that the scores obtained on them are all quite substantially intercorrelated. In short, there is a large general factor, or g, which the tests share in common and which principally accounts for the variance among individuals. When tests are devised to measure this g factor as purely as possible, examination of their item content leads to the characterization of it as requiring an ability for abstract reasoning and problem solving. Tests having quite diverse forms can have equally high loadings on the g factor – for example, the verbal similarities and block design tests of the Wechsler Intelligence Scales are both highly loaded on g. Tests of g can be relatively high or relatively low in degree of 'culture fairness'. (The question 'In what way are a wheel and a penny alike?' is probably more culture fair than the question 'In what way are an oboe and a bassoon alike?') In short, it is possible to assess essentially the same basic intelligence by a great variety of means.

Standard IQ tests measure the kinds of behavior in abstract

and verbal problem situations that we call abstract reasoning ability. These tests measure more of g – the factor common to various forms of intelligence tests – than of any of the other more special ability factors, such as verbal fluency, spatial-perceptual ability, sensory abilities, or mechanical, musical, or artistic abilities, or what might be called social judgment or sensitivity. But a test that measured everything at once would not be very useful. IQ tests do reliably measure one very important, though limited, aspect of human performance.

The IQ qualifies as an appropriate datum for scientific study. If we are to study intelligence, we are ahead if we can measure it. Our measure is the IQ, obtained on tests which meet certain standards, one of which is a high g loading when factor analyzed among other tests. To object to this procedure by arguing that the IQ cannot be regarded as being interchangeable with intelligence, or that intelligence cannot really be measured, or that IQ is not the same as intelligence, is to get bogged down in a semantic morass. It is equivalent to arguing that a column of mercury in a glass tube cannot be regarded as synonymous with temperature, or that temperature cannot really be measured with a thermometer. If the measurements are reliable and reproducible, and the operations by which they are obtained can be objectively agreed upon, this is all that need be required for them to qualify as proper scientific data. We know that individually administered IQ tests have quite high reliability; the reliability coefficients are around 0·95, which means that only about 5 per cent of the total individual differences variance is attributable to measurement error. And standard group administered tests have reliabilities close to 0·90. The standard error of measurement (which is about ∓ 5 points for the Stanford-Binet and similar tests) must always be taken into consideration when considering any individual's score on a test. But it is actually quite unimportant in comparing the means of large groups of subjects, since errors of measurement are more or less normally distributed about zero and they cancel out when N is large. The reliability (i.e., consistency or freedom from errors of measurement) *per se* of the IQ is really not seriously at issue in making comparisons between racial groups when the samples are large. The mean difference between large groups will not include the test's errors of measurement. Moreover, the IQ is a fairly stable measure, especially after individuals have reached school age. The degree to which children maintain their rank order in IQ throughout their development is about the same as the degree to which they maintain their rank order among their age mates in height.

The validity or importance of the IQ derives entirely from its relationship to other variables and the importance we attach to them. The IQ correlates with many external criteria, and at the most general level it may be regarded as a measure of the ability to compete in our society in ways that have economic and social consequences for the individual. In the first place, the IQ accords with parents' and teachers' subjective assessments of children's brightness, as well as with the evaluations of children's own peers. In terms of assessments of scholastic performance, whether measured in terms of school grades, teachers' ratings, or objective tests of scholastic achievement, the IQ accounts for more of the variance among individuals than any other single measurable attribute of the child, and much more, incidentally, than does the child's socio-economic status.

The correlation is quite substantial between IQ and occupations, even when the latter are merely ranked in the order of persons' average judgment of the occupation's prestige. (Correlation is a measure of degree of relationship, on a scale going from 0 [no relationship] to 1·00 [perfect relationship].) Various studies have shown correlations in the range of 0·50 to 0·70. This is sufficiently high that the mean differences between groups of persons in occupations arranged according to a prestige hierarchy (which is highly related to income) show highly significant differences in IQ or other mental test scores. In general, any two groups which differ in possessing what are perceived as 'the good things in life' according to the criteria and values of our society, will be found on the average to differ significantly in IQ.

When groups are selected from the lower or upper extremes of the IQ distribution, the contrasts are enormous. A classic example is Terman's study of gifted children, selected in elementary school, with IQs over 140, a score achieved only by the upper 1 per cent of the population. These 1,528 children have been systematically followed up to middle age (Terman and Oden, 1959). The group as a whole greatly exceeds a random sample of the population on practically every criterion of a successful life, and, interestingly enough, not just on intellectual criteria. On the average the Terman group have markedly greater educational attainments, have higher incomes, engage in more desirable and more prestigious occupations, have many more entries in *Who's Who*, have brighter spouses, enjoy better physical and mental health, have a lower suicide rate, a lower mortality rate, a lower divorce rate, and have brighter children (their average IQ is 133). These results should leave no doubt that IQ is quite related to socially valued criteria.

GENETIC FACTORS

Studies of the relative importance of genetic and environmental factors in individual differences in IQ are based entirely on tests administered to European and North American white populations and cannot be generalized to other populations or used as a basis for inferring the causes of the average difference between racial and cultural groups. But these studies, taken together, do clearly lead to the conclusion that, in the populations sampled, genetic factors are at least twice as important as environmental factors in accounting for the IQ differences among individuals (Jensen, 1969a).

AVERAGE BLACK-WHITE DIFFERENCES IN IQ

It is interesting that most of the general public believe that the differences they observe between whites and blacks in educational and occupational performance are due, not to differences in abilities, whatever the cause of the differences may be, but to differences in motivation or 'will'. Surveys by the National Opinion Research Center have found that the average white American generally thinks about black and white differences in status and achievement in terms of differences in effort and motivation to succeed. Some four out of five white Americans reject the notion that white people are born with higher mental capacity than blacks (Schuman, 1969).

In scientific circles, the causes of behavioral racial differences are an open issue. They are not known in any rigorous, scientific sense, and so the field abounds in speculations. But the differences are viewed by most psychologists primarily as *ability* differences (regardless of whatever their cause may be) rather than as motivational differences. Motivational differences, when they exist at all, are seen as a secondary by-product of frustration, discouragement, failure, and the poor self-esteem that results therefrom. To the extent that these effects may occur, they probably arise largely in school, due in part to the failure of many schools to make adequate provision for the large individual differences that are found in developmental readiness for learning various school subjects and the differences in *patterns* of abilities that children bring to the learning situation. I have emphasized these points in more detail elsewhere (Jensen, 1968d, 1968e).

In terms of what we can measure with our tests, the facts are quite clear and are generally agreed upon by those who have studied the evidence. In the United States persons classed as black by the common social criteria obtain scores on the average about one standard deviation (i.e., 15 IQ points on most standard intelligence tests) below the average for the white population. One standard deviation is an *average* difference, and it is known that the magnitude of black-white differences varies according to the ages of the groups compared, their socio-economic status, and especially their geographical location in the United States. Various tests differ, on the average, relatively little. In general, blacks do slightly better on verbal tests than on non-verbal tests. They do most poorly on tests of spatial ability, abstract reasoning and problem solving (Shuey, 1966; Tyler, 1965). Tests of scholastic achievement also show about one standard deviation difference, and this difference appears to be fairly constant from first grade through twelfth grade, judging from the massive data of the Coleman Report (Coleman, 1966). The estimated median test scores, based on the nationwide Coleman study, for various racial and ethnic groups are shown for first and twelfth grades in Table 6.1.

The scores for all tests are scaled to an overall national average of 50, with a standard deviation of ten points. Table 6.2 shows the national percentages of whites and non-whites of ages 3 to 34 enrolled in schools and colleges.

The IQ difference of one standard deviation is also quite constant

TABLE 6.1. Estimated median test scores (general mean = 50, standard deviation = 10) for 1st- and 12th-grade pupils in the U.S. in fall, 1965

| | RACIAL OR ETHNIC GROUP | | | | | |
	Puerto Ricans	Indian Americans	Mexican Americans	Oriental Americans	Negro	White
1st Grade						
Non-verbal	45·8	53·2	50·1	56·6	43·4	54·1
Verbal	44·9	47·8	46·5	51·6	45·4	53·2
12th Grade						
Non-verbal	43·3	47·1	45·0	51·6	40·9	52·0
Verbal	43·1	43·7	43·8	49·6	40·9	52·1
Reading	42·6	44·3	44·2	48·8	42·2	51·9
Mathematics	43·7	45·9	45·5	51·3	41·8	51·8
General Information	41·7	44·7	43·3	49·0	40·6	52·2
Average of the 5 tests	43·1	45·1	44·4	50·1	41·1	52·0

Source: U.S. Office of Education, Commissioner's report on 'Equality of Educational Opportunity'. July 2, 1966.

TABLE 6.2. Enrollment status of whites and non-whites in schools and colleges, ages 3 to 34, in the United States, October, 1968

| | Percent Enrolled in School | |
Ages (*in Years*)	Whites	Non-whites
3- 4	15·0	19·5
5- 6	88·5	83·3
7- 9	99·1	99·1
10-13	99·1	98·9
14-15	98·1	97·4
16-17	90·8	86·7
18-19	50·0	46·7
20-21	32·8	20·1
22-24	14·5	9·2
25-29	7·4	4·0
30-34	3·9	3·9
Total 3-34	56·6	57·8

Source: U.S. Dept. of Commerce, Bureau of the Census.

over the age range from about 5 years to adulthood. Since the black mean IQ is as far below the white mean (in standard deviation units) at the time of high school graduation as at the beginning of first grade, it means, of course, that the public schools did not create the difference. But neither have they succeeded in narrowing the difference, which, judging from all the available evidence, has remained approximately constant at least as far back as World War I (McGurk, 1967). (Both white and black populations since 1918 have gained in average performance on IQ, scholastic achievement, and military induction tests, but the *difference* between the means has remained close to one standard deviation over the past fifty years.)

CAUSES OF THE DIFFERENCE

While almost no one disputes the existence of the approximately one standard deviation difference between blacks and whites on measures of the kinds of abilities we call intelligence, there is considerable dispute concerning the causes of the difference. Either the existing evidence relevant to this question has not been adequately systematized and analyzed to allow the emergence of any scientifically compelling conclusion or the evidence is still inadequate or inappropriate to yield any generally agreed upon conclusion among the scientific community. There are few, if any, scientists who doubt that the history of blacks in the United States and their poorer social and economic condition are at least partially if not wholly the cause of the observed intellectual differences. But to anyone who has studied the psychological research on this problem thoroughly, it is obvious that the evidence is complex and ambiguous at many points. Most environmental theories are overly simple and do not explain all the facts they are intended to account for. Part of the reason that purely environmental theories of racial differences have not become more refined and rigorous is that they have had virtually no opposition from competing theories for the last two or three decades. In this area, psychologists, sociologists, and anthropologists have not followed the usual methods of scientific investigation, which consist in part of pitting rival hypotheses against one another in such a way that empirical evidence can disprove either one or the other. On the topic of

I

racial differences, social scientists for the most part have simply *decreed* on purely ideological grounds that all races are identical in the genetic factors that condition various behavioral traits, including intelligence. Most environmental hypotheses purporting to explain black-white intelligence differences, therefore, have not had to stand up to scientific tests of the kind that other sciences depend upon for the advancement of knowledge. Until genetic, as well as environmental, hypotheses are seriously considered in our search for causes, it is virtually certain that we will never achieve a scientifically acceptable answer to this question. My view is that we should unrelentingly seek scientific understanding of socially important problems. Of course, there is nothing *inherently* important about anything. Race differences in intelligence are important only if people think these differences, or their consequences, are important. It so happens that in our society great importance is given to these differences and their importance is acknowledged in many official public policies. Racial inequality in educational and occupational performance, and in the social and economic rewards correlated therewith, is clearly one of the uppermost concerns of our nation today.

Most persons are not concerned with those racial characteristics that are patently irrelevant to performance. The real concern results from the observed correlation between racial classification and educational and occupational performance. Persons who feel concerned about these observed differences demand an explanation for the differences. It is apparently a strongly ingrained human characteristic to need to understand what one perceives as a problem, and to ask for answers. People inevitably demand explanations about things that concern them. There is no getting around that. We have no choice in the matter. Explanations there will be.

But we do have a choice of essentially two paths in seeking explanations of intelligence differences among racial groups. On the one hand, we can simply *decree* an explanation based on prejudice, or popular beliefs, or moral convictions, or one or another social or political ideology, or on what we might think it is best for society to believe. This is the path of propaganda. Or, on the other hand, we can follow the path of science and investigate the problem in the same way that any other phenomena would be subjected to scientific study. There is nothing to compel us to one path or the other. This is a matter of personal preference and values. And since persons differ markedly in their preferences and values, we will inevitably see both of these paths being followed for quite some time. My own preference is for a scientific approach to the study of these phenomena. Our experience tells us that the scientific approach, by and large, leads to more reliable knowledge of natural phenomena than any other method that man has yet devised. If solutions to educational problems depend upon recognizing certain psychological realities in the same sense that, say, building a workable spaceship depends upon recognizing certain physical realities, then surely we will stand a better chance of improving education for all children by choosing the path of scientific investigation.

I maintain, therefore, that the causes of observed differences in IQ and scholastic performance among different racial groups is, scientifically, still an open question, an important question, and a researchable one. Official pronouncements, such as 'It is a demonstrable fact that the talent pool in any one ethnic group is substantially the same as in any other ethnic group' (U.S. Office of Education, 1966), and 'Intelligence potential is distributed among Negro infants in the same proportion and pattern as among Icelanders or Chinese, or any other group' (U.S. Department of Labor, 1965), are without scientific merit. They lack any factual basis and can be regarded only as hypotheses. In 1969, in the *Harvard Educational Review*, I challenged this prevailing hypothesis of genetic equality by suggesting that we also scientifically investigate alternative hypotheses that invoke genetic as well as environmental factors as being among the causes of the observed differences in patterns of mental ability among racial groups (Jensen, 1969a). The fact that different racial groups in this country have widely separated geographic origins and have had quite different histories which have subjected them to different selective social and economic pressures make it highly likely that their gene pools differ for some genetically conditioned behavioral characteristics, including intelligence, or abstract reasoning ability. Nearly every anatomical, physiological and biochemical system investigated shows racial differences. Why should the brain be any exception? The reasonableness of the hypothesis that there are racial differences in genetically conditioned behavioral characteristics, including mental abilities, is not confined to the poorly informed, but has been expressed in writings and public statements by such eminent geneticists as K. Matter, C. D. Darlington, R. A. Fisher, and Francis Crick, to name a few. The fact that we still have only tentative conclusions with respect to this hypothesis does not mean that the opposite of the hypothesis is true. Yet some social scientists speak as if this were the case and have even publicly censured me for suggesting an alternative to purely environmental hypotheses of intelligence differences. I have always advocated dealing with persons as individuals, each in terms of his own merits and characteristics and I am opposed to according treatment to persons solely on the basis of their race, color, national origin, or social class background. But I am also opposed to ignoring or refusing to investigate the causes of the well-established differences among racial groups in the distribution of educationally relevant traits, particularly IQ.

Many questions about the means of guaranteeing equality of educational opportunity are still moral and political issues at present. When there is no compelling body of scientific evidence on which policy decisions can be based, such decisions must avowedly be made in terms of one's personal social philosophy and concepts of morality. Many goals of public policy must be decided in terms of values. The results of research are of greatest use to the technology of achieving the value-directed goals of society. The decision to put a man on the moon was not primarily a scientific decision, but once the decision was made the application of scientific knowledge was necessary to achieve this goal. A similar analogy holds for the attainment of educational goals.

The validity of college selection procedures

The question concerning the *causes* of intelligence differences are, in fact, quite irrelevant when it comes to the use of tests for predicting performance in college. Doing well academically in college depends upon a conglomeration of developed abilities, skills, and thinking habits, which scholastic aptitude tests are designed to assess. The important question to the college admissions office is not why students differ on these tests, but whether the tests are valid for their intended purpose, namely, predicting college grades of probability of not flunking out before graduation. Of most importance to the present discussion is whether such tests and other selection criteria are unfair to minority groups.

The *reliability* of a test refers to the consistency and stability of its scores. It is measured by the reliability coefficient, which can have values from 0 to 1. A reliability of 0 means the scores are no more stable than numbers drawn at random in a lottery. A reliability of 1 means the individual's score (or relative standing in a population) is constant from one testing to another. To determine the proportion of error of measurement in test scores, we subtract the test's reliability from 1·00. The reliability of SAT test scores over a ten-months period ranges between 0·85 and 0·90, which is high for a group-administered test. Direct coaching on the SAT results in a gain in score, but not much of a gain – approximately one-tenth of a standard deviation (about 10 points on the SAT), which is less than the test's standard error of measurement.

The *validity* of a test refers to the degree to which it can predict performance in another situation. It, too, is expressed as a correlation coefficient with values from 0 to 1. A good criterion against which to assess the validity of the SAT-V is college grade point average (GPA). Among those students who survive four years of college, the correlation between SAT-V and GPA is above 0·40 (Cronbach, 1960). This is a high validity coefficient, considering that in most colleges the test was used to screen out initially those students with poor prospects of succeeding and that those who left college before their fourth year were not included in the validity estimate.

How should one interpret a validity coefficient? It can be shown that the benefit from a selection program increases in direct proportion to the validity coefficient. To put this fact into easily understood and concrete terms, Cronbach gives an example from industrial personnel selection.

Suppose the 40 applicants out of 100 who score highest on a test are hired. We can consider the average production of randomly selected men as a baseline. An ideal test would pick the forty men who later earn the highest criterion score; the average production of these men is the maximum that any selection plan could yield. A test with validity 0·50, then, will yield an average production halfway between the base level and the ideal. To be concrete, suppose the average, randomly selected worker assembles 400 gadgets per day, and the perfectly selected group of workers turns out 600. Then a test with validity ·50 will choose a group whose average production is 500 gadgets, and a test of validity ·20 will select workers with and average production of 440 gadgets.

The principle is essentially the same in educational selection, except that instead of number of gadgets produced we would be speaking of the amount of knowledge and skills acquired, that is, those aspects of college performance reflected by course grades and scores on achievement tests.

The Law Schools Admission Test (LSAT), which is now in wide use by law schools, correlates about 0·30 with first year law school grade average, and about 0·40 when the LSAT is combinated with students' undergraduate grade point average. Validities would doubtless be higher over the whole course of instruction and if there were no initial selection of students on the basis of LSAT scores and undergraduate grades.

PREDICTIVE VALIDITY OF HIGH SCHOOL GRADES

As a general rule, the best predictor of future performance is past performance in similar situations. We might therefore expect that the best predictor of a student's performance in college is his performance in high school, and, in fact, this is generally true. For most students, high school grades are the best predictor of college grades. Prediction is still far from perfect, of course. But it is so much better than chance that if the same odds were given at Monte Carlo to a gambler with a modest bankroll, he could easily own all of Monaco within a few hours. For example, boys with an A average in high school are seven times more likely than boys with a C average in high school to obtain a B average in college, and A average boys are more than twice as likely to get a B average in college as are boys with a B average in high school (Astin, 1969).

But there are obvious shortcomings with high school grades or rank in high school class. The most serious is the fact that all high schools do not maintain the same grading standards, and a B average in one school might be equivalent to an A average in another in terms of actual scholastic achievement. Schools' grading standards differ on a regional basis and even among schools in the same city. College entrance tests do not have this drawback when they are administered nationwide under standard conditions and on the same dates for everyone, as is the case with the SAT and the LSAT.

Also, it has been found that although high school grades make a greater contribution than SAT scores in predicting college grades for whites, this is not true for blacks (Stanley, 1970). High school grades also have lower validity for black males than for females. Objective examinations, on the other hand, have the same predictive validity for blacks as for whites. Thomas and Stanley state:

> Explanations for the relative ineffectiveness of high school grades in predicting freshman grade point average of black students are a matter of conjecture. A few of the more plausible hypotheses that could be advanced are: (*a*) invalidity of grades [as an index of actual achievement] in high school and/or college, particularly for black males; (*b*) unreliability of grades and grade reporting in black high schools; (*c*) inter-group differences in personality characteristics; and (*d*) restriction in range due to selection processes.

The authors conclude:

> The importance of this research is augmented by the fact that most colleges and universities still rely quite heavily on the high school grade-point average as a criterion for student admission. Many selective institutions are using high school grades without test scores in the belief that the latter are not predictively valid for black college aspirants. Our findings suggest that, on the contrary, academic aptitude and achievement-test scores are often (relative to high school grades) better predictors of college grades for blacks than they are for whites. The best forecasts are made, however, when *both* test scores and high school grades are used optimally to predict college grades.

Popular misconceptions about selection tests

There are a number of common misconceptions about college selection tests, such as the SAT. All of them can be clearly refuted by ample research evidence, although a detailed review of all the relevant research is obviously beyond the scope of the present article, which can present briefly only the most important conclusions.

ARE TESTS UNFAIR TO MINORITIES?

Blacks are the only minority on which there is extensive research concerning the validity of college selection tests (see Boney, 1966; Stanley and Porter, 1967; Cleary, 1968; Hills and Stanley, 1968, 1970; Ruch and Ash, 1969). For predicting college grades, either in predominantly black colleges or in integrated colleges, as well as in selection in industry and in the military, aptitude tests predict performance criteria just as well for blacks as for whites. In technical terms, we can conclude that the regression of scholastic performance (as measured by grade point average) on aptitude test scores is the same for blacks as for whites; the slope and the intercept of the regression line are the same in both groups. This means that the same mathematical formula (regression equation) can be used for predicting the performance of a black student as of a white student, given their individual test scores. In other words, a black student performs academically no better or no worse than a white student with the same score. Most of the few published studies that have not found this to be the case have found just the opposite of the popular misconception that tests underrate the academic ability of black applicants. If the tests err, it is in slightly *over-predicting* the blacks' academic achievement in college; that is, blacks do slightly less well in their courses than whites with exactly the same aptitude test scores. This difference, however, is too small to have any practical significance. What the evidence does indicate is that there is no psychometric basis for 'adjusting' or weighting test scores differently according to the testee's skin color. In short, the tests themselves are quite color-blind in terms of predictive validity.

ARE VERBAL TESTS BIASED AGAINST BLACKS?

One of the commonest misconceptions is that blacks do more poorly on verbal tests as compared with other types of tests, probably because verbal tests are presumed to be more culturally and educationally loaded, thereby reflecting certain environmental advantages that are unequally distributed in the black and white populations. But the fact of the matter is that blacks get higher scores on verbal tests than on almost any other kinds of mental tests – spatial, mechanical, or quantitative. The eleven subtests of the Wechsler Adult Intelligence Scale, for example, can be categorized into verbal and non-verbal (or 'performance') tests. Most studies have shown that blacks obtain relatively lower scores on the non-verbal tests. We have recently completed an analysis of test score data on more than one thousand black and white school children who were given two tests differing markedly in their dependence upon verbal and cultural knowledge. One test, the Peabody Picture Vocabulary Test (PPVT) presents the child with 150 sets of four pictures in each set; the child points to the one picture named by the examiner. The names are words like *wiener, kangaroo, caboose, peacock, capsule, bronco, kayak, amphibian*. The other test was Raven's Progressive Matrices, a non-verbal test consisting of patterns of abstract geometric forms. A part of the pattern is missing in each matrix of figures and the child has to select the missing part necessary to complete the pattern from among six multiple-choice alternatives. The correct choice is dependent not upon perceptual acuity *per se*, but upon logical reasoning – the ability to grasp the principle or general rule governing the overall pattern. It turns out that black children, though performing more poorly than white children on both tests, obtain relatively lower scores on the Matrices Test than on the Picture Vocabulary Test. Mexican-American children in the same schools, on the other hand, showed just the reverse. They scored below the black children on the verbal test and above them on the non-verbal.

The one class of tests that have been found to show the least difference between black and white subjects are tests of immediate and rote memory (Jensen, 1968a, 1968d, 1968e). The differences between blacks and whites referred to here are based on entire

1*

school populations; they are the differences that actually exist in intact groups, not the differences (or possible lack of any difference) if all environmental background factors were controlled. No knowledgeable person would claim that the observed differences do not reflect a host of environmental factors or that genetic factors might not also contribute to the differences. As pointed out previously, scientists have not yet answered this question. But the test differences, whatever their cause, have predictive validity in school and college performance. Verbal aptitude tests predict academic achievement better than other kinds of tests, and so they are the most widely used. The fact that verbal ability is the black's strong point, relative to other mental abilities measured by tests, means that selection based on verbal tests favor blacks more than if nonverbal tests were used.

ARE GRADES OR RATINGS UNFAIR TO BLACKS?

The fact that predictive validities (and regression lines) have been found to be the same for blacks and whites suggests that academic performance, not skin color, affects college grades. At least this seems to be true when the selection procedures are the same for blacks and whites. I have not found any published research studies of college grades when blacks and whites are admitted under different selection procedures. One hears informally of a variety of grading consequences at different colleges having different selection standards for black and white students. Some professors say, for example, that grades on the average are the same for blacks as for whites; others say that grading standards are changed for black students; still others say that grading standards are lowered for *all* students in mixed classes in order to keep very low grades at the same minimal proportion as in unmixed classes. Obviously these casual observations must be evaluated only as speculative hypotheses until someone systematically collects and properly analyzes some actual relevant data.

A grading bias that would systematically lower the course grades of black students, however, seems unlikely. I base this conjecture on some evidence published by the Educational Testing Service which indicates that when whites are asked to rate blacks on their job performance, there is a tendency for them to overrate slightly rather than to underrate blacks as compared with whites. The study was based on large samples of black and white medical technicians employed in 36 Veterans Administration hospitals throughout the country. Supervisors rated the job-knowledge of the medical technicians working under them. The ratings were analyzed in four combinations: blacks rated by blacks, blacks rated by whites, whites rated by blacks, and whites rated by whites. All the technicians were also given a job-knowledge test which sampled only the knowledge that medical technicians must have and that can be picked up on the job. The result was that for any given job-knowledge test score, blacks rated by blacks received the highest rating, blacks rated by whites received the next highest rating, and whites rated by whites received the lowest rating. The ratings of whites by blacks showed absolutely no relationship to job-knowledge test scores, but the average overall rating was about the same as that of blacks rated by blacks. All of the other ratings showed a very substantial correlation with job-knowledge scores. The job-knowledge scores were also compared with the scores on nine aptitude tests that were given to all the technicians. The authors of the study state:

> Scores on every one of the nine aptitude tests predicted scores on the job-knowledge test somewhat better for Negroes than for whites. If there was any bias, it was in the opposite direction from what might be expected. White technicians with any given aptitude score tended to do better on the job-knowledge test than Negro technicians with the same aptitude score. If these aptitude tests were used in selection, the future performance of white technicians would more often be under-estimated (Educational Testing Service, 1969).

DO TESTS MEASURE SOCIO-ECONOMIC STATUS MORE THAN ABILITY?

It is a fact that test scores are correlated with socio-economic status (SES). This had led some critics of tests to claim that tests are a pernicious means of keeping persons in the social class of their origin, especially persons from poor families who, were it not for the tests used by schools and colleges, could move upwards in status educationally, occupationally, and economically. The facts do not bear out this complaint. Any other means of selection or prediction for college-going potential disfavors children of low-SES more than do objective tests. Interviews, ratings, and teachers' judgments are all more subject to influence by the veneer of social-class; objective tests, in effect, 'read through' the superficial appearances associated with socio-economic status and are far more accurate than any other means we presently have for assessing academic aptitude and probability of success in a given college. The use of objective tests is still the best safeguard that persons from a low-SES background will be given a fair chance in the selection procedure. Wider use of tests in schools, combined with wise counseling, would actually *increase* the pool of identified potential college-level candidates from economically disadvantaged backgrounds. Academically gifted children from poor families are much more likely to be identified by tests than by parents or teachers. Aptitude tests, properly used, tend to protect the rights of qualified minority group members. In comparison, the personal interview is notoriously invalid as a selection procedure (Dunnette and Bass, 1963). It is an interesting, but theoretically unexplained, fact that high IQs (i.e., above 120) and consequently high academic potential are somewhat more evenly distributed among social strata than are low IQs (60-80), which are most heavily concentrated in the low-SES segment of the population. Tests can help parents and school authorities to spot the academically talented in disadvantaged groups, children whose abilities might otherwise go unrecognized because of the non-intellectual values of their family environment and the stereotypes many school personnel and employers may hold about the intellectual potential of children of the poor. By the same token, tests identify those students of mediocre academic ability who come from upper-middle class homes that provide the social advantages of proper diction, manners, and the like, which can often be misread by teachers and employers as signs of superior intellectual ability. Some persons have actually objected to selection tests on the ground that they identify low ability in the upper classes as well as in the lower classes. Thus, it is perhaps understandable that tests are criticized from both directions.

If we correlate students' SES and IQ with scholastic performance, we find that IQ accounts for much more of the individual differences in performance than does SES. It is possible statistically to examine the correlation between SES and scholastic achievement with the correlation attributable to IQ eliminated, and the correlation between IQ and achievement with the contribution of SES removed. A typical study, for example, found a correlation of 0·62 between intelligence tests scores and scholastic attainment, with SES held constant, and a correlation of 0·30 between SES and scholastic attainment, with the IQ held constant (Wiseman, 1964). (The magnitude of the difference in the degree of relationship represented by two correlation coefficients is based on the difference between their squares, so a correlation of 0·62 represents more than four times as great a relationship as a correlation of 0·30.) Thus, intelligence contributes a large share of variance in achievement (education, occupation, income) that is *unrelated* to the social class of birth. Findings such as these have led sociologist Otis Dudley Duncan (1968) to the following conclusion:

> In view of the loose relationship between IQ and social class in the United States, it seems that one very constructive function of the ability measured by intelligence tests is that it serves as a kind of springboard, launching many men into achievements removing them considerable distances from the social class of their birth. IQ, in an achievement-oriented society, is the primary leaven preventing the classes from hardening into castes.

ARE RECRUITED STUDENTS THE SAME AS SELF-SELECTED STUDENTS?

Selective colleges sometimes admit a small percentage of applicants with relatively low SAT scores (say, in the 350 to 450 range), or with unpromising high school records. Since some proportion of these students actually succeed in college, it is assumed that there will be approximately the same proportion of successes among students with similar low SAT scores who are *recruited* by the college. This is a false inference. The consequences of recruitment of high risk students must be evaluated empirically; it can not be inferred from data on self-selected students with similar SAT scores. Students who strive to get into a particular college and who, for one reason or another, manage to gain admission despite low test scores or unpromising high school grades, usually have, as they say, 'other things going for them'. They are exceptionally motivated, or under strong family pressures to succeed, or know how to manage their time and study habits exceptionally well, and so on. Consequently a considerably higher percentage of them will succeed than can be expected in any random selection of the college-age population with similar low scores. In terms of statistical probabilities, the student with an SAT in the 350-450 range who gets into a selective college on his own steam is more likely to succeed than a student of the same ability who is simply recruited by the college. The academic performance of recruited 'underqualified' students needs to be evaluated in its own right.

The reason for assuming a probable difference is that self-selected students differ from randomly selected college-age persons on a number of personality and character traits that are related to performance in an academic setting. Using the California Psychological Inventory (CPI), Gough compared groups of high school seniors of similar ability who did and who did not go on to college. Every college-going student was matched with a non-college-going student for sex and IQ, and both groups of students were then compared on each of the eighteen personality scales of the CPI. The groups differed on a number of personality characteristics as assessed by items of the CPI. Examination of the items that discriminate most between the groups led Gough to the following composite description of the college-bound youths, 'mature and rationale, more capable of achieving in a logical and responsible manner'. The non-college youths could more often be characterized as 'poorly organized, less certain of what they can or should do, and . . . less capable of directed and resolute endeavor' (1968). The questionnaire scales that Gough was able to derive from this study would undoubtedly be useful in the recruitment of college students and should add significantly to the predictive validity of the SAT and high school grades.

THE SMALLPOX FALLACY

This particular misconception, also called the 'goiter fallacy', results from the frequent observation in highly selective colleges that there are very few failures or students with overwhelming academic problems. Therefore, it is argued, why do we need any selection tests – since just about everyone makes the grade? This argument is directly analogous to the question, 'We don't see much smallpox, so why urge everyone to be vaccinated?' or 'Who sees anyone with a goiter these days, so why insist on iodized salt?' (In fact, goiter has actually increased in frequency in recent years mainly because of this fallacious reasoning by the public.) When a college's particular selection standards are relaxed, the kinds of problems the selection process was originally intended to minimize can be expected to increase.

Consequences of ignoring selection criteria

In connection with the drive to admit greater numbers of minority students into selective colleges, there has been general recognition of the need to lower admission standards, at least for the minority students, and this has led to much discussion – but so far little or no real research – on the consequences of lowered standards. About all that can be reported at present are the questions, hopes, fears, and speculations of psychologists and educators who, by virtue of their research specialization, are intimately concerned with the selection process. It has been predicted, for example, that racial segregation in American higher education will grow unless different norms are used by the elite colleges in the selection of minority students, since these colleges are becoming more selective and therefore the cut-off is higher up the tail of the ability distribution. The problem is summarized clearly by Professor Lloyd G. Humphreys of the University of Illinois:

> In the ability area in which the highest 25 percent of Caucasians are found, which is the area from which the more distinguished state universities draw their students, only about 5 percent of the Negroes have a competitive ability level.
>
> The emotional response to this is that the tests are "culturally bound" and do not evaluate Negroes "fairly". The data are remarkably consistent, however, in showing that these tests are equally accurate predictors of academic performance for both races during at least the first year in the standard curriculum.
> . . . .
> When the above ratio of 5 to 1 is corrected for the proportion

of Negroes in the population, there is only about one Negro to every 30 Caucasians on a nationwide basis who is in the top 25 percent of our population. In order to obtain more than a token number of Negro undergraduates, admissions standards have to be substantially lowered. When this is coupled with the present severe competition for qualified Negroes, and a crash recruitment program, student quality may deteriorate substantially. The result this past academic year on this campus [University of Illinois, Champaign] was a difference between the means of the two races that was 2·4 times the standard deviation of the Caucasian distribution (1969).

Humphreys goes on to speculate about the possible consequences of such lowered selection standards:

A difference between the means of the races of one standard deviation is difficult to deal with if the goal is something like 15 percent Negro admissions. As the difference increases, difficulties multiply. There will be an intolerable level of dropping of Negro students on academic grounds during the first year unless there is massive intervention. A desirable form of intervention is to establish special sections and special remedial courses. An undesirable form is for the faculty to assign grades in regular racially mixed classes on the basis of skin color rather than on performance. In the present emotional climate, if more desirable forms of intervention are not sufficiently massive, this second type becomes inevitable.

Professor Julian C. Stanley of the Johns Hopkins University has suggested that college revolts by blacks have been fueled by the academic frustration of academically underqualified students exposed to curricula that are impossibly difficult for their developed abilities. He states:

A number of studies have shown that scholastic-aptitude tests are quite resistant to coaching. Claims for remedial courses and tutoring seem largely unsubstantiated. Thus, the college that admits a number of "high-risk" freshmen and looks for academic miracles is probably inviting trouble, unless it provides easier curricula (1969).

Stanley goes on to ask to what extent

many of the black students at Cornell and other highly selective colleges regard most of their courses as "irrelevant" *because those courses are too difficult for them.* Published reports from Cornell and several other selective colleges show that a large percentage of their black freshmen are seriously underqualified academically, compared with most of the freshmen with whom they compete. This factor, almost always ignored in discussions of demands by black students, deserves prominence as probably having potent explanatory value. It seems likely that academic difficulties interact with racial sensitivities to frustrate and infuriate many black students. The percentage of black freshmen in a college who would not have been admitted by a "colorblind" admissions office may be a fairly good index of forthcoming demands by black students who may, of course, be led by academically qualified blacks who themselves are making good grades.

Professor Humphreys expresses a similar concern:

There is another effect of bringing in Negro students who are far below their fellow students in readiness to do academic work. A group of young people who are newly imbued with pride in race are placed in a situation in which they are, by and large, obviously inferior. A scientist qualifies this inferiority by adding "at their present stage of development," but this is slight consolation to the student involved. The causal chain from frustration to aggression is well-established. A large ability difference as a source of aggression cannot be ignored. The universities are damned if they don't admit more Negroes, but they are also damned in another sense if they do (1969).

A much less conspicuous but educationally more consequential effect of lowering admission standards in the most selective colleges is that more of the academically less prepared students are forced into courses and majors that are not of their choosing but are academically easier and thus permit them to get through. This diminishes the number of black professionals who graduate from college, persons with the kind of education that permits them to fill socially and economically important and needed positions as doctors, lawyers, engineers, chemists and the like. In the most selective colleges the pre-professional programs are among the more difficult and competitive majors. By recruiting black students who are not up to this competition academically, selective colleges drain off black talent into the 'black activist' field and create shortages of black professionals – physicians, dentists, lawyers, etc. A greater proportion of these same students could succeed in these majors in somewhat less selective colleges. Ironically, the most intensive recruiting efforts are made by the most prestigious colleges, which offer the least chance for blacks to succeed in their standard curricula, and not by the more average run of colleges in which more blacks might succeed. Programs in 'black studies' and the like will not give black Americans what they most need to gain from higher education. Sir Arthur Lewis has observed:

> The current attitudes of some of our black leaders towards the top white colleges is, therefore, bewildering. In its most extreme form, what is asked is that the college set aside a special part of itself to be the black part: a separate building for black studies, separate dormitories, and living accomodations for blacks, separate teachers, all black, teaching classes open only to blacks. The teachers are to be chosen by the students, and will for the most part be men whom no African or Indian or Chinese university would recognize as scholars, or be willing to hire as teachers.
>
> Doubtless some colleges under militant pressure will give in to this, but I do not see what Afro-Americans will gain thereby. Employers will not hire the students who emerge from this process. And their usefulness even in black neighborhoods will be minimal (1969).

Solutions to the problem

Solutions to the problem of increasing the enrollment of minority students in colleges and universities need to be thought about both in terms of short-range tactics applicable almost immediately and in terms of long-range improvement strategies. Any proposed solutions at this time are bound to be speculative. We are not sure what will work and the only way to find out is to try a variety of proposals. But their results must also be properly evaluated. We are sadly lacking objective information about the actual academic and personal consequences of admitting underqualified students to institutions of higher education. What we do know with great confidence is that when minority students actually meet the same selection standards as the regularly admitted students, they can be expected to perform as well as anyone else with comparable qualifications and therefore their minority status *per se* is of no consequence academically.

If, on the other hand, in the interest of increasing minority enrollments, an institution wishes to admit underqualified students (in terms of its standards for regular students), it must weigh the disparity between the underqualified and the regular students against the institution's facilities and programs for meeting the special needs of those students who cannot compete successfully in the regular curricula. There is no getting around the fact that higher education is a highly competitive affair and, given the values and the needs of our technological society, this fact is not likely to change in the foreseeable future. Therefore, it seems manifestly callous and unfair to admit large numbers of under-qualified students into college programs on a 'sink or swim' basis, without any special provisions of course counseling, remedial classes, tutoring, and the like. Either an inordinate percentage will 'sink' or instructors will alter their standards of evaluation. The latter effect, of course, is often seen as an injustice by those minority students who are qualified by the usual standards and who could earn good grades from a 'colorblind' evaluation. If college grades are no longer indicative of the student's performance in courses, the inevitable consequence will be for graduate schools, professional schools, and employers to rely increasingly on other means of assessment, most probably objective tests.

COMPENSATORY PROGRAMS

There is as yet little published hard evidence on the effectiveness of compensatory and remedial programs in helping academically underqualified students to make the grade in selective colleges. Probably no one in this country has established more contacts and received more information about such programs around the country, or has analyzed the relevant data more thoroughly, than Professor Julian C. Stanley, an expert in educational and psychological measurement at The Johns Hopkins University. It is worth quoting some of his published observations in this area. Referring to Professor Humphreys' concern about the situation at the University of Illinois where specially admitted black students had an average academic aptitude 2·4 standard deviations below the mean of the white distribution, Stanley states:

> In studying various remedial, tutoring, and coaching programs for many years, I have found no evidence that anyone knows how to leap an academic-readiness gap nearly that large.
>
> Especially, the developed verbal and mathematical abilities represented by college-entrance examinations such as the Scholastic Aptitude Test seem highly resistant to accelerated growth at high school and college levels. One hears many anecdotes about academic miracles, but upon closer examination they almost always prove to be unsubstantiated or highly atypical (1970).

Stanley states elsewhere:

> Admissions officers of selective colleges run serious academic risks if they ignore . . . test scores, high school grades, and other such evidences of readiness to succeed in a given college. Enrolees academically underqualified for the institution will need new curricula of suitable difficulty. If these are not offered voluntarily by the college, they will probably be demanded by the black students. Tutoring and remedial courses are not likely to be enough (1969).

In a footnote, Stanley adds:

> The metaphor of the disadvantaged student as an empty vessel waiting to be filled up quickly is implicit in most discussions of the probable benefits of tutoring and remediation at the college level, but I know of no rigorous evidence (though unsubstantiated anecdotes abound) that students initially low in high school grades and academic aptitude test scores "catch up" . . . (1969).

The growth of academically relevant abilities is a long, slow, cumulative process extending continuously all the way from kindergarten (or earlier) up through the college years. The senior year in high school or the college freshman year is a late stage indeed for trying to remedy deficiencies in intellectual habits and skills that take many years to develop, and unfortunately no one has discovered the means of bringing a student with a SAT score of 300 up to the level of a student with, say, 500, after he has reached college age. But at present we also do not know how to do this even beginning in elementary school or the pre-school. Great and massive efforts are being made to improve the scholastic performance of disadvantaged children, but so far no large or lasting effects have been found which would lead one to believe that the present methods will significantly increase the supply of college-level academic talent among the disadvantaged. At present, it seems, the best we know how to do is to identify such talent as exists; this being the case, no efforts or resources should be spared in making sure that potential college-level talent not be overlooked or be allowed to wither for lack of adequate educational stimulation and cultivation.

I have reviewed more extensively elsewhere the results of the best known efforts generally to boost IQ and scholastic achievement at the public school level (Jensen, 1969a). A nationwide survey and evaluation of the large, federally funded compensatory education programs by the U.S. Commission on Civil Rights concluded that these special programs had produced no significant improvement in the measured intelligence or scholastic performance of the disadvantaged children whose educational achievements they were specifically intended to raise. The evidence presented by the Civil Rights Commission leads one to question whether merely applying more of the same approach to compensatory education on a larger scale is likely to lead to the desired results, namely increasing the benefits of public education to the disadvantaged. The well-documented fruitlessness of these well-intentioned compensatory education programs should lead us to question the assumptions, theories, and practices on which they were based. Some small-scale experimental intervention programs have shown more promise of beneficial results, but they have not been in progress long enough to know yet whether the gains are maintained in the later years of schooling. I do not advocate abandoning efforts to improve the education of the disadvantaged. Increased emphasis on this effort is needed, in the spirit of experimentation, with a greater diversity of approaches and more rigorous evaluation in order to increase our chances of discovering the methods that work best.

DISCOVERY AND CULTIVATION OF ACADEMIC TALENT

If we do not know yet how to create or inculcate academic talent in children, we can at least identify it with considerable accuracy. But this talent needs to be discovered early and it must be encouraged and cultivated over a period of years if it is to be of advantage to the student entering college. Even a potential Einstein without the developed intellectual values and acquired scholastic skills would not be able to succeed in college. Therefore, if we are to increase the number of minority and disadvantaged students who can go to college profitably, I would urge that we seek academic talent in these groups as early in their schooling as possible, and then make very certain that it is properly encouraged, stimulated, and cultivated. The less culturally biased tests should assist considerably in this effort, tests like Raven's Progressive Matrices and Cattell's Culture-Fair Tests of g. Children with above-average scores on these kinds of tests, properly administered and given over a period of time in order to overcome test shyness, etc., can be regarded as academically talented, especially if they are more than one standard deviation above the general population mean. Such children, when they are from a disadvantaged background, should be given special attention. They should not be forced to languish in classes with a high percentage of slow learners who demand most of the teacher's attention. The able children especially need the stimulation of smaller classes, better teachers, and tutorial attention from teacher's aids and volunteer college students. The tutorial attention is not so much for purely scholastic reasons as for giving the child intellectually and academically oriented persons with whom he can feel some identification and who can help to fire his enthusiasm for learning and thinking. It is their values and attitudes about intellectual matters, rather than their abilities, that keep many children of the poor from developing the scholastic skills that are needed for college. Greater efforts can be made to prevent the loss of academic potential resulting from unstimulating and discouraging home and school environments.

WIDENING COLLEGE OPPORTUNITIES

Stanley has urged that more colleges representing a much wider range of difficulty levels than is found in the most highly selective 'prestige' institutions make greater efforts to recruit minority students, provide scholarships, and the like. He states:

> A basic principle, applicable across socio-economic levels and races, is that students achieve their academic goals best at institutions where they are not too poorly (or well) prepared to compete academically. Students would not seem to be served best academically by being admitted to those major universities and selective colleges for which they lack even marginal readiness. The some 3000 colleges in this country provide enough variability in academic difficulty to accommodate almost every high school graduate who wishes to be a college student (1969).

Elsewhere he says:

> The old rule of guidance and admissions that a student is well advised to attend a college where he is not almost hopelessly outclassed academically holds for blacks as well as for others. Many colleges and universities exist which are easier than those in the Big Ten, for example. It is cruel psychologically, dangerous racially, costly economically, and unproductive educationally to set up quotas of blacks for selective colleges and universities, however humanitarian that might seem. Most academically quite underqualified students can be got through to degrees there only if easier curricula are developed specially for them, and that needlessly and probably inefficiently duplicates resources already available in state colleges, many private institutions, and open-door community colleges (1968).

ENHANCING THE VALUE OF DIVERSE EDUCATION

The question of selection for higher education finally must be viewed in the total perspective of education for all our nation's youth. Resolving the problem of minority selection in college is but a small portion of the total problems of education. The public schools are actually failing to be of real benefit to a large segment of our youths, particularly minority youths. In Chicago alone it is claimed that some 47,000 school age children are out of school and out of work at any given time. And one thousand drop out of public school each month. In some Chicago high schools the *average* reading level even of those who graduate is seventh grade. In the streets of Harlem there are over 70,000 high school drop outs of college age and younger (*Carnegie Quarterly*, 1968).

Public education has not come to grips with these problems. The solution, I believe, lies in diversified school programs that permit and encourage students with different patterns of abilities and interests to attain employable skills in today's society. College education in the traditional sense is a minority path for *any* racial and socio-economic group. Other educational paths must be made attractive and valuable. Unfortunately the national yearning for educational prestige has forced into college many youths of all races who would have done better in something else. While college enrollments go up, nearly a quarter of the young men and women who turn 18 every year are not educated to the minimum level of employability for the eight out of ten job opportunities which do not require a college education. The federal government invests $14 in the nation's universities for every $1 it puts into vocational education programs; yet it spends up to $12,000 per person in remedial programs to get the unemployed off welfare rolls. Some change in our educational values clearly seems called for, with more emphasis on the needed occupational goals to be met through education and less on the mere prestige value of 'going to college'. Colleges and universities are often criticized as being elitist institutions. So be it. There is nothing wrong with having institutions of higher learning intended for only a small percentage of the population in a democratic society, provided the elitism is one of intellectual merit rather than one of privilege based on social class, race, or family background. But it will take more effort and scrupulous care to make the privilege fully available and accessible, both financially and psychologically, to those of academic promise from socially and economically poor backgrounds. Academic talent and interest must be assiduously sought in all segments of our society and encouraged to fulfillment whenever it is found. This seems the surest way at present of insuring the greatest benefits of higher education to minorities and to society as a whole. Dedication to the ideal of equality of *opportunity* means, at our present point in history, sensitivity and watchfulness for practices, policies, and attitudes which create discrimination disfavoring minorities, and full legal implementation and enforcement, where necessary, to prevent such discrimination. But the ideal of equality of *performance* depends upon strict adherence to dealing with persons, not as members of particular sub-groups in the population, but as individuals, each in terms of his *own* abilities and drives and potentials. Equality of opportunity must apply to all segments of the population and can be evaluated accordingly. But equality of performance, we know, is achieved by persons as individuals, not as a percentage of some socially defined population group. When the individual is lost sight of as merely part of a 'quota', his own achievements and self-esteem are jeopardized. The value of equality of opportunity for all groups in our society is that it permits to the fullest extent the recognition of excellence in performance by individuals, regardless of the group into which they were born.

Do schools cheat
minority children?[1]

Americans' faith in education is tangibly substantiated in the fact
that the American people now invest in educational institutions
annually almost as much as all other nations combined. In the
past two decades educational spending nationwide has increased
fivefold while personal consumption merely doubled. Since World
War II school enrollments have increased 88 per cent, while
school expenditures (in constant dollars) increased 350 per cent.
While employment in private industry increased 38 per cent, it
increased 203 per cent in public education. With such an abundant
outlay for education, the question naturally arises whether the
benefits are equitably distributed to all segments of our population.
A keystone of public education is the promise that no child should
be denied the opportunity to fulfill his educational potential,
regardless of his national, ethnic, or socio-economic background.
When substantial inequalities in educational achievement are
evident between large segments of the population nominally
sharing the same educational system, serious questions are raised,
and rightly so. Numerous attempts have been and are being made
to find the answers to the inequities in the benefits of education.
In California the chief sub-population differences in scholastic
attainments involve majority-minority differences, the minorities
in this case being Negroes and Mexican-Americans.

The causes of educational inequalities, in terms both of input

---

[1] Critical commentaries on this article, by Sir Cyril Burt, H. J. Butcher,
H. J. Eysenck, J. Nisbet, and Philip E. Vernon, were published in
Educational Research, 1972, **14**, 87-100.

and output, cannot be discussed very fruitfully in general terms. There are considerable regional and local differences in educational expenditures and facilities and in their distribution within local districts. In assessing the existence and degree of educational inequities, we must get down to specific cases. That is what is intended in this article. We shall take a rather close look at some of the questions and answers involved in assessing inequalities within a single school system which serves three sub-populations: a majority group, which we shall refer to as Anglos, and two sizeable minorities, Negroes and Mexican-Americans. Before going into the details of this study, however, a few more general points should be reviewed.

School comparisons of academic achievement

The now famous Coleman Report (Coleman *et al.*, 1966), which surveyed 645,000 pupils in more than 3,000 schools in all regions of the United States, found relatively minor differences in the measured characteristics of schools attended by different racial and ethnic groups, but very great differences in their achievement levels. The Report also argued that when the social background and attitudes of students are held constant, per pupil expenditures, pupil-teacher ratio, school facilities and curricula show very little relation to achievement. The Report concluded '. . . that schools bring little influence to bear on a child's achievement that is independent of his background and general social context' (p. 325). A critical examination of this study by Bowles and Levin (1968) led them to the conclusion that Coleman's methodology could have resulted in an underestimation to some unknown degree of the extent of the relationship between school differences and pupil achievement. They also criticize the conclusion of the Coleman Report that 'There is a small positive effect of school integration on the reading and mathematics achievement of Negro pupils after differences in the socio-economic background of the students are accounted for' (pp. 29-30). Bowles and Levin claim that '. . . the small residual statistical correlation between proportion white in the schools and Negro achievement is likely to be due, at least in part, to the fact that the proportion white in a school is a measure of otherwise inadequately controlled social background of the Negro student. Thus, we find that the conclusion that Negro achievement is positively associated with the proportion of fellow students who are white, once other influences are taken into account, is not supported by the evidence presented in the Report.' Here then is one critique of the Coleman Report which suggests just the opposite of the most popularly held conceptions of what was proved by the Report. Bowles and Levin argue that school effects are probably larger than suggested by the study, and racial composition of the school *per se* is probably a more negligible factor than suggested in the Report's conclusions. A smaller-scale but statistically more thoroughly controlled study by Wilson (1967) found that after controlling for other factors, the racial composition of the school had no significant direct association with Negro achievement, thus supporting the conclusion of Bowles and Levin, at least in the one California school district studied by Wilson.

But probably the most compelling argument for requiring racial balance in schools is not the direct effect of a school's racial composition *per se*, but the fact that it could lead to a greater equalization of school facilities for majority and minority groups so that disadvantaged minorities would not be largely confined to schools with inferior resources. This may be a valid argument in some parts of the country. but one may justifiably question whether it is a cogent factor in California schools.

Consider the following evidence. A rather coarse-grained analysis of the relationship between the proportion of minority enrollment and certain school characteristics in California is made possible by the State Department of Education's recent publication of statistics on several scholastic variables for all school districts in the State. The present analysis, carried out by the writer, is based on only the total of 191 school districts in the ten counties of the greater Bay Area.[2]

The variables on which all school districts were ranked were: Grade 6 Reading Achievement (age 11), Grade 10 Reading (age 15), Grade 6 median IQ, Grade 10 median IQ, Proportion of Minority Enrollment, Per Pupil Expenditure, Teacher Salary,

---

[2] Alameda, Contra Costa, Marin, Napa, San Francisco, San Joaquin, San Mateo, Santa Clara, Solano, Sonoma.

Teacher-Pupil Ratio (Grades 4-8), Number of Administrators per 100 Pupils and General Purpose Tax Rate in the school district. The rank order correlations[3] among these variables for the 191 school districts are shown in Table 7.1. We see that minority enrollment has quite negligible correlations with all the school facility variables except number of administrators per 100 pupils (Variable 10), and this correlation is positive. On the other hand, there is a strong negative correlation between minority enrollment

TABLE 7.1. Correlations (Spearman's ρ) among ten educational variables 191 California school districts (decimals omitted)

Variable	2	3	4	5	6	7	8	9	10
Grade 6 Reading (age 11)	81	94	87	−73	23	21	18	−19	−09
Grade 10 Reading (age 15)		75	90	−70	08	06	02	−03	−06
Grade 6 IQ			85	−67	25	21	17	19	−08
Grade 10 IQ				−67	05	05	09	−13	00
Minority Enrollment					02	05	08	−10	17
Per Pupil Expenditure						35	53	42	47
Tax Rate							54	−06	24
Teacher Salary								18	45
Teacher-Pupil Ratio									01
No. Administrators/100									

and the 6th and 10th grade reading and IQ scores. This correlation matrix can be elucidated by factor analyzing it, thereby reducing it to three independent components which account for most of the variance (78 per cent). This was accomplished by a varimax rotation of the first three principal components. The rotated factors are shown in Table 7.2. Factor I is scholastic aptitude (IQ), reading achievement and minority enrollment. Factor II represents the financial resources of the schools, with the highest loading on teacher salary. Factor III is teacher-pupil ratio and that part of per pupil expenditure not associated with Factor II. What this analysis shows most clearly is the absence of any

---

[3] A smaller rank order (e.g., 1) indicates: high reading scores, high median IQ, high proportion of minorities, high expenditure per child, high teacher salaries, high tax rate, high teacher-pupil ratio (i.e., smaller classes), and a larger number of administrators per 100 pupils.

appreciable correlation between the aptitude-achievement variables and the school district's financial outlay. If there were a substantial relationship between the financial resources and the reading achievement of the various school districts, the factors shown in Table 7.2 could not be so clearly separated. Note also that while minority enrollment has a negative correlation (-0.82) with Factor I (IQ-Reading), it has a small positive correlation ($+0.19$) with Factor II (expenditures). The negative correlation (-0.09) between minority enrollment and Factor III indicates a

TABLE 7.2. Rotated factor loadings for ten educational variables in 191 California school districts

	Factors		
Variables	*I*	*II*	*III*
1. Grade 6 Reading (age 11)	0·95	0·12	0·15
2. Grade 10 Reading (age 15)	0·92	0·00	−0·08
3. Grade 6 IQ	0·92	0·13	0·17
4. Grade 10 IQ	0·95	0·06	−0·17
5. Minority Enrollment	−0·82	0·19	−0·09
6. Per Pupil Expenditure	0·10	0·67	0·55
7. Tax Rate	0·11	0·75	0·15
8. Teacher Salary	0·06	0·83	0·17
9. Teacher-Pupil Ratio	0·03	0·01	0·96
10. No. of Administrators	−0·13	0·71	0·01
Per cent of Variance	42·0	22·8	13·6

slight disadvantage to districts with a high proportion of minorities in terms of average class size. Overall, these data suggest that there is no appreciable relationship between these particular school resources and minority enrollment, and if anything the correlation is in just the opposite direction to the popular belief that educational facilities are relatively inadequate in districts with a higher percentage of minority students.

Since this analysis is based on data in which the smallest unit for analysis is the school district, it permits no inference concerning the allocation of educational resources to the various schools, which probably differ in minority enrollments, within the districts. A similar analysis could be performed within a district, using the individual schools as the unit of analysis, but different indices of a school's resources would have to be used, since there would be relatively little variance on such variables as teacher salary and per pupil expenditure *within* any given school district. More fine-grained indices of the school's specific educational facilities should be included. In any case, the first and most obvious step in assessing the equality of educational facilities is to make a direct examination of the facilities, per pupil expenditures, etc. The recreational, hygienic, safety, and aesthetic aspects of the school plant should be considered no less than those facilities deemed to have more direct educational consequences, such as pupil-teacher ratio and special services.

The misuse of national and state norms

School boards, the public, and the press commonly misuse the published and state norms on standardized achievement tests. Schools and districts are compared against 'norms', which are intended to represent national or state averages, as if achieving a close approximation to the norms, if not exceeding them, should be the primary goal of every school system. Deviation from the norm, above or below, is commonly regarded as a credit or a discredit to the particular school system. The fallacy in this, of course, is the fact that the average level of scholastic achievement in a community is highly predictable from a number of the community's characteristics over which the local schools have no control whatsoever. Thorndike (1951), for example, correlated average IQ and an average scholastic achievement index (based on half a million children) with 24 census variables for a wide range of communities, large and small, urban and rural. Eleven of the correlations were significant at the 1 per cent level. Census variables with the highest correlation with IQ and achievement were education level of the adult population (0·43), home ownership (0·39), quality and cost of housing (0·33), proportion of native-born whites (0·28), rate of female employment (0·26), and proportion of professional workers (0·28). In a multiple correlation these census variables predicted IQ and achievement between 0·55 and 0·60. Essentially the same picture is revealed in many other similar studies (Wiseman, 1964, Chapter IV). A school's or district's deviation from the mean achievement predicted from a multiple regression equation based on a host of community characteristics would therefore, make much more sense than a mere comparison of the school's average with national or state norms.

Majority-minority comparisons within a school district

Even when a school district has equalized the educational facilities in all of its schools in terms of physical plant amenities, teacher salaries and qualifications, per pupil expenditures, teacher-pupil ratios, special services, curriculum, and the like, the question may still be asked whether majority-minority differences in scholastic achievement are a product of more subtle and less tangible factors operating in the school situation. We have in mind, for example, such factors as racial and socio-economic composition of the school, and different teacher attitudes and expectancies in relation to majority and minority pupils. Is there any way we can assess the degree to which schools afford unequal educational advantages to majority and minority pupils over and above what can easily be reckoned in terms of pupil expenditures and the like?

I have tried to answer this question as best as I believe it can be answered with the psychometric and statistical methodology now available and with the rather modest resources within the financial means of most school systems. Although it would be impossible to present all the technical details and results of this study within the limits of this paper, it is possible to indicate some of the methods and the most relevant results they have yielded.

The study was conducted in 1970 in a fairly large (35 schools) elementary school district of California. This school district was ideal for this kind of study for four main reasons: (1) the district's school population has substantial proportions of Negro (13 per cent) and Mexican-American (20 per cent) students; (2) the majority (Anglo) population is very close to state and national norms for Anglos in IQ, for both mean and standard deviation, and the same is true for the two minority groups in relation to norms for their respective populations in the U.S.; (3) the schools are largely *de facto* segregated due to rather widely spaced residential clustering of the three ethnic groups, and (4) the district has made a thorough effort to provide equal educational facilities in all of its schools, if anything favoring those schools with the largest minority enrollments to whom additional federal and state funds were allocated for special compensatory programs.

Large representative samples totalling 28 per cent of the school population from kindergarten to the eighth grade (age 13) were selected for study. A total of 6,619 children were tested; more or less equal numbers were tested at each grade. The three main ethnic classifications were Anglo ($N = 2,453$), Mexican-American ($N = 2,263$), and Negro ($N = 1,853$). Approximately half the sample (selected randomly with the classroom as the unit of selection) were tested by a small staff of specially trained testers, and half were tested by their regular classroom teachers. Because of the large sample sizes the tester and teacher results often differ significantly but do not differ appreciably or systematically except that the results of teacher-administered tests consistently have somewhat greater variance and lower reliability which would tend to attenuate intercorrelations among measures and lessen the statistical significance of group differences. Parallel analyses for testers and teachers were run on all the data, which were combined when there were no significant or systematic differences between the two forms of testing. For the sake of simplicity in the present summary only the tester results are reported here when the two two sets of data were not combined.

Rationale of the study

In terms of this study one can think of the educational process as being analogous to an industrial production process in which raw materials ('input') are converted to a specified product ('output'). The output will be a function both of the input and of the effectiveness of the process by means of which the input is converted into output. In the case of schooling, the input is what the child brings with him to school by way of his abilities, attitudes, prior learning, cultural background, and personality characteristics relevant to learning in the classroom. The school itself has relatively little, if any, control over these input variables. The school, however, can have considerable influence on one variable – prior learning – for children who are already somewhere along the educational path, and if the school's instructional program is deficient for some children, the deficiencies in prior learning in

K

earlier grades should show up increasingly in later grades as a cumulating deficit in scholastic achievement.

Whatever else one may say about it, schooling is essentially a process whereby children are helped to acquire certain skills, which are the output of the system. The effectiveness of the process can be judged, among other ways, in terms of the relationship between input and output. Meaningful comparisons cannot be made between the output (scholastic achievement) of different pupils, classes, schools, or school districts without reference to the input variables. The main purpose of the present study is the comparison of the outputs, i.e., educational achievements, of three categories of pupils – Anglo, Negro, and Mexican-American – when these groups are statistically equated on the input variables. In this way we can make some judgment concerning the relative efficiency of the educational process for each of the three groups. The adequacy of the statistical equating of the groups in terms of input depends upon a judicious selection of instruments for measuring the input variables. The chief aims in selecting the input control variables are (1) to represent the domain of educationally relevant abilities, personality and home background factors as broadly as feasible, and (2) to include only those ability and background variables which are not explicitly taught by the schools or are not under direct control of the schools. That is to say, they should represent the raw materials that the schools have to work with. The output, on the other hand, should represent objective measures of those skills which it is the school's specific purpose to teach. These are best measured by standardized tests of scholastic achievement.

The input variables can be classified into three categories: (1) ability or general aptitude tests, (2) motivation, personality, and school-related attitudes, and (3) environmental background variables reflecting socio-economic status, parental education, and general cultural advantages.

Input variables

ABILITY TESTS

Lorge-Thorndike Intelligence Test. This is a nationally standardized group-administered test of general intelligence. In the normative sample, which was intended to be representative of the nation's school population, the test has a mean IQ of 100 and a standard deviation of 16. It is generally acknowledged to be one of the best paper-and-pencil tests of general intelligence.

The Manual of the Lorge-Thorndike Test states that the test was designed to measure reasoning ability. It does not test proficiency in specific skills taught in school, although the verbal tests, from grade 4 (age 9) and above, depend upon reading ability. The reading level required, however, is intentionally kept considerably below the level of reasoning required for correctly answering the test questions. Thus the test is essentially a test of reasoning and not of reading ability, which is to say that it should have more of its variance in common with non-verbal tests of reasoning ability than with tests of reading *per se*.

The tests for grades K-3 do not depend at all upon reading ability but make use exclusively of pictorial items. The tests for grades 4-8 consist of two parts, *Verbal* (V) and *Non-verbal* (NV). They are scored separately and the raw score on each is converted to an IQ, with a normative mean of 100 and *SD* of 16. The chief advantage of keeping the two scores separate is that the Non-verbal IQ does not overestimate or underestimate the child's general level of intellectual ability because of specific skills or disabilities in reading. The Non-verbal IQ, however, correlates almost as highly with a test of reading comprehension as does the Verbal IQ, because all three tests depend primarily upon reasoning ability and not upon reading *per se*. For example, in the fourth grade sample, the correlation between the Lorge-Thorndike Verbal and Non-verbal IQs is 0·70. The correlation between Verbal IQ and the Paragraph Meaning Subtest of the Standard Achievement Test is 0·52. The correlation between the Non-verbal IQ and Paragraph Meaning is 0·47. Now we can ask: what is the correlation of Verbal IQ and Paragraph Meaning when the effects of Non-verbal IQ are partialed out, that is, are held constant? The partial correlation between Verbal IQ and Paragraph Meaning (holding Non-verbal IQ constant) is only 0·29.

The following forms of the Lorge-Thorndike Intelligence Tests were used:

Level 1, Form B		Grades K-1
Level 2, Form B		Grades 2-3
Level 3, Form B	Verbal and Non-verbal	Grades 4-6
Level 4, Form B	Verbal and Non-verbal	Grades 7-8

Figure Copying Test. The Figure Copying Test was given in grades K-6. Beyond grade 6 (age 11) too large a proportion of children obtain the maximum possible score (30) for the test to be useful in making group comparisons. In fact, by grades 5 and 6 group differences are very probably underestimated by this test, since a larger proportion of the higher-scoring group will obtain the maximum score and this 'ceiling' effect will prevent the group's full range of ability from being represented. The ceiling effect consequently spuriously depresses the group's mean and reduces the variance (or standard deviation). Nevertheless, this test is extremely valuable for group comparisons because it is one of the least culture-loaded tests available and successful performance on the test is known to be significantly related to readiness for the scholastic tasks of the primary grades, especially reading readiness.

The Figure Copying Test was developed at the Gesell Institute of Child Study at Yale University as a means of measuring developmental readiness for the traditional school learning tasks of the primary grades. The test consists of the ten geometric forms shown in Figure 7.1, arranged in order of difficulty, which the child must simply copy, each on a separate sheet of paper. The test involves no memory factor, since the figure to be copied is before the child at all times. The test is administered without time limit, although most children finish in 10 to 15 minutes. The test is best regarded as a development scale of mental ability. It correlates substantially with other IQ tests, but it is considerably less culture-loaded than most usual IQ tests. It is primarily a measure of general cognitive development and not just of perceptual-motor ability. Children taking the test are urged to attempt to copy every figure.

Each of the ten figures is scored on a three-point scale going from one (low) to three (high). (A score of zero is given in the rare instance when no attempt has been made to copy a particular figure.) A score of one is given if an attempt is made but the child's drawing completely fails to resemble the model. A score of two is given if there is fair resemblance to the model – the figure need not be perfect but it must be easily recognizable as the model which the child has attempted to copy. A score of three is given for an attempt which duplicates the figure in all its essential

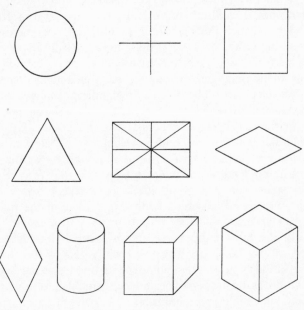

FIGURE 7.1. The ten simple geometric forms used in the Figure Copying Test. In the actual test booklet each figure is present singly in the top half of a $5\frac{1}{2}'' \times 8\frac{1}{2}''$ sheet. The circle is $1\frac{3}{4}''$ in diameter.

characteristics – this is an essentially adult level of performance. Since there are ten figures in all, the possible range of scores goes from 10 to 30 (or 0 to 30 if zeros are counted, but this is rare, since virtually all subjects attempt all ten figures).

The high level of motivation maintained by this test is indicated by the fact that the minimum score obtained in each group at each grade level increases systematically with grade level. This suggests that all children were making an attempt to perform in accordance with the instructions. Another indication that can be seen from the test booklets is that virtually 100 per cent of the children in every ethnic group at every grade level attempted to copy every figure. The attempts, even when unsuccessful, usually show considerable effort, as indicated by redrawing the figure, erasures and drawing over the figure repeatedly in order to improve its likeness to the model. It is also noteworthy about this test that normal children are generally not successful in drawing figures beyond their mental age level and that special instructions and coaching on the drawing of these figures hardly improves the child's performance. This test, in other words, is not very susceptible to training, but measures some fundamental aspects of mental development. The diagnostic significance of this test has been explicated extensively in *School Readiness* (Harper and Row, 1967, pp. 63-129) by Drs Frances L. Ilg and Louise Bates Awes of the Gesell Institute of Child Development at Yale University.

Raven's Progressive Matrices. This non-verbal reasoning test, devised in England, is intended to be a pure measure of g, the general factor common to all intelligence tests. It is a highly reliable measure of reasoning ability, quite free of the influence of special abilities, such as verbal or numerical facility. It is probably the most culture-free test of general intelligence yet devised by psychologists. The test mainly gets at the ability to grasp relationships; it does not depend upon specific acquired information as do tests of vocabulary, general information, etc. The test, which is group-administered, begins with problems that are so easy that all children by third grade can catch on and solve the problems even without instructions.

Two forms of the test were used. The Colored Progressive Matrices, which is the children's form, was used in grades 3 to 6. This test is appropriate even for kindergarten children, but to ensure that all children tested could go through the first few problems without difficulty, giving them a chance to catch on easily and experience success in the early part of the test, we used this test only from the third grade and above. The Colored Matrices consist of 36 matrix problems which are administered without time limit. Children are encouraged to attempt all problems. There is no penalty for guessing.

The Standard Progressive Matrices were used in grades 7 and 8. These begin as easily as the colored matrices but advance in difficulty more rapidly and go up to a level appropriate for average adults. There are 60 matrix problems in all, and the subjects are encouraged to attempt all of them, without penalty for guessing.

Listening-Attention Test. In the Listening-Attention Test the child is presented with an answer sheet containing 100 pairs of digits in sets of 10. The child listens to a tape recording which speaks one digit every two seconds. The child is required to put an X over the one digit in each pair which has been heard on the tape recorder. The purpose of this test is to determine the extent to which the child is able to pay attention to numbers spoken on a tape recorder, to keep his place in the test, and to make the appropriate responses to what he hears from moment to moment. Low scores on this test indicate that the subject is not yet ready to take the Memory for Numbers test which immediately follows it. High scores on the Listening-Attention Test indicate that the subject has the prerequisite skills for taking the digit span (Memory for Numbers) test. The Listening-Attention Test thus is intended as a means for detecting students who, for whatever reason, are unable to hear and to respond to numbers read over a tape recorder. The test itself makes no demands on the child's memory, but on his ability for listening, paying attention, and responding appropriately – all prerequisites for the digit memory test that follows.

It has been found in previous studies using the Listening-Attention Test that the vast majority of subjects from grade 2 and above obtain perfect scores; the median score is 100, and the lower quartile rarely goes below 95. This means that nearly all subjects have the prerequisite skills for the Memory for Numbers test to yield a valid measure of the subject's short-term memory ability.

Memory for Numbers Test. The Memory for Numbers test is a measure of digit span, or more generally, short-term memory. It consists of three parts. Each part consists of six series of digits going from four digits in a series up to nine digits in a series. The digit series are presented on a tape recording on which the digits are spoken clearly by a male voice at the rate of precisely one digit per second. The subjects write down as many digits as they can recall at the conclusion of each series, which is signalled by a 'bong'. Each part of the test is preceded by a short practice test of three-digit series in order to permit the tester to determine whether the child has understood the instructions, etc. The practice test also serves to familiarize the subject with the procedure of each of the subtests. The first subtest is labeled Immediate Recall (I). Here the subject is instructed to recall the series *immediately* after the last digit has been spoken on the tape recorder. The second subtest consists of Delayed Recall (D). Here the subject is instructed not to write down his response until after ten seconds have elapsed after the last digit has been spoken. The ten-second interval is marked by audible clicks of a metronome and is terminated by the sound of a 'bong' which signals the child to write his response. The Delayed Recall condition invariably results in some retention loss. The third subtest is the repeated series test, in which the digit series is repeated three times prior to recall; the subject then recalls the series immediately after the last digit in the series has been presented. Again, recall is signalled by a 'bong'. Each repetition of the series is separated by a tone with a duration of one second. The repeated series almost invariably results in greater recall than the single series. This test is very culture-fair for children in second grade and beyond and who know their numerals and are capable of listening and paying attention, as indicated by the Listening-Attention Test. The maximum score on any one of the sub-tests is 39, that is the sum of the digit series from four through nine.

MOTIVATIONAL AND PERSONALITY TESTS

Speed and Persistence Test (Making Xs). The Making Xs Test is intended as an assessment of test-making motivation. It gives an indication of the subject's willingness to comply with instructions in a group testing situation and to mobilize effort in following those instructions for a brief period of time. The test involves no intellectual component, although for young children it probably involves some perceptual-motor skills component, as reflected by increasing mean scores as a function of age between grades 1 to 5. The wide range of individual differences among children at any one grade level would seem to reflect mainly general motivation and test-making attitudes in a group situation. The test also serves partly as an index of classroom morale, and it can be entered as a moderator variable into correlational analyses with other ability and achievement tests. Children who do very poorly on this test, it can be suspected, are likely not to put out their maximum effort on ability tests given in a group situation and therefore their scores are not likely to reflect their 'true' level of ability.

The Making Xs Test consists of two parts. On Part I the subject is asked simply to make Xs in a series of squares for a period of 90 seconds. In this part the instructions say nothing about speed. They merely instruct the child to make Xs. The maximum possible score on Part I is 150, since there are 150 squares provided in which the child can make Xs. After a two-minute rest period the child turns the page of the test booklet to Part II. Here the child is instructed to show how much better he can perform than he did on Part I and to work as rapidly as possible. The child is again given 90 seconds to make as many Xs as he can in the 150 boxes provided. The gain in score from Part I to Part II reflects both a practice effect and an increase in motivation or effort as a result of the motivating instructions, i.e., instructions to work as rapidly as possible.

Ethnic and social-class group differences on this test are generally smaller than on any other test, with the exception of the Listening-Attention Test (on which there are almost no group *or* individual differences).

Eysenck Personality Inventory-Junior. The EPI-Junior is the children's form of the EPI for adults. It is a questionnaire designed to measure the two factors of personality which have been found to account for most of the variance in the personality domain – Extraversion and Neuroticism. The Extraversion (E) scale represents the continuum of social extraversion-introversion. High scores reflect sociability, outgoingness and carefreeness. The Neuroticism (N) scale reflects emotional instability, anxiety proneness, and the tendency to develop neurotic symptoms under stress. The Lie (L) scale is merely a validity detector consisting of a number of items which are very rarely answered in the keyed direction by the vast majority of subjects. A high score on L indicates that the subject is 'faking good' or is answering the questionnaire items more or less at random, either intentionally or as a result of insufficient comprehension of the items. Naivity is also reflected in elevated L scores, and it is probably mainly this factor which causes a decrease in L scores as children mature.

K*

The EPI scales were included in the present study as a control variable because previous studies had shown the E and N scales to predict a small but significant part of the variance in scholastic performance. Because of the reading level required by the EPI, it was not given below the fourth grade.

Student Self-Report. This 21-item self-report inventory was composed mainly of items in the self concept inventory used by James Coleman in his study, *Equality of Educational Opportunity.* It reveals the student's attitudes towards school, towards himself as a student, and other attitudes affecting motivation and self-esteem. The questionnaire was administered by the classroom teachers to grades 4 to 8. Because of the reading level required, it was not administered below grade 4.

BACKGROUND INFORMATION

The Home Index. This is a 24-item questionnaire about the home environment, devised by Harrison Gough (1949). It is a sensitive composite index of the socio-economic level of the child's family. Factor analysis of past data by Gough has shown that the 24 items fall into four categories, each of which can be scored as a separate scale. Part I (Items 6, 7, 8, 9, 10, 15, 16, 23) reflects primarily the educational level of the parents. Part II (Items 1, 2, 3, 4, 5, 13, 20, 24) reflects material possessions in the home. Part III (Items 17, 18, 21, 22) reflects degree of parental participation in middle- or upper-middle class social and civic activities. Part IV (Items 11 and 19) relates to formal exposure to music and other arts.

OUTPUT VARIABLES: SCHOLASTIC ACHIEVEMENT

Stanford Achievement Tests. Scholastic achievement was assessed by means of the so-called 'partial battery' of the Stanford Achievement Tests, consisting of the following subtests: Word Meaning, Paragraph Meaning, Spelling, Word Study Skills, Language (grammar), Arithmetic Computation, Arithmetic Concepts, and Arithmetic Applications. The Stanford Achievement battery was administered to grades 1 to 8.

Distinction between aptitude and achievement

Can we justify the separation of our tests into two categories, ability or aptitude tests versus scholastic achievement tests, and then regard the former as *input* and the latter as *output*? Do not intelligence or aptitude tests also measure learning or achievement? The answer to this question is far from simple, but I believe there are at least six kinds of evidence which justify a psychological distinction between intelligence tests and achievement tests.

(1) *Breadth of Learning Sampled.* The most obvious difference between tests of intelligence and of achievement is the breadth of the domains sampled by the tests. Achievement tests sample very narrowly from the most specifically taught skills in the traditional curriculum, emphasizing particularly the three Rs. Achievement test items are samples of the particular skills that children are specifically taught in school. Since these skills are quite explicitly defined and the criteria of their attainment are fairly clear to teachers and parents, children can be taught and can be given practice on these skills to shape their performance up to the desired criterion. Because of the circumscribed nature of many of the basic scholastic skills, the pupil's specific weaknesses can be identified and remedied. The skills or learning sampled by an intelligence test, on the other hand, represent achievements of a much broader nature. Intelligence test items are sampled from such a very wide range of potential experiences that the idea of teaching intelligence, as compared with teaching, say, reading or arithmetic, is practically nonsensical. Even direct coaching and practice on a particular intelligence test raises individual's scores on the average by only five to ten points; and some tests, especially those referred to as 'culture fair', seem to be hardly amenable to the effects of coaching and practice. The average 5-year-old, for example, can copy a circle or a square without any trouble, but try to teach him to copy a diamond and see how far he gets! Wait until he is 7 years old and he will have no trouble copying the diamond without any need for instruction. Even vocabulary is very unsusceptible to enlargement by direct practice aimed at increasing vocabulary. This is part of the reason why vocabulary tests are regarded as such good measures of

general intelligence and always have a high *g* loading in factor analyses of various types of intelligence tests. The items in a vocabulary test are sampled from such an enormously large pool of potential items that the number that can be acquired by specific study and practice is only a small proportion of the total, so that few if any are likely to appear in any given vocabulary test. Furthermore, persons seem to retain only those words which fill some conceptual 'slot' or need in their own mental structures. A new word encountered for the first time which fills such a conceptual 'slot' is picked up and retained seemingly without conscious effort, and will 'pop' into mind again when the conceptual need for it arises, even though in the meantime the word may not have been encountered for many months or even years. If there is no conceptual slot needing to be filled, that is to say, no meaning for the individual which the word serves to symbolize, it is very difficult to make the definition of the word stick in the individual's memory, and even after repeated drill, it will quickly fade beyond retrieval, as when a student memorizes a long list of foreign words in order to pass his foreign language exam for the Ph.D. Since intelligence tests assess the learning that occurs in the total life experiences of the individual, they are more general and more valid measures of his learning potential than are scholastic achievement tests. It should come as no surprise that there is a substantial correlation between the two classes of tests, since both measure learning or achievement, one in a broad sphere, the other in a much narrower sphere. In a culturally more or less homogeneous population the broader-based measure called 'intelligence' is more generally representative of the individual's learning capacities and is more stable over time than the more specific acquisitions of knowledge and skill classed as scholastic achievement.

(2) *Equivalence of Diverse Tests.* One of the most impressive characteristics of intelligence tests is the great diversity of means by which essentially the same ability (or abilities) can be measured. Tests having very diverse forms, such as vocabulary, block designs, matrices, number series, 'odd-man out', figure copying, verbal analogies, and other kinds of problems can all serve as intelligence tests yielding more or less equivalent results because of their high intercorrelations. All these types of tests have high loadings on the *g* factor, which, as Wechsler (1958, p. 121) has said,

'. . . involves broad mental organization; it is independent of the modality or contextual structure from which it is elicited; *g* cannot be exclusively identified with any single intellectual ability and for this reason cannot be described in concrete operational terms'. We can accurately define *g* only in terms of certain mathematical operations; in Wechsler's words '*g* is a measure of a collective communality which necessarily emerges from the intercorrelation of any broad sample of mental abilities' (p. 123).

Assessment of scholastic achievement, on the other hand, depends upon tests of narrowly specific acquired skills – reading, spelling, arithmetic operations, and the like. The forms by means of which one can test any one of these scholastic skills are very limited indeed. This is not to say that there is not a general factor common to all tests of scholastic achievement, but this general factor common to all the tests seems to be quite indistinguishable from the *g* factor of intelligence tests. Achievement tests, however, usually do not have as high *g* loadings as intelligence tests but have higher loadings on group factors such as verbal and numerical ability factors and they also contain more task-specific variance. It is always possible to make achievement tests correlate more highly with intelligence tests by requiring students to reason, to use data provided, and to apply their factual knowledge to the solution of new problems. More than just the mastery of factual information, intelligence is the ability to apply this information in new and different ways. With increasing grade level, achievement tests have more and more variance in common with tests of *g*. For example, once the basic skills in reading have been acquired, reading achievement tests must increasingly measure the student's comprehension of more and more complex selections rather than the simpler processes of word recognition, decoding, etc. And thus at higher grades, tests of reading comprehension, for those children who have already mastered the basic skills, become more or less indistinguishable in factorial composition from the so-called tests of verbal intelligence. Similarly, tests of mechanical arithmetic (arithmetic computation) have less correlation with *g* than tests of arithmetic thought problems, such as the Arithmetic Concepts and Arithmetic Applications subtests of the Stanford Achievement battery. Accordingly, most indices of scholastic performance increasingly reflect general intelligence as children progress in school. We found in our study, for example, that up to grade 6, verbal and non-verbal intelligence tests could be factorially separated, with the scholastic achievement tests lining up on the same factor with verbal intelligence. But beyond grade 6 both the verbal and non-verbal tests, along with all the scholastic achievement tests, amalgamated into a single large general factor which no form of factor rotation could separate into smaller components distinguishable as verbal intelligence versus non-verbal intelligence versus scholastic achievement. By grades 7 and 8 the Lorge-Thorndike Non-verbal IQ and Raven's Progressive Matrices are hardly distinguishable in their factor composition from the tests of scholastic achievement. At the same time it is important to recognize that the Lorge-Thorndike Non-verbal IQ and Raven's Matrices are not measuring scholastic attainment *per se*, as demonstrated by the fact that totally illiterate and unschooled persons can obtain high scores on these tests. Burt (1961), for example, reported the case of separated identical twins with widely differing educational attainments (elementary school education versus a university degree), who differed by only one IQ point on the Progressive Matrices (127 versus 128).

(3) *Heritability of Intelligence and Scholastic Achievement*. Another characteristic which distinguishes intelligence tests from achievement tests is the difference between the heritability values generally found for intelligence and achievement measures. Heritability is a technical term in quantitative genetics referring to the proportion of test score variance (or any phenotypic variance) attributable to genetic factors. Determinations of the heritability of intelligence test scores range from about 0·60 to 0·90, with average values around 0·70 to 0·80 (Jensen, 1969a). This means that some 70 to 80 per cent of the variance in IQs in the European and North American Caucasian population in which these studies have been made is attributable to genetic variance, and only 20 to 30 per cent is attributable to non-genetic or environmental variability. The best evidence now available shows a somewhat different picture for measures of scholastic achievement, which on the average have much lower heritability. A review of all twin studies in which heritability was determined by the same methods for intelligence tests and for achievement tests shows an average heritability of 0·80 for the former and of only 0·40 for the latter

(Jensen, 1967). It is likely that scholastic measures increase in heritability with increasing grade level and that the simpler skills such as reading, spelling, and mechanical arithmetic have lower heritability than the more complex processes such as reading comprehension and arithmetic applications. The reason is quite easy to understand. Simple circumscribed skills can be more easily taught, drilled, and assessed and the degree of their mastery for any individual will be largely a function of the amount of time he spends in being taught and in practising the skill. Thus children with quite different learning abilities can be shaped up to perform more or less equally in these elemental skills. If Johnny has trouble with his reading or arithmetic or spelling his parents may give him extra tutoring so that he can be more nearly approximate the performance of his brighter brother. Siblings in the same family differ considerably less in scholastic achievement than in intelligence. Conversely, identical twins reared apart differ much more in scholastic achievement than in intelligence. From these facts we conclude that environmental factors make a larger contribution to individual differences in achievement than in intelligence as measured by standard tests.

(4) *Maturational Aspects of Intelligence.* An important characteristic of the best intelligence test items is that they clearly fall along an age scale. Items are thus 'naturally' ordered in difficulty. The Figure Copying Test (see Figure 7.1) is a good example. Ability to succeed on a more difficult item in the age scale is not functionally dependent upon success on previous items in the sense that the easier item is a prerequisite component of the more difficult item. By contrast, skill in short division is a component of skill in long division. The age differential for some tasks such as figure copying and the Piagetian conservation tests is so marked as to suggest that they depend upon the sequential maturation of hierarchical neural processes (Jensen, 1970b). Teaching of the skills before the necessary maturation has occurred is often practically impossible, but after the child has reached a certain age successful performance of the skill occurs without any specific training or practice. The items in scholastic achievement tests do not show this characteristic. For successful performance, the subject must have received explicit instruction in the specific subject matter of the test. The teachability of scholastic subjects is much

more obvious than of the kinds of materials that constitute most intelligence tests and especially non-verbal tests.

CUMULATIVE DEFICIT AND THE PROGRESSIVE ACHIEVEMENT GAP

The concept of 'cumulative deficit' is fundamental in the assessment of majority-minority differences in educational progress. Cumulative deficit is actually a hypothetical concept intended to explain an observable phenomenon which can be called the 'progressive achievement gap' or PAG for short. When two groups show an increasing divergence between their mean scores on tests, there is potential evidence of a PAG. The notion of cumulative deficit attributes the increasing difference between the groups' means to the cumulative effects of scholastic learning such that deficiencies at earlier stages make for greater deficiencies at later stages. If Johnny fails to master addition by the second grade he will be worse off in multiplication in the third grade, and still worse off in division in the fourth grade, and so on. Thus the progressive achievement gap between Johnny and those children who adequately learn each prerequisite for the next educational step is seen as a cumulative deficit. There may be other reasons as well for the PAG, such as differential rates of mental maturation, the changing factorial composition of scholastic tasks which means that somewhat different mental abilities are called for at different ages, disillusionment and waning motivation for school work, and so on. Therefore I prefer the term 'progressive achievement gap' because it refers to an observable effect and is neutral with respect to its causes.

Absolute and Relative PAG. When the achievement gap is measured in raw score units or in grade scale or age scale units, it is called *absolute*. For example, we read in the Coleman Report (1966, p. 273) that in the metropolitan areas of the northwest region of the U.S. '. . . the lag of Negro scores (in Verbal ability) in terms of years behind grade level is progressively greater. At grade 6, the average Negro is approximately $1\frac{1}{2}$ years behind the average white. At grade 9, he is approximately $2\frac{1}{4}$ years behind that of the average white. At grade 12, he is approximately $3\frac{1}{4}$ years behind the average white.'

When the achievement difference between groups is expressed in standard deviation units it is called *relative*. That is to say, the difference is relative to the variation within the criterion group. The Coleman Report, referring to the findings quoted above, goes on to state: 'A similar result holds for Negroes in all regions, despite the constant difference in number of standard deviations.' Although the absolute white-Negro difference increases with grade in school, the relative difference does not. The Coleman Report states: 'Thus in one sense it is meaningful to say the Negroes in the metropolitan North-east are the same distance below the whites at these three grades – that is, relative to the dispersion of the whites themselves.' The Report illustrates this in pointing out that at grade 6 about 15 per cent of whites are one standard deviation, or $1\frac{1}{2}$ years, behind the white average; at grade 12, 15 per cent of the whites are one standard deviation, of $3\frac{1}{4}$ years behind the white average.

It is of course the absolute progressive achievement gap which is observed by teachers and parents, and it becomes increasingly obvious at each higher grade level. But statistically the proper basis for comparing the achievement differences between various sub-groups of the school population is in terms of the relative difference, that is, in standard deviation units, called sigma (σ) units for short.

Except in the southern regions of the U.S., the Coleman study found a more or less constant difference of approximately one sigma (based on whites in the metropolitan north-east) between whites and Negroes in Verbal Ability, Reading Comprehension, and Maths Achievement. In other words, there was no progressive achievement gap in regions outside the south. In the southern regions, there is evidence for a PAG from grade 6 to 12 when the sigma unit is based on the metropolitan north-east. For example, in the non-metropolitan south, the mean Negro-white differences (Verbal Ability) in sigma units are 1·5, 1·7, and 1·9 for grades 6, 9, and 12, respectively. The corresponding number of grade levels that the southern Negroes lag behind at grades 6, 9, and 12 are 2·5, 3·9, and 5·2 (Coleman, 1966, p. 274). The causes of this progressive achievement gap in the south are not definitely known. Contributing factors could be an actual cumulative deficit in educational skills, true sub-population differences in the developmental growth rates of the mental abilities relevant to school learning, and selective migration of families of abler students out of the rural south, causing an increasing cumulation of poor students in the higher grades.

Cross-Sectional versus Longitudinal PAG. Selective migration, student turnover related to adult employment trends, and other factors contributing to changes in the characteristics of the school population may produce a spurious PAG when this is measured by comparisons between grade levels at a single cross-section in time. The Coleman Report's grade comparisons are cross-sectional. But where there is no reason to suspect systematic regional population changes, cross-sectional data should yield approximately the same picture as longitudinal data, which are obtained by repeated testing of the same children at different grades. Longitudinal data provide the least questionable basis for measuring the PAG. Cross-sectional achievement data can be made less questionable if there are also socio-economic ratings on the groups being compared. The lack of any grade-to-grade decrement on the socio-economic index adds weight to the conclusion that the PAG is not an artifact of the population's characteristics differing across grade levels. (This type of control was used in the present study reported in the following section.)

Another way of looking at the PAG is in terms of the percentage of variance in individual achievement scores accounted for by the mean achievement level of schools or districts. If there is an achievement decrement for, say, a minority group across grade levels, and if the decrement is a result of school influences, then we should expect an increasing correlation between individual students' achievement scores and the school averages. In the data of the Coleman Report, this correlation (expressed as the percentage of variance in individual scores accounted for by the school average) for 'verbal achievement' does not change appreciably from the beginning of the first school year up to the 12th grade. The school average for verbal achievement is as highly correlated with individual verbal achievement at the beginning of grade 1 as at grade 12. If the schools themselves contributed to the deficit, one would expect an increasing percentage of the total individual variance to be accounted for by the school average with increasing grade level. But no evidence was found that this state of affairs exists. The percentage of total variance in individual verbal achievement accounted for by the mean score of the school at grades 12 and 1 is as follows (Coleman *et al.*, 1966, p. 296):

	Grade	
Group	12	1
Negro, South	22·54	23·21
Negro, North	10·92	10·63
White, South	10·11	18·64
White, North	7·84	11·07

PROGRESSIVE ACHIEVEMENT GAP IN A CALIFORNIA SCHOOL DISTRICT

We searched for evidence of a PAG in our data in several ways, which can be only briefly summarized here. Separate analyses for each of the achievement tests did not reveal any striking differences in PAG, so the results can be combined without distortion of the essential results.

Mean Sigma Differences. The mean difference in sigma (standard deviation) units, based on the white group, by which Negro and Mexican-American pupils fall below the white group at each grade from 1 to 8 is shown in Table 7.3. The first three columns show the sample sizes on which the sigma differences are based. The sigma differences (i.e., σ below white mean) for Negroes and Mexican-Americans shown in columns 4 and 5 is the average of all the Stanford Achievement Tests given in each grade. Note that there is a reliable and systematic increase in the sigma difference from grade 1 to grade 3, for both Negro and Mexican groups, after which there is no further systematic change in achievement gap. The mean gap over all grades is $0·66\sigma$ for the Negroes and $0·55\sigma$ for the Mexicans. By comparison, look at columns 6 and 7, which show the mean sigma differences for those non-verbal ability tests in our battery which do not depend in any way upon reading skill and the content of which is not taught in school; this is the average sigma difference for the Lorge-Thorndike Non-verbal IQ, Figure Copying, and Raven's Progressive Matrices. We see that the sigma differences show a slight upward trend

TABLE 7.3. Number of white sigma units by which minority group means fall below the white mean

Grade	Sample Size (N)			Stanford Achievement Tests		Non-verbal Intelligence		Home Index (SES)		Adjusted Achievement Means	
	White	Negro	Mexican	Negro	Mexican	Negro	Mexican	Negro	Mexican	Negro	Mexican
1	285	218	258	0·25	0·34	1·07	0·53	—	—	−0·09	0·15
2	229	162	250	0·57	0·37	1·03	0·70	—	—	0·15	0·06
3	281	207	241	0·83	0·68	0·98	0·53	0·58	1·13	0·11	0·05
4	237	189	239	0·69	0·59	0·95	0·48	0·38	1·18	0·17	0·15
5	242	198	211	0·75	0·54	1·05	0·62	0·70	1·18	0·21	0·10
6	219	169	218	0·84	0·69	1·23	0·67	0·47	1·36	0·09	0·02
7	388	262	305	0·71	0·57	1·13	0·72	0·71	1·36	0·07	0·08
8	356	289	303	0·64	0·62	1·18	0·79	0·77	1·34	0·06	0·08
Mean				0·66	0·55	1·08	0·63	0·60	1·26	0·10	0·09

from the lower to the higher grades. Furthermore, the sigma differences are very significantly larger for the non-verbal intelligence tests than for the scholastic achievement tests in the case of Negroes (1·08σ for non-verbal intelligence v. 0·66 for achievement). The Mexicans show only a slight difference between their sigma decrement in non-verbal ability and in scholastic achievement (0·63 v. 0·55). If we can regard these non-verbal tests as indices of extra-scholastic learning ability, it appears then that these Negro children do relatively better in scholastic learning as measured by the Stanford Achievement Tests than in the extra-scholastic learning assessed by the non-verbal battery. In this sense, the Negro pupils, as compared with the Mexican pupils, are 'over-achievers', although the Negroes' absolute level of scholastic performance is 0·11σ below the Mexicans'. For the Negro group especially, the school can be regarded as an equalizing influence: Negro pupils are closer to white pupils in scholastic achievement than in non-scholastic non-verbal abilities. The mean Negro-white scholastic achievement difference is only 61 per cent as great as the Non-verbal IQ difference. This finding is exactly the opposite of popular belief. The white v. Mexican achievement difference is 87 per cent as great as the Non-verbal IQ difference.

Is there any systematic grade trend in our indices of socio-economic status and home environment? Columns 8 and 9 show the sigma differences below the white group on the composite score of Gough's Home Index, which assesses parental educational and occupational level, physical amenities, cultural advantages, and community involvement. (The Home Index was not used below grade 3.) There is a slight, but not highly regular, upward trend in these sigma differences for both Negro and Mexican groups, as if the students in the higher grades come from somewhat poorer backgrounds. Despite this, the sigmas for scholastic achievement (unlike the non-verbal ability tests) do not show any systematic increase from grade 3 to 8. Note also that on the Home Index the Mexicans, on the average, are further below the Negroes than the Negroes are below the whites. Moreover, the percentage of the Mexican children whose parents speak only English at home is 19·7 per cent as compared with 96·5 per cent for whites and 98·2 per cent for Negroes. In 14·2 per cent of the Mexican homes Spanish or another foreign language is spoken exclusively, as compared with 1·1 per cent for whites and 0·5 per cent for Negroes.

Covariance Adjustments of Achievement Scores. The next step of our analysis consists of obtaining covariance adjusted means on all the achievement tests, using all the ability tests,[4] along with sex and age in months, as the covariance controls. What this procedure shows, in effect, is the mean score on the achievement tests ('output') that would be obtained by the three ethnic groups if they were equated on the ability tests ('input'). Although it is beyond the scope of this paper to explain in mathematical detail just how this kind of covariance adjustment is accomplished, a few words of explanation are in order to remove any mystery that may seem to exist for those who have not studied or used this statistical technique. A simplified illustration will give the reader some notion of what is involved.

The simplest possible illustration consists of two groups, say, Negro and white, who are given two tests, say, an IQ test and an achievement test. What we wish to find out is: what would be the mean achievement scores of the Negro and white groups if they were equated on IQ? What we must determine, in statistical terminology, is the 'covariance adjusted mean' achievement for each group. It is defined mathematically as

$$\hat{Y} = \bar{Y}_G - b(\bar{X}_G - \bar{X}..)$$

In terms of our example,

$\hat{Y}_N$ = adjusted mean achievement score of Negro group
$\bar{Y}_N$ = raw mean achievement score of Negro group
$\bar{X}_N$ = mean IQ of Negro group
$\bar{X}..$ = mean IQ of Negro and white groups combined, i.e., total mean IQ
b = the regression coefficient of Y on X, i.e., of achievement on IQ for both groups combined. The regression coefficient is the slope of the regression line. It is $r_{xy}\dfrac{\sigma_y}{\sigma_x}$, where, r_{xy} is the correlation between the two variables, X and Y (or IQ and achievement) and σ_x and σ_y are the standard deviations of these variables.

---

[4] Lorge-Thorndike Verbal and Non-verbal IQ, Figure Copying, Raven's Matrices, Making Xs, Listening-Attention, and three memory tests.

The situation can be pictured as follows.

For the sake of graphic clarity, this is a greatly exaggerated picture. The so-called regression line is the one straight line about which the squared deviations of all scores are a minimum. Thus, every individual score plays a part in determining the position and slope of the regression line. It is the one best-fitting line to the data of *all* the subjects in both groups. Although the mean raw achievement scores differ markedly for Negroes and whites in this illustration, we see that each group falls only slightly off the common regression line; in this example, the white mean is above the line and the Negro mean is below. The *adjusted* means for the two groups consist of the grand mean plus (or minus) the deviation of the particular group's mean from the regression line. If the means of both groups fall exactly on the common regression line, the adjusted means will be exactly the same and are equal to the grand mean. If there is zero correlation between the input (IQ) and output (achievement) variables, then the regression line will be perfectly horizontal and parallel to the base line, and the adjusted means will consequently be exactly the same as the raw (or unadjusted) means. In the above example, the white adjusted mean would be slightly higher than the Negro adjusted mean, because the white mean is above the regression line and the Negro below. The regression line can be thought of as predicting the most probable achievement score for any given IQ. If the correlation between IQ and achievement were perfect, one could predict achievement from IQ exactly, and vice versa.

The situation is essentially the same for adjusting the means of three or more groups, and one can easily picture another group placed in the illustration (Fig. 7.2). It is much more difficult to picture the situation when more than two variables are involved. In this illustration, we have one output variable (achievement) and only one input variable (IQ). It is possible to have two or three or more input variables. If there are two, then the situation would have to be pictured in three dimensions. The common regression line would no longer be a line on a two-dimensional surface but would become a plane in a three-dimensional cube, and we would be adjusting our means in terms of their deviations from the surface of this two-dimensional plane. If we go to three input variables the situation can no longer be pictured, since we would have to deal with a 'hyper plane' in four-dimensional space. Four input variables require a five-dimensional space, and so on. Although the problem can no longer be pictured graphically beyond two input variables, it can be solved mathematically for any number of input variables (although the point of diminishing returns is rapidly reached). For the sample sizes and the number

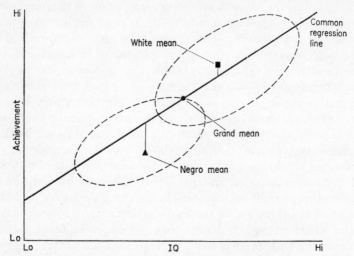

FIGURE 7.2. Simplified correlation scatter diagram illustrating the regression of achievement on IQ and the covariance adjustment of hypothetical white and Negro achievement means.

of input variables used in the present study, the mathematical computations would be virtually impossible without the aid of a high speed computer.

Columns 10 and 11 of Table 7.3 show the sigma difference by which the Negro and Mexican covariance adjusted mean falls below that of the white group. These differences are quite small for both Negroes and Mexicans (averaging 0·10 and 0·09, respectively), and they show no systematic trend with grade level. In other words, when the minority groups are statistically equated with the majority (white) group on the ability test variables, their achievement, on the average, is less than $0·1\sigma$ below that of the white group. On an IQ scale that would be equivalent to 1·5 points, a very small difference indeed. The adjusted decrement is statistically significant, however, which raises the question of why it should differ significantly from zero at all. The reason could be actual differences between minority and majority schools in the effectiveness of instruction, or incomplete measurement of all the input variables relevant to scholastic learning, or some lack of what is called homogeneity of regression for the three ethnic groups, which works against the covariance adjustment. We know the latter factor is involved to some extent, and some combination of all of them are most likely involved. But taken all together, the fact that the majority-minority difference in mean adjusted achievement scores is still less than 0.1σ means the direct contribution of the schools to the difference must be even smaller than this, if existent at all. Surely it is of practically negligible magnitude.

When the personality variables (the Eysenck Personality Inventory-Junior) and the four scales of the Home Index are also included with the ability variables in obtaining covariance adjusted means, the ethnic differences in scholastic achievement are wiped out almost entirely. Two-thirds of the majority-minority differences (for various achievement subtests at various grades) are not significant at the 5 per cent level and are less than 0.1σ. The adjusted mean differences *between* ethnic groups are smaller than the grade-to-grade sigma differences *within* ethnic groups. From this analysis, then, the school's contribution to ethnic achievement differences must be regarded as nil. If the input variables themselves are strongly influenced by the school to the disadvantage of the minority children, we should expect to find a greater sigma difference for Non-verbal IQ at grade 8 (age 13) than at kindergarten. In the present study Negroes are 1.11σ below whites in Non-verbal IQ in kindergarten as compared with 1.17σ in grades 7 and 8 – a trivial difference. Mexican children are 0.98σ below whites in Non-verbal IQ at kindergarten and 0.88σ below at grades 7 and 8. Thus the minority children begin school at least as far below the majority children in non-verbal ability as they are by grades 7 and 8. The schools have not depressed the ability level of minority children relative to the majority, but neither have they done anything to raise it. Differences in Verbal IQ are slightly more likely to reflect the effects of schooling and we note that in grades 7 and 8 Negroes are 1.00σ below the white mean and Mexicans are 0.90σ below.

Paired Ethnic Group Differences. The maximum discrimination that we can make between the three ethnic groups in terms of all of our 'input' variables (ability tests, personality inventories, and socio-economic indexes) is achieved by means of the multiple point-biserial correlation coefficient. The product-moment correlation obtained between a continuous variable (e.g., IQ) and a quantized (dichotomous) variable (e.g., male *v.* female, where male = 1 and female = 0) is called a point-biserial correlation (r_{pbs}). Mathematically it is defined as:

$$r_{pbs} = \frac{\bar{X}_1 - \bar{X}_2}{\sigma_t}\sqrt{pq}$$

where $\bar{X}_2$ and $\bar{X}_1$ = means of groups 1 and 2

σ_t = standard deviation of total (i.e., groups 1 and 2 combined)

p and q = proportions of total sample in groups 1 and 2, respectively. (p + q = 1·00)

It is also possible to compute r_{pbs} in the same manner that one computes the Pearson product-moment correlation between any two continuous variables, except that the dichotomous variable is quantized by assigning 0 and 1 to its two categories. It is also possible to obtain a multiple point-biserial correlation, which gives the maximum possible correlation between the quantized variable and the best weighted combination of a number of 'predictor' variables. The multiple correlation thus represents the maximum degree of discrimination that can be achieved between the two categories of the quantized variables by means of the particular set of predictor variables. Since the multiple correlation capitalizes upon sampling error (chance deviations from population values) to achieve the maximum value of the correlation, it is spuriously inflated by a degree that is inversely proportional to the sample size and the number of variables correlated. For this reason, the obtained multiple correlation should be 'shrunk' down to its estimated population value (i.e., its value if there were no sampling error). The method for doing this is given in most statistics textbooks (e.g., Guilford, 1956, pp. 398-9). All the multiple correlations reported here have thus been 'shrunk' and therefore represent a conservative estimate of the amount of discrimination achieved between the ethnic groups by our battery of 'input' tests.

When the sizes of the samples entering into the quantized variable are large and nearly equal, and when they have nearly equal standard deviations on the predictor variables, it is possible roughly to 'translate' the point-biserial correlation into a linear mean distance in constant sigma units between the two categories

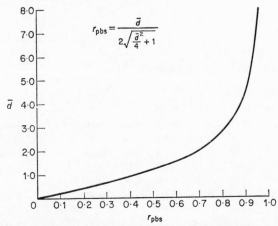

$$r_{pbs} = \frac{\bar{d}}{2\sqrt{\frac{\bar{d}^2}{4} + 1}}$$

FIGURE 7.3. The relationship between the point-biserial correlation (r_{pbs}) and the mean difference ($\bar{d}$) between groups in sigma units on the continuous variable, assuming equal sigmas and equal Ns in the two groups.

of the quantized variable. Figure 7.3 shows the function relating the point-biserial correlation to the mean sigma difference ($\bar{d}$) between groups. The r_{pbs} can attain a value of 1·00 only if the variance within each group diminishes to zero.

Table 7.4 gives the multiple point-biserial correlations between each ethnic dichotomy and all the 'input' variables – first just the ability tests and second the ability tests plus the personality inventory and socio-economic index. Note that the three groups are almost equally discriminable from one another in terms of the multiple correlation, especially after the personality and social background variables are added to the predictors. This is interesting, because it means that the two minority groups, though both are regarded as educationally and socio-economically disadvantaged, actually differ from one another on this composite of all input variables almost as much as each one differs from the majority group. The Negro and Mexican groups each differ from

TABLE 7.4. Point-biserial multiple correlations for 'input' variables and partial correlation for 'output' with 'input' held constant

	'INPUT' All Ability Tests			'INPUT' Ability + Personality + Home Index			'OUTPUT' Stanford Achievement Minus All 'Input' Variables†		
Grade	W-N	W-M	M-N	W-N	W-M	M-N	W-N‡	W-M	M-N
1	0·49	0·28	0·29	—	—	—	—	—	—
2	0·54	0·47	0·37	—	—	—	—	—	—
3	0·54	0·45	0·35	0·62	0·59	0·46	0·06	0·02	0·07
4	0·48	0·38	0·41	0·55	0·60	0·55	0·15	0·07	0·09
5	0·47	0·38	0·27	0·60	0·59	0·36	0·13	0·05	0·11
6	0·53	0·47	0·42	0·69	0·67	0·59	0·14	0·11	0·04
7	0·52	0·42	0·26	0·68	0·70	0·45	0·09	−0·04	0·11
8	0·57	0·42	0·43	0·65	0·66	0·46	0·06	−0·02	−0·07
Mean	0·52	0·41	0·36	0·63	0·64	0·48	0·11	0·05	0·07

† Partial correlations of less than 0·10 are not significant at the 5 per cent level.
‡ The quantized ethnic groups are White = 3, Mexican = 2, Negro = 1, so that for W-N and W-M positive correlations indicate higher achievement scores for the white group, and a positive correlation for M-N indicates higher scores for the Mexican group.

the majority group in a somewhat different way in terms of total pattern of scores, and they differ from one another almost as much. A factor analysis, shown in the next section, helps to reveal the ways in which the three groups differ from one another.

The last three columns in Table 7.4 show the correlation between each ethnic dichotomy and the Stanford Achievement Tests, with all the 'input' variables partialed out, i.e., statistically held constant. These correlations represent the average contribution made to the ethnic discrimination by the Stanford Achievement Tests regarded independently of the 'input' variables. It can be seen that these correlations are very small indeed. For the sample sizes used here, correlations of less than 0·10 can be regarded as statistically non-significant at the 5 per cent level. The proportion of the total variance between the ethnic groups that is accounted for by the achievement tests is represented by the square of the correlation coefficient. Applied to the partial correlations for the Achievement Tests in Table 7.4, this shows how trifling are the ethnic group achievement differences after the ethnic group differences on the input variables have been controlled.

Factor Analysis of All Variables. A factor analysis (varimax rotation of the principal components having Eigenvalues greater than 1) was carried out at each grade level on all test variables obtained at that grade level plus three others: sex, chronological age in months, and welfare status of the parent (whether receiving welfare aid to dependent children). The latter variable was added to supplement the indices of socio-economic status (the four scales of Gough's Home Index). Since grades 4, 5 and 6 had all the measure (27 variables) and the same tests were used at each of these grades, they are the most suitable part of our total sample for factor analytic comparisons. The results are essentially the same at all grade levels, although because the personality inventory and the Home Index were not used in the primary grades, and the Figure Copying Test was not used beyond grade 6, not all of the factors that emerged at grades 4, 5 and 6 come out at one or another of the other grades. Moreover, because of the large number of variables entering into the analysis at grades 4-6, more small factors come out which, in a sense, 'purify' the main factors by partialling out other irrelevant and minor sources of variance.

Factor analyses were performed first on the three ethnic groups separately to determine if essentially the same varimax factors emerged in each group. They did. All three groups yield the same factors, with only small differences in the loadings of various tests. This finding justifies combining all three groups for an overall factor analysis of the total student sample at each grade level. This was done. Eight factors with Eigenvalues greater than 1 emerged at grades 4, 5 and 6, accounting respectively for 67 per cent, 66 per cent and 70 per cent of the total variance.

The first principal component can be regarded as the general or *g* factor for this set of 27 variables. Table 7.5 shows the loadings

TABLE 7.5. Loadings of variables on first principal component for grades 4 to 8 (decimals omitted)

			Grade		
Variable	4	5	6	7	8
1. Sex (M = 0, F = 1)	14	14	03	08	12
2. Extraversion	25	28	46	33	24
3. Neuroticism	00	−06	−21	−12	09
4. Lie Scale	−17	−11	−19	−27	−32
5. Home Index – 1	31	45	41	49	48
6. Home Index – 2	29	30	34	41	45
7. Home Index – 3	36	41	27	50	44
8. Home Index – 4	29	43	28	47	40
9. Aid to Dependent Children	−21	−43	−32	−31	−26
10. Age in Months	−05	−09	−04	−04	−12
11. Lorge-Thorndike Verbal IQ	85	88	85	88	87
12. Lorge-Thorndike Non-verbal IQ	73	75	76	79	83
13. Raven's Progressive Matrices	54	55	54	54	63
14. Figure Copying	45	51	57	—	—
15. Listening-Attention	11	19	21	06	12
16. Memory – Immediate	45	40	36	27	32
17. Memory – Repeat	44	33	24	25	27
18. Memory – Delayed	43	41	41	25	27
19. Making Xs 1st Try	14	02	31	53	10
20. Making Xs 2nd Try	19	14	29	48	19
21. SAT: Word Meaning	83	81	81	—	—
22. SAT: Paragraph Meaning	80	79	89	86	83
23. SAT: Spelling	75	76	78	73	73
24. SAT: Language	83	84	87	78	75
25. SAT: Arithmetic Computation	57	45	63	73	73
26. SAT: Arithmetic Concepts	72	62	80	76	83
27. SAT: Arithmetic Applications	77	71	82	72	71
Per cent of Variance	22	26	29	28	27

of each of the 27 (or 25 in grades 7 and 8) variables on the first principal component in grades 4 to 6. The first principal component is the single most general factor accounting for more of the variance than any other factor. It is most heavily loaded in the Stanford Achievement Tests and Verbal IQ. Inspection of the loadings of the other variables gives an indication of their correlation with this most general achievement factor.

The eight principal components were rotated to approximate simple structure by the varimax criterion. In grades 4, 5 and 6 four substantial and clear-cut factors emerged. The remaining factors serve mainly to pull out irrelevant variance from the main factors. The four main factors that emerge are:

FACTOR I. Scholastic Achievement and Verbal Intelligence

Variables	*Factor Loading*		
	Gr. 4	*Gr. 5*	*Gr. 6*
Lorge-Thorndike Verbal IQ	0·75	0·75	0·85
Word Meaning	0·83	0·69	0·82
Paragraph Meaning	0·83	0·77	0·89
Spelling	0·82	0·77	0·81
Language	0·82	0·79	0·86
Arithmetic Computation	0·64	0·58	0·65
Arithmetic Concepts	0·73	0·69	0·83
Arithmetic Applications	0·77	0·71	0·85

FACTOR II. Non-verbal Intelligence

Variables	*Factor Loading*		
	Gr. 4	*Gr. 5*	*Gr. 6*
Lorge-Thorndike Non-verbal IQ	0·61	0·57	0·32
Raven's Progressive Matrices	0·75	0·75	0·55
Figure Copying	0·69	0·68	0·41

FACTOR III. Rote Memory Ability

Variables	*Factor Loading*		
	Gr. 4	*Gr. 5*	*Gr. 6*
Memory Span – Immediate Recall	0·85	0·81	0·77
Memory Span – Repeated Series	0·85	0·81	0·86
Memory Span – Delayed Recall	0·83	0·79	0·74

FACTOR IV. Socio-economic Status

| Variables | Factor Loading | | |
Home Index:	Gr. 4	Gr. 5	Gr. 6
1. Parental Education and Occupation	0·75	0·74	0·77
2. Physical Amenities	0·69	0·77	0·72
3. Community Participation	0·66	0·76	0·75
4. Cultural Advantages	0·66	0·59	0·66
Receives Welfare Aid to Dependent Children	−0·40	−0·34	−0·46

The remaining four minor factors are: (1) Speed, motivation, persistence as defined principally by the Making Xs Test, (2) Neuroticism, (3) Extraversion, (4) Age in months. These variables, having their largest loadings on separate factors, are in effect partialed out of the major factors. The four major factors listed above are orthogonal, i.e., uncorrelated with one another, and each one is thus viewed as a 'pure' measure of the particular factor in the sense that the effects of all the other factors are held constant.

Ethnic Group Comparisons of Factor Scores. The final step was to obtain factor scores for every student on each of these four main factors. For the total sample, within each grade, these factor scores are represented on a T-score scale, i.e., they have an overall mean of 50 and a standard deviation of 10. Table 7.6 shows the mean and standard deviation of the factor scores for each of the ethnic groups.

Note that the ethnic group differences in Factor I do not show any systematic increase from grade 4 to 6, thus lending no support to the existence of a cumulative deficit in the minority groups. Analysis of variance was performed on the factor scores and Scheffé's method of contrasts was used for testing the statistical significance of the differences between the means of the various ethnic groups at each grade level. The results of these significance tests are shown in Table 7.7. We see that in Factor I (Verbal IQ and Scholastic Achievement) both minority groups are significantly below the majority group, and Negroes are significantly below the Mexican group except in grade 6, where the difference is in the same direction but falls short of significance.

On Factor II (Non-verbal Intelligence) Negroes fall significantly below whites and Mexicans at all grades, and the differences

TABLE 7.6. Mean varimax factor scores for three ethnic groups in grades 4, 5 and 6

| | | | Mean Factor Scores | | | | | | | |
Grade	Group	N	I Verbal IQ and Achievement Mean	SD	II Non-verbal IQ Mean	SD	III Memory Mean	SD	IV Socio-economic Status Mean	SD
4	White	113	55·2	10·7	51·6	8·1	51·6	9·4	53·8	10·3
	Negro	129	47·1	6·5	44·6	8·9	51·0	11·2	51·7	7·9
	Mexican	145	49·5	8·5	51·0	9·3	48·1	7·7	43·6	7·8
5	White	144	54·7	8·7	52·3	8·2	50·4	9·1	54·1	9·2
	Negro	132	45·5	8·4	47·0	11·1	51·1	9·9	49·7	9·5
	Mexican	135	49·6	8·5	50·1	8·5	48·2	9·5	44·6	8·1
6	White	131	55·0	8·8	50·9	7·2	50·7	8·8	53·8	9·4
	Negro	124	47·1	8·3	44·1	10·5	50·5	9·9	51·5	8·0
	Mexican	126	49·1	9·3	51·0	8·7	48·0	10·2	42·5	7·5

L

between Mexicans and whites are non-significant at all grades. It should be remembered that this non-verbal intelligence factor represents that part of the variance in the non-verbal tests which is not common to the Verbal IQ and achievement tests or to the memory tests. The Mexican-white difference is significant on that part of the ability tests variance which has most in common with scholastic achievement and is represented in Factor I.

TABLE 7.7. The significance of ethnic group differences in mean factor scores, by Scheffé's method of contrasts

		Factors			
		I	II	III	IV
		Verbal IQ and	Non-verbal		Socio-Economic
Contrasts (*Means*)	Grade	Achievement	Intelligence	Memory	Status
	4	−**	−**	−NS	−NS
Negro-White	5	−**	−**	+NS	−**
	6	−**	−**	−NS	−NS
	4	−**	−NS	−*	−**
Mexican-White	5	−**	−NS	−NS	−**
	6	−**	+NS	−NS	−**
	4	+*	+**	−*	−**
Mexican-Negro	5	+*	+*	−*	−**
	6	+NS	+**	−NS	−**

*$p < 0.05$. **$p < 0.01$. NS = Not Significant.

Factor III (Rote Memory) shows no significant differences between the Negro and white groups; the Mexican group is significantly below the white at grade 4 and below the Negro at grades 4 and 5. This finding is consistent with the findings of other studies that mean differences between groups of lower and middle socio-economic status are smallest on tests of short-term memory and rote learning (Jensen, 1968b).

Factor IV (socio-economic status) shows relatively small differences between the Negro and white groups, while the Mexican group is significantly below the other two. Again, it should be realized that we are dealing here with 'pure' factor scores which are independent of all the other variables. Thus Factor IV shows us the relative standing of the three ethnic groups in socio-economic status when all the other variables are held constant. What these results indicate is that Negro and white children statistically equated for intelligence, achievement, and memory ability differ very little in socio-economic status as measured by our indices, but that Mexican children, when equated on all other variables with white children or with Negro children, show a comparatively much poorer background than either the white or Negro groups. On the present measures, at least, the Mexicans must be regarded as much more environmentally disadvantaged than the Negroes, and this takes no account of the Mexican's bilingual problem. In view of this it is quite interesting that Mexican pupils on the average significantly exceed the Negro pupils in both verbal and non-verbal intelligence measures and in scholastic achievement.

Equality of educational opportunity: uniformity or diversity of instruction?

The results of our analysis thus far fail to support the hypothesis that the schools have discriminated unfavorably against minority pupils. When minority pupils are statistically equated with majority children for background and ability factors over which the schools have little or no control, the minority children perform scholastically about as well as the majority children. The notion that poor scholastic achievement is partly a result of the pupil's ethnic minority status *per se*, implying discriminatory schooling, is thus thoroughly falsified by the present study. This does not imply that the same results would be obtained in every other school system in the country. Where true educational inequalities between majority and minority pupils exist, we should expect the present type of analyses to reveal these inequalities, and it would be surprising if they were not found in some school systems which provide markedly inferior educational facilities for minority pupils. It should be noted, on the other hand, that the present study was conducted in a school district which had taken pains to equalize educational facilities in schools that serve predominantly majority or predominantly minority populations. The success of this equalization is evinced in the results of the present analyses.

But we can take a bold step further and ask: Is equalization of educational facilities enough? Is the real meaning of equality of educational opportunity simply uniformity of facilities and instructional programs? Is it possible that true equality of opportunity could mean doing whatever is necessary to maximize the scholastic achievement of children, even if it might mean doing quite different things for different children in terms of their differing patterns of ability? Note that I did not say in terms of their ethnic or social class status, but in terms of their individual patterns of ability. The fact that different social classes and ethnic groups show different modal patterns of ability, of course, means that different proportions of various sub-populations will have different patterns of strength and weakness in various mental abilities. Is such a fact to be deplored and swept out of sight, or should it be examined with a view to utilizing the differences in the design of instructional programs that might maximize each individual's benefits from schooling? A couple of years ago I wrote: 'If we fail to take account either of innate or acquired differences in abilities and traits, the ideal of equality of educational opportunity can too easily be interpreted so literally as to be actually harmful, just as it would be harmful for a physician to give all his patients the same medicine. One child's opportunity can be another's defeat' (Jensen, 1968a, p. 3). At that time I suggested that we look for differential ability patterns that might interact with different instructional methods in such a way as to maximize school learning for all individuals and at the same time minimize individual and group differences in scholastic achievement and any other benefits derived from schooling.

In our laboratory research we have discovered two broad classes of abilities which show marked differences in their relation to social class and race (Jensen, 1968b, 1969b, 1970; Jensen and Rohwer, 1968, 1970). Briefly, what we have found is that children of low socio-economic status, especially minority children, with low measured IQs (60 to 80) are generally superior to middle-class children with similar IQs in tests of associative learning ability – free recall, serial rote learning, paired-associates learning, and digit span memory. This finding has been interpreted theoretically in terms of a hierarchical model of mental abilities, going from associative learning to conceptual thinking, in which the development of lower levels in the hierarchy is necessary but not sufficient for the development of higher levels. Our hypothesis states that the continuum of tests going from associative to conceptual is the phenotypic expression of two functionally dependent but genotypically independent types of mental processes, which we call Level I and Level II. Level I processes are perhaps best measured by tests such as digit span and serial rote learning; Level II processes are represented in tests such as the Progressive Matrices. Level I and Level II abilities are distributed differently in upper and lower social classes and in different ethnic groups. Level I is distributed fairly evenly in all sub-populations. Level II, however, is distributed about a higher mean in upper than in lower social classes. The majority of children now called 'culturally disadvantaged' show little or no deficiency in Level I ability but are about one standard deviation below the general population mean on tests of Level II ability. Children who are above average on Level I but below average on Level II ability usually appear to be bright and capable of normal learning and achievement in many life situations, although they have unusual difficulties in school work under the traditional methods of classroom instruction. Many of these children, who may be classed as retarded in school, suddenly become socially adequate persons when they leave the academic situation. But children who are below average on both Level I and Level II seem to be much more handicapped. Not only is their scholastic performance poor, but their social and vocational potential also seem to be much less than those of children with normal Level I functions. Yet both types of children look much alike in overall measures of IQ and scholastic achievement.

These findings are important because they help to localize the nature of the intellectual deficit of many children called 'culturally disadvantaged'. We must ask whether we can discover or invent instructional methods that engage Level I more fully and thereby provide a means of improving the educational attainments of many of the children now called 'culturally disadvantaged'. In our current instructional procedure are we utilizing so exclusively those mental abilities we identify as IQ (Level II) that children who are relatively low in IQ but have strength in other abilities are unduly disadvantaged in the traditional classroom? The whole complex process of classroom instruction as we know it has evolved in relation to a relatively small upper-class segment of Anglo-European stock. The modal pattern of development in learning abilities of this group has probably shaped to a considerable degree the particular educational procedures public education has long regarded as standard for everyone, regardless of differences in cultural background or inherited patterns of ability. But so far we have not successfully met the challenge presented by our ideal of a rewarding education for all segments of the population, with their diverse patterns of ability.

Looking, for example, at the factor scores shown in Table 7.6 we note that the minority groups are not significantly below the majority group on Factor III (Memory), which we would identify with Level I ability. Lest anyone try to argue that these 'pure' factor scores do not correspond to any 'impure' scores that could be obtained with actual tests, we can look at Figures 7.4 and 7.5, showing the grade-to-grade growth curves of a good Level II test (Raven's Progressive Matrices) and a good Level I test (a composite of the three digit memory tests).

The results of both tests have been put on the same scale of T scores, with an overall mean of 50 and a standard deviation of 10 (based on the standard deviation of raw scores in the white group at grade 5). The differences between the growth curves shown in Figures 7.4 and 7.5 are striking. The approximately one standard deviation difference between the Negro and white groups on the Level II test (Matrices) can be seen to have rather drastic implications in terms of grade level comparisons. By drawing a horizontal line from the Negro or Mexican mean at any grade to the point where it crosses the curve for the white group and dropping a perpendicular to the baseline, we can read off the grade equivalent of the minority group mean. The average Negro eighth-grader in this school system, for example, performs on the matrices at a level equivalent to white children at grade 4.5. Mexican children at grade 8 perform at grade 6.3. The grade 6 performance of Negroes and Mexicans is equivalent to the white's performance in grades 3.4 and 4.5, respectively.

On the other hand, note the small differences between the

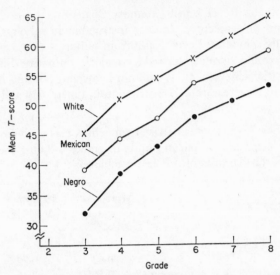

FIGURE 7.4. Mean T scores ($\bar{X} = 50$, $SD = 10$) on Raven's Progressive Matrices in grades 3 to 8.

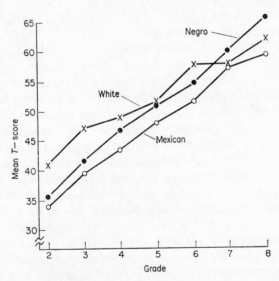

FIGURE 7.5. Mean T scores ($\bar{X} = 50$, $SD = 10$) on composite memory score in grades 2 to 8.

groups on the Level I test (Memory Span) in Figure 7.5. It is interesting to conjecture whether instruction in scholastic skills specifically aimed at Level I ability in children who are low in Level II would significantly reduce majority-minority differences in scholastic achievement. We do not know and can find out only through further research. If instruction is aimed only at Level II

TABLE 7.8. Mean sigmas (based on white group) below white mean of Negro and Mexican pupils in grades 4-8 on Level I-like and Level II-like tests of scholastic achievement

Tests	Negro $(N = 1,107)$	Mexican $(N = 1,276)$
Level I-Like Tests:		
Spelling	0·62	0·52
Arithmetic Computation	0·56	0·36
Level II-Like Tests:		
Paragraph Meaning	0·90	0·75
Arithmetic Concepts	0·71	0·60
Arithmetic Applications	0·72	0·55

ability for all children, we should expect sizable majority-minority differences in achievement. If instruction could somehow be aimed at Level I ability for all those children (regardless of ethnic identification) who are significantly stronger in Level I than in Level II, would their achievement be brought appreciably closer to that of the majority? Or is scholastic learning so intrinsically dependant on Level II ability that no form of instruction attempting to capitalize on Level I ability could possibly succeed beyond the most elementary aspects of any academic subject matter? Again, we do not know. But until these possibilities are explored, schools may be accused of cheating many children, especially large numbers of minority children, by providing uniform facilities but not sufficiently diversified instructional programs to minimize differences in achievement and also maximize the overall level of achievement.

Some scholastic subjects would seem to lend themselves more to Level I processes and instructional methods than any other subjects. For instance, the learning of spelling and arithmetic computation would seem to be less dependant upon Level II ability than, say, reading comprehension, arithmetic concepts or arithmetic applications. If this is true we should expect majority-minority differences to be smaller on the Level I types of subject matter than on the Level II types. Let us make the relevant comparisons in the data of the present study. Table 7.8 shows these comparisons in sigma units. They bear out our hypothesis; the pupils of both minority groups fall below the majority mean about one-fifth of a sigma more on Level II-like scholastic achievement than on Level I-like subjects. Clearly, school subjects which by their nature seem to permit greater utilization of Level I ability show smaller majority-minority differences than those subjects which involve more Level II ability. This raises the interesting question whether all scholastic subjects can be taught in ways that *maximize* their dependence on Level I and *minimize* their dependence on Level II. If this can be done for children who are low in Level II ability – and we will never know without trying – it should reduce not only the scholastic achievement gap between majority and minority children but the achievement differences among all children of every group. If it succeeds, it would do so, not by pulling anyone down toward the common average, but by capitalizing on each child's particular strengths and minimizing the role of his particular weaknesses in learning any given kind of subject matter. This would seem to be an avenue worth exploring in our efforts to achieve not only equality of educational opportunity but greater equality of scholastic performance as well.

L*

Varieties of individual differences in learning

Individual differences and learning research

One thing we can all be quite certain of: Wherever in the vast realm of human learning we wish to look for individual differences, we surely will find them.

What we do about this fact will depend upon several things. First, it will depend upon the strength of our faith that some kind of order and structure do in fact exist in individual differences (IDs) in learning. If we have this faith, it is then up to our fortitude and ingenuity to discover this structure. What we do will depend also upon whether or not we believe that a science of learning can be developed independently of the problem of IDs. If we think it can, we might prefer to ignore IDs except to the extent that anyone planning an experiment must take some account of their nuisance value as 'error variance'.

Since both these points are still regarded by some psychologists as open questions, I shall begin by stating my own biases. On the first issue, I will only say that I have faith that we can eventually make sense out of this realm, which at first glance admittedly looks pretty chaotic. I have made the plunge, and while my groping is still quite untidy, I am not yet discouraged.

On the second issue, I believe that most of what experimental psychologists really want to find out about the nature of learning actually requires an individual differences approach. Often the questions we ask cannot be answered adequately by making statistical comparisons between group means, yet this is the traditional method of assessing the effects and the importance of

322

independent variables on learning. If an independent variable makes for a clear and unanimous difference between experimental and control groups, well and good. But if the group mean difference is meagre, we must ask if the effects of our independent variable have been buried in the error term. The error term contains the Subjects × Independent Variable interaction, whether or not our design has provided for testing its significance. Only if it has been demonstrated that the Subjects × Independent Variable interaction is negligible can we be very sanguine about the psychological importance of a particular independent variable, when our conclusions are based on group mean differences. It is preferable to know what happens to *individuals* under the effect of the independent variable. Experimental psychologists are not interested fundamentally in *group* effects. Our aim essentially is to devise experiments that will yield information capable of narrowing the range of alternative models of the mind. As far as I know, no one ever really thinks of his model or theory as pertaining only to the averaged characteristics of a group of subjects. Yet without adequate recognition of the problem of IDs, psychological theory risks being shaped by the averaged characteristics of the group, which may or may not represent the state of affairs that exists within the individuals. Imagine an independent variable, say some drug, which markedly speeds up learning in some individuals and slows it down in others. Averaging the individual performance scores could result in the false conclusion that the drug has no significant effect on learning. The means and standard deviations of the Drug and No Drug groups could conceivably be identical. Or, in the same type of experiment, a greater proportion of one type of individual might be sampled than of the other type. But what would it mean? Obviously, a different sort of experimental design is required in order to deal properly with this type of problem. It is a rather sobering exercise to keep this analogy in mind while reading much of the experimental literature on learning. The effect of distribution of practice on rote learning may serve as one classic example. Hovland (1939) carried out an experiment which showed an insignificant mean difference between massed and distributed practice in paired-associate learning. He then proceeded to note that some 44 per cent of the subjects in his experiment learned more rapidly under distributed practice, while some 38 per cent learned more rapidly under massed practice; about 18 per cent showed no effect of the independent variable one way or the other. Hovland found similar results in serial learning. Distribution of practice has since become a heavily researched topic; yet, by and large, the mainstream of this research has proceeded without any regard for the Subjects × Independent Variable interaction noted by Hovland. We do not know if this interaction was significant in Hovland's experiment. But would anyone argue that the Subjects × Independent Variable interaction is not the proper place to look if we want to assess the potency of our experimental variable? Underwood (1964, p. 149) has referred to this ID source of variance as producing 'pesky statistical problems resulting from the wide range of scores', even among a supposed homogeneous population of college students. Instead of viewing IDs as merely a pesky statistical problem, I believe the experimental psychology of learning is coming to recognize IDs as the very heart of its subject matter. By making IDs the center of focus, we of course face problems that are staggering as compared with the kinds of statistical problems referred to by Underwood, which can usually be solved simply by increasing our N.

Even for those with no stomach for so messy a subject as IDs in learning and who would want nothing to do with the problem for its own sake, I think it will become apparent that IDs can be *used* in the design of experiments. Individual differences can serve as one additional means of narrowing the range of competing models of the learning process. Any new source of facts is a potential challenge to all existing theories. Some theories fall in the face of the facts and some remain standing, usually with certain modifications. We then search for new facts to challenge these theories, and so on. The process can proceed until, as happened in color theory, two or three competing models stand up equally to all the facts we are capable of producing in the psychological laboratory. Then it becomes necessary to pit the models against facts derived from another realm, which in the case of color theory was retinal neurophysiology, in order to find a basis of choice between our alternative theories. I propose that individual differences might be used in this fashion, as a further source of information for the development and testing of psychological models. Consider, for example, a theory which postulates a single process of inference or response competition to explain both proactive and retroactive inhibition. If measures of individual differences in PI and RI were then found to be only slightly correlated, even after correction for attenuation, we might have grounds for doubting the validity of a uniprocess theory of RI and PI. In this fashion individual differences may be put to work in helping to solve some of the major theoretical issues of general experimental psychology.

Classification of individual differences

Coming back to the title of this paper, to speak of *varieties* of individual differences in learning implies some scheme of classification. Hints for such a scheme may be gleaned from the traditional categories of learning, such as conditioning, discrimination learning, rote learning, perceptual-motor learning, concept attainment, and so forth. Another possible source of suggestions is to look at the labels given to some of the factors derived from factor-analytic studies of IDs in learning. These unfortunately turn out to look exceedingly like the traditional categories of the variables which originally entered into the factor analyses. Thus we again find factors labeled as motor learning, rote learning, conceptual learning, and so on through the list. Now and then we find that some of the factor labels more nearly resemble the titles of psychometric tests, such as the *Primary Mental Abilities*, and we have factors such as verbal conceptual learning, spatial conceptual learning, and so on. All these labels, incidentally, are taken from published factor analyses. The forty or more factor-analytic studies of IDs in learning fall quite short of providing even the rough outlines for a comprehensive taxonomy of IDs. Perusal of this material might even cause us to give up in despair or to conclude, as some investigators have done, that IDs in learning are specific to each and every learning task under each and every condition of learning. Then all we could hope to do successfully would be to measure the final products of learning by means of psychometric tests. The attempt to understand IDs in the learning process itself would be rendered futile by the curse of task-specific variance.

Gaining some perspective on the taxonomy of this problem will help to suggest why the examination of past studies can result in such a gloomy picture. It might also indicate how we can view the total situation in a more hopeful light.

Intrinsic and extrinsic individual differences

The first broad distinction that should be made in order to avoid future confusion, and the lack of which has caused trouble in the past, is the difference between what I call intrinsic and extrinsic individual differences. The essence of the difference is exemplified by the two statements: (*a*) individual differences *in* learning, and (*b*) the effects of individual differences *on* learning.

Extrinsic IDs are those subject variables which operationally bear no resemblance to the learning process as we generally conceive of it. Yet these IDs may influence the individual's performance in a learning situation. Certain attitudes and personality traits are probably legitimately regarded as belonging in this category. We should be explicitly aware of this category, since it is not uncommon for psychologists to identify the whole field of individual differences in learning with this particular category. It is a category I would regard as of relatively minor importance. Yet there is a widespread tendency to think of all individual differences as being phenomena outside the realm of learning, something quite independent, which may at times exert some influence on the subject's performance in a learning task. According to this view, if we could eliminate these kinds of individual differences subjects would all perform alike in laboratory learning tasks. Much of the talk about controlling for individual differences in laboratory experimentation is based on this conception of extrinsic IDs. Chronological age, mental age, IQ, sex, and other personal characteristics are included. We have the picture of the individual as a bundle of traits and mental abilities, as these are assessed by psychometric techniques, and these traits and abilities are seen as acting upon the functioning of the more basic processes of perception and learning, to produce the intersubject variance in performance we see in the laboratory and in the classroom. This view has been a hindrance to the proper appreciation of individual differences in learning. It creates the impression that IDs are really not the learning researcher's business, but someone else's – the differential psychologist's, perhaps, or the personality theorist's. These extrinsic factors are regarded merely as bothersome intruders in the learning domain. The strict control of these extrinsic sources of IDs, however, usually results in disappointingly little reduction in the intersubject variance in our experiments. Psychometric ability measures may at times account for a fair share of the variance in learning, but mental abilities of this type are not properly classed as extrinsic IDs. They fit into another niche in my scheme, and I will save them for a later point in the discussion.

By the term *intrinsic* individual differences I refer to those individual differences which are inherent in learning and which do not exist independently of learning phenomena. In other words, intrinsic individual differences consist of intersubject variability in the learning process itself.

A moment ago I included personality traits in the class of extrinsic IDs. In some cases, however, a personality trait must be regarded on theoretical grounds as belonging to the intrinsic type of IDs, when the development of the personality trait itself is based on some essential variable in the learning domain. A case in point is Eysenck's conception of extraversion, which is hypothesized to develop as a consequence of IDs in the rate of build-up and dissipation of cortical inhibition. Where such forms of inhibition play a role in learning, we should expect to find correlations with the trait of extraversion. In other words, the personality trait and the learning performance both would have some ID 'genotype' in common. On a more superficial level the trait of extraversion might also have extrinsic effects on the subject's performance in a learning situation, and this would occur even when the learning task does not involve any inhibitory factor. It would result from generalized tendencies associated with the extraverted syndrome, such as not taking the experiment seriously, not being conscientious, and wishing to get the whole thing over with as quickly and easily as possible. Separation of the extrinsic and intrinsic aspects of this type of personality trait could presumably be achieved by means of experiments which manipulate the conditions hypothesized to afford an opportunity for the intrinsic or genotypic aspect of the personality trait – in the present case, cortical inhibition – to manifest itself in learning. In the case of extraversion we would select and manipulate tasks in which varying degrees of inhibition were inferred to operate. As another example, the trait of neuroticism or anxiety would be expected to show itself in the learning realm through variations in task complexity, along with the manipulation of instructional variables intended to arouse varying amounts of stress or ego involvement.

A more detailed look at this domain of intrinsic individual differences in learning can be facilitated if we hold in mind the following picture: Imagine a very large cube made up of many small cubes – the sort of diagram you have seen in many of Guilford's recent publications. This three-dimensional figure can be used to represent three major classes of variables and the enclosed three-dimensional space in which almost any particular learning task may be located. We begin with the horizontal dimension, which is labeled 'Content Variables'. This refers to the stimulus classes of the materials to be learned. The columns of this dimension bear labels such as 'verbal', 'spatial', 'numerical', 'perceptual-motor', etc. To avoid adding a fourth dimension to this cube I will also include sensory modality of the learning materials on this horizontal dimension, with the labels 'visual', 'auditory', 'haptic', etc.

Along the perpendicular axis, going from front to back, we can represent types of learning – the traditional categories such as classical and operant conditioning, rote learning, selective trial-and-error learning, concept learning, and so on. On each of the axes I shall leave some columns blank so that anyone can fill in anything else he thinks belongs in this scheme.

Along the vertical axis we have what I will call the procedural variables, such as stimulus duration, CS-UCS interval, task pacing, distribution of practice, degree of intra-task similarity with its associated generalization effects along both primary and semantic generalization gradients, and also the corresponding intra- and inter-task interference effects. Also on this axis we would have variables such as association value of meaningfulness, task complexity, length of task or amount of material to be learned, the stage of practice on a given task or a particular class of tasks, original learning and relearning after some interpolated activity. Instructional variables, such as differentially motivating sets, also may be included on this axis. While each of these variables is allotted a single row, we should think of each one as representing a continuum of values, such as various pacing rates, various degrees of distribution of practice, different degrees of task complexity, and so forth.

Now, in looking at this three-dimensional structure, we may be

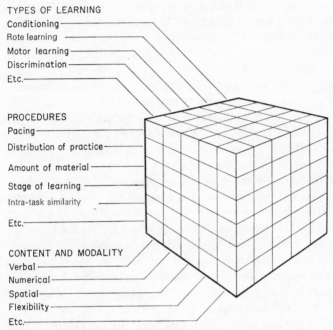

FIGURE 8.1. A representation of the classes of variables in learning tasks.

tempted to conclude that *n* more dimensions are needed to represent adequately all the types of phenotypic variations among all the kinds of learning tasks we can think of. I would not argue about this. I only claim that this simple picture will serve my immediate didactic purpose. After I have made my point with it, it can be discarded altogether. So I shall not bother about its flaws, such as the fact that many of the cells will have to remain empty because certain variables on one axis have no relevance to a particular category on one of the other axes. Also it would be more accurate, but much more confusing, to try to represent all the procedural variables as being completely orthogonal to one another. Obviously, any given learning task can be located in more than one of the rows simultaneously, taking some particular value on each of the procedural variables.

As we contemplate this whole structure, we have to face the awful possibility that each row or column on each of the dimensions could yield significant Subjects × Variables interactions. That is, if we run a group of subjects through all the tasks and conditions represented in this cube, there is the possibility that as we go from cell to cell the rank order of the subjects' learning performance will continually be changing. I am assuming that this change is not due to experimental error in the strict sense and that the different rank orders of subjects are reliable. At present we have no idea just how much shifting of rank order to expect in this situation. Nor do we know which variables will have the greatest interactions with subjects.

This, then, is the task for research on IDs in learning – to delineate the basic dimensions or genotypes of all of the between-subjects variation associated with all of the phenotypes of learning depicted in this three-dimensional scheme. And then some!

I find it useful to keep this scheme in mind while perusing the factor-analytic studies reported in this field. Many such studies have involved a number of learning tasks sampled more or less arbitrarily from here and there in this taxonomic cube. That is to say, one finds batteries of learning tasks which have few if any of their rows or columns in common. Not surprisingly, the correlations between tasks selected under these conditions turn out to be generally meagre. No semblance of a general factor can possibly emerge, and the communalities of the learning measures are nearly always very small. The few factors that emerge are hard to interpret and usually are given uninteresting labels which merely duplicate the names of the learning tasks that entered into the analysis. We thus gain the impression that true genotypes have not been discovered and that at best the factor analysis has only classified the learning tasks along the same obvious phenotypic lines we had previously arrived at by mere inspection of task characteristics. When we sample too widely and too sparsely from the whole learning domain, this is what tends to come of our factor analysis. The analysis indeed reveals hardly more than what we already knew we were putting into it.

It is common practice to 'overdetermine' factors by including several tests for each hypothesized factor. These hypothesized factors have nearly always been named and looked for in terms of the variables listed under content or under the type of learning task. Variance arising from the procedural variables is generally overlooked. For example, even if we had several rote learning tasks, we might not find much factorial communality among them if they all differed from one another on these procedural dimensions. It is primarily to this source of variance that I attribute the meagre communalities that are found in most factorial studies of learning.

What happens when we include psychometric reference tests, such as the *Primary Mental Abilities*, among a battery of learning tasks more or less haphazardly sampled from this cube? We find that the reference tests do absorb some of the variance – usually not very much – and we find that the variance they account for corresponds primarily to the *content* of the learning material. In the factor analysis, therefore, learning tasks tend to line up with reference tests on factors such as verbal rote learning, spatial learning, and so on. Many learning tasks, however, seem to share almost none of this variance. Thus, the total variance in the learning tasks accounted for by the reference tests is generally very small. And how can we expect it to be otherwise? Psychometric tests obviously have little resemblance to most of the procedural variables that are necessarily involved in learning tasks. My hunch is that the largest source of ID variance in learning is connected with these procedural variables. By systematically including variance from this source in our factor analyses, we are apt to discover some of the most basic and pervasive genotypes of individual differences.

At this stage it might be profitable for someone to search the experimental literature on learning with an eye out for Subjects × Independent Variable interactions in the analyses of variance, in order to get some preliminary ideas of the kinds of variables most likely to be important sources of IDs. As we begin to look into this matter, we hopefully may find that some of the variables indicated on the three axes of our cube do not interact with subjects, that is, they might not constitute independent sources of ID variance. Every such variable that we can discover is a blessing, for there will still be plenty of subject interaction variables to keep us all busy for a long time.

In some of my own work, for example, I was happy to find that the sensory modality of the learning task turned out to be unimportant on the genotypic level, at least among normal subjects. I was measuring individual differences in a variety of memory span tasks under variations in the procedural variables, and found that the same genotypes were tapped whether the experiments were conducted in the visual or the auditory modality. Absolute values of certain parameters often differ significantly from one modality to another, but sensory modality in these experiments did not interact with subjects (Jensen, 1971a).

Coming back to this taxonomic cube for the last time, its implications for systematic research seem quite plain. The key idea is to focus on only one or two of the cells in this system in any one study or series of studies. By keeping constant as many sources of variance as we can while manipulating one narrow class of variables at a time, we will be more apt to obtain sets of intercorrelations that have sufficiently substantial structure to reveal the underlying genotypes.

The question immediately arises concerning the role of psychological theory in this search, as contrasted with mere systematic exploration of all possible variables. There is so much work to be done here that in order not to be completely arbitrary in our procedures, I think we will have to plan our experiments around theoretical hunches concerning the nature of the genotypes underlying IDs associated with particular classes of experimental variables. An atheoretical, systematic exploration of Subjects × Independent Variable interactions and the intercorrelations among these interactions is not to be despised, however. For there are probably surprises in store for us in this realm which lie beyond almost anyone's theoretical imagination. Then, too, I would warn of the danger of proliferating *ad hoc* theoretical explanations for IDs in any given learning situation. The basic genotypes we are in search of are probably relatively few in number and enter into phenotypically wide varieties of learning. And the structure or dimensionality of the basic genotypes might well look very different from the structure of the phenotypes we have outlined in terms of task characteristics.

Phenotypes and genotypes

Phenotypes are described in terms of task characteristics, that is, the location of a learning task in our three-dimensional scheme. The genotypes are the underlying factors or basic processes which cause the patterns of intercorrelations among the phenotypes. The primary task of research on IDs consists of discovering these genotypes. Hopefully, the number of these genotypes will be quite limited as compared with phenotypic variations. I am not at all sure what these genotypes will look like once they have been isolated. There are those who might imagine them to look something like the constructs of Hullian theory, with genotypes for habit strength, reactive and conditioned inhibition, drive, oscillation, the threshold of reaction evocation, and so on. Zeaman and Kaufman (1955), using a motor learning task, carried out a now classic study of IDs along Hullian lines. It is one of the few studies of IDs which focused attention on what I have called the procedural variables.

But other genotypes may bear little resemblance in their isolated state to anything we would be inclined to identify as learning. As an example, from some recent research of my own (Jensen, 1965), there appears to be some common genotype or set of genotypes underlying memory span, serial rote learning, and performance on the Stroop color-word test, particularly the speed factor in the Stroop, which is measured by having subjects read the names of colors as fast as they can. It would be interesting to speculate upon why this particular ability to read color names rapidly should be substantially correlated both with memory span for digits and with the speed of serial learning of verbal materials. On the other hand, two types of learning which phenotypically appear very much alike – serial learning and paired-associate learning – have been found not to be significantly intercorrelated in the college population, even when the stimulus materials are identical in both tasks. Furthermore, there seems to be little if any transfer from the paired-associate to the serial list, even when the S-R connections are common to both lists and subjects over-learn the S-R connections in the first task (Jensen, 1963). Such are the kinds of surprises that turn up when we begin looking for the genotypes that underlie phenotypes.

Serial learning has been found to have a great deal in common genotypically with memory span. The two types of tasks, when their intercorrelations are analyzed, have approximately equal loadings – in the range of 0·60 to 0·70 – on the general factor or first principal component. But it would be a mistake to regard even memory span as a unitary ability determined by a single genotype. By putting 14 variations of memory span tasks into one factor analysis, along with an equal number of serial learning tasks, there emerge at least three factors needed to account for the intercorrelations among the various memory span tasks. The nature of these factors can provide clues for the formulation of a psychological model of memory span. Forward span and back-ward span come out on different factors. And memory span, when measured on series which do not appreciably exceed the subject's span, is factorially different from memory span measured in lists that considerably exceed the subject's span; that is, where more items are presented than the subject can possibly recall, but the subject is required to recall as much as he can. This latter pro-cedure increases variance on what I have hypothesized as a factor of susceptibility to interference. This factor is itself far from simple. Individual differences in retroactive inhibition in short-term memory tasks, for example, seem to have a different geno-type than retroactive inhibition in a task like serial learning, where more of the original learning gets consolidated before the inter-fering task is interpolated. Thus we can speak of retroactive inter-ference with the process of consolidation in short-term memory, and interference with the sequential retrieval of a learned series of responses which involves some consolidated or relatively permanent acquisition.

In my factor analysis of the memory span tasks, one of the most striking findings arises from a comparison of the proactive and retroactive inhibition paradigms. We present series A, followed after a brief pause by series B, and then ask the subject to recall series A; and, of course, we get retroactive inhibition as measured against the appropriate control condition. (Each subject is his own control.) If, after the same sequence, we ask the subject to recall series B, we get proactive inhibition. It so happens that the proactive and retroactive inhibition measures come out on different dimensions in the factor analysis. Phenotypically, the RI and PI paradigms look much alike, and the overall magnitude of the inhibition is similar for both. Yet the factor analysis suggests quite different underlying processes in these two types of interference.

One of the most interesting findings is the genotypic change in IDs in serial learning when we go from the original learning of a list to relearning the list after the retention of the original learning has been completely retroactively inhibited by an interpolated interfering task. Though the relearning takes as long or longer than the original learning, and everything looks as though the subject is learning the list for the first time, individual differences in relearning are only barely correlated with individual differences in original learning. Consequently, of course, OL and RL come out on different factors.

I mention these examples without going into further detail only to indicate the kinds of things that turn up when we work within a rather narrow slice of the learning domain and examine one or two tasks under a number of different procedural variations. Investigation of the dimensionality of individual differences just in memory span and serial learning is itself a huge undertaking. My initial investigations in this area have so far just scratched the surface. But certain basic methodological problems have been solved and hypotheses have been generated which will now carry this work forward at a much faster rate.

A word about methodology is in order at this point. First, a great deal more attention has to be paid to the reliability of our measurements in this kind of work than has ever been thought necessary in general experimental work. Another surprise is in store for us if we expect that most of our laboratory phenomena will yield individually reliable measures comparable to those of psychometric tests. A good part of a year was spent on my own project on IDs just trying to solve some of these reliability problems. Correcting correlations for attenuation is one solution, but one likes to know he is correcting intercorrelations with reliabilities that are at least significantly greater than zero. In fact, it has been possible to obtain very satisfactory reliabilities, so that no corrections of the correlation matrix are called for. We have achieved this by eliminating types of learning tasks which tend to elicit strategy types of behavior in subjects, by perfecting our preliminary instructions to subjects, by running subjects through brief pretests consisting of shortened and simplified versions of the experimental tasks in order to make sure that they are behaving in a standard way, and by the use of repeated measurements, made possible by running subjects on a number of parallel forms of every task. We have found, incidentally, that whatever the subject does in his first experience in the laboratory, regardless of the task, correlates with little else he ever does for us in later sessions. Initial performance usually sticks out in a factor analysis and has difficulty fitting anywhere into the factor structure, even though there may be a dozen other similar tests in the battery, all highly intercorrelated. Subjects apparently need some time to simmer down in the laboratory; the between-subjects variance we find in the first half-hour of a learning task reflects little of the learning genotypes manifested in subsequent laboratory performance. It is an interesting thought that so much of the experimental literature on learning is based on subjects' first hour in the laboratory. Subjects do change after this first experience, often quite dramatically. Almost nothing is known concerning the extent to which such changes in subjects affect the interactions among experimental variables. Someone had better look into this matter before long.

Another methodological or analytical risk consists of thinking one has found a source of IDs when in fact none exists. In the simplest case, IDs are thought to be detected when we find a significant Subjects × Independent Variable interaction in our analysis of variance, or when we find a significantly less than perfect correlation between two sets of learning scores (assuming a proper correction for attenuation). Interactions should be examined to determine if they can be removed by some transformation of the scale of measurement. As a simple example, say that subjects' learning scores suffer some decrement under an increase in the rate of stimulus presentation. If the amount of decrement is some constant proportion of the subject's original score or is some exponential function of the original score, analysis of variance or Pearson's r based on the original measures will give the appearance of IDs in the amount of decrement, due to an increase in stimulus pacing. The results would falsely imply that a different genotype is involved in the decrement than that which underlies the original score, while actually there is only one source of variance for both measures. The decrement scores in this case are completely predictable from the original scores, given the proper transformation of the scale. Thus, one should keep an eye out for spurious genotypes of this kind.

My final point on methodology is to recommend sticking with traditional laboratory learning procedures, at least for the time being. We have a considerable advantage if we begin already knowing a good deal about the characteristics of the learning tasks and materials we use in our studies of IDs.

The ultimate genotypes of individual differences will probably have to be described in physiological or biochemical terms. But before we reach that point, let me indulge in some rather unrestrained speculation and suggest some of the kinds of genotypes on the psychological level that we might be apt to find by means of the type of analysis I have indicated. These are some of the kinds of processes underlying individual differences that I imagine we might fathom through the welter of phenotypic variation: (a) the rate of decay of stimulus or associative traces in the absence of rehearsal; (b) the rate of consolidation of stimulus traces; (c) the initial strength of reception of stimuli; (d) proneness to interference with trace consolidation or external inhibition of the trace; (e) the degree of susceptibility of consolidated associations to interference through associative competition; (f) reactive inhibition and stimulus satiation; (g) the degree of spread of primary and semantic stimulus generalization gradients – and individual differences in this might not be general across all sensory modalities; (h) a complex of factors under the heading of drive, arousal, and attention; (i) something which for lack of a better term I will call 'personal tempo' – the sort of variance found in tapping tests and the like – but this could be only a derivative of other processes such as drive and inhibition; (j) oscillation tendency, that is, the tendency for response strength to fluctuate up and down over the course of practice, though again this may be a derivative from more basic processes, probably of the interference type. Even a list as short as this may be further reduced conceptually. IDs in susceptibility to associative competition, for example, might well be based on differences in primary or semantic generalization gradients.

This list suggests that the basic processes from which all phenotypic IDs are generated may be quite few. The big question, of course, is whether this is a false hope or, even if it were theoretically plausible, whether it will ever be at all empirically feasible to penetrate to such a level of elemental basic processes. At the moment, from a purely scientific standpoint, it seems to me a desirable goal.

Primary mental abilities

One of the major tasks of differential and experimental psychology is the theoretical integration of IDs in learning and the structure of mental abilities as represented by tests like the *Primary Mental Abilities*. I see mental abilities measured on this level as less basic and more derivative than the dimensions of individual differences in learning which I have suggested. Therefore, I would not expect to understand individual differences in learning, in any fundamental sense, in terms of psychometric reference tests. What such tests measure is best conceived of as points on the learning curves of various kinds of behavior. The predictive power of psychometric tests is due to the fact that they sample learned behavior and therefore reflect something about the rate of learning in the natural environment. Also, they index the degree of acquisition of certain broad verbal or symbolic mediational systems – systems which are learned in the verbal-symbolic environment and which play an important generalized transfer function in complex learning and problem solving. Furthermore, most psychometric tests are phenotypically closer to the products of learning which we are often interested in predicting, such as ability in school subjects, than are the kinds of variables we generally deal with in the learning laboratory.

But one of the questions that needs to be answered in terms of learning processes is why mental abilities are found to have the particular structure or dimensionality which is more or less consistently revealed by factor analysis. Do the *Primary Mental Abilities*, for example, reflect anything about the structure or functioning of the brain, or are they more properly regarded as a product of a complex interaction among certain classes of stimulus input from the natural and social environment and innate IDs in the basic learning processes?

Among the possible means of working toward a theoretical unification of learning abilities and mental abilities is the developmental study of the dimensionality of these two realms. Further insights might be gained from studies of how various types of aphasia and other disabilities arising from brain damage are manifested in these two spheres of ability measurement. Still another approach is through the experimental study of behaviors which are highly correlated with psychometrically measured abilities and which, at the same time, have some of the phenotypic characteristics of learning tasks. Memory span is a good example of this. It is, of course a subtest of the Stanford-Binet, and the Wechsler intelligence tests and shares at least half its variance in common with the general intellectual abilities measured by these tests. At the same time, various aspects of the memory span test can be manipulated experimentally along many of the procedural variables common to a variety of learning tasks. Discovery of the dimensionality of IDs in memory span in terms of processes common to the learning domain thus affords some link between learning abilities and mental abilities.

Transfer and individual differences

An inevitable and complicating fact we must contend with is that learning abilities also grow out of learning itself. This fact is perhaps best conceptualized in terms of a complex hierarchy of transfer functions. In theory, basic learning abilities, on the one hand, and abilities attributable to transfer from earlier learning, on the other, must constitute a true dichotomy, since something has to be learned initially and some primitive, basic abilities must be present to accomplish this. Beyond a very early stage of life, however, we are forced to think of these basic learning abilities as an idealized point at one end of a continuum of types of learning in which transfer, learning sets, mediational systems, and the like, play an increasingly important role as we move along the continuum. For practical purposes, such as the understanding of IDs in school learning, in problem solving, and in the acquisition of complex skills, the study of transfer hierarchies will be of paramount importance. Basic learning abilities will, of course, be manifested in the sense that they will underlie the rate of acquisition of learning sets, mediational systems, and the like. At the same time, the development of these systems will also facilitate the acquisition of other systems in the hierarchy. The more elemental learning processes and abilities may become thoroughly camouflaged under the elaborate overlay of transfer functions. But if we are interested in the description of IDs in complex learning situations, we would perhaps do best to measure IDs directly in the network of already learned sub-abilities which form the basis for the acquisition of more complex behaviors higher up in the transfer hierarchy.

The effects of early environment on readiness for school learning, and the complex chain of prerequisite learnings throughout the entire educational process are most readily thought of in terms of transfer. The broadest bases of transfer are probably to be found in attentional and discrimination hierarchies and in the processes of verbal mediation. The experimental paradigms that lend themselves to the analysis of individual differences in these processes constitute an immense topic in themselves, which I have elaborated upon elsewhere (Jensen, 1968e). In brief, individual differences in this area can be studied by assessing the properties of the verbal associative network as they are revealed through phenomena such as chained word associations, the degree of subjective organization and associative clustering in the free recall of verbal materials, the differential effects of varying degrees of meaningfulness or association value on the rate of acquisition in verbal learning tasks, and the differential rates of learning in tasks which differ in the amounts and kinds of verbal or symbolic mediation that they involve. Serial and paired-associate learning, for example, apparently stand at different points on this continuum involving degrees of verbal mediation. This fact could partly account for the low correlation between IDs in these two forms of learning (Jensen and Rohwer, 1963; Jensen and Rohwer, 1965; Jensen, 1965).

These, then, are a few of the possible approaches to gaining some theoretical mastery over the multifarious phenomena we find in human learning and the IDs associated with them. Let me conclude by pointing out that in this attempt to offer some description of the domain of IDs in learning at our present state of knowledge, or at least my own state of knowledge, I feel very much like one of the legendary blind men who tried to describe an elephant. At this stage more than one approach is obviously warranted.

Can we and should we study race differences?

Most persons experience some difficulty in discussing the topic of race differences in intelligence – a difficulty over and above that which is ordinarily inherent in the scientific study of any complex phenomenon. There is an understandable reluctance to come to grips with the problem, to come to grips with it, that is to say, in the same straightforward way that we would try to approach the investigation of any other problems in the behavioral sciences. This reluctance is manifested in a variety of 'symptoms' found in most writings and discussions of the psychology of race differences, particularly differences in mental ability: a tendency to remain on the remotest fringes of the subject, to sidestep central questions; to blur the issues and tolerate a degree of vagueness in definitions, concepts, and inferences that would be unseemly in any other realm of scientific discourse; to express an unwarranted degree of skepticism about reasonably well established quantitative methods and measurements; to deny or belittle already generally accepted facts – accepted, that is, when brought to bear on inferences outside the realm of race differences; to demand practically impossible criteria of certainty before even seriously proposing or investigating genetic hypotheses, as contrasted with extremely uncritical attitudes toward purely environmental hypotheses; a failure to distinguish clearly between scientifically answerable aspects of the question and the moral, political, and social policy issues; a tendency to beat dead horses and to set up straw men on what is represented as the genetic side of the argument; appeals to the notion that the topic is either really too unimportant to be worthy of scientific curiosity or too complex, or too difficult, or even forever impossible for any kind of research to be feasible, or that answers to key questions are fundamentally 'unknowable' in any scientifically acceptable sense; and, finally, the complete denial of intelligence and race as realities, or as quantifiable attributes, or as variables capable of being related to one another, thereby dismissing the subject altogether.

These tendencies will be increasingly overcome the more widely and openly the subject is discussed among scientists and scholars. As some of the taboos against the public discussion of the topic fall away, the issues will become clarified on a rational basis, we will come to know better just what we do and do not yet know about the subject, and we will be in a better position to deal with it objectively and constructively.

Is intelligence an attribute?

Intelligence is an attribute of persons. Probably for as long as man has been on earth it has been a common observation that persons differ in brightness, in speed of learning, in ability to solve problems, and so on. Parents, teachers, and employers are able roughly to rank children and adults in terms of a subjective impression of brightness or capability, and there is a fairly high agreement among different observers in the rank order they assign in the same groups of children. It is helpful to think of the subjective perception of intelligence as analogous to the subjective perception of temperatures, which is also an attribute. Before the invention of the thermometer, temperature was a matter of subjective judgment. The invention of the thermometer made it possible to objectify the attribute of temperature, to quantify it, and to measure it with a high degree of reliability. With some important qualifications, the situation is similar in the case of intelligence tests. The most essential difference is that intelligence, unlike temperature, is multidimensional rather than unidimensional. That is to say, there are different varieties of intelligence, so that persons do not maintain the same rank order of ability in every situation or test that we may regard as indicative of intelligence. It so happens that from among the total spectrum of human behaviors that can be regarded as indicative of some kind of 'mental ability' in the broadest sense, we have focused on one part of this spectrum in our psychological concept of intelligence. We have emphasized the abilities characterized as conceptual learning, abstract or symbolic reasoning, and abstract or verbal problem solving. These abilities were most emphasized in the composition of intelligence tests because these were the abilities most relevant to the traditional school curriculum and the first practical intelligence tests were devised to predict scholastic performance. They naturally had a good deal in common with the tests devised for scholastic prediction, since the educational system is intimately related to the occupational demands of a given society. Much the same abilities and skills that are important in schooling, therefore, are important also occupationally. Thus, we find that in industrialized countries practically all intelligence tests, scholastic aptitude tests, military classification tests, vocational aptitude tests, and the like, are quite similar in composition and that the scores obtained on them are all quite substantially intercorrelated. In short, there is a large general factor, or g, which the tests share in common and which principally accounts for the variance among individuals. When tests are devised to measure this g factor as purely as possible (i.e., in a factor analysis including a host of other tests it will have nearly all of its variance loaded on the general factor common to all the other tests and have little or no variance loaded on factors found only in certain tests [group factors]), examination of their item content leads to the characterization of it as requiring an ability for abstract reasoning and problem solving. Raven's Progressive Matrices Test is an example of such a test. Tests having quite diverse forms can have equally high loadings on the g factor – for example, the verbal similarities and block design tests of the Wechsler Intelligence Scales are both highly loaded on g. Tests of g can be relatively high or relatively low in degree of 'culture fairness'. (The question 'In what way are a wheel and a penny alike?' is probably more culture fair than the question 'In what way are an oboe and a bassoon alike?') In short, it is possible to assess essentially the same intelligence by a great variety of means.

Standard IQ tests measure the kinds of behavior in abstract and verbal problem situations that we call abstract reasoning ability. These tests measure more of g – the factor common to various forms of intelligence tests – than of any of the other more special ability factors, such as verbal fluency, spatial-perceptual ability, sensory abilities, or mechanical, musical, or artistic abilities, or what might be called social judgment or sensitivity. But a test that measured everything at once would not be very useful. IQ tests do reliably measure one important, though limited, aspect of human performance. The IQ qualifies as an appropriate datum for scientific study. If we are to study intelligence, we are ahead if we can measure it. Our measure is the IQ, obtained on tests which meet certain standards, one of which is a high g loading when factor analyzed among other tests. To object to this procedure by arguing that the IQ cannot be regarded as being interchangeable with intelligence, or that intelligence cannot really be measured, or that IQ is not the same as intelligence, is to get bogged down in a semantic morass. It is equivalent to arguing that a column of mercury in a glass tube cannot be regarded as synonymous with temperature, or that temperature cannot really be measured with a thermometer. If the measurements are reliable and reproducible, and the operations by which they are obtained can be objectively agreed upon, this is all that need be required for them to qualify as proper scientific data. We know that individually administered IQ tests have quite high reliability; the reliability coefficients are around 0·95, which means that only about 5 per cent of the total individual differences variance is attributable to measurement error. And standard group administered tests have reliabilities close to 0·90.

The standard error of measurement (which is about ± 5 for the Stanford-Binet and similar tests) must always be taken into consideration when considering any individual's score on a test. But it is actually quite unimportant in comparison of the means of large groups of subjects, since errors of measurement are more or less normally distributed about zero and they cancel out when N is large. The reliability (i.e., consistency or freedom from errors of measurement) *per se* of the IQ is really not seriously at issue in making comparisons between racial groups. If the samples are large, the mean difference between groups will not include the test's errors of measurement.

The validity or importance of the measures derives entirely from their relationship to other variables and the importance we attach to them.

M

The IQ correlates with many external criteria, and at the most general level it may be regarded as a measure of the ability to compete in our society in ways that have economic and social consequences for the individual. In the first place, the IQ accords with parents' and teachers' subjective assessments of children's brightness, as well as with the evaluations of children's own peers. In terms of assessments of scholastic performance, whether measured in terms of school grades, teachers' ratings, or objective tests of scholastic achievement, the IQ accounts for more of the individual differences variance than any other single measurable attribute of the child. IQ accounts for about 50 per cent of the variance in scholastic achievement at any single grade level, and over the course of several years or more of schooling it accounts for over 70 per cent of the variance in overall scholastic performance.

Since considerably less than 100 per cent of the variance is accounted for, it means the IQ is not an infallible predictor of the performance of any one individual. When used for individual diagnosis it must be evaluated in terms of many other factors in the child's makeup and background and condition at the time of testing, and even then not too much stock should be placed in the IQ in predicting *for the individual case*, since the predictive validity of the IQ is not sufficiently high to override the effects of possibly unassessed traits or unpredictable unusual future circumstances which may radically alter the course of the individual's development or performance in a statistically small proportion of cases. Thus, I am emphasizing the importance of evaluating the IQ somewhat differently when used for individual diagnosis and prediction than when used in making statistical predictions on large groups of individuals. It is somewhat analogous to actuarial predictions of insurance risks. Predictions for large groups classified by various criteria can be made with high degrees of certainty, while predictions for individual cases are highly uncertain.

Recently I received a letter from a high school senior who described himself as coming from a disadvantaged background. He had a strong desire to go on to college in hopes of becoming a lawyer, and he was wondering about his IQ and how much stock he should put in it in deciding his further course. I doubt if there is much more sense in worrying about one's own IQ than in worrying about the age at which one will die, as predicted by the insurance company's actuarial tables. Among other things, I wrote the following to my student inquirer: 'My own attitude toward tests, when I was a student, was not to give much thought to them but simply to set my sights on what seemed to me a realistic goal and then do my best to achieve it. You find out from those who have already made it what you have to know, what you have to be able to do, what skills you need to develop, and you set about doing these things just as you'd go about doing any kind of job that you know has to be done. If you set your goals too low, it's too easy and you won't develop your potential. If you set goals that are unrealistically high, you become discouraged. I recommend one step at a time, each step being something you really think you can achieve if you really work for it. When you have made the first step successfully, then you will have a better idea of how to take the next step. That way, if you have whatever it takes, you'll make it; if you haven't got whatever it takes, you'll find this out. But you'll never really know without trying your best. I wouldn't let any kind of test score determine what I try for. The reality of your own performance is meeting the competition in striving toward your goals is the only real test. I believe this approach gives one the best chances of finally doing what he is best suited for, and this is one of the conditions for a satisfying life.'

In statistical terms, however, the correlation is quite substantial between IQ and occupations, when the latter are merely ranked in the order of persons' average judgment of the occupation's prestige. Various studies have shown correlations in the range of 0·50 to 0·70. This is sufficiently high that the mean differences between groups of persons in occupations arranged according to a prestige hierarchy (which is highly related to income) show highly significant differences in IQ or other mental test scores. In general, any two groups, which differ in possessing what are perceived as 'the good things in life' according to the criteria and values of our society, will be found on the average to differ significantly in IQ. Upward social mobility is related to IQ: the brighter children in a family tend to move up in socio-economic level and the least bright tend to move down. There are exceptions to the general rule. Those who are born to wealth tend to be less able than those who made it themselves – a quite predictable finding in terms of 'regression to the mean'. Usually the regression of ability is much greater than the regression of cumulated wealth. The most conspicuous exceptions, however, involve various disadvantaged minorities, whose social and economic positions are different from what one would predict in terms of IQ. For example, Negroes earn less income than whites of comparable IQ, education, family background, and work experience (Duncan *et al.*, 1968). And American Indians, though considerable more impoverished then Negroes in the United States, score higher than Negroes on tests of intelligence and scholastic achievement (Kuttner, 1968). Oriental children, who generally score at least as high on IQ as white children, also score considerably higher than would be predicted from their socio-economic status (SES). This appears especially true of low-SES Oriental children, who perform on a par with middle-class white children on non-verbal tests (Lesser, Fifer and Clark, 1965). In predicting scholastic performance in school and in college, however, the evidence indicates that IQ tests and scholastic aptitude tests work with about equal accuracy for all persons from whatever background. In this one respect, at least, the educational system seems to be one of the least discriminatory institutions in our society. For example, there is no evidence that IQ tests predict scholastic performance of Negro children less well than for white children, or that college entrance exams predict college grades less well for Negro than for white students (Jensen 1968c; Stanley and Porter, 1967). The predictive validity of such tests could be lowered or changed, of course, by altering the curriculum such that the predictors would no longer be as relevant and other predictors might then become more valid.

When groups are selected from the lower or upper extremes of the IQ distribution, the contrasts are enormous. A classic example is Terman's study of gifted children, selected in elementary school for IQs over 140, which constitutes the upper 1 per cent of the population. These 1,528 children have been systematically followed up to middle age (Terman and Oden, 1959). The group as a whole greatly exceeds a random sample of the population on practically every criterion of a successful life, and not just intellectual criteria. On the average the Terman group have markedly greater educational attainments, have higher incomes, engage in more desirable and prestigious occupations have many more entries in *Who's Who*, have brighter spouses, enjoy better physical and mental health, have a lower suicide rate, a lower mortality rate, a lower divorce rate, and have brighter children (their average IQ is 133). These results should leave no doubt that IQ is related to socially valued criteria.

Is intelligence inherited?

The evidence on this point is very clear. There is no doubt of a large genetic component in individual differences in IQ. The methodology of determining the heritability of intelligence (or other traits) and the results of the applications of these methods to the study of intelligence have been reviewed in detail elsewhere (Burt, 1958; Jensen, 1967, 1969a and b). Heritability (H) refers to the proportion of individual differences variance in a measurable trait, like intelligence, that can be attributed to genetic factors. $1 - H$, therefore, is the proportion of variance attributable to non-genetic factors. These non-genetic factors are both biological and psychological. Some substantial proportion of the non-genetic IQ variance is unidentifiable, that is, it is due to random environmental effects and to random stochastic biological processes in embryonic development.

The heritability of IQ as estimated from the average of all published studies of the subject is 0·80, which means that on the average the studies show that 80 per cent of the population variance in IQ is attributable to genetic variation, and 20 per cent to non-genetic factors. The value of 0·80 is merely an average of many studies which yield H values that range from about 0·60 to about 0·90. There is no single true value of the heritability of a trait. Heritability is not a constant, but a population statistic, and it can vary according to the test used and the particular population sample tested. H will be affected by the range of genetic and environmental variation that exists in the population. It should be noted that all the studies of the heritability of intelligence have been based on European and North American Caucasian populations. The results cannot strictly be generalized to other populations such as American Negroes. We would need to conduct heritability studies within the Negro population if we are to have any certainty that our IQ tests are measuring a genetic component to the same degree in the Negro as in the white population. (Determining H in both populations still would not answer the question whether the group mean IQ difference between Negroes and whites has a genetic component.)

Non-genetic or environmental sources of variance can be analyzed into two major components: variance attributable to differences *between* families in the population and variance attributable to differences *within* families. The sum of the *between* families and the *within* families variances constitutes the total of the non-genetic or environmental variance. Expressed as a proportion, it is $1 - H = E$, and, as already pointed out, the average value of H reported in the literature is 0·80, making the average value of $E = 0·20$. The conceptually simplest method for estimating E is to obtain the correlation between identical (monozygotic) twins reared apart (r_{MZA}) in uncorrelated environments (families). $E = 1 - r_{MZA}$. The correlation between identical twins reared together (r_{MZT}) in the same family is used to estimate the *within* families environmental variance $E_W = 1 - r_{MZT}$. The *between* families variance is then $E_B = E - E_W$ or $r_{MZT} - r_{MZA}$. When these formulations are applied to all the relevant twin data reported in the literature, the average values they yield are $E = 0·20$, $E_B = 0·12$ and $E_W = 0·08$ (Jensen, 1967). Little, if any, of the E_W is controllable. Some of it is due to prenatal effects related to mother's age, health, accidental perinatal factors, ordinal position among other siblings, etc. In terms of our present knowledge, no prescription could be written for reducing E_W. Some of it, in fact, is almost certainly due to random, stochastic developmental processes in the first weeks after conception, which means that even if we had perfect control over all the identifiable factors usually classified as environmental, genetically identical individuals would still show some differences. The *between* families component, E_B, is probably much more attributable to what we commonly think of as environmental differences in terms of cultural-educational advantages, quality of nutrition, general health care, and the like.

Specific comments on genetics and IQ

To say that an IQ test like the Stanford-Binet 'measures present ability, not inborn capacity' is misleading. Surely it measures present ability or performance. But the fact that the heritability (H) of the Stanford-Binet IQ is about 0·80 in English and North American Caucasian populations also means that the test measures 'innate capacity', if by this term we mean the individual's genotype for intellectual development. Since H is the proportion of variance in IQs (which are phenotypes) attributable to variance in genotypes, the square root of H represents the correlation between phenotype and genotype, and this correlation is about 0·90, a very high correlation indeed. (This is the correlation that exists *after* correction for attenuation, that is, test unreliability.) What the evidence on heritability tells us is that we *can*, in fact, estimate a person's genetic standing on intelligence from his score on an IQ test. If the correlation between phenotype and genotype were perfect (i.e., 1·00), a person's test score would, of course, be an exact index of his genetic potential. But since the correlation is only about 0·90, such statements can only be made on a probabilistic basis.

If education and culturally derived motivation strongly affect intelligence test performance, then these factors should show up as part of the E variance, mostly E_B, i.e., *between* families environmental variance. Heritability studies, as pointed out, show the E variance to be only about 20 per cent of the total and E_B only about 12 per cent of the total. If *group* differences in IQ are to be explained in terms of educational and motivational factors, and if the heritability of IQ were the same in both groups, it would have to be assumed that all the members of one group differed from the mean of the other group by a *constant amount* in these motivational or other environmental variables. More will be said on this point in the later section on proposed genetic research.

The twin method may actually *underestimate*, rather than overestimate, the heritability of IQ. The reason is that there is considerable evidence that twins are more subject to prenatal stresses and nutritional disadvantages than singletons. This is reflected in the much lower birthweight of twins, the higher infant mortality of twins, and the fact that twins average 6 to 7 points lower in IQ than single-born children. One member of the twin pair is usually prenatally favored over the other, and this is especially true for monozygotic twins, as reflected in their differing birthweights. Birthweight of twins is positively correlated with later IQ (Willerman and Churchill, 1967). These prenatal differences, reflected in later IQ differences between the members of twin pairs, are very probably greater for twins than for singletons and therefore suggest a larger component of (prenatal) environmental variance in twins than in singletons. Thus the argument that the twin method of estimating heritability leads to an overestimate and thereby underestimates the environmental component is very weak. A stronger case can be made for just the opposite conclusion. The fact that the estimates of H from the twin methods are in close agreement with estimates based on other kinships indicates that the twin estimates are not very deviant in *either* direction. Indeed, it is the consistency of H estimates arrived at by different methods that makes them so impressive and reinforces their validity and scientific credibility (see Crow, 1969).

Cultural and educational differences are probably the most important *non-biological* sources of individual differences in intelligence, but they are not necessarily the most important *non-genetic* source of differences. It is likely that prenatal and nutritional factors are at least as important sources of variance as social-psychological factors. The sociological emphasis on the non-biological aspects of the environment has resulted in a relative neglect of probably important nutritional factors and maternal factors (age, health, diet, number of births, spacing of births, etc.) which can affect the prenatal and early childhood development of the individual.

In reply to suggestions that our national IQ may be declining due to the possibility that the least able segment of the population is reproducing at a faster rate than the most able segment, some writers draw the familiar analogy between intelligence and physical stature. Both IQ and height are polygenetic traits and the same quantitative genetic model can be applied to both and can predict the various kinship correlations for IQ and height about equally well. It is also known that height, like intelligence, shows a positive correlation with socio-economic status. Thus, if poor people have larger families than the well-to-do, we should expect the average height of the population to decrease over a number of generations. Exactly the same line of reasoning applies also in the case of intelligence. To counter this pessimistic prediction, it has been noted that despite what we should predict from simple genetic principles, the mean height of the population not only has not decreased in the past 200 years or so, but has in fact *increased* by a very significant amount. The increase, it is assumed, is due to environmental factors such as improved nutrition. And the implication is, of course, that intelligence, too, will increase over generations because of improvements in the environmental factors relevant to intellectual development. I believe this line of argument is weak and can lead to an unwarranted complacency about a possibly serious social trend.

First of all, Carter (1962) and Tanner (1965, 1968) have pointed out that much if not all of the increase in adult height in the past 200 years can be attributed to genetic factors, namely, the out-breeding effect. Increase in height is closely associated with the increase in the population's mobility. The offspring of parents from different Swiss villages, for example, are taller than the offspring of parents born in the same village. This outbreeding effect, or hybrid vigor, tends to saturate or level off in the population in a few generations, as has already occurred with respect to height in the United States. Nutritional factors have their greatest effect on *rate* of growth rather than on final adult height. In World War I men reached their full adult height at age 26; today they attain their full height at 18 or 19.

Although it is true that height is positively correlated with socio-economic status (SES) and that low-SES families are larger than high-SES families, these facts alone are not sufficient to warrant the prediction that the mean height of the population should decline. It would have to be shown that the same *numbers* of low-SES persons as high-SES persons have offspring. When this point was investigated for intelligence, it was found that persons of below average IQ have larger families than persons of above average IQ, but that fewer of the below average ever marry or have any children at all (Higgins and Reed, 1962; Bajema, 1963, 1966). The net result is a balance between the low and high IQ groups in the number of offspring they produce. This finding holds only for the white population of the U.S. of a generation ago. No studies of this type have been conducted in the U.S. Negro population. Since the bases for marriage and mate selection may be quite different in various sub-cultures, the

M*

results of investigation of this problem in one group cannot be generalized to other population groups with any confidence. The analogy with height is not convincing, since we have established only a negative correlation between height and family size, but have not taken into account the relative proportion of short and tall persons who never marry or produce offspring. Since we know there is selective mating for height in our population (that is, taller persons are viewed as more desirable) it is likely that fewer short persons marry or reproduce and that therefore a similar equilibrium between reproductive rates of short and tall persons exists as in the case of low and high intelligence. As I have noted elsewhere (Jensen, 1968a, 1969a), certain statistics raise the question of whether Negro intelligence is declining relative to white intelligence as a result of more extreme differential birthrates in lower and upper social classes among Negroes than among whites. Negro middle- and upper-class families have fewer children than their white counterparts, while Negro lower-class families have more. In 1960, Negro women married to professional or technical workers had only 1·9 children as compared with 2·4 for white women in the same circumstances. Negro women of ages 35 to 44 who were married to unskilled workers had 4·7 children compared with 3·8 for non-Negro women in the same situation, and Negro women with incomes below $2,000 per year averaged 5·3 children (Moynihan, 1966). This could mean that the least able segment of the Negro population is reproducing most rapidly, a condition that could alone produce and increase a genetic difference between the Negro and white populations in a few generations. The possible genetic and social implications of these trends have not yet come under investigation and there are no data at present which would warrant complacency about this important question.

Can genetic changes in a population take place only very slowly, so that selective pressures acting over several generations would be of negligible consequence? The answer, of course, depends largely on the degree of selective pressure. We already know enough to permit fairly accurate estimates of genetic trends given certain criteria of selection. If selection were extremely rigorous, an enormous shift in the population mean would be possible, as can be inferred from the average IQ of the offspring of the Terman gifted group. The Terman subjects were selected for Stanford-Binet IQs of 140 and above; they had a mean of 152. There was no selection of their spouses, except by the normal assortative mating that occurs for intelligence in our society (i.e., a correlation of 0·5 to 0·6 between spouses' IQs). The offspring of the Terman gifted had an average IQ of 133 (Terman and Oden, 1959). This is more than two standard deviations above the mean IQ of children born to a random sample of the population. There is a regression from the selected parent generation toward the general population mean, but the regression happens only once, and the offspring of the selected parents will in turn have offspring without further regression, provided, of course, they do not mate outside the group of offspring from the selected parents. Rats have been bred for maze learning ability and it has generally required from six to nine generations of selection to produce two strains of rats whose distributions of maze learning scores are completely non-overlapping.

Is race a variable?

One of the easiest ways of avoiding the issue of race differences in intelligence is to make the claim that there is no such thing as race and therefore it is not a variable that can be related to any other variables. Thus, proponents of this view would claim that the concept of race is merely a myth, not a phenomenon that can be subjected to scientific study. This is, of course, utter nonsense. But it will pay to clarify the concept of race as it figures in comparative studies of intelligence.

There are two general definitions of race: the social and the biological (or genetic). Both are arbitrary, but this need not mean they are unreliable or lacking in precision. Although most of the studies of racial differences in intelligence are based on social definitions of race, it should be noted that there is usually a high correlation between the social and the biological definitions and it is most unlikely that the results of the research would be very different if the investigators had used biological rather than social criteria of race in selecting groups for comparisons.

The social criteria of race are simple: they are the ethnic labels people use to describe themselves and the more obvious physical characteristics such as skin color, hair texture, facial features, and so on, by which persons roughly determine one another's 'race'. Admitted, the social definition is crude. It does not take account of 'borderline' or ambiguous cases that are hard to categorize and which make for some unreliability in classification, and it does not take account of the fact that there are no pure racial types – and especially in the case of American Negroes there is considerable racial admixture. Almost no American Negroes are of pure African descent; most have from 5 per cent to 90 per cent Caucasian genes, the average degree of admixture now being between 20 per cent and 30 per cent. Thus there is great genetic diversity *within* socially defined racial groups.

Does this make the social definition of race useless as a variable? No. In the first place, there is undoubtedly a high correlation between social and biological classification. That is to say, if one were to sort school children, for example, into three socially defined racial groups, Negro, Oriental, and Caucasian, one would find a very high concordance of classification if he used strict biological criteria based on the frequencies of blood groups, anthropometric measures, and other genetic polymorphisms. What one would not have obtained from the crude social classification is degrees of racial admixture. In other words, the major racial categories would be much the same whether constituted by social judgments or strict biological criteria. But if we wanted to go beyond this crude system of classification to make more refined differentiations, we would have to resort to biological criteria. Social judgments of degrees of racial admixture are quite unreliable. The broad categories, however, *are* reliable. They also qualify as variables in the sense that they show significant correlations with other variables such as IQ and scholastic performance. This is not to say that such correlations by themselves tell us anything about a biological or genetic basis for the correlation, which might be due to other environmental, social-class and cultural variables related to the socially defined racial classification. If the crucial variables in IQ differences are not racial classification *per se*, but other correlated environmental factors, then, at least in theory, one should be able to reduce the racial correlation with IQ to zero by partialling out the truly causal factors that are only incidentally correlated with both race and IQ. So far no one has succeeded in doing this as regards Negro-white comparisons. Every combination of environmental variables that anyone has partialled out has always left behind some significant correlation between race (socially defined) and IQ (Shuey, 1965). One can always claim that all the relevant environmental variables were not taken into account. This is a real weakness of such studies and they can be legitimately criticized on this score. It is largely for this reason that our understanding of racial differences will not be greatly advanced until more refined criteria of race based on biological criteria are employed. Specific proposals are made in a later section.

It is strange that those who claim that there are no genetic racial differences in ability are often the most critical of studies that have employed the social criterion of race rather than more rigorous genetic criteria. If the observed IQ differences are due only to social factors, then the social definition of race should be quite adequate, and, in fact, should be the only appropriate definition. If it is then argued that the two socially defined racial groups being compared are not 'pure' and that each group contains some genetic admixture of the other, it can only mean that the biological racial aspects of the observed IQ differences has been *under*estimated by comparing socially defined racial groups.

The biological definition of race is based on gene frequencies. Races are breeding groups which differ in the frequencies of one or more genes. A breeding group is one in which there is a higher proportion of matings among members of the group than of matings in which one member of the pair is from outside the group. Breeding groups result from relative degrees of geographical, racial, and cultural isolation of different population groups. The definition of race by these criteria is arbitrary only in the sense that differences in gene frequencies are a continuous variable, and where one wishes to draw the lines as criteria for classification purposes is not dictated by nature but by the taxonomic considerations of the investigator. Rather than thinking in terms of races, we should think in terms of groups with different gene frequencies. The question we would ask is whether various groups differing in gene frequencies also differ in IQ, other things being, in effect, equal. The major races are simply breeding populations that have a relatively high degree of inbreeding and differ from one another in the relative frequencies of many genes. They differ in so many known gene frequencies, in fact, that it seems highly improbable that they would not also differ in the frequencies of genes related to behavioral traits such as intelligence.

A major block to clear thinking about race is to think of it as a kind of Platonic essence, independent of any particular population group. General statements about the mental abilities of the 'white race', the 'black race', 'the yellow race', and so on, make no sense in terms of any studies that have yet been done or that seem at all feasible for the future. Strictly speaking, to ask if there are race differences in any characteristic is scientifically meaningless if what we mean by race is not clearly specified. All we can do is study samples selected from certain specified populations. These samples cannot be regarded as representative of some Platonic racial groups. They are merely representative (if properly selected) of the clearly specified population group from which they are selected.

We could ask, for example, whether a population sub-group that differs from the general population in its average response to the educational and occupational requirements of our society differs in its gene pool from other population sub-groups which are more successful, and if so, are some of the genetic differences related to ability factors with high heritability?

Population sub-groups which have immigrated are not necessarily representative of their native parent populations. Studies of racial or national groups in the United States, therefore, cannot be generalized abroad, and the reverse is also true. This does not mean, however, that meaningful comparative studies of various population sub-groups within the United States are not feasible.

The notion that there are no genetic mental ability differences among population sub-groups that differ in many other gene frequencies is, in principle, hard to defend. Populations that have been widely separated geographically or socially for many centuries and which have been exposed to climatic and cultural conditions that exert different selective pressures are almost certain to differ genetically in many ways. And, in fact, they do. Nearly every anatomical and physiological system studied has shown race differences. It is not at all necessary to invoke the factor of differential selective pressures to validate or explain some of these genetic differences, many of which confer no discernible advantage or disadvantage to survival or adaptation in any particular environment. A chemical substance, phenylthiocarbamide (PTC), is one illustration. To some persons PTC is completely tasteless; to others it has a very unpleasant bitter taste. Whether a person is a taster is determined by a single gene. This gene has markedly different frequencies in different racial groups. No one knows why this should be. Similarly, blood types have markedly different distributions in various racial groups, although it is not at all clear that one blood type is more advantageous than another in any given environment. In short, genetic diversity is the rule; genetic uniformity is the rare exception. By definition the gene pools of racial groups differ, and it is not at all an unreasonable hypothesis that genetic factors that condition behavioral development also differ.

Biological evolution generally is a slow process, but genetic changes with respect to particular traits can occur relatively fast in response to selective pressure in the environment. In any case, biological evolution, whatever its rate, has resulted in marked genetic differentiation of human populations. Concerning the one standard deviation average IQ difference between Negro and white American populations, one writer stated, 'A review of present knowledge on interracial divergence in man makes it unlikely that a difference as large as the observed one is genetic.' This hardly seems tenable in view of the fact that other traits show even greater racial differences than are found for intelligence. Height, like intelligence, is a polygenically inherited characteristic and is probably less subject to selective pressures than intelligence, and yet we find racial (and even national or regional) differences of more than one standard deviation. In fact, two racial subgroups on the African continent, the Pygmies and the Watusi, differ in height by five to six standard deviations. Obviously biological evolution has, in fact, been sufficient to create marked differences in genetic characteristics.

It is hard to imagine that there have not been different selection pressures for different abilities in various cultures and that these pressures would not be as great for intelligence as for many physical characteristics which are known to differ genetically among racial groups. Individual differences in the abilities most relevant to a particular culture are highly visible characteristics and if they have consequences for the individual's status in the social hierarchy or the culture's system of rewards they will be traits subject to the genetic effects of sexual selection and assortative mating. If a trait is not very relevant to the demands of a particular culture it will not become highly visible, it will not be a basis for selective mating, and its genetic basis will not be systematically affected by pressures in the social environment.

Selective mating refers to the fact that certain characteristics are viewed as desirable in mate selection by virtually all members of the breeding population. The usual consequence is that those standing higher on the desired trait will have greater opportunities for mating and reproduction while those at the lowest end of the distribution on the trait in question will be least likely to find a mate and to leave progeny. The net effect is to boost the mean value of the trait in the population. Assortative mating refers to the fact that like tends to marry (or mate with) like. It is sometimes an inevitable consequence of selective mating with respect to generally desirable traits, but also holds for traits which are merely subject to various individual preferences. It is noteworthy that of all measurable human characteristics the one with the highest coefficient of assortative mating (i.e., the correlation between mates) is intelligence. The correlation between spouses' IQs, for example, is around 0·5 to 0·6 in various studies, as contrasted with a correlation of 0·3 for height and of zero for fingerprints. The high degree of assortative mating for intelligence means that it is highly subject to genetic change through social influences. For example, the variance of the IQ distribution in the population would be reduced by approximately 20 per cent if there were no assortative mating for just one generation. Assortative mating increases the variance of the characteristic in the population, and if there is selective mating (as well as assortative) for the characteristic, the individuals at the lower (least desirable) end of the distribution will be least likely to reproduce. The net effect is to raise the average of the population on the trait in question. Such trends have probably taken place with respect to different traits in different societies for many centuries. While sexual selection may be capricious and non-adaptive with respect to many physical characteristics (e.g., various societies have different criteria of beauty), selection is not likely to be capricious with respect to those abilities which are salient in the competition in a given society. There has probably been quite strong and consistent selection for different patterns of ability in different cultures. A high degree of genetic adaptation to the demands of one environment might not constitute optimal adaptive capabilities to the demands of another, quite different, environment. As stated by Spuhler and Lindzey (1967, p. 413) in their chapter on the behavior-genetics of race difference:

> ... it seems to us surprising that one would accept present findings in regard to the existence of genetic, anatomical, physiological, and epidemiological differences between races and still expect to find no meaningful differences in behavior between races.

They continue to point out that there are

> enormous discrepancies between races in the efficiency with which culture is transmitted (for example, the difference between literate and nonliterate societies). Some of these differences are closely associated with race differences, have existed for many thousands of years, and presumably have been accompanied by very different selection pressures in regard to character potentially relevant to culture transmission, such as 'intelligence'.

Thus, it seems highly improbable that there have been no markedly differing selective pressures on different sub-populations even within the United States. The selective pressures on Negroes must have been very different from those in European immigrant populations. The history of slavery suggests quite extreme selective factors, involving even the deliberate breeding of slaves for certain characteristics which were irrelevant or perhaps even negatively correlated with intellectual prowess. It would be surprising indeed if more than 300 years of slavery did not have some genetic consequences. But since the possible nature of these consequences are highly speculative and cannot be accurately inferred from historical accounts, this retrospective approach to the study of racial differences is too unreliable to be of much real scientific value. Direct genetical studies of present population groups can provide the only really satisfactory basis for the scientific study of genetic differences in abilities.

Are there racial differences in IQ?

In the United States persons classed as Negro by the common social criteria obtain scores on the average about one standard deviation (i.e., 15 IQ points on most standard intelligence tests) below the average for the white population. One standard deviation is an *average* difference, and it is known that the magnitude of Negro-white differences varies according to the ages of the groups compared, their socio-economic status, and especially their geographical location in the United States. Various tests differ, on the average, relatively little. In general, Negroes do slightly better on verbal tests than on non-verbal tests. They do most poorly on tests of spatial ability, abstract reasoning and problem solving (Shuey, 1966; Tyler, 1965). Tests of scholastic achievement also show about one standard deviation difference, and this difference appears to be fairly constant from first grade through twelfth grade, judging from the massive data of the Coleman study (1966). The IQ difference of 1 *SD*, also, is fairly stable over the age range from about 5 years to adulthood, although some studies have shown a tendency for a slight increase in the difference between 5 and 18 years of age. Another point that has been suggested, but which requires much more systematic investigation before any firm conclusions can be reached, is that there is a larger sex difference in IQs for Negroes than for whites (Bronfenbrenner, 1967). The presumed difference favors the females. The point is especially worthy of research because, if true, it would have considerable social and educational consequences, which would be especially evident in the upper tail of the IQ distribution. For example, if girls are a few IQ points higher than boys, on the average, one should expect a greatly disproportionate number of Negro girls to qualify, as compared with boys, in any selection based on cut-off scores well above the mean, such as selection for college. Assuming a general mean of 85, an *SD* of 15, and a normal distribution, a 5 point IQ difference between Negro boys and girls and a college selection cut-off score of 115, for example, we would expect the number of qualified girls to boys to be approximately in the ratio of 2 to 1.

A statistic which has been much less studied than the mean difference is the standard deviation (*SD*), that is, the measure of dispersion of scores within the distribution.

Most studies agree in finding a smaller *SD* in Negro than in white IQs. The single largest normative study of Stanford-Binet IQs in a Negro population, for example, found an *SD* of 12·4 as compared with 16·4 in the white normative sample (Kennedy, Van de Riet, and White, 1963). This study is based on a large sample of school children in five Southeastern states and therefore may not be representative of the Negro population in other regions of the U.S. In general, however, most studies of Negro intelligence have found a smaller standard deviation than the *SD* of 15 or 16 generally found in white samples. The point is of some consequence in considering the relative merits of the opposing hypothesis relating to the *causes* of the observed average IQ difference between Negroes and whites, namely, the hypothesis of genetic equality versus the hypothesis of genetic differences. If the distribution of IQs in the Negro population does, in fact, have a smaller SD than in the white population, and if we hypothesize no genetic differences between the two populations, we must conclude that there is less variance due to environmental differences within the Negro group than within the white group. Since the genetic variance is hypothesized to be exactly the same in both groups, the difference in the variances (i.e., the square of the *SD*) of the groups must be all environmental variance. Thus, if the total variance of Negro IQs is less than of white IQs, the genetic equality hypothesis is forced to predict a higher heritability of IQ in the Negro population than in the white; that is to say, more of the variance in Negro IQs would have to be due to genetic factors. If a study of the heritability of IQ in the Negro population yielded a heritability coefficient equal to or less than that found in the white population, this finding would contradict the genetic equality hypothesis, at least as regards the equality of genetic variance in the two populations.

Let us take another look at the Kennedy *et al.* (1963) data in this connection, to see how the hypothesis of genetic equality of variances comes out for this one set of data comparing the distribution of Negro IQs with the distribution of the white population sample on which are based the norms for the Stanford-Binet Intelligence Test. It will be recalled that the *SD*s for Negroes and whites were 12·4 and 16·4, respectively. The variances are thus $(12·4)^2 = 153·76$ and $(16·4)^2 = 268·96$. Now, the best estimate of the heritability of Stanford-Binet IQs in white population samples similar to that on which the Stanford-Binet was standardized is 0·80 (Jensen, 1969a). This means that 80 per cent of the variance of the white IQ distribution is *genetic* variance: thus, $0·80 \times 268·96 = 215·17$ is the white genetic IQ variance. But this is still greater than the *total* Negro IQ variance. The heritability of IQ in the white group would have to be assumed to be 0·57 for the white *genetic* variance to equal the *total* IQ variance of the Negro group, and surely some of this total variance is non-genetic. Furthermore, no reported study of the heritability of Stanford-Binet IQs is as low as 0·57. Thus, a hypothesis of genetic equality with respect to variances leads to highly untenable conclusions when applied to the data of Kennedy *et al.* (1963). By any canon of statistical and logical reasoning one is forced to reject the hypothesis that the distributions of genotypes for intelligence are equivalent in these two samples. By assuming genetic equivalence, one simply cannot make any sense out of the available data. This is not to say that one cannot question the data with respect to every parameter that is involved in this line of reasoning.[1] But if one accepts the validity of the heritability estimates in the white population and the *SD*s given by Kennedy *et al.*, it logically follows that a genetic equivalence hypothesis is untenable. It is, of course, statistically unwarranted to generalize this conclusion beyond the populations sampled in the study by Kennedy *et al.* The causes of the lesser variance of IQ in the Negro group are

---

[1] For example, one need not accept the IQ scale as the most appropriate. If it could be argued and demonstrated that some transformation of the IQ scale produced more orderly and lawful data in studies of heritability, in the degree of normality of the distribution of scores, and in more closely approximating a genetic model, then such a transformation would be justified. It could very well affect the variances of the distributions in different population sub-groups. Berkeley geneticist Dr Jack King, for example, has suggested that if we assume that the factors (genetic and environmental) that affect intelligence do not behave additively but interact multiplicatively (i.e., a factor adds or subtracts a given *percentage* to the total measure rather than a fixed *amount*) a logarithmic transforma-

not known. One can only speculate and suggest hypotheses. From the evidence on the white population, for example, we know that some 15 to 20 per cent of the total variance is attributable to assortative mating for intelligence; if the correlation between mates' IQs was markedly reduced, the white IQ variance would be substantially reduced. (Variance due to assortative mating is all *genetic* variance.) Also, the covariance of heredity and environment (i.e., there is some correlation between children's genotypes for intellectual development and the quality of the environment in which they are reared) constitutes some 5 to 10 per cent of the total IQ variance in the white population. If environments were more similar, there would be less covariance and this source of variance would be diminished in the total. We could find out if these factors or others, or some combination of factors, are responsible for the lesser variance in the Negro population only by carrying out complex heritability studies in the Negro population.

A point that should be stressed is the fact that neither the white nor the Negro population, by common social classification, is genetically homogeneous. It has already been noted that the American Negro is not of pure African ancestry but has, on the average, an admixture of 20 per cent to 30 per cent Caucasian genes, varying from less than 5 per cent in some regions of the country to 40 per cent or 50 per cent in others (Reed, 1969). The white population contains many different sub-groups which most probably differ genetically in potential for intellectual development. To point to one particular sub-group of one socially defined racial population as being higher or lower in IQ than some sub-group in another racial population proves nothing other than the

---

tion of the IQ scale is theoretically justified. In the multiplicative model, the logarithm of the observed measure is normally distributed. The logarithmic transformation in fact makes the IQ distribution more normal (Gaussian) in a number of studies, and it tends to equalize the variances of the Negro and white distributions, although it also has the effect of pulling their means slightly further apart. The proper transformation is 100 $(1 + \ln IQ/100)$, which leaves the general population mean at IQ 100. ($\ln$ is the natural logarithm.) Past studies of the heritability of intelligence should be re-analyzed using this logarithmic transformation of the IQ scale to see if it gives a closer and more parsimonious fit to a polygenic model.

fact that there exists an overlap between the racial groups. The fact that relatively large mean IQ differences are found between certain sub-groups within the same race does not mean that these differences must be entirely of environmental origin and that therefore racial differences of similar magnitude must also be entirely attributable to environment.

Finally, it should be noted that IQ tests are taken by individuals. There is no such thing as measuring the IQ of a group as a group. Individuals' IQs are obtained as individuals. The basis on which individuals may be grouped is a separate issue, depending upon the purposes of the investigator. When test scores are grouped according to some criteria or racial classification, we find mean differences between the groups. If we group test scores by some criteria of socio-economic status, we find mean differences between the groups. Conversely, if we group persons by levels of IQ, we find the groups differ in their proportions of persons of different races and social classes.

Are race differences important?

There is, of course, nothing *inherently* important about anything. Race differences in intelligence are important only if people think these differences, or their consequences, are important. It so happens that in our society great importance is given to these differences and their importance is acknowledged in many official public policies. Racial inequality in educational and occupational performance, and in the social and economic rewards correlated therewith, is today clearly one of the uppermost concerns of our nation.

Most persons are not concerned with those racial characteristics that are patently irrelevant to performance. The real concern results from the observed correlation between racial classification and educational and occupational performance. Persons who feel concerned about these observed differences demand an explanation for the differences. It is apparently a strongly ingrained human characteristic to need to understand what one perceives as a problem, and to ask for answers. People inevitably demand explanations about things that concern them. There is no getting around that. We have no choice in the matter. Explanations there will be.

But we do have a choice of essentially two paths in seeking explanations of intelligence differences among racial groups. On the one hand, we can simply *decree* an explanation based on prejudice, or popular beliefs, or moral convictions, or one or another social or political ideology, or on what we might think it is best for society to believe. This is the path of propaganda. Or, on the other hand, we can follow the path of science and investigate the problem in the same way that any other phenomena would be subjected to scientific study. There is nothing to compel us to one path or the other. This is a matter of personal preference and values. And since persons differ markedly in their preferences and values, we will inevitably see both of these paths being followed for quite some time. My own preference is for a scientific approach to the study of these phenomena. It is certainly the more interesting and challenging intellectually. And our experience tells us that the scientific approach, by and large, leads to more reliable knowledge of natural phenomena than any other method that man has yet devised. If solutions to educational problems depend upon recognizing certain psychological realities in the same sense that, say, building a workable spaceship depends upon recognizing certain physical realities, then surely we will stand a better chance of improving education for all children by choosing the path of scientific investigation. In facing the issue of race differences in abilities we should heed the statement of John Stuart Mill:

> If there are some subjects on which the results obtained have finally received the unanimous assent of all who have attended to the proof, and others on which mankind have not yet been equally successful; on which the most sagacious minds have occupied themselves from the earliest date, and have never succeeded in establishing any considerable body of truths, so as to be beyond denial or doubt; it is by generalizing the methods successfully followed in the former enquiries, and adapting them to the latter, that we may hope to remove this blot on the face of science.

Once we subscribe to a scientific approach, we are obligated to act accordingly. This means, for one thing, that we entertain alternative hypotheses. To entertain a hypothesis means not just to pay lip service to it or to acknowledge its possible merit and let it go at that. It means to put it into testable form, to perform the test, and report the results with information as to the degree of statistical confidence with which the hypothesis in question can be accepted or rejected. If we can practice what is called 'strong inference', so much the better. Strong inference consists of formulating opposing hypotheses and pitting them against one another by actually testing the contradictory predictions that follow from them. This is the way of science. How much of our educational research, we may ask, has taken this form? How much of the research that we see catalogued in the already gargantuan ERIC bibliography on the causes of the educational handicaps of children called culturally disadvantaged has followed this path? The only sensible conclusion one can draw from a perusal of this evidence is that the key question in everyone's mind about racial differences in ability – are they genetic? – has, in effect, been ruled out as a serious alternative hypothesis in the search for the causal factors involved in inequalities of educational performance. Sundry environmental hypotheses are considered, but rarely, if ever, are alternative genetic hypotheses suggested. If a genetic hypothesis is mentioned, it is usually for the sake of dismissing it out of hand or to point out why it would be impossible to test the hypothesis in any case. Often, more intellectual ingenuity is expended in trying to find reasons why a particular genetic hypothesis could not be tested than in trying to discover a way of formulating the hypothesis so that it could be put to a test. The emotional need to believe that genetic factors are unimportant in individual or group differences in ability can be seen in many statements by dedicated workers in those fields of psychology and education most allied to the problems of children called disadvantaged. For example, Dr Bettye Caldwell, a prominent worker in compensatory and early childhood education, has noted:

> Most of us in enrichment . . . efforts – no matter how much lip service we pay to the genetic potential of the child – are passionate believers in the plasticity of the human organism. We need desperately to believe that we are all born equalizable. With any failure to demonstrate the effectiveness of compensatory experiences offered to children of any given age, one is

entitled to conclude parsimoniously that perhaps the enrichment was not offered at the proper time (Caldwell, 1968, p. 81).

But genetic factors in rate of development are never considered
as a possible part of the explanation.

It is important not to evaluate persons in terms of group
membership if we are to insure equality of opportunity and social
justice. All persons should be treated as individuals in terms of
their own merits, if our aim is to maximize opportunities for
every person to develop his abilities to their fullest capacity in
accord with his own interests and drives. But the result of
individual selection (for higher education, better jobs, etc.) makes
it inevitable that there will be unequal representation of the
parent populations in any subgroup that might be selected whenever there are average differences between parent populations.

Many questions about the means of guaranteeing equality of
educational opportunity are still moral and political issues at
present. When there is no compelling body of scientific evidence
on which policy decisions can be based, such decisions must be
avowedly made in terms of one's personal social philosophy and
concepts of morality. Many goals of public policy must be decided
in terms of values. The results of research are of greatest use to
the technology of achieving the value-directed goals of society.
The decision to put a man on the moon was not a scientific
decision, but once the decision was made the application of
scientific knowledge was necessary to achieve this goal. A similar
analogy holds for the attainment of educational goals.

Can race differences be researched?

It is sometimes argued that even though it is not unreasonable to
hypothesize genetic racial differences in mental ability, we cannot
know the direction or magnitude of such genetic differences and
the problem is much too difficult and complex to yield to scientific
investigation. Therefore, the argument often continues, we should
go on pretending as though there is no question of genetic differences, as was officially stated by the U.S. Office of Education in
1966: 'It is a demonstrable fact that the talent pool in any one
ethnic group is substantially the same as that in any other ethnic
group.'

First, we will never know to what extent research can yield answers on a subject unless we at least try our best to do the research. It is doubtful that any major scientific advances could have been made in any field if it were decided beforehand that the problems could not be researched. I cannot agree that a scientific approach should be restricted to only the easy problems. If all the necessary methodology for studying the genetics of race differences in psychological characteristics is not yet sufficiently developed, this should not be surprising, since so little effort has been made thus far. The methodology of a field of inquiry does not grow in a vacuum. Scientists do not *first* develop a complete methodology for the investigation of a complex area and then apply it all at once to get the final answers. An appropriate methodology evolves as a result of grappling with difficult problems in the spirit of scientific research. Darwin's theory of evolution did not begin with a fully developed methodology adequate to prove the theory, nor did the theory of the inheritance of acquired characteristics – a theory which was later disproved after the development of an adequate methodology, a methodology which would not have developed in the absence of attempts to research this theory. No one would have been inclined to invent the necessary research methods in the absence of the problems these methods were needed to solve. One critic states 'The scientific problem [of genetic race differences in ability] itself seems of dubious validity, if one considers how great are the difficulties . . ., at least on the basis of present techniques.' The same statement could have been made about research on the theory of evolution, the atomic theory, the gene theory, and so on. We do not expect any single study or experiment to reduce all the uncertainty about a complex subject to absolute zero in one bold stroke. But as in dealing scientifically with most other complex phenomena, we should not regard ourselves as so intellectually impotent as to be unable to gradually chip away at the heredity-environment uncertainty with whatever tools that scientists can muster or devise with their present knowledge and ingenuity.

What are some of the thinking blocks in this area? One is the frequent failure to distinguish between raw facts, on the one hand, and inference from the facts in terms of some hypothesis, on the other. The Society for the Psychological Study of Social Issues (SPSSI), for example, in a press release (May 2, 1969) criticizing my article in the *Harvard Educational Review* (Jensen, 1969a), stated, 'There is no *direct* [italics mine] evidence that supports the view that there is an innate difference between members of different racial groups.' Of course there is no *direct* evidence, nor can there be direct evidence if by 'direct' we mean evidence that is immediately palpable to our physical senses. The gradual disappearance of ships over the horizon is not *direct* evidence of anything, but it can be interpreted in terms of the hypothesis that the earth is round. It would be harder to explain if we hypothesized that the earth is flat. So even as relatively simple an hypothesis as that the world is round cannot be proved by direct evidence, but depends upon logical inference from diverse lines of evidence. If all that was needed was direct evidence, even a monkey would know that the world is round, in the same sense that it knows that a lemon is sour. The substantiation of an hypothesis in science depends upon *objective* evidence but does not necessarily depend upon direct evidence.

Another inhibition to thought on this topic is the notion that before research can yield any answers, the environment must be absolutely equal for all groups involved in comparisons. The SPSSI statement went so far as to say that '. . . a more accurate understanding of the contribution of heredity to intelligence will be possible only when social conditions for all races are equal and when this situation has existed for several generations'. Since no operationally testable meaning is given to 'equal' social conditions, such a statement, if taken seriously, would completely preclude the possibility of researching this important question, not just for several generations, but indefinitely. Actually, large environmental differences between racial groups can be revealing when the environmental ratings are positively correlated with IQ or scholastic performance *within* the groups but show a negative correlation *between* the groups. If group A on the average has a poor environment in terms of variables claimed to be important to intellectual development and group B has a good environment, and if group A performs better than group B on intelligence tests which are appropriate to the experience of both groups, this is evidence that some factors other than the measured environmental variables are involved in the relatively higher intellectual performance of group A as compared with group B. If environmental factors cannot be found that will account for the difference, it is presumptive evidence in favor of the genetic hypothesis. Genetical tests of the hypothesis are preferable, of course. (These are discussed in a later section.) But what one also looks for are consistencies among various lines of evidence, especially lines of evidence that lead to opposite predictions from different hypotheses.

Many investigators now would question the view that the lack of early stimulation in the pre-school years can be counted among the chief causes of the poorer IQ performance of Negro children, since when children are grouped in several categories according to their parents' socio-economic status, the Negro children in the highest SES category still score two to three IQ points below white children in the lowest SES level (Shuey, 1966). Thus, what we generally think of as a reasonably good environment is apparently not sufficient to equalize the performance of Negro and white groups.

Such findings lead to hypothesizing increasingly subtle and hard to measure environmental effects. But it should be recognized that at present most of the environmentally 'damaging' effects that are assumed to be accountable for performance differences are hypothetical and not factual. Poor self-concept and alienation are among the currently prevailing explanations, but what has not yet been satisfactorily explained is why such general motivational dispositions should affect some cognitive abilities so much more than others. Performance is not uniformly low on all tasks, by any means. There are distinct high and low points in the profile of various abilities in different ethnic groups (Stodolsky and Lesser, 1967), and no one has yet attempted to explain how such profile differences, which are invariant across social classes, could come about as a result of differences in generalized attitudes and motivation in the test situation.

Finally, unnecessary difficulties arise when we allow the scientific question to become mixed up with its possible educational, social, and political implications. The scientific question and its solution should *not* be allowed to get mixed up with the social-political aspects of the problem, for when it does we are less able to think clearly about either set of questions. The question of whether there are or are not genetic racial differences in intelligence is independent of any questions of its implications, whatever they may be. But I would say that the scientific question should have priority and the answer should be sought through scientific means. For although the answer might have educational and social implications, and there are indeed grave educational and social problems that need to be solved, we must first understand the causes of problems if we are to do anything effectively toward solving them. Gaining this knowledge is a scientific task. As it is accomplished, we are then in a better position to consider alternative courses of action and evaluate their feasibility and desirability in terms of society's values and goals. This moves the problem into the realm of public policy, where all the answers cannot be scientifically derived. But policy cannot be wisely or effectively formulated unless it is informed by the facts. No matter how well intentioned it may seem to be, it can only be less effective and less beneficial if it is based on false premises or in contradiction of reality.

Genetic research to reduce the heredity-environment uncertainty

Today there is virtually no uncertainty among those who have attended to the evidence that individual variation in intelligence is predominantly conditioned by genetic factors and that environmental factors account for a lesser proportion of the phenotypic variance. One can point to variations among studies that have estimated the heritability of intelligence. Such variations in estimates of the proportion of variance attributable to genetic factors are to be expected in view of the great variety of populations sampled and the differences among the variety of tests of mental ability that have been used. Despite these expected variations in heritability estimates, it is important to note that no major study contradicts the conclusion that heredity contributes something more than twice as much to the variance in IQ as environment in *white* European and American populations. (We do not have good heritability data on other populations.)

The term 'heredity-environment uncertainty' refers mainly to the question of race differences in intelligence. The answer to this question is still in the realm of uncertainty in terms of the normal scientific meaning of this word. *Absolute* certainty is never attained in an empirical science. Absolute certainty can be had only in pure mathematics, the certainty of which rests upon the fact that pure mathematics is, as Bertrand Russell pointed out, just one vast tautology. Empirical science deals in probability statements, and 'certainty' refers to a high degree of probability that a proposition is 'true', meaning that certain objective consequences can be predicted from the proposition with a stated probability. A decisive increase in this probability with respect to any given scientific proposition rarely results from a single experiment or discovery. I take exception to the impression that might be given by some writers that unless a scientific study can be perfect and 100 per cent certain, we cannot know anything. This is not how scientific knowledge advances. We do not devise perfect methods or obtain complete answers on the first try. Certainty, in the sense of probability, is generally increased very incrementally in science. Research aims to add reliable increments to statements of probability.

This we must continue to do with respect to the question of genetic race differences in intelligence. It is still an open question by all reasonable scientific standards. The existing evidence is in all cases sufficiently ambiguous, due largely to the confounding of racial and environmental factors, as not to permit statements with a sufficiently high probability such that all reasonable and qualified persons attending the evidence will agree that it is conclusive. The issue of genetic race differences may be likened to theories of the moon's craters – whether they were caused by volcanic eruptions or by the impact of meteors. All the evidence obtainable by astronomers could support either interpretation, and different scientists could argue for one theory or the other. A substantial increment could be subtracted from this uncertainty only by obtaining new evidence not obtainable through telescopic study, namely, directly obtaining and analyzing material from the surface of the moon.

I believe that, similarly, the heredity-environment uncertainty about race differences in IQ will be substantially reduced only by obtaining new evidence – new *kinds* of evidence. Exclusive reliance on anthropological, sociological, and psychological evidence would probably not substantially advance our knowledge. I believe that application of the methods of biometrical genetics (also called population genetics or quantitative genetics) to the question of race differences will substantially reduce our uncertainty.

Someone suggested that the only way one could prove race differences in intelligence would be to dye one member of a pair of white identical twins black and adopt it out to a Negro family while the co-twin is reared by a white family. How much difference would it make in their IQs? Better yet is the suggestion of Professor Arthur Stinchcombe (1969): find pairs of identical twins in which one member of each pair is Negro and one is white, separate them at birth and rear them in Negro and white families and see how their IQ differences compare with those found for twins where both are of the same race! These suggestions sound ridiculous; one is unfeasible and the other is impossible. Yet as conceptual experiments they are good, because they suggest the necessary ingredients of the information we must obtain to reduce the heredity-environment uncertainty. Both examples rightly recognize skin color (and, by implication, other visible racial features) as a part of the individual's environment. They are based on comparing genetically equivalent persons reared in different environments. Another possibility consists of rearing genetically and racially different persons in essentially similar environments – including the factor of skin color, etc. Is such a study possible? Yes.

Geneticists already know the frequencies of a large number of genetically independent blood groups in European and African populations. On the basis of such data, it is entirely possible to determine the proportion of Caucasian genes in a population sample of Negroes, socially defined. Furthermore, it should be possible by the same means to classify individuals on a probabilistic basis in terms of their relative proportions of African and Caucasian genes. Since the *average* admixture of Caucasian genes for American Negroes is between 20 and 30 per cent, there should be enough variance to make it possible to assign large numbers of individuals to at least several categories according to their amount of admixture, and the probable error in classification could be quite definitely specified. A sufficient number of blood groups or other genetic polymorphisms with known frequency distributions in African and Caucasian populations would have to be employed to insure a high degree of statistical certainty that the categories represented different degrees of genetic racial admixture. A wide range of admixtures probably exists among Negroes living in highly similar environments, so that it should be quite possible in such a study to obtain samples which do not differ across the admixture categories in a number of socioeconomic or other environmental indices. What about skin color? It is polygenetic and is very imperfectly correlated with the amount of Caucasian admixture. Individuals, for example, whose genes are derived in equal (50-50) proportions from African and Caucasian ancestors evince the full range of skin colors from white to black, including all the shades between. This makes it possible statistically to control the effect of skin color; that is, one can compare a number of persons all of whom have the same skin color but different degrees of African/Caucasian admixture, or conversely, the same degree of admixture but different skin colors. (Skin color can be quantified precisely and objectively by means of a photoelectric device which measures reflectance.) The question, then, would be: do the mean IQs (or any other mental ability tests) of the several categories of racial admixture differ significantly and systematically? The genetic equality hypothesis would predict no difference; the genetic inequality hypothesis would predict a difference between the groups.

A further refinement, in order to insure greater equality of environmental conditions across the admixture categories, *including* prenatal environment, would be to include in the study a large number of half-siblings all related through the mother and reared together. Some half-siblings will inevitably fall into different admixture categories. Do they differ significantly on mental tests when skin color is controlled? Birth order, maternal age, and other factors would have to be noted, but in large samples these factors would probably tend to be random with respect to racial admixture. One would also want a white control group with no African admixture in order to rule out the remote possibility that the blood groups themselves are causally related to IQ, since they are intended in this study only as genetic markers or indices of racial admixture. Such a study would go further toward answering the question of Negro-white genetic differences in intelligences than the sum total of all the other studies that we now have.

The possibility has been suggested of using genetic linkages for studying the inheritance of intelligence and race differences, but evaluation of its potential merits will have to be decided by geneticists. If the genes for some clearly identifiable physical trait are located on the same chromosome as the genes for some measurable mental ability, we should expect to find a marked correlation in the population between the appearance of the physical characteristic and the mental attribute whose genes share the same chromosome. The physical characteristic would thus serve as an objective genetic marker for the mental trait.

The major difficulty with this approach may be that what we call intelligence is so polygenetic that the relevant genes are carried on most or all of the chromosomes, so that specific linkages could never be established. If intelligence consists of a large number of sub-abilities, each of which is conditioned independently by a very limited number of genes which are carried on a single chromosome, then it may be possible to study linkages, provided we can realiably measure the sub-abilities. I have described elsewhere how psychologists might make their measurements of abilities of greater interest and value to researchers in genetics (Jensen, 1968c). Briefly, it would consist of the fractionation of mental abilities to the most extreme limits that reliability of measurement will permit, and then seeing if these sub-abilities show any signs of relatively simple genetic inheritance (such as showing Mendelian ratios) or genetic linkages.

Are there any known linkages between physical and mental characteristics in the normal distribution of intelligence? I do not know of any established examples. We should begin looking for such possible mental linkages with blood groups, biochemical variations, and other physical traits. One set of interesting findings concerns the association between uric acid level in the blood and intellectual achievement. Whether this is an instance of genetic linkage or whether there is a causal connection between uric acid and brain functions is not yet established. Stetten and Hearon (1958) reported a correlation between serum uric acid concentration and scores on the Army intelligence test of 817 inductees. A study of serum urate levels of 51 University of Michigan professors found a positive correlation with drive, achievement, and leadership (Brooks and Mueller, 1966), and high school students have been found to show a similar relationship (Kasl, Brooks, and Cobb,

N

1966). It would be interesting to know if these correlations are found within other racial groups and also if there are differences between groups in serum uric acid levels. Every bit of such various kinds of information, if it points consistently in the same direction, reduces to some extent the heredity-environment uncertainty.

There are other promising approaches to this problem through biometrical genetics, but explication of the technical aspects of these methods is clearly beyond the possible scope of the present discussion.

Implications for education

Since educators have at least officially assumed that race and social class differences in scholastic performance are not associated with any genetic differences in growth rates or patterns of mental abilities but are due entirely to discrimination, prejudice, inequality of educational opportunity, and factors in the child's home environment and peer culture, we have collectively given little if any serious thought to whether we would do anything differently if we knew in fact that all educational differences were not due solely to these environmental factors.

There have been and still are obvious environmental inequities and injustices which have disfavored certain minorities, particularly Negroes, Mexican-Americans, and American Indians. Progress has been made and is continuing to be made to improve these conditions. But there is no doubt still a long way to go, and the drive toward further progress in this direction should be given top priority in our national effort. Education is one of the chief instruments for approaching this goal. Every child should receive the best education that our current knowledge and technology can provide. This should not imply that we advocate the same methods or the same expectations for all children. There are large individual differences in rates of mental development, in patterns of ability, in drives and interests. These differences exist even among children of the same family. The good parent does his best to make the most of each child's strong points and to help him on his weak points but not make these the crux of success or failure. The school must regard each child, and the differences among children, in much the same way as a good parent should do.

I believe we need to find out the extent to which individual differences, social class differences, and race difference in rates of cognitive development and differential patterns of relative strength and weakness in various types of ability are attributable to genetically conditioned biological growth factors. The answer to this question might imply differences in our approach to improving the education of all children, particularly those we call the disadvantaged, for many of whom school is now a frustrating and unrewarding experience.

Individuals should be treated in terms of their individual characteristics and not in terms of their group membership. This is the way of a democratic society, and educationally it is the only procedure that makes any sense. Individual variations within any large socially defined group are always much greater than the average differences between groups. There is overlap between groups in the distributions of all psychological characteristics that we know anything about. But dealing with children as individuals is not the greatest problem. It is in our concern about the fact that when we do so, we have a differentiated educational program, and children of different socially identifiable groups may not be proportionately represented in different programs. This is the 'hang-up' of many persons today and this is where our conceptions of equal opportunity are most likely to go awry and become misconceptions.

Group racial and social class differences are first of all individual differences, but the causes of the *group* differences may not be the same as those of the *individual* differences. This is what we must find out, because the prescription of remedies for our educational ills could depend on the answer.

Let me give one quite hypothetical example. We know that among middle-class white children, learning to read by ordinary classroom instruction is related to certain psychological developmental characteristics. Educators call it 'readiness'. These characteristics of readiness appear at different ages for different kinds of learning, and at any given age there are considerable individual differences among children, even among siblings reared within the same family. These developmental differences, in middle-class white children, are largely conditioned by genetic factors. If we try to begin a child too early in reading instruction, he will experience much greater difficulty than if we waited until we saw more signs of 'readiness'. Lacking readiness, he may even become so frustrated as to 'turn off' on reading, so that he will then have an emotional block toward reading later on when he should have the optimal readiness. The readiness can then not be fully tapped. The child would have been better off had we postponed reading instruction for six months or a year and occupied him during this time with other interesting activities for which he was ready. Chances are he would be a better reader at, say, 10 or 11 years of age for having started a year later, when he could catch on to reading with relative ease and avoid the unnecessary frustration. It is very doubtful in this case that some added 'enrichment' to his pre-school environment would have made him learn to read much more easily a year earlier. If this is largely a matter of biological maturation, then the time at which a child is taught in terms of his own schedule of development becomes important. If, on the other hand, it is largely a matter of pre-school environmental enrichment, then the thing to do is to go to work on the pre-school environment so as to make all children equally ready for reading in the first grade. If a child's difficulty is the result of both factors, then a combination of both enrichment and optimal developmental sequencing should be recommended.

There is a danger that some educators' fear of being accused of racial discrimination could become so misguided as to work to the disadvantage of many minority children. Should we deny differential educational treatment to children when such treatment will maximize the benefits they receive from schooling, just because differential treatment might result in disproportionate representation of different racial groups in various programs? I have seen instances where Negro children were denied special educational facilities commonly give to white children with learning difficulties, simply because school authorities were reluctant to single out *any* Negro children, despite their obvious individual needs, to be treated any differently from the majority of youngsters in the school. There was no hesitation about singling out white children who needed special attention. Many Negro children of normal and superior scholastic potential are consigned to classes in which one-fourth to one-third of their classmates have IQs below 75, which is the usual borderline of educational mental retardation. The majority of these educationally retarded children benefit little or not at all from instruction in the normal classroom, but require special attention in smaller classes that permit a high degree of individualized and small group instruction. Their presence in regular classes creates unusual difficulties for the conscientious teacher and detracts from the optimal educational environment for children of normal ability. Yet there is reluctance to provide special classes for these educationally retarded children if they are Negro or Mexican-American. The classrooms of predominantly minority schools often have 20 to 30 per cent of such children, which handicaps the teacher's efforts on behalf of her other pupils in the normal range of IQ. The more able minority children are thereby disadvantaged in the classroom in ways that are rarely imposed on white children for whom there are more diverse facilities. Differences in rates of mental development and in potentials for various types of learning will not disappear by being ignored. It is up to biologists and psychologists to discover their causes, and it is up to educators to create a diversity of instructional arrangements best suited to the full range of educational differences that we find in our population. Many environmentally caused differences can be minimized or eliminated, given the resources and the will of society. The differences that remain are a challenge for public education. The challenge will be met by making available more ways and means for children to benefit from schooling. This, I am convinced, can come about only through a greater recognition and understanding of the nature of human differences.

The phylogeny and
ontogeny of intelligence

Phylogeny of adaptive behaviour

Are there qualitative as well as quantitative differences in the behavior-adaptive capabilities of animals at different levels of the phyletic evolutionary sequence? That is to say, are there differences not only in the *speed* of learning but also in the complexity of what the organism can learn at all, given any amount of time and training? Are there discontinuities as well as continuities in capacities to perceive, to learn, and to manipulate the environment as we ascend the phyletic scale?

The answer to these questions is now empirically quite clear. There are indeed discontinuities and qualitative differences in learning (i.e., behaviorally adaptive) capabilities as we go from one phyletic level to another. Behaviorally, the phylogenetic hierarchy is best characterized in terms of an increasing complexity of adaptive capabilities and an increasing breadth of transfer and generalization of learning, as we move from lower to higher phyla. It is a fact that every animal, at least above the level of worms, has the capacity to learn, that is, to form stimulus-response associations or conditioned responses. But the degree of complexity and abstractness of what can be learned shows distinct 'quantum jumps' going from lower to higher phyla. Simpler capacities, and their neural substrate, persist as we move from lower to higher levels, but new adaptive capacities emerge in hierarchical layers as we ascend the phyletic scale. Each phyletic level possesses all the learning capacities (although not necessarily the same sensory and motor capacities) of the levels below itself in addition to new emergent abilities, which can be broadly conceived as an increase in the complexity of information processing. For example, studies by Bitterman (1965) of animals at various levels of the phyletic scale (earthworms, crabs, fishes, turtles, pigeons, rats, and monkeys) have clearly demonstrated discontinuities in learning ability among different species and the emergence of more complex abilities corresponding to the phylogenetic hierarchy. In the experimental procedure known as habit reversal, a form of learning to learn in which the animal is trained to make a discriminative response to a pair of stimuli and then has to learn the reverse discrimination and the two are alternated repeatedly, a fish does not show any sign of learning to learn (i.e., each reversal is like a completely new problem and takes as long to learn as the previous problems), while a rat improves markedly in its speed of learning from one reversal to the next. When portions of the rat's cerebral cortex are removed, thereby reducing the most prominent evolutionary feature of the mammalian brain, the learning ability of the decorticate rat is exactly like that of the turtle, an animal with little cortex, and would probably be like that of the fish if all the rat's cortex could be removed. Harlow and Harlow (1962) have noted similar discontinuities at high levels of learning among rhesus monkeys, chimpanzees, and humans. Again, situations that involve some form of learning to learn are most sensitive to differences in capacity. No animals below primates have ever learned the so-called oddity-non-oddity problem no matter how much training they are given, and more complex variations of this type of problem similarly differentiate between rhesus monkeys and chimpanzees. The species' differences are not just in *speed* of learning but in whether the problem can be learned at all, given any amount of training. This is essentially what is meant by a hierarchical conception of learning ability. There is much evidence for this conception, which Jensen (1970b) has summarized more extensively elsewhere. The evolution of humans from more primitive forms is now believed to be intimately related to the use of tools and weapons (Ardrey, 1961). The mental capabilities involved in the use of implements for gaining ever greater control of the environment, in lieu of sheer physical strength, were just as subject to the evolutionary effects of natural selection as are any genetically mutated organs. More specifically, according to Haskell (1968, p. 475), 'What primarily evolves in man is the nerve structure which confers the capacity to invent, to borrow, and to adapt culture traits.'

Ontogeny of human mental abilities

In humans does mental development of the individual occur in qualitatively different stages that are hierarchically related? Are there ontogenetic discontinuities in mental development just as there are phylogenetic discontinuities?

There is now much evidence, exemplified in the work of Piaget (1960) and substantiated in numerous experiments by other child psychologists both here and abroad (for reviews, see Flavell (1963), Kohlberg (1968), and Phillips (1969)), that individual cognitive development proceeds by distinct, qualitatively different stages in children's modes of thinking and problem solving at different ages. Piaget and others have demonstrated that children's thinking is not just a watered-down or inferior approximation to adult thinking; it is radically and qualitatively different. The stages of mental development form an invariant sequence or succession of individual development. Each stage of cognitive development is a structured whole; mental development thus does not consist of the mere accretion of specific stimulus-response associations. Cognitive stages are hierarchically integrated; higher stages reintegrate the cognitive structures found at lower stages. Also, as Kohlberg (1968, p. 1021) points out, 'There is a hierarchical preference within the individual . . . to prefer a solution of a problem at the highest level available to him.' In reviewing the experimental literature on children's learning, Sheldon White (1965) has amassed evidence for two broad stages of mental development, which he labels *associative* and *cognitive*. The transition from one to the other occurs for the vast majority of children between 5 and 7 years of age. In the simplest terms, these stages correspond to *concrete-associative* thinking and *abstract-conceptual* thinking. The latter does not displace the former in the course of the child's mental development; in older children and adults the two modes co-exist as hierarchical layers.

Individual differences in mental development

Are individual differences in the rate and the asymptotic level of mental development genetically conditioned?

Mental development, as indexed by a wide variety of tests, is known to take place at different rates among children, and the final level of ability attained can be viewed as a hierarchical composite of earlier developed abilities, each level of the hierarchy being necessary but not sufficient for development of the next higher level. At maturity, individuals differ with respect to the relative prepotence of different modes in the hierarchy of abilities and thus show different capabilities for different kinds of learning and problem solving. The difficulty level of items in most standard intelligence tests (especially tests of the culture-fair variety, such as Raven's Progressive Matrices and Cattell's Culture-Fair Tests of *g*) reflects increasing dependence of the problem's solution upon higher mental processes.

Over the past half-century, numerous studies (for reviews, see Jensen (1967a, 1968c, and 1969a)) based on a wide variety of tests of mental ability administered to persons of varying degrees of genetic and environmental relatedness, sampled from European and North American Caucasian populations, lead to the now generally accepted conclusion that in these populations genetic factors are approximately twice as important as environmental factors in accounting for individual differences in mental ability. This means, among other things, that variations in mental abilities can be, have been, and still are subject to selective and assortative mating, just as is true of physical characteristics that display genetic variation.

Sub-population differences in mental development

Are there genetically conditioned differences among population *groups* both in the overall average level of mental development and in the pattern of relative strengths of various mental abilities?

Sub-groups of the population which are relatively isolated geographically, culturally, or socially can be regarded as breeding populations to varying degrees (i.e., mating within groups has a higher occurrence than mating between groups). To the extent that breeding populations have been subjected to differential selective pressures from the environment, both physically and culturally, differences in gene frequencies can be expected to exist, especially for adaptive characteristics, physical and behavioral,

N*

but also for possibly non-adaptive pleitropic characters (i.e., seemingly unrelated phenotypic effects caused by the same gene). Racial groups and, to a lesser degree, social classes within a society can be regarded as breeding populations.

Social classes as defined largely in terms of educational and occupational status are subject to differential selection for mental abilities. Since these have genetic as well as environmental components, they are transmitted to the offspring, and because of a high degree of assortative mating for mental traits in Western cultures the gene pools for different social classes will differ in the genetic factors related to ability. The evidence for phenotypic mental ability differences among social classes, along with evidence for genotypic differences, has been reviewed extensively elsewhere (Eckland, 1967; Jensen, 1970e; Jensen, 1970b). It is now generally accepted by geneticists, psychologists, and sociologists who have reviewed the evidence that social class differences in mental abilities have a substantial genetic component. This genetic component should be expected to *increase* in an open society that permits and encourages social mobility. Phenotypically, of course, social class differences in patterns of mental ability are firmly established. Jensen (1968c) has found that lower-class and middle-class population samples differ much less in abilities that are lower in the ontogenetic hierarchy, such as associative learning and memory span, than in higher cognitive abilities, such as conceptual learning and abstract reasoning. A different pattern of correlations between lower and higher abilities also is found in lower-class and middle-class groups, implying that the lower abilities are necessary but not sufficient for the development and utilization of higher-level abilities.

Scientific knowledge concerning the genetic aspect of ability differences among racial groups, having been generally shunned as a subject of scientific study in modern genetics and psychology is far more ambiguous and more in dispute than social class differences. The uncertainty in this area will be reduced only through further appropriate research using the most advanced techniques of behavior-genetic analysis. Phenotypically, racial differences in abilities are well established, both with respect to overall average level of performance and to the pattern of relative strengths of various abilities (Lesser *et al.* 1965). Both social class and racial (Caucasian, Negro, and Oriental) differences have been found in rates of cognitive development as assessed by Piagetian test procedures, such as ability to grasp concepts of conservation of number, quantity, and volume (Tuddenham, 1970). Some indication of the role of genetic factors in the Piagetian indices of level of cognitive development is shown in a study of Australian aboriginal children, the majority of whom, if full-blooded aborigines, do not show ability for grasping the concepts of conservation of quantity, weight, volume, number, and area, even by the time they have reached adolescence, while the majority of Caucasian children attain this level of mental development by 7 years of age. However, aboriginal children having (on the average genetically) one Caucasian great-grandparent, but reared in the same circumstances as the full-blooded aborigines, performed significantly better (i.e., showed higher levels of cognitive development) than the full-blooded aborigines (De Lemos, 1969).

Personality correlates of ability

Do human behavioral traits other than ability have a genetic component, thereby also being subject to selection, and do such traits become associated, through genetic selection, with intellectual abilities?

Here the evidence is somewhat less well established than that which was adduced in answer to the previous questions. Eysenck (1967) has amassed extensive evidence for the existence of two broad dimensions or factors of personality, called extraversion-introversion (E-I) and neuroticism (N). The former (E-I) is related to outgoingness and carefreeness; the latter (N) is related to emotional and autonomic instability. Both dimensions have been shown to have physiological correlates and a substantial genetic component comparable to that found in mental abilities. Together, these factors, E-I and N, account for most of the individual differences variance in a wide variety of personality assessments. Certain combinations of these traits appear to have socially important consequences. For example, high extraversion combined with high neuroticism is significantly associated with antisocial behavior (Eysenck, 1964).

In a social system such as ours, that tends to sort out people according to their abilities, it seems most likely that those traits of personality and temperament which complement and reinforce the development of intellectual skills requiring persistent application, practice, freedom from emotional distraction, and resistance to mental fatigue and to boredom in the absence of physical activity should become genetically assorted and segregated, and thereby correlated, with those mental abilities requiring the most education for their full development – those abilities most highly valued in a technological culture. Thus ability and personality traits will tend to work together in determining individuals' overall capability in the society. Cattell (1950, p. 98-9) has, in fact, shown that certain personality variables are correlated to the extent of about 0·3 to 0·5 with a general ability factor. Cattell concludes: 'There is a moderate tendency ... for the person gifted with higher general ability, to acquire a more integrated character, somewhat more emotional stability, and a more conscientious outlook. He tends to become "morally intelligent" as well as "abstractly intelligent".'

The heritability of intelligence

Since the dawn of history people have noticed differences in intelligence among individuals and have wondered about the causes of these obvious differences. Intelligence has been described by many different words – brightness, cleverness, reasoning power, judgment, and quickness in learning, in grasping abstract concepts, and in solving problems. Every parent, teacher, and employer has observed differences among children and adults in all these characteristics that we call 'intelligence'. A few persons appear extremely 'bright', a few appear extremely 'dull', and the vast majority falls somewhere between these extremes. There is a continuous gradation of mental ability from the one extreme to the other, from idiot to genius. Just as we see a continuous gradation of differences in other characteristics of humans, such as physical stature, so too there is a similar gradation of differences in intellectual ability. Indeed, individual variation is a fundamental aspect of all living things. Without individual variation, biological evolution as we know it could not have occurred.

The question of why people differ in intelligence has been asked for centuries, but a scientifically acceptable answer did not become wholly possible until psychologists devised techniques for measuring intelligence quantitatively and objectively. The first really useful intelligence test was devised in 1905 by the French psychologist Alfred Binet. Binet's early test was later revised and improved by Lewis Terman at Stanford University; the now-famous test that resulted from these efforts is known as the Stanford-Binet Intelligence Scale. It is still the most widely used test of general intelligence.

There are also many other intelligence tests, and although many of them appear to be quite different from one another, all actually

389

measure much the same general ability. That is to say, if we administer several seemingly quite different intelligence tests to a large number of persons, their scores on all the tests will be in pretty much the same rank order. Those who score high on one test will tend to score high on the others, and those who score low on one test will usually score low on all the others. This fact of correlation among all tests of intelligence led Charles Spearman, the famous English psychologist, to conclude that there is a general factor, 'g', which is common to all tests of intelligence. We know that it is practically impossible to make up a mental test having any degree of complexity which does not involve 'g'. We can perhaps most clearly characterize 'g' as an ability for abstract reasoning and problem solving, for seeing relationships, and for grasping concepts.

A person's score on an intelligence test is usually expressed as an IQ (for Intelligence Quotient). The test is standardized in the general population in such a way that the average IQ at any age is set at 100, and the middle 50 per cent of the population falls within the so-called average range of IQs going from 90 to 110.

Significance of the IQ

Can the IQ tell us anything of practical importance? Is it related to our commonsense notions about mental ability as we ordinarily think of it in connection with educational and occupational performance? Yes, indeed, and there is no doubt about it. The massive evidence from psychological, educational, and industrial research, and research in the armed forces, in unequivocal. We know, for example, that no other single fact that we are now able to ascertain about a child gives us a better prediction of his future scholastic performance than his IQ obtained after age 5 or 6. (Below this age IQ tests become less accurate indicators of the child's later mental development, and below 2 or 3 years of age test scores have practically no predictive value.)

The IQ obtained after 9 or 10 years of age also predicts final adult occupational status to almost as high a degree as it predicts scholastic performance. When various occupations are ranked for average income and for the general public's average judgment of the occupation's prestige and desirability, this rank order is found to be highly related to the average IQ level of the persons in these occupations. There is of course a wide spread of IQs in nearly every occupation, but the *average* IQ of persons within a particular occupation is closely related to that occupation's standing in terms of its average income and the amount of prestige accorded to it by the general public.

One of the most convincing demonstrations that IQ is related to 'real life' indicators of ability was provided in a classic study by Terman and his associates at Stanford University. In the 1920s they selected a total of 1,528 children with Stanford-Binet IQs above 140. The average IQ of the group was 152. These children were investigated periodically over the years up into their adulthood. (Most of them are now in their 50s.) Terman found that for the most part these high-IQ children in later adulthood markedly excelled the general population on every indicator of achievement that was examined: a higher level of education completed; more scholastic honors and awards; higher occupational status; higher income; production of more articles, books, patents, and other signs of creativity; more entries in *Who's Who*; a lower mortality rate; better physical and mental health; and a lower divorce rate. Also, they have much brighter children than the average; their average IQ is 133, a level which is exceeded by only 2 per cent of children in the general population.

Findings such as these establish beyond a doubt that IQ tests measure characteristics that are obviously of considerable importance in our present technological society. To say that the kind of ability measured by intelligence tests is irrelevant or unimportant would be tantamount to repudiating civilization as we know it.

The causes of IQ differences

The layman usually asks: 'Is intelligence due to heredity *or* environment?' The scientist promptly answers: 'Both'. Without heredity *and* environment there simply is no intelligence. Obviously every person must have had a biological inheritance of genes from his parents and must have grown in an environment, or he wouldn't even be here to take an IQ test. So, of course, both heredity and environment are essential for the existence of the individual or any of his physical and mental characteristics.

But when scientists actually study this problem, we find that they do not even ask the layman's question. The question to which scientists have sought an answer can be stated as follows: How much of the *variation* among persons in a given population is attributable to differences in their environments and how much to differences in their genetic endowments?

Numerous studies conducted by psychologists and geneticists over the last 40 or 50 years provide an answer to this question. The answer is unambiguous and is generally agreed upon by all scientists who have considered all the evidence. This evidence strongly supports the conclusion that genetic factors are much more important than environmental influences in accounting for *individual differences* in IQ. How much more important? The evidence indicates that genetic factors account for at least *twice* as much of the variation in IQs as environmental factors. This conclusion has one main limitation. Since all of the major studies in this field were conducted with samples of Caucasian European and North American populations, we cannot confidently generalize their conclusions to other populations, especially those with very dissimilar environments.

What are the kinds of evidence that lead to the conclusion that genetic differences outweigh environmental differences in accounting for individual differences in IQ? Most of this evidence, as it is found in the scientific literature, depends upon quite technical methods of analysis developed in a specialty known as quantitative genetics or population genetics. Some of these methods were devised originally to analyze the roles of heredity and environment in agriculture and animal breeding.

Experiments in animal breeding

Experiments in which we explicitly try to breed for some specific trait give us the most certain evidence that variation in the trait has a genetic component. Psychologists have bred rats for speed of learning mazes, which is a good indicator of rat intelligence. By always mating the fast-learning males with fast-learning females, and mating slow-learning males with slow-learning females, it is possible, within six to ten generations, to produce two quite distinct strains of rats in respect to maze-learning ability.

The slowest learning rat of the 'bright' strain will learn mazes faster than the fastest rat of the 'dull' strain. The two strains will differ markedly in the number of tries they need to learn how to run through a maze efficiently, avoiding the blind alleys. These experiments definitely prove that not only physical characteristics but some behavioral traits as well are largely inherited through the parental genes. Thus we should not be surprised to find in humans that differences in some behavioral characteristics, including intelligence, are a product of genetic inheritance.

Identical twins reared apart

One of the most important lines of evidence for the inheritance of intelligence in humans comes from studies of identical twins who were separated shortly after birth and reared in different homes. Identical twins originate from a single fertilized ovum which splits in the course of early development to form two individuals. Each member of the pair of twins therefore has exactly the same complement of genes. Consequently, any difference between the twins must be due entirely to non-genetic or environmental differences.

Twins separated shortly after birth are often reared in families that differ markedly in social class, and the range of environmental differences observed in their foster homes is fairly typical of the environmental variations seen in the general population.

Four major studies of identical twins reared apart, conducted in England, Denmark, and the United States, and totaling 122 pairs of twins, are in remarkably close agreement in showing that twins reared in different homes are still much more alike in IQ than are *fraternal* twins reared together. Fraternal twins are merely siblings who happen to be conceived and born at the same time, and therefore half of them are of opposite sex. In IQ and other traits they resemble one another no more than do ordinary siblings born at different times.

Identical twins reared apart differ, on the average, by only 6 to 7 IQ points. But even if we test the very same person on two occasions a week apart, we find that his test score will vary, on the average, by 2 or 3 IQ points. This is the test's 'measurement error'. When we eliminate this error from the twin data, we find that the twins differ only 4 or 5 points in IQ. Identical twins reared *together* differ by only 2 or 3 points, not including measurement error. The largest IQ difference ever found in a pair of identical twins reared apart is 24 points. More than 17 per cent of siblings reared together differ by more than 24 IQ points. The same is true of fraternal twins. But siblings (and fraternal twins) have only half of their genes in common, and they differ on the average by 12 IQ points (excluding measurement error), even when reared together.

The studies of identical twins show clearly that individuals who are genetically identical are almost as much alike in mental ability as they are alike in physical traits, and this is true even when they have grown up in different environments.

Unrelated children reared together

The opposite situation to identical twins reared apart is that of genetically unrelated children adopted at birth by foster parents and reared together. Such children differ from one another, on the average, by 15 to 16 IQ points (excluding measurement error). Compare this with the 17 to 18 points difference between unrelated children reared in *different* homes, or the 15 to 16 points difference between unrelated children brought up in different homes but in the same socio-economic class. We see that unrelated children brought up together in the *same* home differ from one another in IQ at least three or four times more than genetically identical twins reared in *different* homes. And the unrelated children reared together differ almost as much in IQ as unrelated children simply picked at random from different homes.

The IQs of adopted children also show little or no relationship to the IQs of their adopting parents, but they are almost as closely related to the IQs of their natural parents as we find in the case of children who are reared by their natural parents.

Children reared in the common environment of an orphanage differ from one another in IQ to approximately the same degree as children picked at random from the total population. The IQs of orphanage children who have never known their own parents show almost the same degree of correlation with their parents' level of ability as we find in the case of children reared by their own parents.

Resemblance between parents and children

Now and then we notice that very bright parents can have an intellectually mediocre child, or that rather dull parents can have an exceptionally bright child. These observations are often pointed to mistakenly as evidence that intelligence is not inherited. But the fact is that genetic theory predicts precisely that we should find such discrepancies between parents and their offspring. For example, parent-offspring differences in height are of about the same relative magnitude as their differences in IQ. Children resemble their parents physically and in mental ability to about the same degree that they resemble their own siblings. The average IQ difference between a parent and his (or her) child is the same as the difference between siblings – that is, about 12 IQ points. The difference between a child and the average of both of his parents' IQs is about 10 points.

A parent with a high IQ will usually, but by no means always, have children whose IQs are somewhat lower than his own but are still above the average for the general population. A parent with a low IQ, on the other hand, will usually, but not always, have children whose IQs are somewhat higher than his own but are still below the average of the population. This phenomenon, discovered by Sir Francis Galton, is called 'regression towards the mean', and it holds true for height and other inherited physical traits as well as for IQ.

IQs of husbands and wives

It is interesting that in our society husbands and wives are at least as much alike in IQ as brothers and sisters. If men and women picked their mates strictly at random, as by a lottery, spouses would differ by an average of 18 IQ points. But in fact men and women choose one another partly for intelligence, and so spouses differ by only 10 or 11 points in IQ.

The effect of inbreeding on IQ

Every person harbors a number of mutant, recessive genes. Most of these are defective genes. They are passed on from parent to child, but they usually will not produce any harmful effects to the child unless the other parent also contributes exactly the same defective gene. The reason this usually does not occur is that each parent's normal genes are dominant over the other parent's defective, recessive genes. When mating occurs between a man and a woman who are blood relations, however, the chances are much greater that they will both possess many of the same defective genes. When these defective genes are paired together in the related couple's children, they subtract unfavorably from the traits that are controlled by these genes under normal conditions. This depression due to inbreeding is known to occur in inherited physical traits, such as stature, and the same thing has been found for IQ. It is well established, for example, that cousin marriages produce children who, on the average, have lower IQs than children whose parents are unrelated but are matched with the married cousins on IQ, age, educational level, and socio-economic status. More extreme are the cases of children who have resulted from incestuous relationships, such as father-daughter and brother-sister matings. These children show a much higher incidence of severe mental retardation than children born to the same parents when they have mated with unrelated persons. These interesting findings are entirely predictable from basic principles of genetics that apply to all living beings. Moreover, it is virtually impossible to explain such facts without concluding that IQ differences are very strongly influenced by genetic mechanisms.

The relative effects of heredity and environment

How can we summarize briefly what is now known about the relative importance of heredity and environment in causing individual differences in IQ? In the terminology of genetics a summary answer consists of saying that the 'heritability' of IQ is close to 0·80. This means that 80 per cent of the 'variance' in IQs in the general population is attributable to genetic differences and 20 per cent is attributable to non-genetic or environmental differences.

'Variance' is essentially a quantitative index of the total amount of differences that exist among all members of some population. So instead of talking about variance we can more easily describe our conclusions in terms of average differences.

If we should determine the differences in IQ between every person in the population and every other person, the average of all these differences would turn out to be 18 IQ points. These differences are due both to genetic and to environmental factors. Now we can ask theoretically: What would be the average IQ difference among all persons in the population if everyone had grown up in identical environments from the moment of conception, while genetic differences remained as they are? Under this hypothetical condition of completely equal environments for everyone, the average IQ difference would be 16 points. Thus, there would be a reduction of 2 points in the average difference that now exists. Let us now ask the reverse: What would be the average difference if everyone had exactly the same genetic endowment, but environmental differences remained unchanged? Under this hypothetical condition of complete genetic equality the average IQ difference among persons would be only 8 points, or just half the difference that would exist with equal environments.

So the conclusion we come to – which is certainly valid at least in the white European and North American populations in which the research was conducted – is this: In accounting for the causes of the differences among persons in IQ, the genes outweigh the effects of environment by 2 to 1. As environmental conditions are improved and made more alike for all persons in the society, the average intelligence level of the population will be somewhat increased, and the IQ differences among persons will be slightly reduced. But of course the differences that remain will inevitably be due even more to genetic factors.

Heritability and teachability

Heritability and teachability

It has been said that the heritability of learning ability or of intelligence is irrelevant to teachability, or as the *Bulletin of the ERIC Information Retrieval Center on the Disadvantaged* (1969, 4, no. 4) printed in boldface: 'Teachability is not a function of heritability'. In support of this statement we see it pointed out that a child or a group of children show some response to training, and this is held up as evidence against the heritability of intelligence or learning ability.

Heritability (h^2) is a technical term in genetics which refers to the proportion of the population variance in a phenotypic characteristic or measurement that is attributable to genetic variation. It has also been called the coefficient of genetic determination. It can take any value from 0 to 1. It is not a constant but differs for different traits, different measurements, and in different populations. Its value can be estimated by a number of methods in quantitative genetics. Like any population statistic, it is subject to measurement error and sampling error. Since it is based essentially on the analysis of variance, it can tell us nothing at all about the causes of the particular value assumed by the grand mean of the population. It only analyzes the variance (or squared deviations) *about* the grand mean. And it tells us what proportion of this total variance is *genetic* variance and what proportion is *non-genetic*, i.e., due to environmental factors of all kinds and to errors of measurement. Most estimates of the heritability of IQ in the European and North American populations on which we have good data fall in the range from 0·60 to 0·90 and most of these estimates are in range from 0·70 to 0·80 (not corrected for test unreliability).

The fact that IQ has high heritability surely does *not* mean that individuals cannot learn much. Even if learning ability had 100 per cent heritability it would not mean that individuals cannot learn, and therefore the demonstration of learning or the improvement of performance, with or without specific instruction or intervention by a teacher, says absolutely nothing about heritability. But knowing that learning ability has high heritability does tell us this: if a number of individuals are all given *equal* opportunity – the same background, the same conditions, and the same amount of time – for learning something, they will still differ from one another in their rates of learning and consequently in the amount they learn per unit of time spent in learning. That is the meaning of heritability. It does not say that individuals cannot learn or improve with instruction and practice. It says that given equal conditions, individuals will differ from one another, not because of differences in the external conditions but because of differences in the internal environment which is conditioned by genetic factors. 'Teachability' presumably means the ability to learn under conditions of instruction by a teacher. If this is the case, then it is true that heritability has nothing to do with teachability. But was this ever really the question? Has anyone questioned the fact that *all* school children are teachable? The important question has concerned *differences* in teachability – differences both among individuals and among sub-groups of the population. And with reference to the question of *differences*, the concept of heritability is indeed a relevant and empirically answerable question.

We have heard it said that 'teachability is not inversely related to heritability'. Such a statement simply ignores the central fact that heritability deals with differences. The degree to which equal conditions of teaching or instruction will diminish individual differences in achievement *is* inversely related to the heritability of the 'teachability' of the subject in question, and various school subjects probably differ considerably in heritability.

The fact that scholastic achievement shows lower heritability than IQ means that more of the variance in scholastic achievement is attributable to non-genetic factors than is the case for IQ. Consequently, we can hypothesize what the sources of the environmental variance in scholastic achievement are, and possibly we can manipulate them. For example, it might be hypothesized that one source of environmental variance in reading achievement is whether or not the child's parents read to him between the ages of 3 and 4, and we can obviously test this hypothesis experimentally. Much of the psychological research on the environmental correlates of scholastic achievement have been of this nature. The proportion of variance indicated by $1-h^2$, if small, does in fact mean that the sources of environmental variance are skimpy under the conditions that prevailed in the population in which h^2 was estimated. It means that the *already existing* variations in environmental (or instructional) conditions are not a potent source of phenotypic variance, so that making the best variations available to everyone will do relatively little to reduce individual differences. This is not to say that as yet undiscovered environmental manipulations or forms of intervention in the learning or developmental process cannot, in principle, markedly reduce individual differences in a trait which under ordinary conditions has very high heritability. By the same token, low heritability does not guarantee that most of the non-genetic sources of variance can be manipulated systematically. A multitude of uncontrollable, fortuitous microenvironmental events may constitute the largest source of phenotypic variance in some traits.

The heritability of individual differences and of group differences in scholastic performance in the total population is therefore relevant if we are at all interested in the causes of these differences. To say that heritability is trivial or irrelevant is to say also that the complement of heritability, $1-h^2$, or the proportion of variance attributable to non-genetic or environmental factors is also trivial. To dismiss the question of heritability is to dismiss concern with the causes of educational differences and their implications for educational practices. As I read it, what most educators, government officials, and writers in the popular press who discuss the present problems of education are in fact referring to is not primarily dissatisfaction with some *absolute* level of achievement, but rather with the large group *differences* in educational attainments that show up so conspicuously in our educational system – the achievement gaps between the affluent and the poor, the lower-class and the middle-class, the majority and the minority, the urban and the suburban, and so on. Educational *differences*, not absolute level of performance, are the main cause of concern.

Whether we like to admit it or not, the problem of achievement differences today is where the action is, where the billions of dollars of educational funds are being poured in, where the heat is on, and where the schools are being torn apart. Are we not trying to understand more about the causes of these differences? But as Carl Bereiter (1970, p. 298) has commented: 'It is necessary to avoid both the oversimplification that says if there are genetic group differences nothing can be accomplished through educational improvement and the oversimplification that says if group differences in IQ are environmentally caused they can be eliminated by conventional social amelioration. The possibility that cultural differences are related to heredity, however, adds force to the need for schools to come to grips with the problem of providing for cultural pluralism without separatism or segregation. This may well be the major policy problem facing public education in our time.'

It is mistaken to argue that heritability has no implications for the probable effects of environmental intervention. Since $1 - h_c^2$ (h_c^2 is h^2 corrected for attenuation) is the proportion of trait variance attributable to environmental factors, the square root of this value times the *SD* of the 'true score' trait measurement gives the *SD* of the effect of existing environmental variations on the particular trait. For IQ this is about 6 points; that is to say, a shift of 1 *SD* in the sum total of whatever non-genetic influences contribute to environmental variance (i.e., $1 - h_c^2$), will shift the IQ about 6 points. (There is good evidence that environmental effects on IQ are normally distributed, at least in Caucasian populations (Jensen, 1970b, 1971).) Thus the magnitude of change in a trait effected by changing the allocation of the existing environmental sources of variance in that trait is logically related to its heritability. This applies, of course, only to existing sources of environmental variance in the population, which is all that can be estimated by $1 - h_c^2$. It can have no relevance to speculations about as yet non-existent environmental influences or entirely new combinations of already existing environmental factors. With respect to IQ, I believe Bereiter (1970) states the situation quite correctly: 'What a high heritability ratio implies, therefore, is that changes within the existing range of environmental conditions can have substantial effects on the mean level of IQ in the population but they are unlikely to have much effects on the spread of individual differences in IQ within the population. If one is concerned with relative standing of individuals within the population, the prospects for doing anything about this through existing educational means are thus not good. Even with a massive redistribution of environmental conditions, one would expect to find the lower quarter of the IQ distribution to be about as far removed from the upper quarter as before' (p. 288). Bereiter goes on to say: 'A high heritability ratio for IQ should not discourage people from pursuing environmental improvement in education or any other area. The potential effects on IQ are great, although it still remains to discover the environmental variables capable of producing these effects.'

Reaction range of IQ

Heritability can be understood also in terms of what geneticists refer to as the reaction range of the phenotypic characteristic. In the case of intelligence, for example, this is the range through which IQ varies in the population due to non-genetic influences. It is best expressed in terms of probabilities under the normal curve. There is good reason to believe that the *effects* of non-genetic factors on IQ in the population are normally distributed in the IQ range above 60 (Jensen, 1970b). If the heritability of IQ is 0·80, say, then we can picture the phenotypic reaction range, and the total distribution of environmental effects on IQ, as shown in Figure 12.1. The shaded curve is the normal distribution of IQs in the population. If we remove the 80 per cent of the variance due to genetic factors and leave only the 20 per cent of variance due to non-genetic factors, we see in the unshaded curve the resulting total distribution of IQs for identical genotypes that express phenotypic IQs of 100 in average environmental conditions. You can see that this distribution ranges from about IQ 80 to IQ 120. (The unshaded curve's variance is only 20 per cent of the shaded curve's variance.) This is the reaction range of IQ in populations in which the heritability of IQ is 0·80. Figure 12.2 shows the converse situation. Again, the shaded curve is the actual distribution of phenotypes. The unshaded curve is the distribution of genotypes when the environment is held constant

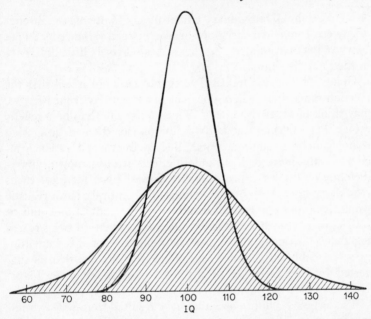

FIGURE 12.1. Shaded curve is distribution of IQs in the population. Unshaded curve is hypothetical distribution if all genetic variance (when $h^2 = 0.80$) were removed.

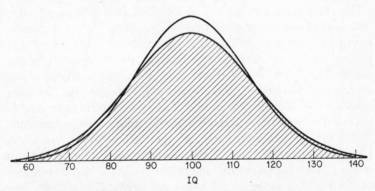

FIGURE 12.2. Shaded curve is distribution of IQs in the population. Unshaded curve is hypothetical distribution if all environmental variance (when $h^2 = 0.80$) were removed.

or identical for all individuals. Under these conditions, the absence of any environmental variation shrinks the total variance by 20 per cent. As Bereiter pointed out, this makes relatively little difference in the total distribution.

Going back to Figure 12.1, it should be emphasized that the reaction range shown here does not result entirely from what we may think of as 'environment'. Thus, I use the term non-genetic rather than environmental. By definition, for the geneticist what is not genetic is environmental. But environmental variance includes many more or less random effects with unknown, unpredictable, or (as yet) uncontrollable causes. Even identical twins reared together are not phenotypically identical. How realistic would it be to hope that all members of the population could be subject to as little environmental variance as identical twins reared together? The manipulable or equalizable aspects of the environment probably effect much less of the IQ variance than is suggested by our depiction of the total reaction range in Figure 12.1.

The largest IQ differences that have resulted from very extreme manipulations of the environment – extremes that very likely fall outside the limits of the middle 99 per cent of the distribution of naturally occurring environments – have shown IQ changes of some 20 to 30 points. These changes have been observed only in very young children, with few, if any exceptions.

The important experiment of Dr Rick Heber illustrates this reaction range concept of mental development. He has compared two groups of genotypically similar children in the Milwaukee ghetto, one group reared from birth in what may well be the lowest 1 or 2 per cent of environmental conditions found in our society and the other group reared experimentally in the most mentally stimulating environment that psychologists know how to devise; it is beyond the scale of naturally occurring environments. These two groups of children are now about 5 or 6 years old. Heber finds IQ differences between the groups of some 20 to 30 points, which is about what one might predict from our estimate of the reaction range of IQ when the heritability is 0·80. The Heber results have recently been held up in the popular press as evidence that genetic factors are of negligible importance, and some writers have even pointed to the Heber experiment as a refutation of 'jensenism'. Yet, interestingly enough, the results are within the range that would have been predicted from a genetic model assuming a heritability of 0·80.

The famous old study of Skodak and Skeels (1949) is repeatedly subjected to the same kind of misinterpretation by environmentalists who would like to deny the importance of genetic factors in causing intellectual differences. The Skodak and Skeels study is usually held up as an example of evidence which supposedly contradicts the high heritability of intelligence. The fact that the adopted children in the Skodak and Skeels study turned out to have considerably higher IQs than their biological mothers is thought to constitute a disproof of the conclusion from many heritability studies that genetic factors are more important than environmental factors (in the ratio of about 2 to 1) in the causation of individual differences in IQ. (Another way of saying this is that the heritability of intelligence is about 0·80, i.e., about 80 per cent of the IQ variance is attributable to genetic factors. The 20 per cent of the variance due to environmental differences can be thought of as a normal distribution of all the effects of environment on IQ, including prenatal and postnatal influences. This normal distribution of environmental effects has a standard deviation of about 7 IQ points since the total variance of IQ in the population is $15^2 = 225$ and the 20 per cent of this which is attributable to environment is $0·20 (225) = 45$, the square root of which gives $SD = 6·71$.) Is there anything in the Skodak and Skeels data that would contradict this conclusion? Skodak and Skeels based their study on 100 children born to mothers with rather low IQs (a range from 53 to 128, with a mean of 85·7, SD of 15·8). The children were adopted into what Skodak and Skeels described as exceptionally good, upper-middle-class families selected by the adoption agency for their superior qualities. Of the 100 true mothers, 63 were given the 1916 form of the Stanford-Binet IQ test at the time of the adoption. Their children, who had been reared in adoptive homes, were given the same test as adolescents. The correlation between the mothers' and children's IQs was 0·38. Now, the *difference* between the mothers' IQs and the children's IQs is not really the relevant question. Yet it is on this point that the interpretation of this study has so often gone wrong. What we really want to know is, how much do the children differ from the IQs we'd predict from a genetic model? Using the simplest model, which assumes that the children represent a random selection of the offspring of mothers having a mean IQ of 85·7 and are reared in a random sample of homes in the general population, the children's average predicted IQ would be 96. In fact, however, their average IQ turns out to be 107, or 11 points higher than the predicted IQ. If 20 per cent of the IQ variance is environmental, and if one standard deviation of environmental influence is equivalent to about 7 IQ points, then it might be said that the Skodak and Skeels children were reared in environments which averaged $1\frac{1}{7}$ or about 1·6 standard deviations above the average environment of randomly selected families in the population. This would be about what one should expect if the adoption agency placed children only in homes they judged to be about one standard deviation above the average of the general population in the desirability of the environment they could provide. From what Skodak and Skeels say in their description of the adoptive families, they were at least one standard deviation above the general average in socio-economic status and were probably even higher in other qualities deemed desirable in adoptive parents. So an 11-point IQ gain over the average environment falls well within what we should expect, even if environmental factors contribute only 20 per cent of the IQ variance. But this 11 IQ points of apparent gain is more likely to be an overestimate to some extent, since these children, it should be remembered, were selected by the agency as suitable for adoption. They were not a random selection of children born to low IQ mothers. Many such children are never put out for adoption. (Most of the children were illegitimate, and as indicated in Leahy's (1935) study, illegitimate children who become adopted have a higher average IQ than illegitimate children in general or than legitimate children placed for adoption.) Even so, it is interesting that Skodak and Skeels found that the eleven adopted children whose true mothers had IQs below 70 averaged 25 points lower than the eight adopted children whose true mothers had IQs above 105. There are also certain technical, methodological deficiencies of the Skodak and Skeels study which make its results questionable; these deficiencies were trenchantly pointed out many years ago in critiques by Terman (1940, pp. 462-7) and McNemar (1940). In summary, the

Skodak and Skeels study, such as it is, can be seen to be not at all inconsistent with a heritability of 0·80 for intelligence.

Heritability and individual IQs

Heritability is said to be a population concept because its value cannot be determined independently of the population. That is to say, it is a statistical construct. But does this mean that it is irrelevant when we consider an individual measurement, such as a score on an IQ test? No. The reliability of a test score is also a statistical construct, being the proportion of 'true score' variance in the population of obtained scores. Now, just as the square root of a test's reliability coefficient tells us the correlation between obtained scores and true scores, so the square root of a test's heritability tells us the correlation between obtained scores (i.e., the phenotypes) and 'genetic values' (i.e., genotypes) on the trait being measured. ('Value' refers here to a scaled quantity; it implies no 'value judgment'.) Without an absolute scale (as is the case for practically all psychological measurements), these values must be expressed merely as deviation scores, i.e., as deviations from a population mean. For the 'genetic value' to have any valid meaning, it must be expressed (and interpreted) as a deviation from the mean of the population in which the heritability was estimated and also in which the individual in question is a member. Given these conditions, we can determine the standard error of a test score's 'genetic value', analogous to the standard error of measurement. (The analogy is not perfect, however, since true scores and measurement errors are by definition uncorrelated, while genetic (G) and environmental (E) components may be correlated. But this is a soluble problem. The covariance of G and E can be independently estimated and may or may not be included in the estimates of h^2, depending upon the interpretation one wishes to give to h^2. Roberts (1967, pp. 217-18) has suggested that the environment should be defined as affecting the phenotype independently of the genotype. Thus, if individuals' genotypes influence their choice of environments, the environmental variation resulting therefrom would be considered a part of the total genetic variance.) It is simply $SE_G = SD\sqrt{1-h^2}$, where SE_G is the standard error of the genetic value, SD is the standard deviation of the test scores, and h^2 is the heritability (not corrected for attenuation due to test unreliability). For IQ, assuming $SD = 15$ and $h^2 = 0.75$, the standard error of the genetic value is 7·5 IQ points. This can be interpreted the same as the standard error of measurement. It means that 68 per cent of our estimates of individual's genetic values will differ less than 7·5 points from this phenotypic IQ, 95 per cent will differ less than 15 (i.e., 2 SE_Gs), and 99·7 per cent will differ less than 22·5 points (3 SE_Gs). In other words, the probability is very small that two individuals whose IQs differ by, say, 20 or more points have the same genotypes for intelligence or that the one with the lower IQ has the higher genetic value. The individual's estimated genetic value, $\hat{G}_i$, expressed as a deviation score, is $\hat{G}_i = h^2(P_i - \hat{P}_p) + \hat{P}_p$ where P_i is the individual's phenotypic measurement (e.g., IQ), and $\hat{P}_p$ is the population mean.

The statement that an individual's test score is within, say, $\pm x$ points of his 'true score' with a probability p is no less probabilistic than saying his test score is within $\pm x$ points of his 'genetic value', with a probability p. In the individual case, of course, we may be able to take account of a variety of other information in addition to the individual's test score in order to obtain a more accurate assessment. Such adjustments in individual assessments, as Burt (1958) has indicated, can increase the heritability of the scores and consequently reduce the standard error of estimate of individual genotypic values. The use of less culture-loaded tests could have a similar effect.

Heritability and group differences

I have been falsely accused of claiming that the high heritability of IQ inevitably means that the mean differences in IQ between social class groups and racial groups must be due to genetic factors. I have never made this incorrect inference. What I have said is this: While it is true, indeed axiomatic, that heritability *within* groups cannot establish heritability *between* group means, high *within* group heritability increases the *a priori* likelihood that the *between* groups heritability is greater than zero. In nature, characteristics that vary genetically *among* individuals within a population also generally vary genetically *between* different breeding populations of the same species. Among the genetically conditioned traits known to vary between major racial groups are body size and proportions, cranial size and cephalic index, pigmentation of the hair, skin, and eyes, hair form and distribution on the body, number of vertebrae, fingerprints, bone density, basic metabolic rate, sweating, fissural patterns on the chewing surfaces of the teeth, numerous blood groups, various chronic diseases, frequency of dizygotic (but non-monozygotic) twinning, male-female birth ratio, ability to taste phenylthiocarbomide, length of gestation period, and degree of physical maturity at birth (as indicated by degree of ossification of cartilage). In light of all these differences, Spuhler and Lindzey (1967) have remarked '. . . . it seems to us surprising that one would accept present findings in regard to the existence of genetic anatomical, physiological, and epidemiological differences between the races . . . and still expect to find *no* meaningful differences in behavior between races' (p. 413). The high within groups heritability of certain behavioral traits, such as intelligence, adds weight to this statement by Spuhler and Lindzey.

In fact, it is quite erroneous to say there is no relationship whatsoever between heritability *within* groups and heritability *between* group means. Jay Lush, a pioneer in quantitative genetics, has shown the formal relationship between these two heritabilities (Lush, 1968, p. 312), and it has been recently introduced into the discussion of racial differences by another geneticist, John C. DeFries (1972). This formulation of the relationship between heritability *between* group means (h_{B}^2) and heritability *within* groups (h_{W}^2) is as follows:

$$h_{\text{B}}^2 \simeq h_{\text{W}}^2 \frac{(1-r)\rho}{(1-\rho)r}$$

where: h_{B}^2 is the heritability *between* group means.

h_{W}^2 is the average heritability *within* groups.

r is the intraclass correlation among *phenotypes* within groups (or the square of the point biserial correlation between the quantized racial dichotomy and the trait measurement).

ρ is the intraclass correlation among *genotypes* within

o

groups, i.e., the within-group genetic correlation for the trait in question.

Since we do not know ρ, the formula is not presently of practical use in determining the heritability of mean group differences. But it does show that if for a given trait the genetic correlation among persons within groups is greater than zero, the between group heritability is a monotomically increasing function of within groups heritability. This is illustrated in Figure 12.3, which shows between groups heritability as a function of within group heritability for various values of the within-group genetic correlation when the mean phenotypic difference between the two groups involved is one standard deviation.

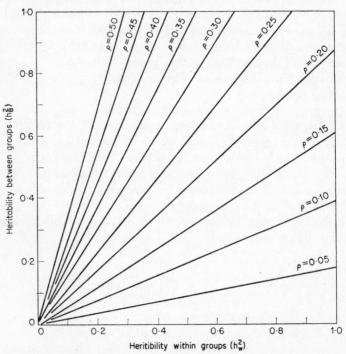

FIGURE 12.3. Heritability between groups as a function of average heritability within groups for different values of within-group genetic correlation (ρ) for two populations which differ phenotypically by one standard deviation.

As I have pointed out elsewhere, other methods than heritability analysis are required to test the hypothesis that racial group differences in a given trait involve genetic factors and to determine their extent (Jensen, 1970c).

Analysis of group mean differences

It may be instructive to express the magnitude of the differences between group means in terms of *within-group* environmental effects on the trait in question, which can be estimated from heritability analysis. For illustrative purposes I shall use the heritability value for IQs obtained from the combined studies of identical twins reared apart (Jensen, 1970b). For the sake of simplicity in this illustration, I will assume the same heritability in white and Negro populations. This is not a necessary assumption and in practice we would obtain estimates of heritability in both populations. At this point I am focusing only upon the logic of a particular kind of analysis rather than making a case for the particular quantitative values involved. Also, I assume that the total variance is the same in both populations and that the environmental effects on IQ are normally distributed in both populations. This can be shown to hold true in the twin samples in which heritability was determined, but in practice it would of course have to be empirically determined in both populations.

Figure 12.4 shows this kind of analysis. The top figure shows the total distribution of IQs in two populations with means of 85 and 100, respectively. The standard deviation, σ, in each group is 15 points. The middle set of curves show the shrunken distribution of IQ when the genetic variance in each population is eliminated. Thus, while the groups differ phenotypically by 1σ (upper curves), they differ in terms of total environmental effects on IQ by $3 \cdot 2\sigma$. The standard deviation of environmental effects (with error of measurement removed) within groups is only 4·74 IQ points. But this represents the total nongenetic or environmental effect, much of which is 'microenvironmental', i.e., unsystematic and unsusceptible to systematic control. If we regard environmental differences *within* families, such as birth order effects, and the like, as largely constituting this source of unsystematic microenvironmental variance, we can estimate it by appropriate methods and

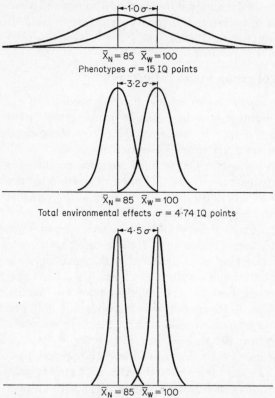

FIGURE 12.4. The top curves represent two IQ distributions each with $\sigma = 15$ IQ points and the means differing by 15 points or 1σ. The middle set of curves shows the effect of removing all genetic variance, leaving only the total environmental variance; the means then differ by $3\cdot2\sigma$ of total environmental effects. The lower curves show the effect of removing both the genetic and the within-families environmental variance, leaving only between-families environmental variance; the means then differ by $4\cdot5\sigma$ of between-families environmental effects. The area under all curves is the same.

eliminate it statistically, leaving only the distribution of *between-*families environmental effects on IQ. This has a standard deviation of 3·35 IQ points and, as shown in the lower curves of Figure 12.4, the population mean difference can be expressed as a difference of 4·5σ of between-families environmental effects. These are the effects we are most likely to have in mind when we talk about changing environments. The between-families environmental effects are the systematic environmental differences we associate with socio-economic status, nutritional conditions, child rearing practices, cultural advantages, and the like. It can be seen here that these effects as estimated from twin studies account for only a small part of the within-population variance (about 12 per cent), and that if one were to explain all of the 15 IQ points difference entirely in terms of this source of environmental effects, it would have to be granted that the populations differ on a scale of these effects by 4·5σ. This is an enormous difference, implying almost no overlap between the two populations in the distribution of systematic environmental effects on IQ. A warranted conclusion would be that it is highly improbable that the group mean difference is entirely attributable to the environmental variations that make for differences between separated twins reared in different families. To argue otherwise would require us to believe that on a scale of environmental effects the average Negro is reared under conditions 4·5σ below those of the average white twin. If we call the latter's environment about average for the white population, we would conclude that the *average* Negro environment is 4·5σ below this level, that is, something below the 0·003 percentile of systematic environmental effects on IQ in the white population. This strongly suggests that if one is to explain the average 15-point Negro IQ deficit in wholly non-genetic terms, it will probably be necessary to posit some environmental factors other than those we normally think of as the environmental factors affecting intelligence in the white population. Moreover, if the heritability of IQ is not appreciably different in the Negro and white populations, these hypothesized environmental effects responsible for the lower average Negro IQ would have to be assumed to produce little or no variance *within* the Negro population, unless one wanted to assume that virtually none of the environmental proportion of IQ variance *within* the Negro population was attributable to the same kinds of environmental effects that contribute to environmental variance in the white population. Such an entirely cultural explanation would seem to make the Negro population too incredibly different. The amount of genetic difference that would have to be hypothesized to explain what we already know is quite small as compared with the fantastically great environmental and cultural differences between the American Negro and the white populations that must be hypothesized in order to maintain a wholly non-genetic theory. The average amount of genetic difference that would have to be hypothesized to explain the data is about the same as the average difference in genotypic IQs between ordinary siblings in the same family. Do parents view this as such an awful difference among their own children? Yet this is about the amount of difference that would need to be hypothesized by a genetic theory for all that we now know about Negro-white IQ differences to be accounted for. How else essentially does science advance our knowledge than by trying out various hypotheses for how well they accord with the evidence?

The storm of criticism that has been leveled at me has been a result of my expressing serious *doubts* that this racial IQ difference is entirely explainable in terms of culture-bias in tests, unequal educational opportunities, social discrimination, and other environmental influences. My position is that there is now sufficient evidence seriously to question the 100 per cent environmental theories of the mean white-black intelligence difference. Are there any responsible scientists today who claim that this position can be ruled out on the basis of evidence or ruled out *a priori* by any principle of genetics? How many scientists today express little or no doubt that all of the racial IQ difference is attributable to environment? And on what evidence do those who claim no doubt base their certainty? I have not found any 100 per cent environmental theory which can explain the facts or which stands up when its major premises are critically examined in the light of evidence. Therefore, I regard this issue scientifically as an open question which can be eventually answered in a scientific sense only if we are willing to consider all reasonable hypotheses. It is a reasonable hypothesis that genetic factors are involved in the average white-black IQ difference, and my study of the research evidence bearing on this question leads me to believe that a preponderance of the evidence is more consistent with a genetic hypothesis, which, of course, does not exclude the influence of environment.

Heritability in the Negro population

Unfortunately, we still have no adequate estimates of the heritability of intelligence in the Negro population, although two interesting studies have made a beginning in this direction (Nichols, 1970; Scarr-Salapatek, 1971). The statistical problems and the nature of the data in both studies make their results rather tentative, but essentially they found that the heritability of the mental test scores are about the same in the Negro and white samples or possibly slightly lower in the Negro group, and definitely lower in the lower social classes of both racial groups. Scarr-Salapatek's results have been misrepresented in some popular accounts (e.g., *Psychology Today*, March, 1972, p. 20) as refuting my position. Nothing could be further from the truth. In fact, one of the main points about Negro-white differences that I made in my *Harvard Educational Review* (Winter, 1969) article finds impressive support in Scarr-Salapatek's study. Scarr-Salapatek emphasizes the point that the heritability of the mental tests is less in her lower social class groups of both races than in the middle-class groups. This fact she apparently interprets as being consistent with an explanation of the mean Negro-white IQ differences in terms of environmental factors such as cultural deprivation. She states: 'The lower mean scores of disadvantaged children of both races can be explained in large part by the lower genetic variance in their scores' (p. 1293). She adds: 'If most black children have limited experience with environmental features relevant to the development of scholastic skills, then genetic variation will not be as prominent a source of individual phenotypic variation; nor will other between-family differences such as SES [socio-economic] level be as important as they are in a white population' (p. 1294).

The data shown in Scarr-Salapatek's Table 3 (p. 1288), however, make this interpretation extremely questionable. These data allow comparison of the mean scores on the combined aptitude tests for Negro children whose parents' level of education and income are both *above* the median (of the Negro and white samples combined) with the mean scores of white children whose parents' education and income are both *below* the common median. The lower status white children still score *higher* than the upper status Negro children on both the verbal and the non-verbal tests. Although non-verbal tests are generally considered to be less culture-biased than verbal tests, it is the non-verbal tests which in fact show the greater discrepancy in this comparison, with the *lower* status whites scoring higher than the *upper* status Negroes. But in this comparison it is the upper status Negro group that has the higher heritability (i.e., greater genetic variance) on both the verbal and non-verbal tests. Thus the lower heritability which Scarr-Salapatek invokes to infer that Negroes' generally poorer performance is attributable to environmental deprivation applies to the lower status white group in this particular comparison. Yet the lower status white group out-performs the upper status Negro group, which has the highest heritability of any of the sub-groups in this study (see Table 9, p. 1292).

This finding seems more difficult to reconcile with a strictly environmental explanation of the mean racial difference in test scores than with a genetic interpretation which invokes the well-established phenomenon of regression toward the population mean. In another recent article in *Science* (1971, p. 1226), Scarr-Salapatek clearly explicated this relevant genetic prediction, as follows:

> Regression effects can be predicted to differ for blacks and whites if the two races indeed have genetically different population means. If the population mean for blacks is 15 IQ points lower than that of whites, then the offspring of high-IQ black parents should show greater regression (toward a lower population mean) than the offspring of whites of equally high IQ. Similarly, the offspring of low-IQ black parents should show less regression than those of white parents of equally low IQ.

In other words, on the average, an offspring genetically is closer to its population mean than are its parents, and by a fairly precise amount. Accordingly, it would be predicted that upper status Negro children should, on the average, regress *downward* toward the Negro population mean IQ of about 85, while lower status white children would regress *upward* toward the white population mean of about 100. In the downward and upward regression, the two groups' means could cross each other, the lower status whites, thereby being slightly above the upper status Negroes. Scarr-Salapatek's data (Table 3) are quite consistent with this genetic prediction. Scarr-Salapatek's finding is not a fluke; the same phenomenon has been found in other large-scale studies which I pointed out in my *HER* article (pp. 83-4).

Controlling for social class

In the past year two widely publicized studies, one by George W. Mayeske and the other by Jane Mercer, have claimed that racial differences in intelligence and scholastic achievement can be explained entirely in terms of the environmental effects of the lower socio-economic status of Negroes in the United States. They showed that by statistically controlling a large number of social variables associated with socio-economic status, they were able to 'explain' practically all of the scholastic achievement gap between Negroes and whites. This procedure is what I have termed the 'sociologist's fallacy'. It is based on the unwarranted and untenable assumption that all the socio-economic and environ-mental variables on which the racial groups have been matched or statistically equated are direct *causal* factors, when in fact they are merely *correlates* of IQ. If some part of the SES difference within racial groups has a genetic basis, then statistically equating racial groups on social class equates them also to some degree on the genetic factors involved in intelligence. Indeed, it is theoretically conceivable that if one equated racial groups on a large enough number of *correlates* of IQ, one could statistically eliminate all of the IQ differences between them. But it would prove nothing at all about the *causes* of the mean IQ difference between the total populations. Many environmental indices are undoubtedly cor-related with genotypes. Educational level of the parents, for example, is often included as an environmental variable affecting the child's mental development. But it almost certainly includes also some genetic component which is common to both the parents and their children. If the environmental variables used for statistical control account for more of the IQ variance *within* racial groups

o*

than the complement of the heritability (i.e., $1 - h^2$) within the groups, then it is virtually certain that the environmental indices also reflect correlated genetic factors. Controlling SES thus partials out too much of the difference between the racial groups. Matching for SES, in short, matches not only for certain environmental factors but also for genetic factors as well. It is interesting also that when such matching is carried out, it is noted that the average skin color of the Negro groups becomes lighter in the higher SES categories, indicating that genetic factors covary with SES, for whatever reason. Genetic SES intelligence differences are firmly established within the white population. Matching Negro and white groups on SES, therefore, is certain to minimize genetic as well as environmental differences. For this reason, studies that control for SES are probably biased in favor of the environmentalist hypothesis and can contribute nothing to elucidating the nature-nurture problem.

Several lines of evidence support with a high level of confidence the conclusion that social classes, on the average, differ to some degree in the genetic factors involved in intellectual development. Social classes may be viewed as Mendelian populations that have diverged genetically. When the population is stratified into five or six socio-economic status (SES) categories, mainly according to occupational criteria, the mean IQs of the *adults* so classified, from the highest SES category (professional and managerial) to the lowest (unskilled labor), span a range of some 30 to 40 points. The standard deviation of IQs *within* SES groups averages about 9 or 10 points for the adult population, as compared with $SD = 15$ for the whole population. Children born into these SES groups, on the other hand, show a mean IQ difference, from the lowest to the highest class, of only 20 to 30 points; and the SD *within* classes for children is about 13 or 14 IQ points, which means there is almost as much IQ variation among children *within* social classes as we find in the total population.

The cause of the higher degree of correlation between SES and IQ among adults than among children is the high level of social mobility in each generation. In England and in the United States, more than 30 per cent of the adult generation are found to be of a different SES than that of their own parents (Burt, 1961; Gottesman, 1968; Maxwell, 1969). In each generation some individuals move up in SES and some move down. Those who move up have higher IQs, on the average, than those who move down.

Since the heritability, h^2 (i.e., the proportion of genetic variance) of IQ in the total population is between 0·70 and 0·80, and since the correlation between phenotypes and genotypes is the square root of the heritability, it follows that the IQ estimates genotypic intelligence with a reliability of between $\sqrt{0\cdot70}$ and $\sqrt{0\cdot80}$, i.e., between about 0·84 and 0·89 (Jensen, 1967, 1969). Conversely, the reliability with which IQ measures the *non*-genetic component of intelligence variation is $\sqrt{1-h^2}$, or between about 0·45 and 0·55. If only non-genetic factors determined individuals' SES, then the maximum correlation that could exist between SES and IQ would be in the range of 0·45 to 0·55. In fact, however, the correlations generally found are between 0·30 and 0·50 for children and between 0·50 and 0·70 for adults (depending largely upon how fine-grained the SES measure is). Now, if the correlation between IQs and genotypes is between 0·84 and 0·89, and the correlation between IQ and SES is between 0·50 and 0·70, the correlation between SES and genotypes must be greater than zero. To maintain a strictly environmental hypothesis, at the very least one would have to assume that only the environmental component of intelligence played a part in persons' educational and occupational attainments (the chief determinants of SES). If we admit no genetic component in SES differences in IQ and still admit the high heritability of IQ, we are logically forced to argue that persons have been fitted to their SES (meaning largely educational and occupational attainments) almost *perfectly* according to their environmental advantages and disadvantages, which constitute only 20 to 30 per cent of the variance in IQ; and it would have to be argued that persons' innate abilities, talents, and proclivities play no part in educational and occupational selection and placement. This is a most unlikely state of affairs.

Consider other, more direct, evidence:

1. Adopted children show only about half as much dispersion in mean IQ as a function of SES of the adopting parents as that of children reared by their own parents (Leahy, 1935).

2. Children reared from infancy in an orphanage, with no

knowledge of their parents, show nearly the same correlation between their IQs and their fathers' occupational status (graded into five categories) as children reared by their own parents (Lawrence, 1931).

3. Most of the IQ difference between siblings reared together is attributable to differences in genetic inheritance. (The genetic correlation between siblings is about 0·5 to 0·6.) When siblings who are reared together move into different social strata, as adults it is the sib with the higher IQ who is more likely to move up and the sib with the lower IQ who is more likely to move down the SES scale (Gibson, 1970).

4. Sons whose IQs differ most from their father's IQ are more likely to change SES, the higher IQs moving up, the lower moving down (Young and Gibson, 1963). Waller (1971) found a correlation of $0·368 \pm 0·066$ between the father-son disparity in IQ (both tested as school children) and father-son disparity in SES as adults, when only the middle three of five SES classes were considered (since in Classes I and V mobility is restricted to only one direction).

5. Genetically identical twins who are separated in infancy and reared apart in homes of different SES (over a range of six categories, from professional to unskilled), differ on the average by only 1 IQ point per each SES category difference, with a total range of about 6 IQ points difference between the highest and lowest SES categories (Burt, 1966). Compare this difference, in which genetic factors play no part, with the difference of 20 to 30 IQ points generally found between children in the lowest and highest SES classes.

All this evidence is highly consistent with a model of social mobility in which the genetic factors involved in mental ability, through the processes of segregation and assortment, become selected into somewhat different gene pools in various social and occupational classes.

Environmentalist hypotheses

Those environmentalist hypotheses of the Negro-white IQ difference which have been most clearly formulated and are therefore subject to empirical tests are the only ones that can be evaluated within a scientific framework. The most frequently cited environmentalist hypotheses which are sufficiently clear to put to an empirical test and which already have been put to a test have not proven adequate to the explanatory function they were intended to serve. A number of lines of such evidence casts serious doubt on purely environmental and cultural theories of the racial IQ difference.

NEGATIVE CORRELATIONS BETWEEN ENVIRONMENT AND ABILITY

A number of environmental factors which correlate positively with mental ability *within* various population groups have been shown to correlate *negatively* with IQ differences *between* certain groups. On all of the many measurable factors which environmentalists have invoked to explain the Negro-white IQ difference, both American Indians and Mexican-Americans have been found to be much more disadvantaged than Negroes. Yet on non-verbal intelligence tests (which are more fair for bilingual groups such as Mexicans and Indians) and in scholastic performance, Indians and Mexicans significantly outperform Negroes. This finding is neutral with respect to a genetic theory, in the sense that no prediction could have been derived from genetic principles; but it contradicts those environmental theories that invoke measurable environmental factors known to correlate with IQ within population groups as the cause of the lower Negro IQ. The only attempts of environmentalists to rationalize these findings have invoked highly speculative cultural and attitudinal factors which have not yet been shown to be correlated either with IQ or with race.

CULTURE-BIASED TESTS

Intelligence tests can be rank-ordered according to certain generally agreed upon criteria of their cultural loading. Within a given culture, tests are better described as differing in *status-fairness*. Environmentalists who criticize intelligence tests usually give as examples those tests which are most obviously loaded with what is presumably white, middle-class factual knowledge, vocabulary, and the like, as contrasted with more abstract figural material such as compose Raven's Progressive Matrices and Cattell's Culture-Fair Tests of *g*. Yet it is on the latter type of tests that Negroes perform most poorly, relative to whites and other minority groups. Disadvantaged minorities, such as American Indians and Mexican-Americans, perform on tests showing different degrees of status bias in accord with the environmentalist hypothesis. Negroes do the opposite. 'Translation' of tests such as the Stanford-Binet into the Negro ghetto dialect also does not appreciably improve scores.

The scholastic and occupational predictive validity of IQ tests is the same for Negroes as for whites, and item analyses of tests showing large average group mean differences do not reveal significant differences in rank order of item difficulty or in choice of distractors for error responses. Test-taking attitudes and motivational factors appear unconvincing as an explanation of the group difference in view of the fact that on some tests which make equal demands on attention, persistence, and effort, such as various memory tests, Negroes do perform quite well relative to whites. When various diverse tests and test items are ordered in terms of the degree to which they discriminate between Negroes and whites, the one feature which is common to the most discriminating tests and items is the conceptual and abstract nature of the test material, or the degree to which they accord with the classic definitions of the psychological nature of *g*, the general factor common to all complex tests of mental ability.

In 1968 I proposed that the heritability of a test be considered as one objective criterion of the test's culture-fairness or status-fairness (Jensen, 1968). Since then, M. B. Jones (1971) also has advocated the use of heritability as a criterion in psychological test construction. I also suggested that one might test competing genetic and environmental hypotheses of a particular group difference by comparing the performance of the two groups in question on tests which differ in heritability. The environmental hypothesis should predict a smaller mean difference between the groups on those tests with the higher heritability than on tests with lower heritability; a genetic hypothesis would predict just the opposite. So here we have the possibility of strong inference, since the two competing theories are pitted against each other in yielding opposite predictions.

To see the rationale of this kind of hypothesis, consider the fact that various mental tests differ in their sensitivity to environmental influences. For example, a test which is very sensitive to reflecting environmental influences will show smaller differences between genetically dissimilar and unrelated children who have been adopted and reared together in the same home than between genetically identical twins who have been separated in infancy and reared apart in different homes. Such a test which strongly reflects environmental influences has low heritability. On the other hand, a test with high heritability (or low sensitivity to environmental effects) will show larger differences between unrelated children reared together than between identical twins reared apart.

In order to obtain statistically reliable estimates of the environmental sensitivity of tests I used siblings rather than twins, because siblings are more plentiful. We identified all siblings in grades K to 6 in an entire California school district. A variety of 16 mental tests of abilities and achievement, many of them standard tests, were administered to the eight thousand children in the study, and the correlations among siblings (r_s) were obtained on each test. Now we know that if only genetic factors were involved in the test variance, the sibling correlation should be very close to 0·50. (This is the sibling correlation, for example, for number of fingerprint ridges, which, we know, are virtually unaffected by environmental factors.) Any departure of the correlation from 0·50, above or below, therefore, is an indication of environmental variance. So we can employ as a index of environmental influence, E, on test scores the absolute difference from 0·50 of the obtained sibling correlation, thus $E = |r_s - 0·50|$. This E index was obtained for white siblings and for Negro siblings. Next we obtained the mean white-Negro difference on each test, and to put the differences all on the same scale of standard scores, the mean difference was divided by the same standard deviation of the tests' scores in the white sample. Thus, on every test the mean white-Negro difference was expressed in white standard deviation units. We then obtained the correlation and regression lines of the mean difference on the environmental sensitivity index for whites and for Negroes. An environmentalist hypothesis should predict a positive correlation. In fact, however, the correlations are negative. The negatively sloping regression lines are

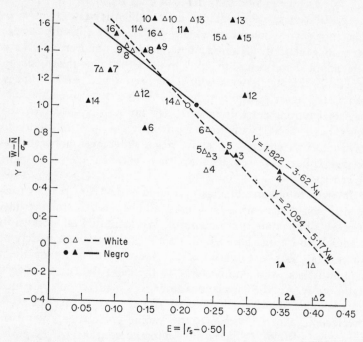

FIGURE 12.5. The regression lines (for whites and Negroes) show-ing the mean white-Negro difference in white sigma units (Y) on 16 ability tests (numbered 1 to 16) as a function of the absolute difference from 0·50 of the sibling correlation for each test (E). Circles indicate the bivariate means; triangles indicate the various tests, which are numbered as follows: 1. Making Xs (Neutral instructions); 2. Making Xs (Motivating instructions); 3. Memory – Immediate recall; 4. Memory – After repetition; 5. Memory – Delayed recall; 6. Figure Copying; 7. Lorge-Thorndike IQ, Levels I and II (Pictorial); 8. Lorge-Thorndike, Verbal IQ; 9. Lorge-Thorndike, Non-verbal IQ; 10. Stanford Achievement: Word Meaning; 11. Stanford Achievement: Paragraph Meaning; 12. Stanford Achievement: Spelling; 13. Stanford Achievement: Language (Grammar); 14. Stanford Achievement: Arithmetic Computation; 15. Stanford Achievement: Arithmetic Concepts; 16. Stanford Achievement: Arithmetic Applications.

shown in Figure 12.5. The correlation between the Negro and white values of the E index is 0·71. This means that the various tests are quite similar for whites and Negroes in the degree to which they reflect non-genetic influences. The correlation between the Negro-white difference and the E index is $-0·80$ for whites and $-0·61$ for Negroes. Clearly, the results are more in accord with a genetic hypothesis than with a cultural hypothesis as an explanation of the mean white-Negro differences on the various tests. It should be noted that in general the scholastic achievement tests are more sensitive to environmental influence than the standard intelligence tests.

Is this finding merely a result of the particular selection of tests used in this study? I doubt it. The essential design has been replicated by Nichols (1970) at the University of Minnesota. Nichols used an entirely different battery of tests comprised mostly of the various subtests of the Wechsler Intelligence Scale for Children as well as several other tests (e.g., Bender-Gestalt, Illinois Test of Psycholinguistic Abilities, Draw-A-Man, and three scholastic achievement tests). Nichols used Negro and white sibling correlations to obtain an estimate of heritability for each test; this corresponds closely to the complement of our E index, i.e., $1 - E$. So in Nichols's study the genetic hypothesis would predict a positive correlation between the racial difference (again expressed in standard deviation units) and the heritability of the tests. The correlation obtained by Nichols was $0·67 +$ (the average for whites and Negroes). The correlation of socio-economic status differences with heritability was $+0·86$, which is consistent with the hypothesis of a high degree of genetic variance in SES differences in mental abilities. Two independent large-scale studies, therefore, have yielded results that are strikingly more consistent with a genetic than with an environmentalist hypothesis. I know of no other way that scientific investigation can proceed in this field at the present time than by testing a variety of hypotheses in this fashion, one by one, and sizing up the converging lines of evidence. I have examined the most often repeated environmentalist hypotheses in the light of relevant evidence. I can here only briefly summarize some of my observations. All the points made in these summaries are fully documented in my book *Educability and Group Differences*.

LANGUAGE DEPRIVATION

This is an unconvincing explanatory hypothesis in view of the fact that Negroes perform best on the most verbal parts of intelligence tests and poorest on the least verbal materials. All other disadvantaged minority groups within the American population show the opposite trend. Children who are born deaf are the most verbally deprived subjects we can study. They show marked verbal deficits on intelligence tests. Yet they perform at an average level on non-verbal tests, thus showing a pattern of abilities opposite to that of Negroes.

Another important difference between low-SES children and children who are verbally deprived because of deafness is that while the former begin to lag in linguistic and intellectual development after beginning school, the latter show a gradual catching up to the average level as they progress in school – it merely takes them longer to acquire information because of their severe sensory handicap. But once it is acquired, normal mental development ensues. A study of the developing conceptual capacities of the deaf concluded '. . . the differences found between deaf and hearing adolescents were amenable to the effects of age and education and were no longer found between deaf and hearing adults. Dissociation between words and referents, verbalization adequacy, and (conceptual) level of verbalization were not different for deaf and hearing subjects. Our experiments, then, have shown few differences between deaf and hearing subjects. Those found were shown to fall along a normal developmental line and were amenable to the effects of increased age and experience, and education' (Kates, Kates, and Michael, 1962, pp. 31-2).

POOR MOTIVATION

There is no consistent evidence that Negroes are less motivated in a test situation than are other groups. Some groups (e.g., Indians) whose general educational aspirations and self-concepts are poorer than those of Negroes actually perform better on tests and in school. Also, on performance tests specially devised to maximize the influence of motivational factors and to minimize the test's dependence upon abstract or complex cognitive functions which would involve g, Negroes do not perform significantly below whites. The 'expectancy' or 'self-fulfilling prophecy' theory has not been empirically demonstrated, and when put to proper tests it has failed to be substantiated.

NON-COGNITIVE TESTS

Certain perceptual-motor tests such as choice reaction time and pursuit rotor learning (which has a very high heritability) show large Negro-white differences even under very highly controlled experimental conditions, and the results are independent of the race of the tester. Moreover, the magnitude of the racial difference has been shown to be related to the degree of Caucasian admixture in the Negro sample as assessed by physical indices. If genetic racial differences in behavioral tests other than intelligence tests are admitted, by what principle can one exclude the same possibility for types of tests labeled as measures of intelligence? There is no reason why intelligence tests should be categorically excluded from the possibility of showing genetic race differences when such differences in other physical and behavioral traits can be found.

NUTRITIONAL DEFICIENCIES

The fact that severe malnutrition, especially protein deficiency, during prenatal development and in infancy and childhood can impair mental as well as physical growth is not at issue. Studies from the nutritionally most deprived segments of populations in Africa, Mexico, and South America would support this conclusion. There are no data, however, which would support the hypothesis that malnutrition contributes any appreciable fraction to the average Negro-white IQ difference. In Negro communities where there is no evidence of poor nutrition, the average Negro IQ is still about 1 SD below the white mean. When groups of Negro children with IQs *below* the general Negro average have been studied for nutritional status, no signs of malnutrition have been found. Physical evidence of malnutrition found to be correlated with lower IQs in studies conducted in Africa, Mexico, and Guatemala have not been found even in the poorest and lowest IQ segments of the American Negro population. On the basis of present evidence, the hypothesis that lower average Negro IQ is due to poor nutrition is not tenable.

The nutritional and health care status of American Indian children, as indicated by much higher rates of infant mortality, is much poorer than that of Negroes; yet Indian children in the first grade in school (age 6) have been found to score about 1 *SD* above Negroes on non-verbal ability tests.

PRENATAL AND PERINATAL DISADVANTAGES

The higher rate of fetal loss and infant mortality in the Negro population may indicate disadvantages related to prenatal health care of the mother and undesirable conditions attending birth. These conditions prevail in the poorer segment of the Negro population and probably contribute to the incidence of neurological handicap among Negro children. All of the causes of high fetal loss, however, are not understood, for there are some relatively disadvantaged populations which have shown lower rates of fetal loss than is found in the white majority – Orientals, for example. There is now evidence that the degree of genetic heterogeneity of the fetus' ancestors is directly related to the probability of fetal loss, and thus genetic factors may be involved even in this seemingly environmental phenomenon. Disadvantaging forms of birth trauma such as anoxia, low birthweight and prematurity are reflected in subnormal performance on infant tests of perceptual-motor development. But larger representative samples of Negro children show no depression of scores on these tests and generally perform at slightly higher levels than middle-class white children. Prenatal and perinatal factors, though differing in Negro and white populations, do not begin to account for such phenomena as the six times higher rate of mental retardation (IQs below 70) in the Negro than in the white population. Unless one hypothesizes the existence of genetic factors, in the vast majority of cases the causes of the mental retardation must be categorized as 'unknown' or 'unidentified'.

Educational implications

At present, neither I nor anyone else, I'm afraid, has any more than rather general notions concerning the educational implications of the wide range of apparent differences in educability in our population. Since the heredity-environment issue is not likely to reach a general consensus among qualified scientists for quite some time to come and after much more genetical and psychological research has been completed, it is probably wise for educators to assume an openly agnostic position with regard to the genetic issue as it involves racial differences, at the same time recognizing that whatever may be the causes of the difference, we do not at present know of any measures or methods within the power of the schools that will appreciably or permanently diminish either individual or group differences in intelligence or scholastic achievement. There is fundamentally, in my opinion, no difference, psychologically and genetically, between individual differences and group differences. Individual differences often simply get tabulated so as to show up as group differences – between schools in different neighborhoods, between different racial groups, between cities and regions. They then become a political and ideological, not just a psychological, matter. To reduce the social tensions that arise therefrom, we see proposals to abolish aptitude and achievement testing, grading, grade placement, special classes for the educationally retarded and the academically gifted, neighborhood schools, the classroom as the instructional unit, the academic curriculum, and even our whole system of education. There may be merit in some of these proposals. But I think they are too often aimed at covering up problems rather than coming to grips with them. We can urge doing away with classification and groups, and enforce laws against racial discrimination in educational opportunities and employment and housing; we can and must insist upon considering only persons' individual characteristics rather than their group membership as a basis for educational treatment and in social relations in general. Well and good. I trust there is no disagreement on this. What we may not accomplish by these means, however, is equality of performance in school or in the acquisition of certain skills deemed valuable by society and rewarded accordingly. If we repeatedly look for the causes of differences in ability to acquire an educationally valued skill such as reading, for example, in the external environment and are hard put to find a convincing explanation there, but we also refuse to consider any other than external factors as possible causes of these differences, perhaps we only sow the seeds of a kind of social paranoia – a need to find strictly external causes to blame for the observed differences.

In terms of what we now know in educational research and in terms of what seems immediately feasible, I would suggest further consideration of three main educational approaches. They are not at all mutually exclusive. (The desirability and necessity of eliminating racial discrimination and of generally improving the environmental conditions and educational and occupational opportunities of all disadvantaged persons in the population are taken for granted.) These approaches have nothing to do with race *per se*, but are concerned with individual differences in those characteristics most relevant to educability. Their success in improving the benefits of education to Negro children, however, may depend in part upon recognizing that racial differences in the distribution of educationally relevant abilities are not mainly a result of discrimination and unequal environmental conditions. None of the approaches that seem to me realistic is based on the expectation of the schools' significantly changing children's basic intelligence.

Seeking aptitude × training interactions

This means that some children may learn better by one method than by another and that the best method may be quite different for different children, depending on their particular aptitudes or other personological characteristics. It implies that the same educational goals can be accomplished to the same degree for children of different abilities provided the right instructional variations are found. This is merely a hope, and the relevant research so far gives little basis for optimism that such aptitude × training interactions will be found which can overcome to any marked degree the importance of IQ level for educability. But since this type of research has been underway only a few years, it is much too soon to discount the possibilities it may turn up – especially if one expects not miracles, but only positive, if modest, benefits from this approach.

Greater attention to learning readiness

The concept of developmental readiness for various kinds of school learning has been too neglected in recent educational trends, which have been dominated by the unproved notion that the earlier something can be taught to a child, the better. Forced early learning, prior to some satisfactory level of readiness (which will differ markedly from one child to another), could cause learning blocks which later on practically defy remediation. The more or less uniform lock-step sequencing of educational experiences may have to be drastically modified for the benefit of many children, but the recent massive insistence on 'earliness' and equality of educational treatment of all children has militated against large-scale research on the implications of readiness for children with below-average educability within the traditional school system.

Greater diversity of curricula and goals

Public schools, which aim to serve the entire population, must move beyond narrow conceptions of scholastic achievement to find a greater diversity of ways for children over the entire range of abilities to benefit from their schooling – to benefit especially in ways that will be to their advantage when they are out of school. The academic goals of schooling are so ingrained in our thinking and our values that it will probably call for radical efforts to modify public education in ways such that it will maximally benefit large numbers of children with very limited aptitude for academic achievement. I believe that a well-intentioned but misconceived social egalitarian ideology has prevented public education in the United States from facing up to this challenge.

The belief that equality of educational opportunity should necessarily lead to equality of performance, I believe, is proving to be a false hope. It is the responsibility of scientific research in genetics, psychology, and education to determine the basis for realistic solutions to the problems of universal public education. Though it may be premature to prescribe at present, I venture the prediction that future solutions will take the form not so much of attempting to minimize differences in scholastic aptitudes and motivation, but of creating a greater diversity of curricula, instructional methods, and educational goals and values that will make it possible for children ranging over a wider spectrum of abilities and proclivities genuinely to benefit from their years in school. The current zeitgeist of environmentalist equalitarianism has all but completely stifled our thinking along these lines. And I believe the magnitude and urgency of the problem are such as to call for quite radical thinking if the educational system is truly to serve the whole of society. We have invested so much for so long in trying to equalize scholastic performance that we have given little or no thought to finding ways of diversifying schools to make them rewarding to everyone while not attempting to equalize everyone's performance in a common curriculum. Recommendations have almost always taken the form of asking what next we might try to make children who in the present school system do not flourish academically become more like those who do. The emphasis has been more on changing children than on revamping the system. A philosophy of equalization, however laudable its ideals, cannot work if it is based on false premises, and no amount of propaganda can make it appear to work. Its failures will be forced upon everyone. Educational pluralism of some sort, encompassing a variety of very different educational curricula and goals, I think, will be the inevitable outcome of the growing realization that the schools are not going to eliminate human differences. Rather than making over a large segment of the school population so they will not be doomed to failure in a largely antiquated elitist oriented educational system which originally evolved to serve only a relatively small segment of society, the educational system will have to be revamped in order to benefit everyone who is required by the society to attend school. It seems incredible that a system can still survive which virtually guarantees frustration and failure for a large proportion of the children it should intend to serve. From all the indications, public education in such a form will not much longer survive.

But we should not fail to recognize that to propose radical diversity in accord with individual differences in abilities and interests, as contrasted with uniformity of educational treatment, puts society between Scylla and Charybdis in terms of insuring for all individuals equality of opportunity for the diversity of educational paths. The surest way to maximize the benefits of schooling to all individuals and at the same time to make the most of a society's human resources is to insure equality of educational opportunity for all its members. Monolithic educational goals and uniformity of approaches, however, guarantee unnecessary frustration and defeat for many. On the other hand, educational pluralism runs the risk that social, economic, ethnic background or geographic origin, rather than each child's own characteristics, might determine the educational paths available to him. The individual characteristics appropriate for any one of a variety of educational paths and goals are to be found everywhere, in every social stratum, ethnic group, and neighborhood. Academic aptitudes and special talents should be cultivated wherever they are found, and a wise society will take all possible measures to insure this to the greatest possible extent. At the same time, those who are poor in the traditional academic aptitudes cannot be left by the wayside. Suitable means and goals must be found for making their years of schooling rewarding to them, if not in the usual academic sense, then in ways that can better their chances for socially useful and self-fulfilling roles as adults.

References

Alvord, R. W. Learning and transfer in a concept-attainment task: A study of individual differences. Technical Report No. 4. Project on individual differences in learning ability as a function of instructional variables, School of Education, Stanford University, February, 1969.

Anastasi, A. Culture-fair testing. *Educational Horizons*, Fall, 1964, 26-30.

Ardrey, R. *African genesis*. New York: Delta, 1961.

Armor, D. J. The evidence on busing. *The Public Interest*, Summer, 1972, 90-126.

Astin, A. W. Folklore of selectivity. *Saturday Review*, Dec. 20, 1969, 57.

Bajema, C. Estimation of the direction and intensity of natural selection in relation to human intelligence by means of the intrinsic rate of natural increase. *Eugenics Quarterly*, 1963, **10**, 175-187.

——Relation of fertility to educational attainment in a Kalamazoo public school population: A follow-up study. *Eugenics Quarterly*, 1966, **13**, 306-315.

Bayley, N. Comparisons of mental and motor test scores for ages 1-15 months by sex, birth order, race, geographical location, and education of parents. *Child Development*, 1965, **36**, 379-411.

Bereiter, C. Academic instruction and preschool children. In *Language programs for the disadvantaged*. National Council of Teachers of English, 1965. Pp. 195-203.

——Genetics and educability: Educational implications of the Jensen debate. In J. Hellmuth (Ed.) *Disadvantaged child*, Vol. 3. *Compensatory education: A national debate*. New York: Brunner-Mazel, 1970. Pp. 279-299.

434

BEREITER, C. & ENGELMANN, S. *Teaching disadvantaged children in the preschool.* Englewood Cliffs, New Jersey: Prentice-Hall, 1966.

BERNSTEIN, B. Social structure, language and learning. *Educational Research*, 1961, **3**, 163-176.

BIALER, I. Primary and secondary stimulus generalization as related to intelligence level. *Journal of Experimental Psychology*, 1961, **62**, 395-402.

BINET, A. & SIMON, T. *The development of intelligence in children.* (Trans. by Elizabeth S. Kite). Baltimore: Williams and Wilkins, 1916.

BITTERMAN, M. E. The evolution of intelligence. *Scientific American*, 1965, **212**, 92-100.

BLANK, M. & SOLOMON, F. A tutorial language program to develop abstract thinking in socially disadvantaged preschool children. *Child Development*, 1968, **39**, 379-389.

BLOOM, B. S. *Stability and change in human characteristics.* New York: Wiley, 1964.

BONEY, J. D. Predicting the academic achievement of secondary school Negro students. *Personnel and Guidance Journal*, 1966, **44**, 700-703.

BOUSFIELD, A. K. & BOUSFIELD, W. A. Measurement of clustering and of sequential constancies in repeated free recall. *Psychological Reports*, 1966, **19**, 935-942.

BOUSFIELD, W. A. The occurrence of clustering in the recall of randomly arranged associates. *Journal of General Psychology*, 1953, **49**, 229-240.

BOWLES, S. & LEVIN, H. M. The determinates of scholastic achievement – an appraisal of some recent evidence. *Journal of Human Resources*, Winter, 1968.

BRACHT, G. H. Experimental factors related to aptitude-treatment interactions. *Review of Educational Research*, 1970, **40**, 627-645.

BRONFENBRENNER, U. The psychological costs of quality and equality in education. *Child Development*, 1967, **38**, 909-925.

BRONSON, G. The hierarchical organization of the central nervous system: Implications for learning processes and critical periods in early development. *Behavioral Science*, 1965, **10**, 7-25.

BROOKS, G. W. & MUELLER, E. Serum urate concentrations among university professors. *Journal of the American Medical Association*, 1966, **195**, 415-418.

BURT, C. *The backward child.* London: University of London Press, 1937.

——The evidence for the concept of intelligence. *British Journal of Educational Psychology*, 1955, **25**, 158-177.

——The distribution of intelligence. *British Journal of Psychology*, 1957, **48**, 161-175.

——The inheritance of mental ability. *American Psychologist*, 1958, **13**, 1-15.

——Class differences in general intelligence: III. *British Journal of Statistical Psychology*, 1959, **12**, 15-33.

——The gifted child. *British Journal of Statistical Psychology*, 1961, **14**, 123-139. (a)

——Intelligence and social mobility. *British Journal of Statistical Psychology*, 1961, **14**, 3-24. (b)

——Is intelligence disturbed normally? *British Journal of Statistical Psychology*, 1963, **16**, 175-190.

——The genetic determination of differences in intelligence: A study of monozygotic twins reared together and apart. *British Journal of Psychology*, 1966, **57**, 137-153.

BURT, C. & HOWARD, M. The multifactorial theory of inheritance and its application to intelligence. *British Journal of Statistical Psychology*, 1956, **9**, 95-131.

CALDWELL, B. The fourth dimension in early childhood education. In R. Hess and R. Bear (Eds.), *Early education: Current theory, research and action*. Chicago: Aldine Publishing Co., 1968.

Carnegie Quarterly. Where failures make the grade: Two schools for dropouts. *CQ*, 1968, **16**, No. 4.

CARROLL, J. B. Instructional methods and individual differences. In R. M. Gagné (Ed.), *Learning and individual differences*. Columbus, Ohio: Merrill, 1967. Pp. 40-44.

CARTER, C. O. *Human heredity*. Baltimore, Maryland: Penguin Books, 1962.

CASSIRER, E. *An essay on man*. Garden City, New York: Doubleday, 1953.

CATTELL, R. B. *Personality*. New York: McGraw-Hill, 1950.

——*Handbook for the culture fair intelligence test: A measure of 'g.'* Champaign, Illinois: Institute for Personality and Ability Testing, 1959.

——Theory of fluid and crystalized intelligence: A critical experiment. *Journal of Educational Psychology*, 1963, **54**, 1-22.

CLEARY, T. A. Test bias: Prediction of grades of Negro and white students in integrated colleges. *Journal of Educational Measurement*, 1968, **5**, 115-124.

COFER, C. N. & FOLEY, J. P. Mediated generalization and the interpretation of verbal behaviour: 1. Prolegomena. *Psychological Review*, 1942, **49**, 513-540.

COLEMAN, J. S. *et al. Equality of educational opportunity*. U.S. Dept. of Health, Education, and Welfare, 1966.

COOPER, G. D., YORK, M. W., DASTON, P. G., & ADAMS, H. B. The Porteus Test and various measures of intelligence with Southern Negro adolescents. *American Journal of Mental Deficiency*, 1967, **71**, 787-792.

CORAH, N. L. *et al.* Effects of perinatal anoxia after seven years. *Psychological Monographs*, 1965, **79**, Whole No. 596.

CRONBACH, L. J. *Essentials of psychological testing*. (2nd ed.) New York: Harper, 1960.

——How can instruction be adapted to individual differences? In R. M. Gagné (Ed.), *Learning and individual differences*. Columbus, Ohio: Merrill, 1967. Pp. 23-39.

CROW, J. F. Genetic theories and influences: Comments on the value of diversity. *Harvard Educational Review*, 1969, **39**, 301-309.

CROW, J. F. & FELSENSTEIN, J. The effects of assortative mating on the genetic composition of a population. *Eugenics Quarterly*, June, 1968.

DEFRIES, J. C. Quantitative aspects of genetics and environment in the determination of behavior. In Lee Ehrman, G. S. Omenn, & E. W. Caspari (Eds.), *Genetics, environment and behavior: Implications for educational policy*. New York: Academic Press, 1972.

DE LEMOS, M. M. The development of conservation in aboriginal children. *International Journal of Psychology*, 1969, **4**, 255-69.

DEUTSCH, M. Social and psychological perspective for the facilitation of the development of the preschool child. Prepared for the Arden House Conference on Pre-School Enrichment of Socially Disadvantaged Children. (mimeo.)

DREGER, R. M. & MILLER, K. S. Comparative psychological studies of Negroes and whites in the United States. *Psychological Bulletin*, 1960, **57**, 361-402.

DUNCAN, O. D. Ability and achievement. *Eugenics Quarterly*, 1968, **15**, 1-11.

DUNCAN, O. D., FEATHERMAN, D. L., & DUNCAN, B. Socioeconomic background and occupational achievement: Extensions of a basic model. Final Report, Project No. 5-0074 (EO-191) U.S. Dept. of Health, Education, and Welfare, Office of Education, Bureau of Research, May, 1968.

DUNNETTE, M. D. & BASS, B. M. Behavioral scientists and personnel management. *Industrial Relations*, 1963, **2**, 115-130.

DURNING, K. P. Preliminary assessment of the Navy Memory of Numbers Test. Unpublished Master's thesis, San Diego State College, 1968.

ECKLAND, B. K. Genetics and sociology: A reconsideration. *American Sociological Review*, 1967, **32**, 173-194.

EDUCATIONAL TESTING SERVICE. Are aptitude tests unfair to Negroes? ETS investigates two kinds of 'bias.' *ETS Developments*, 1966, **14**, 1.

——Bias in selection tests and criteria studied by ETS and U.S. Civil Service. *ETS Developments*, Princeton, New Jersey, 1969.

EELLS, K. *et al. Intelligence and cultural differences.* Chicago: University of Chicago Press, 1951.

EICHENWALD, H. Mental retardation. *Science*, 1966, **153**, 1290-1296.

ELKIND, D. Piagetian and psychometric conceptions of intelligence. *Harvard Educational Review*, 1969, **39**, 319-337.

ELLIS, N. R. (Ed.) *Handbook of mental deficiency.* New York: McGraw-Hill, 1963.

ENTWISLE, D. R. *Word associations of young children.* Baltimore: Johns Hopkins Press, 1966.

ERLENMEYER-KIMLING, L. & JARVIK, L. F. Genetics and intelligence: A review. *Science*, 1963, **142**, 1477-1479.

ERTL, J. P. Evoked potentials and intelligence. *Revue de l'Université d'Ottawa*, 1966, **36**, 599-607.

EYSENCK, H. J. *Crime and personality.* Boston: Houghton-Mifflin, 1964.

——*The biological basis of personality.* Springfield, Illinois: Charles C. Thomas, 1967. (a)

——Intelligence assessment: A theoretical and experimental approach. *British Journal of Educational Psychology*, 1967, **37**, 81-98. (b)

FISHER, J. The twisted pear and the prediction of behaviour. *Journal of Consulting Psychology*, 1959, **23**, 400-405.

FLANAGAN, J. C. & COOLEY, W. W. Project Talent one-year follow-up studies. University of Pittsburgh, 1966.

FLAVELL, J. *The developmental psychology of Jean Piaget*. New York: Van Nostrand, 1963.

FLAVELL, J. H., BEACH, D. R., & CHINSKY, J. M. Spontaneous verbal rehearsal in a memory task as a function of age. *Child Development*, 1966, **37**, 283-299.

FOX, W. L. & TAYLOR, J. E. Adaptation of training to individual differences. Paper presented at the North Atlantic Treaty Organization Conference on 'Manpower Research in the Defense Context,' 14-18 August, 1967, London. (Hum RPO Division No. 3, Presidio of Monterey, California.)

FROST, J. L. & HAWKES, G. R. *The disadvantaged child*. New York: Houghton-Mifflin, 1966.

FREEMAN, R. The concept of accountability in education. *The University Bookman*, 1971, **11**, 75-89.

GAGNÉ, R. M. *The conditions of learning*. New York: Holt, Rinehart & Winston, 1965.

——Contributions of learning to human development. *Psychological Review*, 1968, **75**, 177-191.

GATES, A. I. & TAYLOR, G. A. An experimental study of the nature of improvement resulting from practice in mental function. *Journal of Educational Psychology*, 1925, **16**, 583-593.

GHISELLI, E. E. *The measurement of occupational aptitude*. University of California Publications in Psychology, Vol. 8, No. 2. Berkeley, California: University of California Press, 1955.

GIBSON, J. B. Biological aspects of a high socioeconomic group: I. IQ, education, and social mobility. *Journal of Biosocial Science*, 1970, **2**, 1-16.

GLASMAN, L. A social-class comparison of conceptual processes in children's free recall. Unpublished Doctoral dissertation, University of California, Berkeley, 1968.

GOTTESMAN, I. I. Biogenetics of race and class. In M. Deutsch, I. Katz, & A. R. Jensen (Eds.), *Social class, race, and psychological development*. New York: Holt, Rinehart, & Winston, 1968. Pp. 11-51.

GOUGH, H. G. A short social status inventory. *Journal of Educational Psychology*, 1949, **40**, 52-56.

——A nonintellectual intelligence test. *Journal of Consulting Psychology*, 1953, **17**, 242-246.

GOUGH, H. G. College attendance among high-aptitude students as predicted from the California Psychological Inventory. *Journal of Counseling Psychology*, 1968, **15**, 269-278.

GOUGH, H. G. & DOMINO, G. The D 48 Test as a measure of general ability among grade school children. *Journal of Consulting Psychology*, 1963, **27**, 344-349.

GOUGH, H. G. & McGURK, E. A group test of perceptual acuity. *Perception and Motor Skills*, 1967, **24**, 1107-1115.

GRAHAM, F. K. Development three years after perinatal anoxia and other potentially damaging newborn experiences. *Psychological Monographs*, 1962, **76**, Whole No. 522.

GRAY, S. W. & KLAUS, R. A. An experimental preschool program for culturally deprived children. Reprint from *Child Development*, 1965, **36**, 887-898.

GREENBERG, I. M. Project 100,000: The training of former rejectees· *Phi Delta Kappan*, 1969, **50**, 570-574.

GUILFORD, J. P. *Fundamental statistics in psychology and education.* (3rd ed.) New York: McGraw-Hill, 1956.

――Zero correlations among tests of intellectual abilities. *Psychological Bulletin*, 1964, **61**, 401-404.

――*The nature of human intelligence.* New York: McGraw-Hill, 1967.

GUINAGH, B. J. An experimental study of basic learning ability and intelligence in low socioeconomic population. Unpublished Doctoral dissertation, Michigan State University, 1969.

HARLOW, H. F. The development of learning in the Rhesus monkey. *American Scientist*, 1959, **47**, 459-479. (a)

――Learning set and error factor theory. In S. Koch (Ed.), *Psychology: A study of a science*, Vol. 2. New York: McGraw-Hill, 1959. Pp. 492-537. (b)

HARLOW, H. F. & HARLOW, M. K. The mind of man. In *Yearbook of science and technology*. New York: McGraw-Hill, 1962.

HARTMAN, T. F. Dynamic transmission, elective generalization, and semantic conditioning. In W. F. Prokasy (Ed.), *Classical conditioning: A symposium*. New York: Appleton-Century-Crofts, 1965. Pp. 90-106.

HASKELL, E. F. *Assembly of the sciences*, Vol. 1, *Scientia Generalis*, 1968. (mimeo.)

HESS, R. D. & SHIPMAN, V. Early blocks to children's learning. *Children*, **12**, 189-194.

HIGGINS, J., REED, S., & REED, E. Intelligence and family size: A paradox resolved. *Eugenics Quarterly*, 1962, **9**, 84-90.

HILLS, J. R. & STANLEY, J. C. Prediction of freshman grades from SAT and from Level 4 of SCAT in three predominantly Negro state colleges. *Proceedings, 76th Annual Convention, American Psychological Association*, 1968, 241-242.

——Easier test improves prediction of Negroes' college grades. *Journal of Negro Education* (in press).

HOLT, S. B. Inheritance of dermal ridge patterns. In L. S. Penrose (Ed.), *Recent advances in human genetics*. London: Churchill, 1961.

HONZIK, M. P. Developmental studies of parent-child resemblances in intelligence. *Child Development*, 1957, **28**, 215-228.

HORN, J. L. Intelligence – why it grows, why it declines. *Transaction*, Nov., 1967, 23-31.

——Organization of data on life-span development of human abilities. In P. B. Baltes & L. R. Goulet (Eds.), *Life-span development psychology*. New York: Academic Press, 1970.

HOVLAND, C. I. Experimental studies in rote-learning theory. V. Comparison of distribution of practice in serial and paired-associate learning. *Journal of Experimental Psychology*, 1939, **25**, 622-633.

HULL, C. L. Knowledge and purpose as habit mechanisms. *Psychological Review*, 1930, **37**, 511-525.

HUMPHREYS, L. G. Racial differences: Dilemma of college admissions. *Science*, 1969, **166**, 167.

HUMPHREYS, L. G. & DACHLER, P. Jensen's theory of intelligence. *Journal of Educational Psychology*, 1969, **60**, 419-426. (a)

——Jensen's theory of intelligence: A rebuttal. *Journal of Educational Psychology*, 1969, **60**, 432-433. (b).

HUNTLEY, R. M. C. Heritability of intelligence. In J. E. Meade & A. S. Parkes (Eds.), *Genetic and environmental factors in human ability*. New York: Plenum Press, 1966.

HUSÉN, T. *International Study of Achievement in Mathematics*, Vol. 2. Uppsala: Almquist & Wiksells, 1967.

ILG, F. L. & AMES, L. B. *School readiness*. New York: Harper and Row, 1964.

JENCKS, C. *Inequality*. New York: Basic Books, 1972.

JENKINS, J. J. Mediated association: Paradigms and situations. In C. N. Cofer & B. S. Musgrave (Eds.), *Verbal behavior and verbal learning*. New York: McGraw-Hill, 1963, Pp. 210-245.

P

JENSEN, A. R. Learning abilities in Mexican-American and Anglo-American children. *California Journal of Educational Research*, 1961, **12**, 147-159.

——Learning ability in retarded, average, and gifted children. *Merrill-Palmer Quarterly Journal of Behavior and Development*, 1963, **9**, 123-140. (a)

——Transfer between paired-associate and serial learning. *Journal of Verbal Learning and Verbal Behavior*, 1963, **1**, 269-280. (b)

——*Individual differences in learning: Interference factor.* Cooperative Research Project No. 1867, U.S. Office of Education, 1965. (a)

——Rote learning in retarded adults and normal children. *American Journal of Mental Deficiency*, 1965, **69**, 828-834. (b)

——Social class and perceptual learning. *Mental Hygiene*, 1966, **50**, 226-239. (a)

——Verbal mediation and educational potential. *Psychology in the Schools*, 1966, **3**, 99-109. (b)

——Estimation of the limits of heritability of traits by comparison of monozygotic and dizygotic twins. *Proceedings of the National Academy of Sciences*, 1967, **58**, 149-157. (a)

——Varieties of individual differences in learning. In R. M. Gagné (Ed.), *Learning and individual differences.* Columbus, Ohio: Merrill, 1967. Pp. 117-135. (b)

——Another look at culture-fair tests. In *Western Regional Conference on Testing Problems, Proceedings for 1968*, 'Measurement for Educational Planning.' Berkeley, California: Educational Testing Service, Western Office, 1968. Pp. 50-104. (a)

——Patterns of mental ability and socioeconomic status. *Proceedings of the National Academy of Sciences*, 1968, **60**, 1330-1337. (c)

——Social class, race, and genetics: Implications for education. *American Educational Research Journal*, 1968, **5**, 1-42. (d)

——Social class and verbal learning. In M. Deutsch, I. Katz, & A. R. Jensen (Eds.), *Social class, race and psychological development.* New York: Holt, Rinehart, & Winston, 1968. Pp. 115-174. (e)

——How much can we boost IQ and scholastic achievement? *Harvard Educational Review*, 1969, **39**, 1-123. (a)

——Intelligence, learning ability, and socioeconomic status. *Journal of Special Education*, 1969, **3**, 23-35. (b)

——Jensen's theory of intelligence: A reply. *Journal of Educational Psychology*, 1969, **60**, 427-431. (c)

——Reducing the heredity-environment uncertainty. In 'Environment, heredity and intelligence'. *Harvard Educational Review*. Reprint Series No. 2, 1969. Pp. 209-243. (d)

——Can we and should we study race differences? In J. Hellmuth (Ed.), *Disadvantaged child*, Vol. 3: *Compensatory education: A national debate*. New York: Brunner/Mazel, 1970. Pp. 124-157. (a)

——Hierarchial theories of mental ability. In B. Dockrell (Ed.), *On intelligence*. London: Methuen, 1970. (b)

——IQs of identical twins reared apart. *Behavior Genetics*, 1970, **1**, 133-148. (c)

——Race and the genetics of intelligence: A reply to Lewontin. *Bulletin of the Atomic Scientists*, 1970, **26**, 17-23. (d)

——A theory of primary and secondary mental retardation. In N. R. Ellis (Ed.), *International review of research in mental retardation*, Vol. IV. New York: Academic Press, 1970. (e)

——Individual differences in visual and auditory memory. *Journal of Educational Psychology*, 1971, **62**, 123-131. (a)

——The race × sex × ability interaction. In R. Cancro (Ed.), *Contributions to Intelligence*. New York: Grune & Stratton, 1971. Pp. 107-161. (b)

JENSEN, A. R. & FREDERIKSEN, J. Social-class differences in free recall learning. *Journal of Educational Psychology*, 1973.

JENSEN, A. R. & ROHWER, W. D., Jr. The effect of verbal mediation on the learning and retention of paired-associate by retarded adults. *American Journal of Mental Deficiency*, 1963, **68**, 80-84. (a)

——Verbal mediation in paired-associate and serial learning. *Journal of Verbal Learning and Verbal Behavior*, 1963, **1**, 346-352. (b)

——Syntactical mediation of serial and paired-associate learning as a function of age. *Child Development*, 1965, **36**, 601-608.

——Mental retardation, mental age, and learning rate. *Journal of Educational Psychology*, 1968, **59**, 402-403.

——An experimental analysis of learning abilities in culturally disadvantaged children. Final Report, Office of Economic Opportunity. Contract No. OEO2404, 1970.

JOHN, V. P. The intellectual development of slum children. Paper presented at American Orthopsychiatric Association, 1962.

JONES, H. E. The environment and mental development. In L. Carmichael (Ed.), *Manual of child psychology*. (2nd ed.) New York: Wiley, 1954. Pp. 631-696.

JONES, M. B. Heritability as a criterion in the construction of psychological tests. *Psychological Bulletin*, 1971, **75**, 92-96.

KASL, S. V., BROOKS, G. W., & COBB, S. Serum urate concentrations in male high school students. *Journal of the American Medical Association*, 1966, **198**, 713-716.

KATES, S. L., KATES, W. W., & MICHAEL, J. Cognitive processes in deaf and hearing adolescents and adults. *Psychological Monographs*, 1962, **76**, Whole No. 551.

KENDLER, H. H. & KENDLER, T. S. Vertical and horizontal processes in problem solving. *Psychological Review*, 1962, **69**, 1-16.

KENNEDY, W. A., VAN DE RIET, V., & WHITE, J. C., Jr. A normative sample of intelligence and achievement of Negro elementary school children in the Southeastern United States. *Monographs of the Society for Research in Child Development*, 1963, **28**, No. 6.

KIDD, A. H. & RIVOIRE, J. L. The culture-fair aspects of the development of spatial perception. *Journal of Genetic Psychology*, 1965, **106**, 101-111.

KOHLBERG, L. Early education: A cognitive-developmental view. *Child Development*, 1968, **39**, 1013-1062.

KUENNE, M. R. Experimental investigation of the relation of language to transposition behavior in young children. *Journal of Experimental Psychology*, 1946, **36**, 471-490.

KUSHLICK, A. Assessing the size of the problem of sub-normality. In J. E. Meade & A. S. Parkes (Eds.), *Genetic and environmental factors in human ability*. New York: Plenum Press, 1966. Pp. 121-147.

KUTTNER, R. E. Letters to and from the editor. *Perspectives in Biology and Medicine*, 1968, **11**, 707-709.

LASHLEY, K. S. Persistent problems in the evolution of mind. *Quarterly Review of Biology*, 1949, **24**, 28-42.

LAWRENCE, E. M. An investigation into the relation between intelligence and inheritance. *British Journal of Psychology*. Monograph Supplement, 1931, **16**, No. 5, p. 80.

LEAHY, A. M. Nature-nurture and intelligence. *Genetic Psychology Monographs*, 1935, **17**, 241-305.

LEE, S. S. & JENSEN, A. R. The effect of awareness on three-stage mediated association. *Journal of Verbal Learning and Verbal Behavior*, 1968, **7**, 1005-1009.

LEMKAU, P. V. & IMRE, P. D. Epidemiology of mental retardation in a rural county: The Rose County study. Progress Report, The

Johns Hopkins University, Department of Mental Hygiene, July 18, 1966.

LESSER, G. S., FIFER, G., & CLARK, D. H. Mental abilities of children from different social-class and cultural groups. *Monographs of the Society for Research in Child Development*, 1965, **30**, No. 4.

LEWIS, A. The black man's route to the top. *Reader's Digest*, August, 1969.

LINE, W. & KAPLAN, E. The existence, measurement and significance of a speed factor in the abilities of public school children. *Journal of Experimental Education*, 1932, **1**, 1-8.

LOEHLIN, J. C. Psychological genetics, from the study of human behavior. In R. B. Cattell (Ed.), *Handbook of modern personality theory*. New York: Aldine, 1971.

LUDLOW, H. G. Some recent research on the Davis-Eells Games. *School and Society*, 1956, **84**, 146-148.

LURIA, A. R. *The role of speech in the regulation of normal and abnormal behavior*. New York: Liveright, 1961.

——*The mind of a mnemonist: A little book about a vast memory*. Translated from the Russian by Lynn Solotaroff. New York: Basic Books, 1968.

LUSH, J. L. Genetic unknowns and animal breeding a century after Mendel. *Transactions of the Kansas Academy of Science*, 1968, **71**, 309-314.

MANDLER, G. & HUTTENLOCKER, J. The relationship between associative frequency, associative ability and paired-associate learning. *American Journal of Psychology*, 1956, **69**, 424-428.

MAXWELL, J. *Social implications of the 1947 Scottish Mental Survey*. London: University of London Press, 1953.

——Relative influences of social class and IQ on children's education and occupation. *International Newsletter* (Educational Testing Service, Princeton, New Jersey) Issue VIII, December, 1969, 5-6.

McCARTHY, D. Language development in children. In L. Carmichael (Ed.), *Manual of child psychology*. New York: Wiley, 1946. Pp. 467-581.

McGURK, F. C. J. A scientist's report on race differences. *U.S. News & World Report*, September 21, 1956.

——The culture hypothesis and psychological tests. In R. E. Kuttner (Ed.), *Race and modern science*. New York: Social Science Press, 1967. Pp. 367-381.

P*

McNemar, Q. A critical examination of the University of Iowa studies of environmental influences upon the IQ. *Psychological Bulletin*, 1940, **37**, 63-92.

Medical World News. Using speed of brain waves to test IQ. *MWN*, 1968, **9**, 26.

Moynihan, D. P. Employment, income, and the ordeal of the Negro family. In T. Parsons & K. B. Clark (Eds.), *The Negro American*. Cambridge: Houghton-Mifflin, 1966. Pp. 134-159.

Moynihan, D. P. & Mosteller, F. *On Equality of Educational Opportunity*. New York: Random House, 1972.

Nichols, P. L. The effects of heredity and environment on intelligence test performance in 4 and 7 year old white and Negro sibling pairs. Unpublished doctoral dissertation. University of Minnesota, 1970.

Olson, D. R. *Cognitive development: the child's acquisition of diagonality*. New York: Academic Press, 1970.

Orr, D. B. & Graham, W. R. Development of a listening comprehension test to identify educational potential among disadvantaged junior high school students. *American Educational Research Journal*, 1968, **5**, 167-180.

Osgood, C. E. *Method and theory in experimental psychology*. New York: Oxford University Press, 1953.

Osler, S. F. & Cooke, R. E. *The biological basis of mental retardation*. Baltimore: Johns Hopkins Press, 1965.

Page, E. B. How we *all* failed in performance contracting. *Educational Psychologist*, 1972, **9**, 40-42.

Pasamanick, B. & Knobloch, H. Retrospective studies on the epidemiology of reproductive casualty: Old and new. *Merrill-Palmer Quarterly*, 1966, **12**, 7-26.

Pearson, K. On the inheritance of the mental and moral characters in man, and its comparison with the inheritance of physical characters. *Journal of the Anthropological Institute*, 1903, **33**, 179-237.

Phillips, J. L., Jr. *The origins of intellect: Piaget's theory*. San Francisco: W. H. Freeman, 1969.

Piaget, J. The general problem of the psychobiological development of the child. In J. M. Tanner & B. Inhelder (Eds.), *Discussion on child development*, Vol. 4. New York: International Universities Press, 1960.

PYLES, M. K. Verbalization as a factor in learning. *Child Development*, 1932, **3**, 108-113.

RAINWATER, L. & YANCEY, W. (Eds.) *The Moynihan Report and the politics of controversy.* Cambridge, Massachusetts: MIT Press, 1967.

RAPIER, J. The learning abilities of normal and retarded children as a function of social class. *Journal of Educational Psychology*, 1968, **59**, 101-110.

RAVEN, J. C. *Guide to using Progressive Matrices.* London: Lewis, 1952.

REED, T. E. Caucasian genes in American Negroes. Unpublished manuscript. March, 1969.

ROBERTS, R. C. Some concepts and methods in quantitative genetics. In J. Hirsch (Ed.), *Behavior-genetic analysis.* New York: McGraw-Hill, 1967. Pp. 214-257.

ROHWER, W. D., Jr. Social class differences in the role of linguistic structures in paired-associate learning. Cooperative Research Project No. 5-0605, U.S. Office of Education, 1967.

——Mental mnemonics in early learning. *Teachers College Record*, 1968, **70**, 213-226. (a)

——Socioeconomic status, intelligence and learning proficiency in children. Paper presented at the annual meeting of the American Psychological Association, San Francisco, California, 1968. (b)

——Learning, race, and school success. Paper presented at a symposium, 'Race and intelligence: Implications for education,' at the annual convention of the American Educational Research Association, Los Angeles, California, February 6, 1969.

——Prime time for education: Early childhood or adolescence? *Harvard Educational Review*, 1971, **41**, 316-341.

ROHWER, W. D., Jr. & LYNCH, S. Retardation, school strata and learning proficiency. *American Journal of Mental Deficiency*, 1968, **73**, 91-96.

ROHWER, W. D., Jr., LYNCH, S., LEVIN, J. R., & SUZUKI, N. Pictorial and verbal factors in the efficient learning of paired associates. *Journal of Educational Psychology*, 1967, **58**, 278-284.

ROHWER, W. D., Jr., LYNCH, S., SUZUKI, N., & LEVIN, J. R. Verbal and pictorial facilitation in paired-associate learning. *Journal of Experimental Child Psychology*, 1967, **5**, 294-302.

——Grade level, school strata and learning efficiency. *Journal of Educational Psychology*, 1968, **59**, 26-31.

ROSENBERG, L. A., ROSENBERG, A. M., & STROUD, M. The Johns Hopkins Perceptual Test: The development of a rapid intelligence test for the preschool child. Paper presented at the Eastern Psychological Association annual meeting, New York. New York, April, 1966.

ROTH, E. Die Geschwindigkeit der Verarbeitung von Information und ihr Zusammenhang mit Intelligenz. *Zeitschrift für experimentelle und angewandte Psychologie*, 1964, **11**, 616-622.

RUCH, F. L. Comments on psychological testing. *Columbia Law Review*, 1969, **69**, 610-612.

RUSSELL, W. A. & STORMS, L. H. Implicit verbal chaining in paired-associate learning. *Journal of Experimental Psychology*, 1955, **49**, 287-293.

SCARR-SALAPATEK, S. Race, social class, and IQ. *Science*, 1971, **174**, 1285-1295.

SCHUMAN, H. Sociological racism. *Trans-action*, 1969, **7**, 44-48.

SHUEY, A. M. *The testing of Negro intelligence.* (2nd ed.) New York: Social Science Press, 1966.

SKEELS, H. M. Adult status of children with contrasting early life experiences: A follow-up study. *Child Development Monographs*, 1966, **31**, No. 3, Serial No. 105.

SKEELS, H. M. & DYE, H. B. A study of the effects of differential stimulation on mentally retarded children. *Proceedings & Addresses of the American Association on Mental Deficiency*, 1939, **44**, 114-136.

SKODAK, M. & SKEELS, H. M. A final follow-up study of one hundred adopted children. *Journal of Genetic Psychology*, 1949, **75**, 85-125.

SPUHLER, J. N. & LINDZEY, G. Racial differences in behavior. In J. Hirsch (Ed.), *Behavior-genetic analysis.* New York: McGraw-Hill, 1967. Pp. 366-414.

STANLEY, J. C. Letter to the Editors. *Harvard Educational Review*, 1967, **37**, 475.

——Achievement by the disadvantaged. *Science*, 1969, **163**, 622. (a)

——Confrontation at Cornell. *Trans-action*, 1969, **7**, 54. (b)

——Letter to the Editors. The Johns Hopkins *Newsletter*, October 17, 1969, 10. (c)

——How can we intervene 'massively'? *Science*, 1970, **167**, 123.

STANLEY, J. C. & PORTER, A. C. Correlation of scholastic aptitude test scores with college grades for Negroes versus whites. *Journal of Educational Measurement*, 1967, **4**, 199-218.

STERN, C. *Principles of human genetics.* San Francisco: W. H. Freeman, 1949.

STETTEN, D., Jr. & HEARON, J. Z. Intellectual level measured by Army classification battery and serum acid concentration. *Science*, 1969, **129**, 1737.

STEVENSON, H. W., ISCOE, I., & MCCONNELL, C. A developmental study of transposition. *Journal of Experimental Psychology*, 1955, **49**, 278-280.

STINCHCOMBE, A. L. A critique of Arthur R. Jensen's 'How much can we boost IQ and scholastic achievement?' *Harvard Educational Review*, 1969, **39**, no. 3.

STODOLSKY, S. S. & LESSER, G. Learning patterns in the disadvantaged. *Harvard Educational Review*, 1967, **37**, 546-593.

STORMS, L. H. Rationales for the 'twisted pear.' *Journal of Consulting Psychology*, 1960, **24**, 552-553.

TALLAND, G. A. *Deranged memory: A psychonomic study of the amnesic syndrome.* New York: Academic Press, 1965.

TANNER, J. M. The trend towards earlier physical maturation. In J. E. Meade & A. S. Parkes (Eds.), *Biological aspects of social problems.* New York: Plenum Press, 1965. Pp. 40-66.

——Earlier maturation in man. *Scientific American*, 1968, **218**, 21-28.

TERMAN, L. M. Personal reactions of the Yearbook Committee. In G. M. Whipple (Ed.), *Intelligence: Its nature and nurture*, 39th Yearbook of the National Society for the Study of Education, Part I. 1940. Pp. 460-467.

TERMAN, L. M. & ODEN, M. *The gifted group at mid-life.* Stanford: Stanford University Press, 1959.

TERMAN, L. M. *et al. Genetic studies of genius.* 5 vols. Stanford: Stanford University Press, Vol. 1, 1925; Vol. II, 1926; Vol. III, 1930; Vol. IV, 1947; Vol. V, 1959.

TERRELL, G. The role of incentive in discrimination learning in children. *Child Development*, 1959, **29**, 231-236.

TERRELL, G. DURKEN, K., & WIESLEY, M. Social class and the nature of the incentive indiscrimination learning. *Journal of Abnormal and Social Psychology*, 1959, **59**, 270-272.

THOMAS, C. L. & STANLEY, J. C. Effectiveness of high school grades for predicting college grades of black students: A review and discussion. *Journal of Educational Measurement*, in press.

THORNDIKE, R. L. Community variables as predictors of intelligence and academic achievement. *Journal of Educational Psychology*, 1951, **42**, 321-338.

TUDDENHAM, R. D. A 'Piagetian' test of cognitive development. In B. Dockrell (Ed.), *On Intelligence*, pp. 49-70. London: Methuen, 1970.

TYLER, L. E. *The psychology of human differences* (3rd ed.). New York: Appleton-Century-Crofts, 1965.

UNDERWOOD, B. J. Laboratory studies of verbal learning. In E. R. Hilgard (Ed.), *Theories of learning and instruction*. Chicago: National Society for the Study of Education, 1964.

VERNON, P. E. *The structure of human abilities*. New York: Wiley, 1950.

——Environmental handicaps and intellectual development: Part I and Part II. *British Journal of Educational Psychology*, 1965, **35**, 1-22.

VYGOTSKY, L. F. *Thought and language*. Cambridge, Massachusetts: M.I.T., 1962.

WALLER, J. H. Achievement and social mobility: Relationships among IQ score, education, and occupation in two generations. *Social Biology*, 1971, **18**, 252-259.

WATSON, J. B. *Behavior: An introduction to comparative psychology*. New York: Holt, 1914.

WECHSLER, D. *The measurement and appraisal of adult intelligence* (4th ed.). Baltimore: Williams & Wilkins, 1958.

WHITE, S. H. Evidence for a hierarchial arrangement of learning processes. In L. R. Lipsitt and C. C. Spiker (Eds.), *Advances in child development and behavior*, Vol. 2. New York: Academic Press, 1965, Pp. 187-220.

——Changes in learning processes in the late preschool years. Paper presented at a symposium, Early Learning, at the American Educational Research Association Convention, Chicago, 1968.

WILLERMAN, L. & CHURCHILL, J. A. Intelligence and birth weight in identical twins. *Child Development*, 1967, **38**, 623-629.

WILSON, A. B. Educational consequences of segregation in a California community. *Racial isolation in the public schools*, Appendices, Vol. II, p. 185. U.S. Commission on Civil Rights, Washington, D.C., 1967.

WISEMAN, S. *Education and environment*. Manchester: Manchester University Press, 1964.

WOLFF, J. L. Concept-shift and discrimination-reversal learning in humans. *Psychological Bulletin*, 1967, **68**, 369-408.

WRIGHT, S. Systems of mating. III. Assortative mating based on somatic resemblance. *Genetics*, 1921, **6**, 144-161.

YOUNG, M. & GIBSON, J. In search of an explanation of social mobility. *British Journal of Statistical Psychology*, 1963, **16**, 27-36.

YOUNG, M. & GIBSON, J. B. Social mobility and fertility. In J. E. Meade & A. S. Parkes (Eds.), *Biological aspects of social problems*. Edinburgh: Oliver and Boyd, 1965.

ZEAMAN, D. & HOUSE, B. J. The relation of IQ and learning. In R. M. Gagné (Ed.), *Learning and individual differences*. Columbus, Ohio: Merrill, 1967. Pp. 192-212.

ZEAMAN, D. & KAUFMAN, H. Individual differences and theory in a motor learning task. *Psychological Monographs*, 1955, **69**, No. 6 (Whole No. 391).

ZIGLER, E. Familial mental retardation: A continuing dilemma. *Science*, 1967, **155**, 292-298.

Author index

453

Subject index

457